the
VENDETTA

the VENDETTA

FBI Hero Melvin Purvis's
War Against Crime,
and J. Edgar Hoover's
War Against Him

Alston Purvis

WITH ALEX TRESNIOWSKI

PublicAffairs
New York

Book design by Jane Raese

Library of Congress Cataloging-in-Publication Data
[TK]

FIRST EDITION

2 4 6 8 10 9 7 5 3 1

dedication TK

Contents

1

LEGACY

Some memories have a terrible power beyond any telling of them, beyond our ability to harness what they mean. One such memory is of a boy on a raw winter's morning, summoned from school and told he must go home. The boy, bundled in the back of a car, stares blankly at the landscape rushing past, at familiar homes that are different now, at stately magnolias that now stand forlornly along the driveway to his home in Florence, South Carolina. Apprehension weighs on his chest until the boy believes he cannot breathe. When at last the car arrives at the back of the columned colonial house, the boy sees something he will remember the rest of his life—a small Oriental scatter carpet drenched a deep crimson and draped over a clothesline in the backyard. The family's chauffeur and butler, Charlie Vivians, is washing the stains with a garden hose, causing a puddle of red water to form in the grass at his feet. "I'm so sorry," Charlie tells the boy. "I think your mama needs you now."

The blood on the carpet was my father's blood. The boy was me. I was sixteen.

That was how it ended for my father—with a .45-caliber bullet fired through his jaw. He was found lying in his own blood, the same end that befell John Dillinger and Pretty Boy Floyd and all the others he had pursued to their deaths so many years before. A man who in life knew great peril and great glory—who had the adulation of an entire citizenry—had become, in the end, bitter and broken. And now his home, his Carolina sanctuary, had become the last killing ground.

———

Around 11:00 that morning a single gunshot pierced the quiet inside the house. My mother Rosanne had just put clothes in the washer and was in the kitchen planning dinner with the cook, Evelyn Cyrus, when she heard the shot and raced upstairs. My father had taken his breakfast in bed at shortly after 8:00, and his empty tray sat on the night table. Folded carefully over the footrest were a clean shirt and a suit. But nothing else was normal about the scene that greeted my mother at the top of the stairs. She found my father in the hallway outside his bedroom, dressed in pajamas and a red housecoat, lying on his right side with his knees slightly bent. Blood poured from a one-inch wound under his jaw, on the left side and just behind the point of his chin. She saw a cigarette beside his body, half-smoked and stubbed. Bits of plaster littered the hardwood floor, dislodged from the ceiling by the bullet that had passed through the top of my father's skull. Near his left hand lay a nickel-plated, pearl-handled Colt .45 automatic pistol that had belonged to Gus Winkler, a Chicago contract killer my father had used as an informant. The pistol, one of some 300 guns in his collection, was not normally kept upstairs; only his favorite weapon, the .38-caliber Colt revolver he used in his work, was stashed in his bedroom dresser, alongside a tray of bullets. So it was odd to see Winkler's polished old pistol claiming an improbable last victim.

My mother telephoned my father's physician, Dr. Walter R. Mead, telling his secretary, "Send Walter quick. Melvin has shot himself." Then she sat beside my father's body for several long minutes until Dr. Mead arrived and sent her to a bedroom.

Mamie and Ed Day Charles, family friends, came to get me at McClenaghan High School. I thought I was being summoned to the principal's office because of my spotty attendance record or for some other transgression. Then I saw Mamie, her face drained of color. The principal rose from his chair and told me, "Your father died this morning." Nothing else was said.

I was the first of my father's three sons to arrive at our family's twenty-acre estate on Cherokee Road. My older brother Melvin, age twenty, got the call at the University of South Carolina, while ten-year-old Christopher was retrieved from elementary school.

News of the tragic events in Florence soon traveled several hundred miles to the north. At 5:24 that afternoon, the special-agent-in-charge of the Federal Bureau of Investigation's Savannah office sent an urgent memorandum to Director J. Edgar Hoover, the man who once had taken my father under his wing and chosen him to be his top agent. "Information received through division that Melvin Horace Purvis committed suicide today," the memo read. "Further details will be submitted." Not much later, C. D. DeLoach, an assistant to Hoover, provided more information through one of my father's friends, a former agent: "Purvis has not looked well for the last several weeks, had not been eating and last week came down with the flu." Purvis, it read, "feared that osteomyelitis (bone disease) had been spreading through his system." It was true my father had been ill, suffering from chronic back pain and debilitated by an unshakable case of the Asian flu. He was weak and lethargic, and only a few days before his death had almost fallen on the steps while getting off an airplane. He had trouble sleeping and could not regain his strength despite eating three solid meals a day. "He expressed many times the feeling of the futility of trying to go ahead with so many circumstances against him," Dr. Mead would later say. At home he seemed increasingly more distant, dejected, and dependent upon alcohol and pain-killing drugs.

Even so, the memo to Hoover noted that only days before his death, Melvin Purvis declared he would never take his own life—"I've got too much to live for," he had said. The memo ended with a recommendation that the organization to which my father had devoted his finest years not send a letter of condolence to his stricken widow, now the mother of three fatherless sons. Incredibly, Hoover scribbled "right" in the margin of the memo, and no such letter was sent.

Hoover, however, was not content merely to remain silent upon hearing of the death of his former friend and favorite agent. On that day, February 29, 1960, he had the Bureau dispatch a brief memo to the press stating categorically that Melvin Purvis had committed suicide—this, before autopsy, coroner's report, medical investigation, or official inquest into the shooting. In the days that followed, there were indeed serious questions raised about the circumstances of my father's death. Why was the pistol found near his left hand when he was right-handed? Did the amount of powder burns indicate the pistol had been fired from a distance? My father had scheduled meetings for that day with Dr. Mead; his lawyer, Hugh L. Willcox; and business partner A. P. Skinner; and he had told the cook that morning that he felt fine. Further, he detested automatic weapons like Winkler's pistol, which used an ammunition clip containing several shells; one shot still would leave the gun loaded and ready to be fired again. Why would a man obsessed with gun safety use such a dangerous weapon for his wife or whoever discovered him to pick up when he could have used his service revolver loaded with a single bullet? And why was there no suicide note? My father had a habit of writing notes and leaving them everywhere; he always carried a number-one pencil in his right pocket for that purpose.

Such details did not matter to Hoover, who hurriedly announced the suicide of the former agent he had not spoken to in twenty-five years. His bulletin made no mention of my father's accomplishments, his sacrifices for the Bureau, his place in history. There were no elegant phrases proffering gratitude, no expressions of sadness or sympathy. The sparseness of the bulletin, as well as its swiftness, suggested a trace of gloating. Hoover simply could not wait to publicize what was to him a long-awaited victory—the final silencing of a man he considered his nemesis.

For more than a quarter century, the nation's top law-enforcement officer waged a secret vendetta against my father. Hoover could not tolerate that my father achieved fame after the killings of John Dillinger and Pretty Boy Floyd, could not bear that the media made Melvin Purvis a hero while funneling diminished credit to Hoover. He railed against editorials that called for Purvis to replace him as head of the Bureau, and he viewed my father as a threat long after it was reasonable to do so. For these reasons, Hoover undertook myriad spiteful activities against my father. He drove him from the Bureau, blocked him from getting jobs, ordered agents to dig up dirt on him, invented stories that impugned his character, and deleted him from official FBI histories. Don Whitehead's Bureau-authorized 1956[ck] history, *The FBI Story*, does not even mention Melvin Purvis, who at the time was easily the Bureau's most famous former agent. Hoover tried to give sole credit for Dillinger's death to another agent, insisting Melvin Purvis had been little more than a bystander at the event. It is difficult to think of another instance in American history when such a powerful government official used the full weight of his office to crush a former colleague who had been a national hero, and did so solely out of personal animus. Hoover's well-documented vindictiveness, coupled with his unchecked power, gives my father's story the arc and the heft of Greek tragedy.

Of course, Hoover was only one player in the drama. No hero is without flaws. To be sure, my father was 1a complicated man, driven by contradictory impulses. Melvin Purvis never wanted to become a law-enforcement officer, never played cops and robbers as a boy, and went to work at the Bureau only after discovering the Department of State had no openings. He stood a mere five feet nine inches and weighed only 140 pounds, and the papers took to calling him Little Mel. Yet he had a powerful presence that commanded people's attention whenever he walked into a room. He was a courtly Southern gentleman, a lawyer who loved the theater, opera, and ballet. Yet he was expert at making contacts among underworld figures, earning their respect as a straight-talking man of his word. He was a fine marksman, yet he loathed the prospect of engaging in gun battles, fearing that civilians might get caught in the crossfire. He disdained cheap publicity and insisted on keeping a low profile, yet he had an irrepressible showman's streak and unquestionably enjoyed the opportunities his exploits later brought him. He was preternaturally confident, unflinchingly sure of himself, and a born leader, yet he was never a glory-hound, preferring to share credit with his devoted men and insisting that Hoover do the same. A meticulous analyst, he was known for his "never ignore anything" philosophy and for his obsessive interest in criminology. Yet he seemed oblivious to the blatant persecution Hoover leveled at him, believing to the end that Hoover was his friend.

Most famously, he showed uncommon candor in confessing to being afraid in times of crisis, though more for the lives of his men than for his own. His well-known fearfulness—he admitted to shaking with nerves during the Dillinger raid—led the press to dub him "Nervous Purvis." But he never once shirked his duty or shied away from confrontation. Carved on my father's gravestone are the Latin words *Saepe timui sed numquam curri:* "I was often afraid, but I never ran."

Melvin Purvis was also fiercely loyal. I later discovered his weathered 1920 yearbook from Timmonsville High School, where he had been a two-sport athlete as well as president of the literary society. Alongside his formal photograph, in which he looks intently to the future and appears much younger than his sixteen years, was the legend, "Trust in all things high comes easy to him." In light of how his life would unfold, this catchphrase was eerily ironic. But his trust in authority initially served my father well, for it made him an ideal protégé to the powerful man who would shape his destiny.

The 1930s were a crucial period for America, and with nothing less than the nation's sense of its worth on the line, Melvin Purvis and J. Edgar Hoover became one of history's great crime-fighting teams. The two men played to each other's strengths. Hoover's professionalism and ferocious resolve were inspirations to my father, giving him the higher purpose for which he abandoned his hometown and his legal career. To Hoover, Melvin Purvis personified everything he wanted in his new breed of federal agent: He was educated, efficient, dedicated, well-mannered—a true gentleman crime-buster. He also was handsome and charming, a formidable presence, capable of swagger—qualities the graceless Hoover so obviously lacked. Those traits attracted Hoover to my father, and his fondness for him was reflected in the many affectionate, personal letters he sent him, addressing him as Mel and signing off as Jayee. Their surprising and at times almost touching friendship fueled a successful professional partnership. Hoover asked for absolute devotion and received it; in exchange he expressed a bolstering confidence in my father, handpicking him for the Bureau's premier job: running the dangerous and highly visible Chicago field office—ground zero in the war on gangsters. Together the two men seemed capable of great things, and indeed their crime-fighting accomplishments during a mere twenty-month span from 1933 to 1935 forever changed the perception of law enforcement in America.

Those twenty months also profoundly changed both men; they proved a watershed not only for the nation but for Hoover and Purvis as well. Events of the time set them on vastly divergent and irreversible paths. Hoover—who early in his tenure as Bureau director was steadfast and incorruptible in shedding the agency of its scandal-scarred past—used his successes against gangsters to turn the FBI into his fiefdom, ruling it for fifty years and ensuring his dominion by maintaining secret files on presidents and other powerful people. In these pursuits, he became perhaps a more villainous figure than any gangster he pursued. My father, however, had no such lengthy history. Within nine months of cornering Pretty Boy Floyd on the Conkle farm in eastern Ohio—the second top public enemy he took down in just three months—he was out of the Bureau, his tenure as its most celebrated agent over as swiftly as it began. Perhaps what happened in those twenty months was at once Hoover's greatest triumph and his original sin, defining both the scope of his power and the lengths to which he would go to keep control of his world. By the end of that period, my father and Hoover had ceased to be friends, their partnership dissolved even as it achieved its grandest success. How this could have happened—how the fates of two men were forged in this remarkable moment in history—is the story of this book.

Of course, it is not the entire story, though the rest is not the sort of discussion to be found in history books. After walking away from the FBI, my father went on to other careers. He wrote an autobiography, *American Agent,* which covered his short but eventful time in the Bureau. He resumed the practice of law in San Francisco; he started a newspaper in Florence, South Carolina, where he eventually bought a radio station, WOLS. He enlisted in the Army during World War II and rose to the rank of colonel; after the war he was dispatched to hunt down fugitive Nazis such as Martin Bormann and to interview war criminals during the Nuremberg trials. Years later he would become counsel to the Senate Judiciary Committee, his final job. In each of these endeavors he accomplished good things. But none came close to matching the glamour and the glory of his crime-fighting days.

He also married and started a family. After years of distance, he returned to his hometown sweetheart, Rosanne Willcox, whom he had left behind fourteen years before when he set out on the adventure that would make him internationally famous. Never mind that she was married to another man; as soon as she divorced, they wed in 1938. They had three sons and lived in the brick two-story colonial house my father had built on farmland once owned by his wife's parents. He named the place Melrose, for Melvin and Rosanne.

It was an idyllic tableau, at least on the outside, but this part of the story has its downside too. I was almost three years old when I first laid eyes on my father, who had been overseas during the war. I was on our front lawn to greet him upon his arrival from the train station and saw a figure in a gleaming white colonel's uniform climb out of the car. I can still recall the impact of this first impression of my father. Before he hugged me or even said hello he took off his white colonel's hat and tossed it several feet away. Then he instructed me to fetch it. My father was a military man, accustomed to having his orders followed, but I was too young to know this was a spontaneous test of my obedience. Rather than get it, I hid behind my mother's knee. My father reached down and spanked me for ignoring his command. The wall erected between us right there on the lawn would, over the years, never be fully torn down.

There were warm, wonderful moments, to be sure, between my father and his three boys, but the true satisfaction of getting to know him seemed to elude us all. Besides his rigid nature, his reticence about his days with the Bureau distanced him from us. Our friends at school knew about his G-man exploits and were fascinated by them, but to us they seemed irrelevant, vague, forgotten. It was not disinterest—it was a necessary posture born of his reluctance to share his stories with us. Those days seemed to matter little to him; why should they matter to us? Of course, we did not know then that the reason he was loath to relive his time chasing gangsters was that he had been saddled with a murky legacy. We did not know that Hoover's efforts to diminish my father in the public eye had, to a large extent, laid waste to my father's belief in himself. There was about my father an uncertainty, a restlessness—a drive to complete a story that could never be completed. Instead of basking in his youthful accomplishments and allowing his sons to share in that pride, he wrestled with his self-worth and dwelled not on his bravery but on his failures. "I hope none of my sons do what I did," he once said to Dolly Coker, our nanny and intimate friend, and my father's confidant.

"What's that?" she asked.

"Reach for the moon and miss it."

And because my father was a hero who died believing he was

something less, his sons assumed this cloak of insecurity as part of our inheritance. We, too, were all driven to prove something—to him, to ourselves. All fathers are heroes to their sons, but all fathers eventually betray their sons, because the day comes when we realize that fathers too are human. We must abandon our notion of them as infallible and replace it with something less potent but ultimately truer, deeper, and more satisfying. The question, of course, is, replace it with what? What happens if we cannot reconcile the reality and the myth, cannot discern who our fathers really are? And what if the father himself cannot sort through the fact and the fiction? Is such a father himself ultimately unknowable?

I struggled with those questions for years, as I suppose my brothers, Melvin III and Christopher, did as well, though resolution for me remained out of reach. My mother grieved, enduring her sad widowhood until she died in 1978. Then, in 1984, my brother Christopher got into his battered Chevrolet, parked along a deserted road, and, fueled by alcohol, drugs, and depression, slit his wrists. A week later passersby discovered his body, which had badly decomposed in the broiling sun. Christopher was thirty-four. Two years later, Melvin—a new father and as happy as he had been in a long while—suffered a fatal heart attack while playing with his four-year old son. Melvin was only forty-six.

Thus my father's premature death had parallels in my brothers' lives. Their deaths stunned me and left me to wonder how everything had gone so wrong. Was this our fate, to be destroyed by life as our father had been? My brothers and I should have been the happy and confident sons of one of America's true heroes, buoyed by our affection and admiration for him. But some terrible fissure along the way threw all our lives off course.

At the time it was all terribly sad, but I could see nothing to do to make sense of it. What recourse did I have but to continue to live my life and make my own way? I had found a niche in the art world far from my father's line of work, and with each passing year my connection to him seemed to grow a little fainter. I carried his name but little else that linked me to him. Now I had even lost my brothers, the only other individuals who could fathom the mixed blessing of being his son. My impulse was to retreat further from the wreckage, rather than attempt to sort through it. And in this way my father, Melvin Purvis, became part of a distant past.

Then a remarkable event occurred. In 1996 my wife, Susan, and I had a son—my first child, named Alston after me. His birth stirred in me the feeling that my son's future was inextricably bound to my family's past. Suddenly my father's legacy, which had dwindled in importance to me, seemed critical to the fate of my own boy. I could not allow him to grow up with the same clouded past that had tormented me and my brothers; I had to pass on to him a more resolved version of the family mythology. One day he would want to know who his grandfather was. How could I tell him if I did not really know myself?

And so, almost without realizing it, I began to gather the loose strings of my father's life. I searched Internet auction sites and found many of his letters and papers (my brothers had sold such items, perhaps as a means of healing). I pursued collectors and wrote to relatives and obsessively tracked down every newspaper clipping and magazine article that dealt with my father's career. I petitioned the FBI and claimed copies of every file the Bureau had preserved concerning Melvin Purvis—thousands of pages, enough to fill fifteen four-inch-thick folders. I catalogued every letter J. Edgar Hoover ever sent to my father, an illuminating eight-year trail of correspondence. I spoke to people who knew my father when he was with the Bureau, most notably Doris Lockerman, who joined him in Birmingham, Alabama, and was his devoted secretary when he ran the Chicago Bureau office. Now in her nineties and living in Atlanta, she helped me rediscover the things about my father that had intrigued me as a child—what he stood for, what he meant to the country, why he should be remembered.

"Melvin Purvis was an absolute hero, at a time when America was desperate for one," Doris told me. "He was a romantic figure with a remarkable aura, and of course it was that aura that ended his career. He knew there was drama to what he was doing and he did it with some dash, and so the whole world came to know who he was. And Hoover wound up with a hero who was more charming than him." Nearly seven decades after my father left the Bureau, Doris was still indignant about his treatment at the hands of a man he initially idolized. "What is truly tragic is that your father never managed to escape Hoover's clutches," she said. "He could not believe Hoover would turn on him, and he tried too long to be what Hoover wanted him to be, long after he was being blackballed.

Other agents managed to shake off Hoover's malevolence, but poor Melvin never did. He just took his duty too seriously. To the end he still hoped he could do the best job that he could."

This dedication, I came to realize, was a key to my father's story. I believe he had, as my mother once said, loved Hoover, as a loyal soldier loves his general. These feelings clouded his judgment; the full breadth of Hoover's betrayal was something he simply could not comprehend. My father never uttered a public condemnation of Hoover, and he kept a framed photo of the director in his office to the day he died. To the end he refused to believe that Hoover would attempt to ruin his career out of petty jealousy. It was this deep but sadly misplaced sense of loyalty to Hoover that prevented my father from coming to terms with his own accomplishments. Hoover's reality became the only one that mattered.

As I pored through my father's records, I became incensed that Hoover had been able to ruin a man's life. My suppressed anger over the deaths of my father and brothers coalesced into a fierce resolve to discover the truth. To this end, I emulated my father and became a manhunter. If I failed to understand him while he was alive, I now had the chance to discover his meaningful life. His story did not have to stay maddeningly unfinished. Yes, Hoover diminished my father's role, but Melvin Purvis was there in the clover patch where Pretty Boy Floyd took his last breath, and at the theater where John Dillinger finally met his end. My father *was* at these places—indeed, was in charge of these operations—and so his story had been severely undermined. I could no longer stand either Hoover's version of the truth, or my father's distorted estimation of himself. My father had been subverted by his own myth, his humanity lost in the jumble of a tainted history. Still, his humanity had not been lost forever. It could be retrieved.

And so that task fell to me. I am the only one left to tell my father's full story, the only one who can offer testament to what he achieved. Perhaps I am the only one who can try to make sense of his death—who can venture some theory about what happened in that house the day he died. Perhaps some will say I am the wrong person for this task, too close to the subject of the story, too prone to want to acclaim my father. Certainly this book will not be dispassionate. The story is painful and difficult, and there will be some anger in its unfolding. I have no interest in glorifying my father; I simply want to understand him. He was a good man who did good things; he made sacrifices, risked his life, performed his duty. He does not deserve to be forgotten.

This, then, is the story of a man who was summoned by history and answered the call. It is the story of an American family with all its mysteries and ghosts. It is the story of a complex friendship that went tragically wrong, and a story of what it means for a man to be a hero. I hope that it is the real story, at long last. And I hope that, with its telling, the world will know my father did not miss the moon after all.

2

NORTH TO AMERICA'S CAPITAL

July 22, 1934
CHICAGO, ILLINOIS

First we go back—to a time of gangsters and G-men, of spats and submachine guns, of tramps and boxcars and bread lines, of newsreels and New Deals. A time of despair and deep longing, of cautious hope and tested faith, of some vast, vague belief in the goodness of a place called America.

And here comes John Dillinger, in his crisp straw boater and his silver-rimmed specs, strolling out of the Biograph movie theater like any other cinema patron. He has a loaded Colt .38 handgun in the right rear pocket of his gray trousers and an unwrapped La Corona–Belvedere cigar, never to be smoked, in the breast pocket of his white Kenilworth shirt. His crooked smile and leering eyes adorn a million wanted posters in stores and post offices across the country, but there is something different about his familiar face this night. Seven weeks recovered from a grisly plastic surgery, he has had his famous chin dimple plugged with tissue from behind his ear and a telltale ridge on his nose hammered flat. His eyebrows have been plucked and, like his hair, dyed dark brown. Still, the practiced eye can pick him out. And if not him, the woman with him, Anna Sage, wearing an orange dress that prophetically glows blood red under the lights of the Biograph marquee.

The tug of the departing crowd carries Dillinger onto Lincoln Avenue. Waiting for him there, just south of the box office, is Bureau of Investigation special-agent-in-charge Melvin Purvis. It is his job to identify Dillinger and give the signal for his capture, mobilizing a squad of agents poised around the theater. Purvis wears a single-breasted, buttoned blue jacket and cuffed white slacks, and he has two pistols tucked into his waist, one just above his left pocket, the other above his right. He, too, has a cigar, unlit but chewed thoroughly and wedged between his teeth. In one hand he holds a tiny match; in the other, the packet it came from. He scans the mass of moviegoers until he fixes on one face. It is 10:40 P.M. when Melvin Purvis recognizes John Dillinger.

On this day, a Sunday, Chicago is staggering under the weight of an epic heat wave, with oppressive hundred-degree temperatures suffocating the Midwest. Two days later, on July 24, an all-time high—105 degrees—will be recorded at the city's downtown weather office. The city's elderly are hit hardest, and hundreds die alone in their airless homes. On this day alone, heat prostration claims twenty-three lives. Everywhere, desperate apartment dwellers search for relief—a meager rooftop breeze, a rare electric fan. Many flock to theaters such as the Biograph, which gives the technology of its controlled climate—"Cooled by Refrigeration," "Iced Fresh Air"—larger billing than its featured attraction, a Clark Gable gangster movie called *Manhattan Melodrama.* Heat—a great, searing, hellish heat—is the very theme of the day.

Outside the Biograph, Purvis looks hard at Dillinger. The agent has thought of little else for the past ten months. Purvis is not married, has no children. He works long hours and counts few friends outside the Bureau. He is uncommonly devoted to his job and to his mentor, Director J. Edgar Hoover, who has designated Dillinger Public Enemy Number One and made his capture the Bureau's top priority. Hoover, in his tenth year as director, is a masterful motivator, a paternalistic despot who commands the attention of his youthful agents through the sheer force of his will. He has imposed his own black-and-white moralism on the agency, so that to be loyal to the Bureau means to be loyal to Hoover. No one wants to fail at a mission, for that would be to disappoint Hoover. Thus, capturing Dillinger is in every way a personal matter, to Hoover, to his men in the field, to Purvis.

And now there they are, the hunter and the hunted, converging on a crowded city street where the swell of weaving bystanders is the backdrop to the drama—the worst possible scenario of people being in the path of harm. But good and evil tend to meet in disorderly ways. Purvis, in his third hour of standing in the sweltering heat, shines with sweat. His throat is parched from the taste of his cigar, and his eyes are bleary from examining faces. He worries about the women and children forming an inadvertent shield around Dillinger. His knees feel weak; he can hear his heart thumping in his chest. He is, he will later admit, afraid. The cigar shakes in Purvis's mouth as he strikes the match and raises it to his lips. Flame touches tobacco. The signal has been given.

January 1, 1927
FLORENCE, SOUTH CAROLINA

Seven and a half years earlier, Melvin Purvis commenced his plan B late on New Year's Day, 1927. At 8:00 P.M. he boarded the Atlantic Coast Line's Palmetto Limited, which normally stopped only in Florence but this day made a special stop in Purvis's hometown of Timmonsville, a few miles west. His mother and father and his seven sisters and one brother waved goodbye from the station platform. For the next fourteen hours, the train traveled northward up the eastern seaboard. Had he been traveling in summertime, a gritty layer of dust and cinders would have covered his hair and clothes because the train's windows would have been opened against the stifling heat of the steam engine. Dirt kicked up by hundreds of horsepower would have invaded every car, and an experienced porter could tell where a train had come from by the color of its dust; a reddish clay meant out west, a grayish cover meant up north. But in the dead of winter, Purvis enjoyed a clean and relatively quiet trip. The locomotive churned through vast stretches of backwoods and scrub pine and farmland, encountering no city of more consequence than Richmond, Virginia, on its 413-mile route. Toward the end of his journey, Purvis might have glimpsed, through smudged glass, the symbol of his future world—the stately dome of the U.S. Capitol building, visible as he arrived at Union Station midmorning on January 2.

Purvis was twenty-three but looked years younger. Fellow passengers could have mistaken him for a college freshman heading back to school. Close attention, however, would have revealed his striking countenance, the straightness of his posture, the perpetual upward jut of his prominent chin. Years later, a supervisor evaluating his performance with the Bureau of Investigation observed that Purvis "has only one major fault—that of being overconfident." Indeed, "Melvin knew that he could cut a figure," recalled secretary Doris Lockerman. "He had a sense of drama. There are people who can command a room when they walk into it. And Melvin was such a person. He had a lot of dash and self-confidence."

He would need every bit of it, as he was traveling to Washington to interview for a job for which he was technically ineligible. Moreover, it was not a job he had ever pursued. The decision to seek it was, essentially, an afterthought. At the time, Purvis was an attorney apprenticing at the Willcox and Hardee law firm, where, except for defending two hopelessly guilty murder suspects, he mainly ran title searches, adjusted insurance claims, and pored through thick law books. Purvis drew no salary and earned only a modest part of the fees for cases he worked. After twenty months, his patience for the job had worn thin. Plan A was to jettison this dreary routine and find adventure in far-off lands. "I wanted to wear white suits and a pith helmet," he would later say, "to get into the diplomatic service and be sent to foreign ports." So it was that in early December 1926, Purvis took his first trip to Washington, D.C., and walked unannounced into the Department of State, confident of both his calling and his aptitude as a diplomat.

His brashness was no match for the steel-door bureaucracy of the nation's capital. A State Department worker curtly told Purvis there were no openings, nor were any expected in the foreseeable future. The best the official could do was put his name on file and usher the would-be diplomat on his way. "It could not have been more negative unless I had been physically tossed out the front door," Purvis recalled. The long train ride back to Timmonsville gave him time to ponder working another twenty months in the purgatory of title searches and insurance claims.

Purvis wasted little time fretting. He quickly asked Allard Gasque, a close friend of his father's as well as the congressman from his local district, for help in cracking Washington's tight ranks. Gasque suggested Purvis forget about diplomacy and apply to the Department of Justice's Bureau of Investigation (it would not be renamed the FBI until 1935). The Bureau was a relatively new agency, headed by an anonymous young federal bureaucrat, J. Edgar Hoover. For years it had been plagued by corruption and inefficiency, and Hoover's mandate was to swab the decks. It would be easier to find an audience there, in an agency seeking fresh blood, Gasque advised, than at the venerable Department of State.

It took Purvis no time at all to deem himself fit for work as a special agent of the Bureau. On December 18, 1926, within days of being turned away at State, he sent a letter to "Mr. Hoover" asking to be considered for the position of investigator. This time he bolstered his case, mentioning in the letter that Congressman Gasque had provided him with the application. Two days later Gasque sent Hoover his own letter: "It is very seldom that I ever ask a favor of any of the Departments along this line," he wrote, "but in this case I know the applicant so well and know that he is a deserving young man." Purvis also enlisted U.S. Senator Ellison Durant "Cotton Ed" Smith, another family acquaintance and one of South Carolina's most influential politicians, to recommend him to Hoover, which Smith did in a December 22 letter. Young Melvin, it seemed, had quickly grasped the rules of engagement in Washington, where youthful bravado, on its own, was inadequate currency.

Even so, Hoover sent a standard reply to all three men—Purvis, Gasque, and Smith—advising that there were no openings and assuring them that Purvis's application would be placed on file.

At the same time, Hoover—even at age thirty-one supremely attuned to the political value of a well-placed favor—set in motion the vetting process that would bring Purvis back to Washington. Shortly before Christmas he dispatched special agent Lewis Baley of the Atlanta Bureau field office to run the requisite background check and to interview Purvis in Timmonsville. Everyone from the head of the law firm, Fred Willcox, to his Methodist minister, S. W. Henry, provided testimonials to Purvis's brightness and promise. Willcox touted Purvis as a candidate by slighting his potential as an attorney. "He [Willcox] said that he doubted that Applicant would make any great success in the practice of law as he was not aggressive enough in going after the dollars," Baley later wrote of Willcox's assessment. "Not that he was not industrious and ambitious, but he did not

believe he was cut out for a money maker." Baley's impression of
Purvis was favorable. "Agent believes him to be a young man of excellent character, good intelligence and manner, and that he can be
developed into a good Agent."

There was one major problem: Purvis was technically ineligible to
become a special agent. Bureau rules called for agents to be at least
age twenty-five and at least five feet nine inches tall, but he was only
twenty-three and just barely met the height requirement. Still, he
forged ahead with his plan B and returned to Washington to interview at Justice.

When Purvis arrived in the capital January 2, 1927, the town was
still in many ways a provincial city, far less cosmopolitan than other
world capitals. Prohibition had been in effect since 1920, and there
was no nightlife to speak of. Yet Purvis was smitten. Washington, he
would later say, seemed to him to be the very center of the world.
On January 5 he made his way to the elegant, triangular Denrike
Building on K Street and Vermont Avenue—headquarters for the
Bureau of Investigation. The Bureau occupied merely the third
floor and part of the fourth; Hoover could do no better than an office across the hall from the mailroom. At the time, the Bureau had
only 386 agents and a support staff of 208, spread out over several
field offices.* Special agents were not authorized to carry guns or
make arrests, and they busied themselves primarily with investigative legwork. Purvis was not walking into a prestigious seat of power;
in a way, he would be trading one paper-pushing job for another.
Still, he took no chances. This time he did not storm the castle
alone. For his January 5 meeting with Hoover's second-in-com-
mand, Assistant Director Harold "Pop" Nathan, Purvis arrived with
John L. McMillan and Alfred "Bunt" Lawton, the personal secre-
taries, respectively, to his sponsors, Congressman Gasque and Senator Smith, and formidable men in their own right (McMillan would
eventually be elected to Congress and, as chairman of the Committee on the District of Columbia, become known as the "mayor of
Washington"). This time, Purvis was warmly received.

Then came his big moment as he sat across from Nathan over an
imposingly wide desk. Fatherly and unflappable, known for wearing
suspenders, smoking a pipe, and vacationing in museums, Nathan

*Today the FBI has more than 10,000 agents.

was a pillar of the Bureau, a rare holdover from its pre-Hoover days. A New York City–born opera buff, he joined the Bureau in 1917 and survived Hoover's early purge of investigators, a downsizing that left Nathan as one of its few Jewish agents. Overall, he would log forty-two years in federal government, twenty-eight of them at the Bureau. His gentle and reasoned nature allowed him to serve as a counterbalance to Hoover, whose ambition to overhaul the Bureau often produced impractical ideas. In this way Nathan earned the director's respect and became, if not his top adviser, the only one who could be trusted to be consistently blunt. Nathan was the furthest thing from a yes man, and that alone made him an exceptional figure in Hoover's Bureau. When he fixed his attention on the thin young man parked nervously in his guest chair, Nathan's paternal side took over. "What kind of experience do you have, son?" he asked Purvis. "You look pretty much like a kid."

"Well, I've had a lot of experience," Purvis replied.

"Traveled a lot?"

"Yes, quite a bit."

Nathan smiled and said, "Probably all over the state of South Carolina." Then he did his best to talk Purvis out of the job. He told him he would not be stationed in South Carolina, that he would likely be sent far away from his family, that he would have few chances to return home—that he basically would need to sever all ties to his previous life. Purvis didn't blink. "He stated that such procedure would be entirely agreeable to him," Nathan later told Hoover. Something about Purvis touched Nathan in that meeting; perhaps it was Purvis's glint-eyed gumption, his brash naïveté. The mutual fondness that was evident that day would last each man his lifetime. Purvis had succeeded in making his technical ineligibility irrelevant. "I was favorably impressed with this applicant," Nathan wrote to Hoover, "and although he is slightly below the age limit, I recommend favorable consideration."

Only one hurdle remained. On January 22, 1927, Purvis's completed application—affixed with reference interviews and Nathan's recommendation—reached the desk of Nathan's boss: the director of the Bureau of Investigation, J. Edgar Hoover.

Tryouts for Central High School's football team in Washington, D.C., were open to all students, of any shape and size. Yet one boy was turned away on sight; he was deemed too small and skinny to warrant a further look. It took some time for the student to overcome his hurt feelings and, with few other options, apply instead to Central High's Brigade of Cadets. But this unit, too, was selective. Only students of obvious gifts would be considered to wear the regal uniforms of the marching brigade: pressed gray trousers, navy blue jacket, and, on the shoulders, gold epaulets signifying rank. The boy—nothing if not determined—somehow earned a spot, though he was buried in the very rear rank of the squad, the spot assigned to the brigade's smallest cadets. This did not matter to the boy. In the brigade's insistence on order and discipline, he had found something that fit. By the end of his fourth year at Central High, John Edgar Hoover was not only captain of his company but class valedictorian as well. The six squads he led marched in all their splendor at the inauguration of President Woodrow Wilson.

Hoover had learned his strengths early, and just four years later he would find a more permanent home at the Department of Justice. The man known to relatives as Edgar needed no lengthy train ride to reach the Justice building, where, as a twenty-two-year-old law school graduate, he began work as a $990-a-year entry-level clerk in 1917. He merely hopped on the trolley that ran from Seward Square—his birthplace and home for the first forty-three years of his life—to nearby K Street. In every sense it was a very short ride for Hoover, who grew up almost literally in the shadow of the U.S. Capitol. His great-grandfather had been the first Swiss consul in Washington, and a great-uncle had helped build the Capitol. Young Edgar seemed to absorb into his bloodstream the byzantine workings of federal government. Hoover was born to be a bureaucrat.

Born in 1895, in a coal-heated home in a quaint Victorian neighborhood of cobblestone streets and brick sidewalks, Hoover was thrust into a role he would play for four decades—as the replacement for a sister who died eighteen months before. Sadie Marguerite was only three years old when she succumbed to diphtheria, and Hoover's birth interrupted his family's mourning. For this reason, Hoover would remain inordinately close to his mother, Anna Margaret, who sheltered him and dressed him in precious outfits during his childhood. Hoover had no similar close connection to his father. Dickerson Hoover, an engraver for the U.S. Coast and Geodetic Survey—one of the oldest federal agencies—possessed few qualities of interest to his son. He was dour and pinched, and absolutely lacking in the kind of charisma that might have enticed Edgar from his mother's embrace. Their lack of closeness only became more pronounced as Dickerson slipped deeper and deeper into depression late in his life. When the elder Hoover wound up in a sanitarium for several months, his teenage son, by all accounts, behaved as if it had never happened. This crippling imbalance in Edgar's relations with his parents would undoubtedly shape his character. Unable to replace the mother he clung to, he never married and seldom thought highly of other women; deprived of an adequate male role model, he became a compassionless authoritarian.

His inheritance also included an uncompromising Swiss Calvinist moralism and a pugnacious patriotism. These qualities would define his successful stewardship of the Bureau in its early years, but they would also explain the righteousness that came to define his tenure. In addition, Hoover knew instinctively how to handle the convoluted federal bureaucracy. Anticipating a career in government, he never voted or even joined a political party, a neutrality that enabled him to find work in any administration. His chief attribute, however, was an uncommon diligence. "He had an exceptional capacity for detail work and he handled small chores with enthusiasm and thoroughness," read a 1937 *New Yorker* profile of Hoover. Within a few months of starting his clerkship at Justice in 1917, Hoover was promoted to special agent, largely due to logging twelve-hour days and seven-day weeks. He first drew notice hunting subversives on U.S. soil just after World War I, and as head of the Bureau's Radical Division engineered the arrest of 5,000 suspected dissidents in a twenty-four-hour period in 1920. He survived charges of unethical conduct for his use of blank arrest warrants—and his reliance on evidence he knew to be false to deport one anarchist. So immersed was Hoover in his work that he was apparently too busy to pay even a single visit to his father in his drab room at the Laurel Sanitarium. Dickerson died in 1921—the official cause was melancholia—but there was no funeral or memorial service. The loss of his father barely caused Hoover to break stride.

Hoover's unbending devotion to his work paved the way for his final ascent to power. He had the good fortune of entering the Bureau of Investigation—founded in 1908 as a small federal detective force—at a time when its reputation was at its lowest. Little more than a bureaucratic old-boy's network riddled by incompetent leadership and vastly inadequate record keeping, it inspired next to no public confidence. In 1923 its involvement in the Teapot Dome scandal—a morass of rigged government bids, suppressed federal investigations, and illegal surveillance of U.S. senators by Bureau agents—convinced then-President Calvin Coolidge that wholesale reform was in order. In this nest of scandal and corruption, one Bureau employee stood out. Tireless, unimpeachable, and a skilled administrator—thanks to a mastery of advanced filing methods he acquired while clerking at the Library of Congress—Hoover was a man for the moment. On May 10, 1924, shortly before noon, newly appointed U.S. Attorney General Harlan F. Stone named Hoover the acting director of the Bureau of Investigation. Hoover thereafter would be the most powerful man in the agency.

Once "acting" was dropped from his title in December 1924, Hoover sought to reshape the Bureau to match his idealized vision of strength and masculinity. Hoover's elite agents would be youthful, bright, educated, mannered—a new paragon of decency. Besides revamping the Bureau's administrative structure and instilling a rigorous standard of conduct—arguably his best and most lasting achievements—Hoover changed the very shape of his investigative army by handpicking his special agents, a practice he would continue even as the Bureau grew in size and scope in the 1940s and beyond. Not only were applicants required to have law, accounting, or chemistry degrees, but a clear premium was placed on appearance as well. Some criteria were subtle—Hoover liked agents who were clean-cut and athletic. Some criteria were not—Hoover kept blacks and women out of the Bureau. The director made all the hiring decisions, and all his decisions were final. It was an unapologetically autocratic process. "If an applicant for special agent is not the kind of man I would invite into my home," Hoover said, "I don't want him." Former special agent William Turner, who joined the FBI in 1951, remembered his class of new recruits being ushered single file into Hoover's office for inspection. "We were instructed not to speak to him other than to say, 'Good morning, Director,' unless he initiated a conversation," Turner said. "Sometimes he talked to an agent because he liked him, but others times it was so he could later tell the class counselor, 'That one guy that I talked to looks like a truck driver. Get rid of him.'"

One of the less orthodox criteria was a candidate's height. Hoover, short and stocky, was famously insecure about his stature and "did not like agents who were too tall," Turner recalled, adding that his fellow rookies were arranged in order of ascending height before being paraded before the director, presumably to make it easier for him to cull out the giants. Media queries about his height received the official response that he was "just a shade under six feet," but in fact he was a rounded five feet nine inches. One official biographer, resorting to tortured logic, described Hoover as "tall, but sufficiently well-proportioned to make his height less apparent." Acutely conscious of his image in and out of the Bureau, Hoover seldom allowed himself to be dwarfed by a taller man. To handle emergencies, he kept a dais under his desk.

Hoover's idiosyncratic hiring formula, its integrity ensured by his insistence on personally reviewing all applications, delivered to him the elite investigative force he coveted. Fortunately, Melvin Purvis was unaware of this daunting screening process; he might otherwise have been discouraged, because when he applied the Bureau was downsizing, part of its ongoing effort to eliminate deadwood. What chance did an unknown young man from Timmonsville, South Carolina, have of entering this elite men's club? Yet Hoover surely must have noticed the similarities between Purvis and himself: Both men were members of the national Kappa Alpha fraternity; both had captained their high school cadet corps; both stood significantly less than six feet tall. And how could Hoover have overlooked the glowing references from a senator and a congressman?

Even before Purvis could submit results of his physical exam as part of his application, Hoover had made up his mind. He wrote to Purvis January 29, 1927:

There is enclosed herewith a letter notifying you of your
appointment as a Special Agent in the Bureau of Investigation of this
Department, with salary at a rate of $2700 per annum, CAF-8. You
will also be allowed your actual expenses of travel and operation and
$4.00 per diem in lieu of subsistence when absent from official

headquarters, which are fixed temporarily at Atlanta, GA., and following your general assignment will be fixed from time to time at such places as may be deemed advisable.

The letter was no surprise to Purvis. "I never doubted that my application would be accepted," he would later say. "I had a complete and ignorant confidence in my own abilities." On February 2, 1927, he dispatched a short Western Union telegram to his new boss: "Will accept," it read. "Will go to Atlanta Friday February 4th."

That very month, thirty miles northeast of Indianapolis, John Dillinger—born the same year as Melvin Purvis—was serving the third of nine straight years in jail for armed robbery. Deep in the Oklahoma hills, Charles Arthur "Pretty Boy" Floyd was savoring his freedom after serving half of a three-year sentence for similar offenses. And Lester J. Gillis, later known as George "Baby Face" Nelson, was just beginning his career of crime, slipping in and out of prison for parole violations. It would be years before the nation knew their names.

As for young Melvin Purvis, a new world beckoned. All that remained was for him to sever his ties to Timmonsville. He promptly resigned from the Willcox law firm, but that was the easy step. Far more difficult separations loomed. He would have to say goodbye to his parents and to his brother and sisters. He would have to leave the house he grew up in and the horses he rode so many mornings. He would have to say goodbye to Rosanne Willcox, the woman he loved. He would have to give up a way of life that had once fit him well—give it up, he thought then, forever.

3

"HOME OF THE GODS"

Summer 1913

Timmonsville—a one-square-mile speck in northeast South Carolina, was a quintessential tobacco town of two thousand "where the farmers and plantation owners tied their horses to hitching posts and everybody knew everybody else," Purvis later recalled. The tiny town and its rigid values would influence his behavior for the rest of his life. Of all the things that shape a man, surely the land on which he is raised is among the most vital. And Purvis was always a good son of the South. He was born in the very cradle of secession—in the first state to announce its withdrawal from the Union. He grew up just three counties north of where, on April 10, 1861, Brigadier General P.G.T. Beauregard demanded the surrender of federal forces at Fort Sumter in Charleston Harbor, triggering the first skirmish of the Civil War. He was raised only a few miles from the historic town of Camden, which fell victim to William Tecumseh Sherman's merciless march through the South, burned down in 1865 for the sins of a state held responsible for the whole ungodly conflict. "South Carolina cried out the first for war, and she shall have it to her heart's content," one Union soldier later wrote. Sherman himself made no attempt to hide his consuming hatred for the state. "When I go through South Carolina it will be one of the most horrible things in the history of the world," he declared. "The devil himself couldn't restrain my men in that state."

Several Purvises had donned the gray wool garb and flattened caps of the Rebel Army, true to the military legacy of their ancestor Major Purvis, who, records show, served on George Washington's staff during the Revolutionary War. Not long before that war, the first Purvis made his way to the new continent. The family's forebears were among the landed gentry of Great Britain 'and descended from the venerable Scottish house of Purves. The family came to England with William the Conqueror; a William Purvoys De Mosspennach, twelfth-century proprietor of the lands of Mosspennach, was the first family name in the records. The first Purvises to arrive in America likely were part of a group of Scots who sailed to the shores of North Carolina and settled there. In 1765, John Purvis, a farmer, married a woman named Ann and moved to the area that is now Darlington County in South Carolina—land that would host the Purvis family for the next two centuries.

It was there in rich tobacco country that the first Melvin Purvis raised a family. Born four years after the end of the Civil War, Melvin Horace Purvis Sr. married Janie Elizabeth Mims in 1894. Janie Elizabeth was herself descended from survivors of a 1695 shipwreck off the Carolina coast.

The couple lived in a classic A-frame, two-story colonial in Timmonsville, on the corner of a lot that abutted Main Street, only yards from the railroad tracks that split the town. The handsome house had a columned porch that surrounded its left side and wrapped around back, opening onto a generous lawn and overlooking the garage and carriage house. The grand dining room extended onto the back porch, an arrangement that allowed for indoor or outdoor dining. In a state known for vast mansions and sprawling plantations, this was the home of a man of modest affluence. Purvis Sr. was not born rich; his family struggled during Reconstruction. But he was a bold investor, a believer in himself, and by the time he married he had extensive land holdings throughout Darlington and neighboring Florence counties. He was also director of a local bank and held the deed to four farms, one on each corner of Timmonsville. He employed several servants who lived on his property; one of them, Dolly, was descended from a slave family that was linked to the Purvis family for more than two centuries. Dolly would eventually work for Melvin Purvis in his home in Florence, becoming, in effect, a cherished and vital family member.

An intractable smoker who battled emphysema in later years, Purvis Sr. was a commanding figure, with a gravelly voice that could rattle the walls and an authoritative manner that gave him prominence in his community. By contrast, Janie Elizabeth was soft-spoken and gentle. Her husband with his stentorian tone ruled by decree, but hers was a quiet authority. Both hailed from large families: Janie was one of eight children, Melvin one of thirteen. In turn, the couple had a large family of their own: eight children, six girls and two boys. The fifth of these, and the first son, was Melvin Horace Purvis Jr., born October 26, 1903.

There was something exceptional about Melvin and his siblings, and to understand it calls for understanding the Carolina Lowcountry. America is a land of divides, of geographic splits and continental demarcations. People who live west of a mountain differ from those to its east; this side of a river or that defines the character of a city. Even in the relatively small inverted triangle that is South Carolina, there is a schism. Draw a horizontal line through the state capital, Columbia, from border to border; everything north of the line is Upcountry, and all to the south, including the entire coast, is Lowcountry.

This distinction is not pejorative in any way. It is sociological, honed over generations. People from Upcountry, the thinking goes, are brought up under a Protestant ethic; they work hard and accomplish good things, and that, they believe, is the chief end of man. Those in the Lowcountry, on the other hand, learn from an early age to enjoy life. An Upcountry host might serve coffee or tea; in the Lowcountry an afternoon toddy is more likely. Upcountry Carolinians are practical; Lowcountry dwellers have a more spiritual outlook on life.

Geographically, Timmonsville is just a few miles north of the dividing line. Curiously, however, it is deemed Lowcountry. Perhaps this straddling of the two cultures sheds light on the Purvis clan, because its members exhibited characteristics of both. They ran the gamut from serious and industrious to frivolous and eccentric.

Melvin Horace Purvis may have been the most blessed of all his twelve siblings. Beyond his financial successes, the family he raised in Timmonsville was uncommonly close, loving, and happy, buoyed by their affection for one another and an inherent exuberance. The confidence his children exhibited later in their lives had its roots in their sibling loyalty and parental attention. "The children loved their father and they absolutely adored their mother," said Ann Marion. "We know this not just from one of them but from all of them. It was just a wonderful family living in this wonderful home. It was as if nothing ever went wrong in that house. Someone once referred to it as the 'Home of the Gods.'"

The six sisters were especially close, a sorority unto themselves. The eldest, Nell Eulalia, was the unquestioned leader of the children—a strong, decisive woman; she and her sister Callie Mims were known by the others as Judge and Jury. "Callie, don't you think Melvin should be punished for what he did?" Nell might ask. "Why yes, Nell, I do," would come the reply. Stubborn as she was, Nell generally accepted the noisy discipline of her father, and very rarely went against the wishes of her mother, who never raised her voice in dealing with her children. But on occasion Nell's fiery temperament could not be subdued. A heavy snowstorm that swept through Timmonsville on the night of a dance the sisters planned to attend prompted their father to forbid them to go. "It's too bad," he said simply, "but you're not going anywhere." One of the sisters cried; another pouted. Nell gave a speech. "I got this dress specifically for this dance and Miss McSween is our chaperone and they're going to come and pick me up and I'm going to the dance and I will see you when I get back," she informed her father, and with that she was off. He chose not to put up a fight. Their father ran his family like a benevolent general, but his children—particularly Nell—could always find the chinks in his armor.

The brothers—Melvin and Guy—reveled in outdoor activities, learning to ride horses at an early age. The boys and their friends played cowboys and Indians, racing across fields and lassoing unlucky cattle. Melvin never lost his love of horses, and would continue to ride wherever he lived. "Bridle-path riding was no fun," Melvin later wrote. "We preferred cross-country galloping, jumping fences and ditches." The brothers also learned to shoot and hunt, traditional boyhood pursuits in the South. Ducks, quail, doves, rabbits, and raccoons were all targets, though not, in Melvin's case, particularly vulnerable ones. "One might well have thought that my prime consideration was wild-game conservation," he wrote, "for all the damage I did."

In this way childhood for the Purvis siblings was typical of life in a small Southern town. Commerce in Timmonsville comprised a very short list: two drugstores, a handful of dry-good stores, a blacksmith, a livery stable, a hardware store that carried everything from rifles to buggy-whip mounts, an ice house, a filling station, and an infrequently used railway depot. The town also had a small hospital, a public school, several seasonally active tobacco warehouses, and a very few ceiling-fanned restaurants.

Melvin worked an after-school job behind the soda fountain at the Cole Drug Company, on a corner of Main Street, and friends who stopped by might get some Whitman's Sampler on the house. Timmonsville's telephone operator, Eva Lawhon, not only knew all the townspeople but also knew their affairs. Her office window overlooked Main Street, allowing her to track everyone's comings and goings. If young Melvin called his father at the bank, Lawhon might tell him, "He's not at the office right now. I just saw him walk into the drugstore." And when Melvin asked her to patch him through to a girl he fancied, Lawhon saved him the trouble: "Sorry, honey, but if you're looking for a date she's already going out with Henry White."

Bolstered by his family's affection, young Melvin developed a fine sense of himself. Despite his small stature, he was outgoing, confident, and occasionally mischievous. He was educated at the Timmonsville School, of which his father was a trustee. Students attended for ten years; the last three were considered high school. Melvin enrolled in 1910, the year the school moved from a small brick Tudor-style building to a wide and squat two-story edifice constructed in 1909. "We went to the old building that morning and marched from there to the new building," he later wrote in the 1920 Timmonsville yearbook. "We didn't like this change so much because in the old building four of us could sit in one of those large desks and now we have to sit alone in the little new desks." One of fifteen students in his class, he was its designated historian, and as graduation neared he recounted his memories of life at the school. "We were always punished for talking," he recalled; he also confessed to misspelling words in a contest purposely to keep from advancing in a line of students. We would "spell well enough to stand where we wanted to," he wrote, "that is, beside the girl we liked best." Melvin eventually found a way to beat the system. Banished to the cloakroom for talking in class, he and other miscreants smuggled in food and made a party of it. "One day [the teacher] decided that we liked that too well," he wrote. "She began sending us to the office"—of Superintendent M. M. Wilkes, bow-tied, bespectacled, and not a little imperious. "We despised this, for we heard many sad and woeful tales from older boys who had been sent in there." The specter of Wilkes's harsh punishment proved little deterrent, however, and in the seventh grade "we were sent to the office more frequently and in larger numbers than ever before."

In fact Melvin was no more troublesome than any student, and certainly was busier and more popular than most. He was elected captain of the high school military company and was thought to be interested in a military career—the 1920 yearbook listed his ambition as "to go to Annapolis" (it also listed his greatest accomplishment as "bluffing teachers"). Melvin's interest was actually in the dynamics of leadership; he had a belief he should be a decision-maker in any group he chose to join. Undersized but undeterred, Melvin played both sports offered at the school—football and baseball. A comment in the 1920 yearbook indicates that Melvin's classmates found him both charming and charmed, possessed of a certain finesse that allowed him to navigate the world with grace: "Whenever all the class is dull and stupid, he always thinks of something cute to say." Another remark countered, "But still, why so sarcastic?" Certainly students saw that Melvin had a restlessness about him; that he had a sense of entitlement and a propensity for big dreams; that he was likely to live some sort of extraordinary life. His friend Evelyn Coker, dubbed the Class Prophet, anticipated the future for all of her classmates and closed with her projections for Melvin. "I now behold . . . acres and acres of cultivated fields, green and inviting in the early morning sun, surrounding a large colonial home. I look again, and to my astonishment, I see my carefree friend and classmate, Melvin Purvis, who has inherited an immense fortune, master of the scene of enchantment. On one side of the house is a large, open field. I soon discover that this is an aviation field and that Melvin has devoted his entire time to aeroplanes."

Of course, nothing is quite so optimistic as a high school yearbook. The Timmonsville class of 1920 had reason to feel good about its prospects. America was finished with World War I and still years away from the Great Depression. In 1920 one in three households owned an automobile, up from one in thirteen at the start of the war. A new invention called the radio was finding its way into more and more homes; the first commercial radio broadcast was in November 1920. The world, it seemed, was opening up—opportunity was everywhere. What reason did Melvin and his classmates have to feel cynical? They could look forward and reasonably expect to have their fondest wishes fulfilled. Certainly Melvin must have felt nothing but unwavering wonder about his future. The innocence of that time was captured in the poem selected by Melvin's classmate Dorothy Keith in her 1920 valedictory speech:

Don't look for the flaws, as you go through life,
And even when you find them,
It's nice and kind to be somewhat blind,
And look for the virtues behind them.

The tragedy of Melvin Purvis is that he believed these lines.

———

Only two sentences—a mere forty-two words—served Melvin Purvis to describe his college experience in his memoir *American Agent*. "I went off to the University of South Carolina with every intention of becoming a businessman, and took a few law courses as part of my business education," he wrote. "Somewhat to my own surprise, I found myself graduating in law five years later."

Perhaps the experience was less than memorable for him, with hours spent scouring dull textbooks deep into the night. More likely the two sentences reveal Purvis's normal reticence about his personal life. His years at the university in Columbia, some sixty miles west of Timmonsville, represented his first significant time away from home and his first exposure to anything approaching a cosmopolitan environment. Yet the broadening of his horizon did little to focus his ambition; he remained unsure of his calling even after five years of college. Neither business nor law engaged him in any real way; nor did he develop any compelling interests while at school. He joined the southern branch of the Kappa Alpha fraternity, something of a rite of passage. He was also briefly the second-string quarterback on the university's football team until he broke a leg and settled for being the assistant manager of the football and baseball associations. Despite professing a deep boredom with law school, he received his law degree in 1925, and on June 10 of that year, he passed the South Carolina bar. Melvin Purvis was a lawyer.

His desire to return to the Timmonsville area to practice left only one real option: the law office of Willcox and Hardee, in nearby Florence. Perhaps the most prestigious law firm in eastern South Carolina, it was founded by a giant of the profession—Philip Alston Willcox, "the ablest lawyer I ever saw in action," wrote Judge E. C. Dennis, a highly regarded circuit judge in Darlington County. "I have heard and known many able lawyers, but the greatest of them all was P. A. Willcox." Short, stout and balding, Willcox was nevertheless enormously magnetic, and capable of swaying judges and juries with his genial disposition and easy charm. He never browbeat a witness or raised his voice to the bench; instead he allowed his polished manner, dapper clothes, and uncanny grasp of the subject at hand to so dazzle spectators that they could not help but convert to his point of view.

It was his firm that Melvin Purvis joined as a junior member in 1925, though by that time P. A. Willcox was gone. In 1921, the same year that he delivered a memorable Founders Day speech before the American Bar Association in Cincinnati—a speech many believed was a prelude to his being offered the presidency of the bar—Willcox, a diabetic, contracted influenza. He never recovered and died at the age of fifty-six. He left behind a wife and three children: two sons, Philip and St. George, and, in between, a twelve-year-old daughter, Rosanne.

How Melvin Purvis met Rosanne Willcox is unclear, but they must have known each other even before Purvis began work at her late father's firm. She was raised in a two-story house on Irby Street in downtown Florence, which was ten miles east of Timmonsville. After her father died, the family fortune quickly dwindled. Her mother, Marie, parted with such luxuries as a private railway car, a stable of horses, and a mountain retreat in Saluda, North Carolina. Their home in Florence also was sold, and Marie built a smaller home on property the family owned on Cherokee Road. The law firm provided a small stipend, but it was not enough; Marie took the first job of her life, as a librarian at the Florence Public Library. Still, her children had a pleasant, small-town childhood. Rosanne attended dances in Florence and took trips with her friends to Myrtle Beach. One such social occasion was likely when she encountered a small, confident, sharp-featured fellow from Timmonsville. Melvin Purvis, who traveled frequently to Florence to escape the tedium of his hometown, "was absolutely crazy about Rosanne," said Mamie Charles, a Florence native who knew both Melvin and Rosanne well. "She was such a precious girl and so perfectly lovely and just the dearest, sweetest person you could imagine. And he was crazy in love with her."

Rosanne was indeed lovely. She had short, wavy brown hair and a shy, hesitant smile, and she spoke with a slight lisp that made her seem playful and carefree. There was a softness to her manner, an alluring blitheness, which Melvin—surrounded by headstrong sisters—had not much experienced. "She was one of the more fascinating women I have known," recalled Melvin's niece Ann Marion. "She was so vibrant and so full of life. Everybody loved her because she was so much fun to be around."

Rosanne attended Winthrop College in Rock Hill, in northern South Carolina, and spent some weekends at the home of Melvin's sister Nell, who lived with her husband in Chester, twenty miles from the Winthrop campus. Nell's daughter, Ann Marion, remembered her mother describing these visits: "When Rosanne stayed with us Melvin would come up here to see her. He would call and make a date and then he would come up from Timmonsville and take her out somewhere. He came up all the time." No one knows the extent or duration of their dating or even their activities; in later years neither Melvin nor Rosanne spoke much of their early courtship. But family histories make it clear that Melvin was smitten with Rosanne. "I think Melvin was always in love with her," said Ann Marion. "Rosanne was the love of his life."

Yet there were problems. Melvin, five years older than Rosanne, was a less than ideal suitor. For one thing, he had no money of his own; his job at the law firm paid him next to nothing. "He was from Timmonsville, and that was considered a backwater town," Mamie Charles said. Ironically, the Purvis family was far more prosperous than the Willcoxes were at the time. But that did not change the fact that Melvin was not thought to be a good catch. It would not have been a simple thing for Rosanne to announce that she planned to marry him; in those days a woman's choice of a husband affected not only her but her family as well. For that reason, the blossoming romance between Melvin and Rosanne was, in some ways, doomed before it began.

Melvin was in no position to ask for her hand in marriage. "He fell in love with Rosanne but he could not afford to marry anybody," said Ann Marion. He might have proposed to her anyway, or he might have continued the courtship for as long as it took to earn a good salary and prove that his prospects were bright. But that would entail staying at the law firm, and this was something Melvin Purvis had no desire to do. He had an idea he was destined for something extraordinary in life, and he was convinced he would not find it inside a law book. He had an impulse for action—a yearning for adventure. But for that he would have to leave Timmonsville—and Rosanne.

It was February 4, 1927, when Melvin Purvis took a train from Timmonsville to Atlanta, where he would take his first oath of office as a special agent for the Bureau of Investigation. He was twenty-three years old. Back in Florence, Rosanne Willcox could not be expected to wait for him to make his mark on the world, and she did not. She met a man named Archie Taylor, a vice president for Standard Oil who was passing through Florence on business. He was handsome and charming, and he drew a large salary. Rosanne's mother found him to be an ideal suitor, and when he proposed Rosanne said yes. A wedding date was set, and a rehearsal dinner was planned for the night before. But even then Rosanne realized she was making a mistake.

Still, the wedding went forward; the two were married in a ceremony at St. John's Episcopal Church in Florence on August 22, 1931. "Rosanne never raised up her eyes when she came into that church," recalled Mamie Charles, who attended the wedding as a young girl. "She kept her head down the whole time." Few details about the wedding have survived in family lore. But it has been said that all the bridesmaids wept during the wedding. "They were not crying because they were happy," said Ann Marion. "They were crying because they knew that Rosanne was marrying the wrong man."

———

Far from Timmonsville, in the largely Quaker village of Mooresville, Indiana, a handsome twenty-year-old man hid in the dark back steps of the Mooresville Christian Church late on September 6, 1924. He was half drunk on moonshine, and he held a heavy bolt wrapped in a handkerchief in his hand. An Iver Johnson .32 pistol was stashed inside his waistband. The man watched from his lair as Frank Morgan, sixty-five-year-old proprietor of the West End Grocery, walked home after getting a haircut. Morgan had the weekend's receipts—$150—in his pocket, and the man in the shadows knew this. The old grocer, in his straw hat, walked past the church at around 10:00 P.M. He never saw the figure lurching toward him from the steps.

Life had not been terrible for the twenty-year-old up to that point, but neither had it been easy. Born in 1903—the same year as Melvin Purvis—he was only three years old when his mother suffered an apoplectic stroke and died after an operation. At her funeral, relatives found her young son standing on a chair beside her coffin and shaking her cold body. He lived with his widowed father and grew into a rebellious teenager, full of mischief but not so bad as to cause alarm. But when he dropped out of school in the eighth grade, the tide turned. His first criminal act was stealing a brand-new car as its owners prayed inside Mooresville's Friends Church. He joined the Navy and became a fireman third class, but went AWOL, received a court-martial, and ultimately deserted. He was later arrested for stealing forty-one chickens and avoided prison only when his father persuaded police to drop the case. Yet he was only a small-time crook, still capable of straightening out his life.

Then came the night of September 6, 1924. He might have simply pulled his gun on the old grocer and demanded the cash. But something drove him to violence on the street outside the church. With a full swing he crashed the heavy bolt into Morgan's head, then hit him again as he went down. Morgan fell but did not stay down; his straw hat saved him from unconsciousness. Instead he grappled with his assailant and fought him for the gun. During the struggle the Iver Johnson fired into the ground, and the shot brought neighbors out of their houses. The man ran away, empty-handed.

Enough people had seen him around town that night to lead Deputy Sheriff John M. Hayworth to his father's farm the next morning. Young John Dillinger was questioned and arrested, and eventually he implicated the ex-convict who had been his accomplice, Edgar Singleton. Singleton hired a lawyer and pled not guilty;

at trial he was found guilty and received a sentence of two to fourteen years. He was back on the streets within two years. The outcome was different for Dillinger. At his father's urging, he pled guilty, believing his lack of a criminal record would convince the judge to go easy on him. His father even said court officials had promised him such leniency. But he had the misfortune of drawing Judge Joseph Williams, known as the toughest jurist in the county. With no defense lawyer to persuade him otherwise, Judge Williams delivered the harshest sentence he could—ten to twenty years. The convicted boy's older sister cried as sheriffs drove him past her home on the way to the Indiana State Reformatory at Pendleton. "The judge and the prosecutor took him out and told him if he would tell certain things they would let him off with a lighter sentence; they didn't keep their word," Indiana Governor Paul V. McNutt said of the case ten years later, calling it a terrible injustice. "This made a criminal out of [him]."

Indeed, his time in prison taught Dillinger how to be a proper thief, as he had the chance to absorb the lessons of hardened criminals. He would learn how to be cool under pressure, how to terrorize his victims, how to be brazen in choosing his targets, how to disregard human life. It was in prison—from which he would not emerge for more than nine years—that he would be transformed from a common thug into a true criminal. When the steel bars of his Pendleton cell first slammed shut, young John Dillinger slipped forever to the dark side.

4

"HE IS POSSESSED OF SNAP"

February 1927

A brash new employee bounded into the Bureau's Atlanta field office early on February 4. Melvin Purvis shook hands with special-agent-in-charge Lewis J. Baley and reported for duty. Purvis took the oath of office and learned he would leave later that day for the Dallas field office, where he would receive his first assignment. He was eager to get started on the good and worthy work of fighting crime.

But first some of the more experienced agents in Atlanta pulled the youthful recruit aside and gave him pointers. Over lunch one agent offered a tip on how to get along with the chief of detectives in Dallas. "He said it would be very difficult to gain admittance to the chief's office and that such admittance must be gained in as secret a fashion as possible," Purvis recalled. "He said the real name of the chief of detectives was Hughes, but that I should cautiously approach the information desk and state that I desired to see 'Mr. Love.'" Purvis nodded and thanked him for the tip. Only when he ran it by some agents in Dallas did he realize the Atlanta old-timers were having "some fun at the rookie's expense."

That was the extent of the fun. Purvis learned quickly that the special agent's life was "not a happy one." The business of chasing criminals placed enormous demands on the relative handful of agents across the country. They were, first and foremost, expected to be on call twenty-four hours a day, and could expect to be roused at any hour to follow a lead or stage a raid. An agent's chief attribute was the ability to live lightly. Because he might need to travel at a moment's notice to spend the next week or month in a far-off city, he had to put down as few roots as possible. To agents, the standard nine-to-five workday was unknown; besides the early mandatory start time, their workday could last anywhere from ten to twenty hours or longer. Casework could become so demanding that the idea of going home for a shower and a meal sometimes seemed a distraction. The nature of the work was mostly investigative and often tedious but required absolute absorption in the task. Essentially, agents were asked to surrender themselves to the Bureau completely and make its work the most important thing in life. "These men were absolutely devoted to the work—they consecrated it," said Doris Lockerman. "The stress and tension never subsided; it was there twenty-four hours a day year after year. These young men could not take their eyes off their targets for a second. This was their mission, and it was not about one great moment of capture or death but about endless days of maximum effort to bring people to justice."

Purvis, for one, found such devotion rewarding. "Like the artist or architect, the special agent can see his plans grow and take form until finally his case is complete," he would say. "He can have the satisfaction that follows an effort toward the end." In his very first case as a special agent, Purvis learned the importance of such diligence and follow-through effort. He arrived in Dallas February 6 and was immediately assigned one of several cold cases languishing in the files. The case involved an automobile stolen in Denver, Colorado, and investigation had led nowhere despite the thick file.

Like all new agents in the early days of the Bureau, Purvis had received no investigative training beyond reading and memorizing a standard-issue rulebook. Still, as a lawyer, he was skilled at culling volumes of information down to their crucial core. While he was flipping through the car-theft file, one small reference caught his attention—an indication that the suspected thief might have once visited a little restaurant on an out-of-the-way side street in Dallas. Purvis noticed the lead had not been followed. He grabbed his coat, found the place, and questioned the woman who ran it. Not surprisingly, she claimed not to know the man. Purvis persisted. Finally, he recalled, "She indicated with a shrug of her shoulders that I might find his telephone number by looking on the wall near the telephone."

Purvis checked the wall and found dozens of numbers scrawled around the telephone. He wrote down six or eight of them and returned to the office. It wasn't much to go on, but it was all he had. Purvis called the numbers and, on one of his last tries, was surprised when the woman who answered said that, yes, this was the home of the suspect, and that she was his wife. Purvis remembered from the case file that the suspect had worked as a cement mixer; he explained he was calling because he needed someone for a construction job. The woman told Purvis her husband would be home by 6:30 that evening. Since special agents did not yet have the power to arrest people, Purvis phoned the Dallas police department and asked for two officers to meet him at the address. The suspect showed up right on time. "He was arrested and sent to jail for his crime," Purvis recalled. "Catching this criminal was luck, beginner's luck."

Nevertheless, he had cracked his first case, and his superiors took notice. It was standard protocol for new agents to be evaluated after thirty days, and after thirty-eight days J. Edgar Hoover wrote the Dallas office asking for Purvis's efficiency statement. The new special-agent-in-charge, W. D. Bolling, provided Purvis's first Bureau evaluation. "Agent Purvis has a very pleasing personality and pays a great deal of attention to the details of an investigation," Bolling wrote on March 24. "I feel sure he will make a competent Agent." Hoover felt confident enough to transfer Purvis to the New York office to begin training in antitrust investigations, which, in the pre-gangster days of 1927, were among the Bureau's most important cases. After two weeks of training, Purvis was on his way to the field office in Norfolk, Virginia. He scored 92 out of 100 in his six-month efficiency rating, with top marks in dependability, industry, loyalty, and, of course, personal appearance.

Three weeks after Purvis's transfer to Norfolk, the special-agent-in-charge there, G. H. Hennegar, received an urgent telegram advising that Purvis's mother was seriously ill; his family wanted him in Timmonsville immediately. Hennegar reached Purvis in Roanoke, where he was on assignment, and told him to catch a train home. For years Janie Elizabeth Purvis had suffered from high blood pressure, and on her doctor's orders she spent summers in a resort in rural Glen Springs. The water there, went the thinking, would bring her blood pressure down. "One morning Janie Elizabeth came down for breakfast but in the middle of it she said she did not feel well and she went back upstairs," said her granddaughter Ann Marion. "And that was it. [My aunt] Edith found her upstairs. She died in bed that day."

Purvis learned of his mother's death as soon as he reached Timmonsville. He found a devastated family. "My God, the children worshiped their mother," said Ann Marion. "But it was their father who took it the worst. I remember one of my aunts telling me, 'My father missed my mother so much he had no idea we were grieving, too.'" At the time, all of the children were grown, and only two lived at the Timmonsville house. But after their mother's death, they reconvened to support one another and bolster their shaken father. "He was in awful shape," Ann Marion recalled. "Once the rest of the children left, only Mary Beth and Janie remained with him, and they would always say how terrible things were. The poor man was just lost."

In Washington, J. Edgar Hoover dictated his first personal letter to Melvin Purvis. "I have just learned of the death of your mother and I hasten to express to you my deepest sympathy," it read. "I well realize how inadequate words are at such a time to alleviate the sufferings which one experiences, but I did want you to know that my sympathy was with you. If there is anything that I can do, either personally or officially, do not hesitate to let me know." When Purvis returned to Norfolk on August 24, he handwrote a reply: "I desire to thank you for your kind note . . . it was indeed good of you and I cannot tell you how much I appreciate it."

By the end of his first year at the Bureau, Purvis had put himself firmly on Hoover's radar. He mainly worked on antitrust investigations in the movie industry, interviewing exhibitors, examining the minutes of film board meetings, and compiling investigative reports. None of it was glamorous work, but Purvis showed an eye for detail and a keen persistence. "He creates in the party whom he interviews respect for the Department and himself," one supervisor told Hoover, "although somewhat handicapped for trust work by reason of his very youthful appearance." Hoover had heard enough. On November 25, 1927, he instructed that Purvis be released from any further antitrust work. "It is my intention," he wrote, "to order [Purvis] on general assignment and to develop [him] for executive positions."

Over the next three years, Purvis worked in several field offices—
New York, Atlanta, Chicago, Connecticut, Ohio—living out of hotels
and only rarely renting an apartment. Periodic raises and grade
bumps brought him by March 1931 to a grade CAF-12 (from CAF-
8) and an annual salary of $5,000 (from $2,700). Because of his legal background, he soon resumed investigating antitrust cases,
conducting hundreds of interviews, meeting with state attorneys
general, and attending trials as part of the prosecutor's staff. Along
the way, glowing reviews kept landing on Hoover's desk. "He has
taken hold of the general investigative work in an excellent fashion
and his attitude has been unusually good," one special-agent-in-
charge observed. "He is possessed of snap and goes after his work
aggressively." Purvis "exercises excellent judgment, has much initia-
tive and force and has been exceedingly industrious," wrote L. C.
Schilder, the special-agent-in-charge of the Columbus, Ohio, office,
for whom Purvis served as top assistant. "I am very glad to have
Agent Purvis here, especially as I have been in dire need of a number one man." Purvis is "conscientious, loyal, energetic and of splendid appearance," a December 1929 report observed. Purvis
"possesses an exceptional memory, is highly intelligent, intensely
loyal to the Bureau and possesses . . . the requisite executive ability
to make a successful Special Agent in Charge," read another. Surely
Hoover—who favored unquestioning devotion above all else—
found magic words in a March 1931 report: "He made a grade of
100% on the Manual of Rules and Regulations, and 100% on the
Manual of Instruction . . . I believe he is 100% Bureau-minded."

Hoover began grooming Purvis in earnest. In December 1929,
Hoover asked Schilder to release Purvis from Cincinnati to attend
ten days of special executive training in Washington, telling
Schilder to designate another number-one man temporarily.
Schilder replied, "No Agent attached here excepting Mr. Purvis is so
qualified." Hoover nevertheless had Purvis brought to Washington
for a training program for agents designated for advancement.
When Purvis returned to Cincinnati in January 1930, he was officially named acting special-agent-in-charge for times Schilder was
absent from the office. Almost precisely three years from the day he
began work at the Bureau, Purvis, only twenty-six, had been entrusted to run a field office.

Purvis's quick ascension to a leadership position roughly coincided with a defining event in his career—and in America's history. In early October 1929, Yale University economist Irving Fisher confidently declared, "The nation is marching along a permanently high plateau of prosperity." His optimism would prove dramatically unfounded in only five days. On Monday, October 21, stock prices began to slide, alarming Wall Street investors. Three days later even the hardiest of them had lost all confidence as stock prices dropped even lower. That Friday, a group of bankers helped stabilize the market, but only for one last weekend. On October 29, 1929—a day that would soon be known as Black Tuesday—millions of stocks lost all value. Within two weeks nearly $30 billion of the nation's wealth vanished. The first of some 85,000 businesses failed; the first of millions of people lost their jobs. In Chicago one disconsolate banker was found hanged in his hotel room. The Roaring Twenties had ended. The Great Depression had begun.

The worst financial crisis in America's history scarred the country in profound ways. Its image of itself was badly damaged; its very landscape was transformed. Suddenly there were long bread lines, beggars on every corner, hoboes hopping trains, "For Sale" signs everywhere. Once hearty and robust, the nation fell into despair. Men with no criminal inclinations turned to crime out of helplessness; men predisposed to break the law became hardened criminals. Men who had shown a particular penchant for theft and graft matured into a new breed of evildoer: the supercriminal, the fearless, phantom menace—the American gangster.

Poring through his dreary antitrust records, Melvin Purvis had no inkling such monsters were being loosed—that from jails across the country were springing the most daunting nemeses the Bureau had ever encountered. Soon he would know it all too well. A great conflict loomed, a reckoning, a clash of wills, as a nation torn by hardship spawned uncommon villains and heroes.

———

On November 5, 1930, Hoover sent Purvis a one-sentence letter: "This is to advise you that you are hereby designated Special Agent in Charge of the Cincinnati Bureau Office." At twenty-seven, he was the youngest field office chief in the Bureau. In Cincinnati, Purvis presided over twelve agents, five accountants, and six stenographers

packed into a cramped office on the fourteenth floor of a downtown building. They had no conference room, no storage area for
files, and only a single large space for all twelve agents. There were
over 300 active cases and more than 100 undeveloped leads, a staggering burden for the small staff; one inspection found eleven cases
had been neglected altogether. Still, once Purvis assumed leadership of the Cincinnati agents, he was deemed "to be vigorously ad-
ministering the affairs of the office," according to an inspector.
What's more, the inspector told Hoover, "I am absolutely convinced
of his entire loyalty to you." There was no question: Purvis was the
rising star of the force.

For the next two years, Hoover shuffled Purvis around the country in a sort of prolonged executive audition. In May 1931, Purvis
took over in Washington, D.C., the field office most directly under
Hoover's watchful gaze. That August, Purvis became acting chief of
the Division of Identification, the Bureau's fingerprint squad. Just a
month later, he assumed control of the Oklahoma City field office.
In May 1932, Hoover made him special-agent-in-charge in Birmingham, Alabama. At every stop, inspectors were struck by his energy
and confidence. "I was particularly impressed with the rapid, snappy
way in which Purvis handled his correspondence and reviewed his
reports," one noted. "I believe the trouble with many of our offices
is that our Agents in Charge are somewhat foggy mentally." By 1932
there was no question Hoover had a trusted foot soldier in Purvis.
"His loyalty is intense," inspector Hugh Clegg observed in March
1932. "He has a feeling that as part of the Bureau it is his organization, and he is willing to go to the limit for the organization and for
anyone connected with it, from administrative officials down to the
lowest salaried clerical employees; yet, if an employee gets off the
reservation he is equally alert to protect the Bureau's interests."

Purvis, aware that his youthful looks might mark him as a
pushover, proved his mettle by coming down hard on anyone who,
as Clegg put it, got "off the reservation." As head of the Cincinnati
office, Purvis convened a formal hearing to investigate charges
against an agent who had failed to brief supervisors about a case. After the hearing, the agent caught up with Purvis on the street outside the field office. "He stated that he hoped I would 'go easy,'"
Purvis noted in a letter to Hoover. Instead, Purvis recommended
the man be fired.

Raised to feel unbending allegiance to his family, Purvis arrived at the Bureau with a strong sense of duty intact. Once he adopted the Bureau as his new family, it is not surprising he became its sworn supporter. Hoover saw in Purvis the perfect reflection of his own commitment to the Bureau. Time and again, Purvis proved that he was, as Clegg put it, willing to go to the limit for Hoover, and Hoover expected nothing less than this. By early 1932 Purvis's audition was close to ending.

Not that there weren't rough spots along the way. Purvis was undoubtedly a Hoover loyalist, but he was not a sycophant. It was not in his nature to be one. The same confidence that allowed him to become a leader despite his age also prevented him from accepting rules and strictures he felt were frivolous. In all his time at the Bureau, Purvis never stopped chafing under Hoover's impossibly stringent regulations. For instance, Bureau policy held that being even one or two minutes late meant an agent had to submit a leave slip for a full hour. Purvis deplored this rule. He preferred conducting Bureau business on the way into his office, while Bureau policy required agents to stop by the office first unless authorized to do otherwise. In November 1927 an inspector reprimanded Purvis for arriving at the office at 9:15 instead of nine sharp. His explanation—that he stopped on the way to conduct an interview—was no excuse. On February 15, 1928, Purvis arrived at the office at 8:58 A.M. by his watch, but an inspector's watch showed 9:02. Purvis grudgingly submitted a leave slip for one hour. If the rule was intended to teach agents a hard lesson, it did not work with Purvis: Over the years he would receive several reprimands for being late. Purvis never accepted the notion that agents who were asked to devote nearly every waking hour to their jobs could not, on occasion, be a few minutes late getting to work.

Nor did Purvis bow to Hoover's demand for the impeccable administration of paperwork. Hoover cleaned up the Bureau by stressing clerical efficiency and implementing a rigid filing system to ensure accountability. He truly believed adherence to this layered bureaucracy produced better results in the field. But Purvis felt Hoover placed undue emphasis on clerical matters. In March 1929, Hoover scolded Purvis for his continued disregard of a certain procedure. "I have conveyed these instructions to you verbally several times, but I find that a number of cases have arisen in which these rules have not been followed," Hoover wrote. "I want you to take immediate steps to see that my orders upon this matter are carried out at once." A month later, Hoover wrote, "It has been necessary to call your attention before to the insufficient information provided in the briefs of applicants and I desire that you give this matter your personal attention so that this may not occur again." In March 1930, Hoover berated Purvis for scoring only 82 out of 100 on a test of his knowledge of Bureau rules and regulations. On another occasion, Hoover returned a memorandum to Purvis because it contained a single typographical error. "Please advise me as to the identity of the person responsible for this error," Hoover demanded, "and why the same was not carefully checked before being sent to me for signature."

Purvis, whose administrative skills improved little despite a steady stream of warnings, found a way to repay Hoover for his pettiness. When Washington issued a new Manual of Instructions in August 1930, Purvis searched for mistakes and promptly sent Hoover a letter listing seven typographical errors in the manual, most in the spelling of legal terms. "Statue should be statute," he lectured Hoover. "Testimony is misspelled testamony; subornation [of perjury] is misspelled as subordination."

Purvis's positive qualities, however, made it easy for Hoover to overlook what more than one inspector called the flaw of overconfidence. Hoover had a vision of his ideal agent, and Purvis came as close as anyone to matching that vision. The director showed utmost faith in the young Purvis by promoting him to a top field position when most agents were just entering the Bureau and studying their manuals at night. By early 1932, Purvis had risen so quickly through the Bureau's ranks that only one position remained to which he could rise as an agent. The most high-profile field office of all, the place that handled the most dramatic cases, the city that cradled the most sinister criminals, was Chicago.

Few cities could speak of such a rich history of crime and bloodletting. Chicago's neighborhoods had names that reflected the evil within them—Hell's Half Acre, Little Hell, the Bad Lands, the Black Hole. Its underworld was, for a century, the most ruthless and colorful criminal element in America, with the possible exception of San Francisco's Barbary Coast. Chicago teemed with gangs and gangsters of exceptional renown: the vicious turn-of-the-century saloonkeepers Roger Plant and John Ryan; the swarming hoodlums who looted the city after its great 1871 fire; the gleefully thieving prostitutes Black Susan Winslow and Lizzie Clifford; the belligerent fence and knockout-drink artist Mickey Finn; the gruesome serial killer H. H. Holmes; the conglomeration of murderous gangs known collectively as the Black Hand; the early underworld bosses Big Jim Colosimo and Johnny Torrio; and, of course, the most feared and famous Chicago gangster of all—Al Capone, who was sentenced to eleven years in prison in October 1931.

Quite simply, no other city was like it. "Chicago is the hurly-burly, rough-and-tumble, guns-and-girls front page hero town of the U.S.," one writer observed. Well before it became home to a new breed of criminal in the 1930s—the Depression-era gangsters, who treated the city as a sort of headquarters while waging their roving sprees of robbery and terror—Chicago was a cauldron of crookedness and vice, unmanageable by its corrupt police, ungovernable by its shady politicians. Hoover's Bureau had no greater challenge in the country than the entrenched and sensational Chicago underworld.

To lead the Chicago office in that dangerous time, Hoover chose his favorite agent and most dependable man—Melvin Purvis. On October 25, 1932, Hoover informed Purvis he was being transferred from Birmingham to serve as special-agent-in-charge in Chicago. The youthful Purvis, with only five years of investigative experience, would be seen as Hoover's Golden Boy, groomed for greatness and given the Bureau's most glamorous job. And yet, said Doris Lockerman, in many ways "Melvin Purvis was absolutely the wrong man for the job. Here was this genteel attorney from the South who looked like he was fresh out of college, and Hoover put him in the toughest spot there was. He was not like these rugged police-types who usually worked in Chicago; he was a soft-spoken gentleman who wore elegant suits. He could not have been a more atypical choice for Hoover to make. And yet Hoover saw something in Melvin Purvis that made him right for the job. And of course Purvis never doubted for a moment that he could pull it off."

The adventure Purvis had dreamed of was truly about to begin. Purvis gathered up his new fox terrier puppy, put him in the passenger seat of his shiny Pierce-Arrow sedan, and drove from Birmingham to Chicago. By then, Purvis would later write, "I had traveled in every one of the 48 states except Vermont; I had been the special agent in charge of federal bureaus in a number of cities." Even so, he would say, once he arrived in Chicago, "I soon discovered that I still had a great deal to learn."

———

Why did Hoover choose Purvis to be his top field agent and then to head the critical Chicago office? Why, when so many more experienced agents were available, did the diminutive, soft-spoken Purvis garner so much of Hoover's attention? It was likely because, ironically, he rebelled against Hoover's directive that his agents be interchangeable. In Hoover's deliberately homogenized army of special agents, Purvis stood out. Purvis was bristly, bursting with purpose, youthfully audacious; this energy was hard to resist or ignore. "He is a little impatient for things to happen," one report noted, "whether it be an investigation which he is conducting or work which he desires to have turned out of any other nature." As Henry Adams once said of Theodore Roosevelt, "He was pure act," and some of this thrust-chest urgency was present in Purvis, too.

Not for a moment, though, should this quality be mistaken for the capacity or intention to intimidate. Purvis, though a pursuer of the nation's most feared criminals, may have been the least intimidating law-enforcement officer in American history. Melvin Purvis simply had no weight to throw around. "He is not of the rugged type who impresses one as being a forceful character," E. J. Connelley, special-agent-in-charge of the Cincinnati office, once observed. "I never once saw him blow up," Doris Lockerman said. "I think I saw him flare on occasion, but never at an agent. He might have been angry, but if he was he would call on the agent personally and handle the problem. There were never any angry or belittling remarks about any of his men. Melvin did not diminish anyone."

No, Purvis did not adopt his boss's style of roaring disapproval to get results. Purvis worked the other side of the street: He relied on his charm. He had an ability to make people overlook his shortcomings and a way of winning them over with his confidence and style. He was, quite simply, not afraid to be the man he was. His fondness for horses gave him a cultivated air; he kept a silver horse figurine on his glass-top desk and often took his palomino mare out for Sunday canters in Lincoln Park. Most agents drove modest Fords, if they drove at all; Purvis preferred his long, eight-cylinder Pierce-Arrow. He employed a black valet named President to run his apartment, be a trusted confidant, act as chauffeur, and handle his affairs—a practice born of his Southern upbringing and well outside the lifestyle of the typical agent, who tended to share an apartment with several other agents to save on expenses. Purvis liked having a country dog and so brought his terrier to Chicago; this, too, seemed unusual for a single and ostensibly hard-boiled federal agent. Bureau regulations required that all agents wear suits, but Purvis was an unabashedly elegant dresser—dapper to the point of foppishness. He managed to come across as aristocratic without seeming arrogant. Doris Lockerman brought him lunch one day from the modest coffee shop in the Bankers Building lobby. "I'll be glad," Purvis remarked, "when I get someplace where a baked ham sandwich is not considered a gentleman's lunch."

Purvis, said Lockerman, "saw himself as a gentleman, which he was. He had a full-blown sense of himself when he arrived. Those of us who worked with him recognized a kind of showmanship in him, and yet it wasn't phony or faked. He saw himself as doing a very important job and doing it with some dash." Surely these qualities helped Purvis advance quickly through the Bureau.

Purvis and Hoover were very different men, sprung from different pasts. Hoover's family circumstances were more complicated than Purvis's. Hoover adored his mother and she him, but there was something compensatory about their closeness. They had an almost exclusive relationship, an intense doting that continued long after Hoover reached manhood; when Annie Hoover fell ill it was her son Edgar who took care of her in their Washington, D.C., home until she died—with him at her bedside—when he was forty-three. This appears to have affected how Hoover viewed other women. "I think he regarded women as a kind of hindrance," Hoover's niece Margaret Fennell told the writer Ovid Demaris. "You know, they sort of got in your way when you were going places." In general, Fennell explained, Hoover "had a fear of becoming personally involved with people. He was always very gracious and fed you a lot of kidding and everything, but I think a lot of it was surface . . . I think you would have to say he was not a family person." Indeed, the adult Hoover—who even in high school never had a single date—confined himself to the company of colleagues, all of them men.

In his twenties Hoover had only one close friend—Thomas Franklin Baughman, a fellow law student at George Washington University. Baughman more than fit the bill—he was handsome, charming, passionate, with a movie-star smile and an irresistible intensity. Hoover brought Baughman into the Bureau and saw to it that his friend progressed swiftly through its ranks; in exchange he had the pleasure of countless lunches and dinners with his popular friend. Of particular interest to Hoover, according to Richard Hack, was "the ease with which Baughman handled himself, the way he leaned into a conversation no matter how unimportant." This is not to say that Hoover was uninteresting or entirely graceless, for he was not. Those who spent time with him insisted he was courteous, witty, and engaging. Still, he was a far cry from the men he most admired—men who were suave, attractive, confident, and magnetic, particularly to the opposite sex. "The perception of Hoover at the Bureau was that he was not a whole person," said Doris Lockerman. "He needed someone else to buoy him. That was why he always had to have a man follow him around."

There is no way of knowing precisely why Hoover preferred the company of men, or what lay behind his specific attraction to charismatic men. Certainly Hoover never addressed these issues. Perhaps he envied these men their easy charm; perhaps he fancied himself to be like them; perhaps it was an impulse he never fully understood. But what is clear is that once he found someone he admired, he assumed the role of the mentor, and the other man that of the protégé. And because Hoover was a powerful person, his mentorship was no small matter. His interest in Baughman launched the latter's career at the Bureau; the same was true of the handsome Clyde Tolson, who parlayed a chance meeting with Hoover in the Mayflower Hotel in 1927 into a decades-long career as Hoover's right-hand man. Shortly after joining the Bureau in 1928, Tolson was transferred to Washington, where he was designated chief clerk—a position that placed him under Hoover's watchful eye. Hoover's interest in Tolson coincided with another significant event in his life—the surrender by his friend Thomas Baughman of the one factor that made him an ideal companion: his bachelorhood.

If Baughman's marriage created a void, it is possible Hoover summoned Tolson to Washington as a way to audition him for becoming the director's new protégé. Hoover's motivation is unknown, but it was not uncommon for him to rotate agents in and out of Bureau headquarters, presumably to gain insight into their capabilities. Tolson's assignment to chief clerk was a sure sign of Hoover's curiosity about him. But on March 26, 1929, Hoover replaced Tolson with Melvin Purvis, effective April 1.

Tolson was transferred to Buffalo, New York, but less than a week later was resummoned to Washington—a good illustration of Hoover's whimsical, whirlwind personnel decisions. Ultimately, of course, Tolson, not Purvis, won the role of Hoover's new confidant; after returning to the capital he would never again leave Hoover's side. Still, Purvis's appointment as chief clerk gave Hoover his first real chance to evaluate this rising star. Though they almost surely met when Purvis first joined the Bureau and probably met again during his antitrust training, records indicate their first significant encounter likely occurred when Purvis assumed Tolson's duties as chief clerk in April 1929. Hoover's decision to take the highly qualified Purvis out of the field and assign him to a clerical position in Washington was transparently guided by a desire to give him a closer look. Less than six weeks later, Hoover admitted he had made a flawed decision in putting a legally trained agent in a clerical position, and he wrote to Purvis that because of "heavy demand for investigative assistance in the field on a number of special matters, it was desirable to assign you to field duty."

That short six-week stint in Washington was long enough for Purvis to make an impression on the director. In the letter advising Purvis of his transfer to a field office in Norfolk, Virginia, Hoover also wrote, "I will want to talk with you as to some special work in the field which I am desirous of having you take up." Purvis's replied: "I shall be glad when I arrive [in Washington] and can see you about it." Purvis had earned something not easily won: Hoover's trust.

The history of their relationship—which began in earnest during those six weeks in 1929 and intensified in the following years—is told almost entirely through the letters the two men exchanged. The letters were classified until only a few years ago, and most of them have never before been published. There are no telephone records to supplement them, no accounts of their friendship in the books written by either man, no published observations made by others who served in the Bureau at that time. There are only the letters—several hundred of them spanning eight years. The portrait of the friendship that emerges from them is rich and layered and surprising; the letters contain an intimacy and jocularity that are difficult to detect in any of the tens of thousands of official letters and memos Hoover composed in his five decades of public service.

After Purvis was posted to Norfolk, it would be nearly two more years before some hint of their burgeoning friendship found its way into their correspondence. Hoover visited the Cincinnati field office in February 1931 to meet with Purvis, then special-agent-in-charge. Very few agents were on a first-name basis with the director, but Hoover's note to Purvis following their meeting was the first of many he would address "Dear Melvin."

This marked the beginning of Hoover's continuing and occasionally sophomoric fascination with Purvis's appeal to women, beginning a prolonged stretch of teasing about Purvis's attractiveness—and particularly about his irresistibility to Hoover's personal secretary, Helen Gandy. In February 1932, Purvis sent Hoover a publication that featured a photo taken at a meeting of the Committee of the International Association of Chiefs of Police. "You will no doubt recognize the person above whose photograph has been placed the question mark, and who appears to be wearing a toupee," Purvis wrote. "They insisted that I stand in the front row in this photograph, because they said I was not as tall as some of the others. However, I don't appear to be so small, and the photograph would, beyond a doubt, have been far better had I been in the rear." Hoover replied:

> I do wish that in the future when you send anything of this kind to me, if your picture appears in it, that you be kind enough to cut it out and not send the photograph along for it has disrupted my office this morning. My secretary has been floating around in the air, so to speak, and has been saying how "SWEET" you look. I don't expect to get any work out of her today. It is a crime what effect you have upon the fair sex.

That July, Hoover again raised the subject of Gandy's infatuation with Purvis. "I have done everything in my power to suppress a piece of poetry which is coming out in the next issue of the *Investigator*, the official organ of the Bureau's Athletic Association," Hoover wrote. "But I, unfortunately, don't have as much drag with the editors as I thought I had. After this issue is released I don't see how my secretary and you can help but embark upon the matrimonial sea." One week later, he expounded on his theme:

> You no doubt by this time have received the issue of the[**TK**] *Investigator* and I am certain that you well appreciate the fact that there is but one thing for you to do and that is to embark upon the matrimonial sea. . . . Consequently I think you owe it not only to yourself and the lady but it would be of great assistance to the efficiency of my office to get this matter straightened out and straightened out as early as possible.

On August 4, 1932, Hoover took his goading of Purvis to another level:

> The last report from the battle front, which will be incorporated in the next issue of the[**TK**] *Investigator,* following the baseball game of yesterday, is that the front office was further disgraced publicly and I personally have been exceedingly humiliated and embarrassed and I know that you will feel crushed at the news in view of the relations pending between you and my secretary. The facts are that Mr. Keith, otherwise know as the Dean or Sir John of Ivanwold, had precipitated upon his lap at the initiation of my secretary one Helen Gandy and so overwhelmed was the chauffeur of the car—it not being my car however—that he drove around the Ellipse twice not being able to find the outlet; the chauffeur having lived in Washington all his life. During this episode John Keith kept saying sweet nothings to one Helen inspired by her actions and the event has now resulted in much speculation as to whether Sir John of Ivanwold will be chal-lenged to a duel by one Melvin of Birmingham. I am informed that this so-called "snaking" in the car continued all the way in to the city.
>   I thought it my duty, as your friend, to at once advise you of this. Miss Gandy has pleaded with me with tears in her eyes not to write you but I could not have you deceived any further.

Purvis responded on August 11:

> I have read with much interest and mixed feelings your last two letters. The *Investigator* finally arrived and the poems were likewise read with the same interest and feeling. In spite of the poet's attempt

it cannot be said that the poem is iambic pentameter; the last verse is like the newspaper poems entitled "More truth than Poetry."

Hoover had found a sparring partner, and he was delighted. But he was also disappointed that Purvis insisted on addressing his letters "Mr. Hoover." In one letter he wrote, "I am always glad to hear from you, notwithstanding the formality with which you still address your letters, but I suppose there is no use trying to teach an old dog new tricks." Shortly after that: "I am now getting some hopes of being able to teach an old dog new tricks, as I note you have at least dropped the title of 'Mr.,' although you have addressed me as 'Chairman'—of what, I don't know, unless it is the Moral Uplift Squad." Hoover himself had begun signing his letters to Purvis with just "J.E." and, on occasion, "Ed." He urged Purvis to be less formal and as a reminder addressed one of his "Gandy" letters, with impatient irony, "Dear MISTER Purvis."

> I took the liberty of advising my secretary of your comment that the last verse was "more truth than poetry" and since I told her that she has phone calls, mail and everything else mixed up. I shall not again advise her of any such expressions upon your part for it seems to have a most disquieting effect and I believe it will be some days before she comes down to earth again. I am enclosing, for your information as well as edification, two recent poems which have been composed by persons familiar with the Alabama-Gandy situation. The reference in these potential efforts has relation to the recent incident following the baseball game of the Bureau's team when Mr. Keith took Miss Gandy home and had her sit on his lap. I know how this will make you gnash your teeth but you may rest assured that the Dean's activities will be properly circumscribed by Mrs. Keith who bears a very watchful eye over him.

The occasion of a Halloween Ball in 1932 again gave Hoover an opportunity to needle his agent by notifying him in September to be ready for the upcoming event in October. The message read, "My secretary . . . has indicated to me that she will not attend that festivity unless she can go in your company. So you may make your plans accordingly to be here in sufficient advance to accompany her to the Halloween Ball." Though the letter was from Hoover, it was signed "Sincerely yours, Miss Helen W. Gandy." In pen Hoover scribbled "By J.E.H. per H.G." and doodled four crosses and eight circles with x's in them below the signature line. A day later, after learning Purvis would attend the Ball, he wrote again:

> Following our talk I told Miss Gandy you said you would be here with bells on and she said she can hardly wait until that time. Incidentally the ball is to be a masquerade affair and Miss Gandy has promised she will wear a cellophane gown. You can look forward to seeing all of Miss Gandy.

Even the dignified Assistant Director Harold Nathan enjoyed Hoover's crack about the gown. He wrote to Purvis, "It is understood, of course, that you will be in Washington on the 29th, in order to take Miss Gandy to the Masquerade. Please don't apply a match to her cellophane garment. The fire might be extinguished, but, oh well."

Purvis played along in a September 24 letter to Hoover:

> I am looking forward to coming to the Grand Ball to be given at the Willard on October 29th. I am especially glad to note that the affair is to be a masquerade because those are the kinds of Balls at which I am most successful. I am sure Miss Gandy would look extremely well in a cellophane gown. . . .
>
> What do the crosses with circles and crosses without circles at the bottom of your letter mean? Is it some cryptic signal to watch for the lady in the cellophane gown? Don't be so mysterious and tell me their significance. I can't figure them out.

Hoover hurried a reply to explain the strange symbols in his letter.

> With reference to the crosses with circles, etc., at the bottom of my letter to which you refer, I had absolutely no knowledge of these but upon a vigorous cross-examination on my secretary I ascertained that she had placed them on the letter and from my past knowledge of amorous symbols, gained in my young days, I recall that such symbols were indicative of osculatory intentions. Of course, this is a matter entirely between you and my secretary but I have made certain that in the future she will not affix such symbols to my

communications. She will have to send them to you herself in a separate letter.

Hoover then insisted he had not even signed the letter. He maintained that he dictated it but left the office and his secretary signed it and "took the liberty of affixing these symbols for your edification." Yet the initials "J.E.H." on the letter were in the same distinctive script Hoover used in every other letter he signed that way. Helen Gandy probably did not sign Hoover's initials, though it is possible she added the crosses and circles with x's.

In any case, Hoover had not bored of teasing Purvis about his secretary. On October 14 he wrote:

I have just read the article appearing in the *Birmingham News* of last Sunday and want to congratulate you upon the very excellent presentation which you caused to have made of the Bureau and its work. I think this article will do the Bureau a great deal of good in the South. I have been unable, since the article was received, to get very much work out of Miss Gandy since she persists in viewing your photograph which graces the article and has gone into a kind of a stupor since she first saw it.

Hoover then pressed Purvis to send an autographed photograph of himself "for my personal rogues' gallery." He received the requested picture a week later, then again quipped in a return letter that Miss Gandy had requested some time off to recover from "viewing your sheik-like appearance." Hoover closed that letter saying he hoped he and Purvis could meet shortly.

Four days later, on October 25, 1932, even as his bantering about Gandy continued, Hoover bestowed on Purvis the biggest prize an agent could receive: appointment as special-agent-in-charge of the Chicago office.

———

The joking continued once Purvis was settled into his new position. In July 1933, Purvis sent Hoover a letter that included an erroneous reference by his secretary to his being married. Hoover seized the moment July 15, needling Purvis in a letter that the agent had been remiss in failing to disclose his marital status, and that although everyone wished him well, "many of us do feel you have treated some of the ladies rather shabbily letting them believe that you were still a bachelor. However, I assume they will get over it, but they will never look the same."

Purvis responded with a letter addressed "Dear J.E.," explaining that he had talked with his secretary and she acknowledged she "had a splitting headache" when the letter was typed and she could not explain making the error about Purvis's marital status. Purvis acknowledged that he "signed the letter without reading it."

Hoover refused to let Purvis off the hook, writing him tongue-in-cheek that he discounted the secretary's story: "It is easy enough for you to lay the responsibility upon your stenographer but frankly I believe she transcribed what you gave her." Hoover needled Purvis for "trying now to cover up the situation. My advice to you, however, is that you watch your step and not be guilty of committing bigamy."

The good-natured joshing between the two men continued over other topics as well. In August 1933 Purvis delivered a speech at a convention of the Fraternal Order of Police in Gary, Indiana. The organization's official publication listed Purvis as "Director" of the Bureau, a blunder that had occurred before. Purvis wrote to Hoover on September 23 claiming to be "at a loss" to understand the mistake and hazarding a guess "that they invited you originally and since I was second choice, they decided to make me feel good, although I probably wouldn't feel good if I were Director."

Far from being offended or threatened, Hoover had fun with the mistake:

I received your letter of September 23rd . . . and note the public acceptance of you as Director of the Department of Justice. In some respects I am greatly relieved, while in others I am somewhat concerned. There are times when I feel strongly the need of having two or three pairs of shoulders upon which the burdens and responsibilities of the Directorship might rest, particularly when the Director is expected to be possessed of psychic powers. On the other hand I am, as I have said, somewhat concerned because of your well-known proclivities along certain lines. I fear that my good reputation as Chairman of the Moral Uplift Squad may become seriously affected by reason of confusing your activities with those of mine, the latter always being above any reproach.

I want to say in conclusion that I bow with humble acceptance to
you and your title as Director.

Hoover was by then aware that Purvis was an increasingly popular
figure, and that the combination of his good looks and his high-profile position in Chicago guaranteed he would continue to receive
greater attention than any special agent had before. For the moment, Hoover seemed thrilled by the attention, in that it reflected
well on the Bureau. In April 1934, Hoover forwarded to Purvis a
flattering newspaper article :"What intrigues me . . . is the description of our Agent in Charge at Chicago. No doubt you will soon
have several movie propositions made to you, for I don't know how
the movies could miss a 'slender, blond-haired, brown-eyed' gentleman. All power to the Clark Gables of the service!"

Many other letters reflect the fondness Hoover developed for
Purvis. Some show that Hoover felt protective of him, and that—
aware Purvis was sensitive to outside criticism—he sought to boost
his spirits whenever he could. In a February 1934 letter, Hoover enclosed a Washington newspaper article and wrote:

One of the bits of philosophy entitled "Silence" by Bruce Barton . . .
so adequately expresses the wise philosophy that one should try to
follow, particularly the closing paragraph: "No active man gets
through life without being subjected to a certain amount of
unfounded criticism. But not very many men learn what an
unanswerable answer is silence."

When I read this it brought to my mind our talk of a few Sundays
ago, and I think is a bit of philosophy that each of us might follow
with good results. I know how distressing it is to be the subject of
attacks both vicious and unfounded, and while it takes quite some
patience and quite some time to develop the attitude suggested by
Bruce Barton, I know that in the long run his advice is sound.

Purvis, in his reply, concurred with Hoover's assessment and offered his own addition: "I remember having read that Calvin
Coolidge once said that 'I have never been hurt by something I did
not say.' I believe that is a very good policy to follow."

On other occasions Hoover showed a deep, often paternalistic
concern for Purvis's health. On May 10, 1933, he wrote, "You seem
to be having quite some trouble with [your throat], and you will

have to watch it carefully." Two weeks later, Purvis was sick at home, and Hoover wrote again, admonishing his agent to stay home from work to get well: "I cannot too strongly insist upon your remaining from the office and disassociating your attention with any matter concerning your work, until you have fully recovered your health and regained your strength." Hoover noted his awareness that Purvis's sister was staying with her brother, and he prodded his agent to forgo his obstinate streak in favor of recovering his health: "No doubt, you are just as stubborn in complying with her requests as you are in complying with mine, but between the two of us we might be able to get some sense into your head and make you realize you must take care of yourself, first and foremost."

Despite these admonishments, Purvis left his sickbed to oversee a Bureau exhibit at the Chicago World's Fair that spring. In another letter, Hoover played the stern father:

I was astounded this morning when I received a letter from Mr. Smith advising me as to certain phases of the exhibit at the Fair, and informing me you had come to the office yesterday to look after some of these matters. He stated in his letter you were in a very weakened condition. I wrote you yesterday expecting that you would stay at home, and stating the reason I had not called you by telephone—I feared you would insist upon coming to the phone. It never dawned on me you would actually go to the office. I had given you credit for more intelligence. As soon as I received Mr. Smith's letter this morning I called the Chicago office to see whether you had been fool enough again to come down today, and I was informed you were expecting to be there in about an hour; so, consequently, I called you at your home.

I don't know whether I made any impression upon you, but I want to say very definitely and emphatically that you are to stay at home and not have anything to do with any official matters in Chicago before next Monday, and not then unless your condition is greatly improved. You are certainly old enough to have sufficient sense to take care of yourself. . . .

What someone should do is crack you over the head with a blackjack, and if I were near I would welcome the opportunity of doing that. It distresses me considerably to see you act this way. I know that you are tremendously interested in taking care of the things in Chicago, but as I have previously said, I am much more interested in having your health restored than I am in having these matters taken care of.

Nearly a year later, in February 1934, Hoover blamed himself when Purvis was again stricken with a cold.

I have been thinking about you and have been very much concerned. . . . I do want to urge, though I assume that it is useless for me to do so, that you remain home and not only recover from your present illness, but try to build up some resistance, before you try to return to the office. However, I realize that I am talking to a very stubborn individual when I give this advice. I feel somewhat responsible for your present illness in that I directed you to proceed to Sioux Falls in connection with the Sankey matter, and I believe that had you remained at Chicago you probably would not have contracted the cold.

The Hoover-Purvis letters also show that as their friendship grew, Purvis frequently provided Hoover with gifts. In February 1933, Hoover wrote thanking Purvis for a music box to add to his collection. That November the director thanked Purvis for an unusual paper cutter, which he also planned to add to his antique collection. Hoover commended Purvis's generosity: "You are always doing something for someone, and I just don't know how to thank you for your kindness. I do deeply appreciate it." Christmas 1933 brought a note from Hoover thanking Purvis for another gift.

The following spring came a letter that stands above all the others for its personal expression of close friendship. On April 3, Hoover sat at his broad desk and handwrote a note to Purvis thanking him for several gifts. Obvious from the letter's tone is the affection Hoover and Purvis had for each other, their waggish and occasionally puerile interplay, and their obvious camaraderie. Its closing line is the most resonant comment to emerge from the entirety of their correspondence.

Dear Melvin:
  I received the Tru-Vue and films, bombs, magic tricks and your sassy note. What did the Tru-Vue and films cost? I asked you to get

them for me and I intend to pay for them. The films were both educational and uplifting but I thought they would include a series on "A Night in a Moorish Harem" or was it a "Turkish Harem." Nevertheless it was some night and I am still looking forward to you producing a set. Of course my interest is solely as a censor or as chairman of the Moral Uplift Squad.

The bombs are the best yet. I have already caused Miss Gandy to jump two feet and that is something considering the fact that she is now in the heavyweight class. The damned magic trick has me almost "nuts" trying to figure out how it is done. I probably will take it apart to find out.

The cartoon is swell. Can you get me the original from the magazine? I have started to collect some cartoons particularly pertinent to our work and I would like to add this for it tells a real story.

Well, son, keep a stiff upper lip and get Dillinger for me and the world is yours.

Sincerely and affectionately,

Jayee

"Get Dillinger," Hoover told Purvis, "and the world is yours." That statement would prove to be one of history's great false promises.

———

The correspondence between the two men demonstrates that in addition to thinking highly of Purvis's capabilities, Hoover also came to like him very much as a person. Hoover's fatherly interest in Purvis's health cannot be interpreted as anything other than genuine concern. Beyond this, the nature of the teasing in his letters demonstrates that, at the very least, Hoover trusted Purvis enough to show a side of himself that he had not shown before and would not show again. Such suggestive schoolboy banter about a woman and her desirability may have been common among special agents, who, after all, were mostly young, single, and lonely. That the director of the Bureau not only participated in it but in fact instigated it is, to say the least, unusual. Stranger still is that the object of Hoover's risqué comments was his secretary, Helen Gandy, who had to transcribe and type up his letters. Hoover was a self-positioned

paragon of virtue—a man of rigid morality and utter professionalism. What, then, was Melvin Purvis to make of the surprisingly juvenile tone of Hoover's letters? What was he to think of Hoover's
seemingly undue attention to his agent's looks? Certainly Hoover
spent far more time and shared more of his life with Clyde Tolson—
his best friend and closest colleague for more than three decades—
than he did with Melvin Purvis. But the looseness, intimacy, and
sheer humanness evident in Hoover's correspondence are unique
in the voluminous annals of the Bureau's history.

As such, the letters invite speculation: What, exactly, motivated
Hoover to write them? Were they simply expressions of friendship
from someone who lacked experience in making friends? Were the
schoolboy comments simply the efforts of a clumsy man to appear
to be one of the guys? Or, as at least one Hoover historian has suggested, are the letters evidence that Hoover had some kind of sexual
attraction to Purvis? At the time he wrote them—1933 and 1934—
Hoover was not yet the subject of rampant speculation about his sex-
uality. "We did not think that he was homosexual or anything like
that," recalled Doris Lockerman. "We simply thought that he felt
more comfortable in the company of men." Several years after
Hoover's death, though, a book by journalist Anthony Summers implied the director had been gay, and that Tolson had been his lover.
Summers also suggested that Hoover's letters to Purvis were more
than just expressions of friendship. "It is hard to interpret the correspondence as anything other than a homosexual courtship," Summers wrote in *Official and Confidential,* "even though Purvis is not
known to have had any such tendencies." Summer's theories were
harshly rebutted by Hoover's former deputy director, Cartha De-
Loach, in his book *Hoover's FBI.* DeLoach, who worked with the director for nearly three decades, argued that Hoover was
asexual—and that he was, in fact, incapable of having an adult relationship. Even Tolson, he said, was "an almost indispensable figure
at bureau headquarters, but not quite [Hoover's] friend. The only
person for whom he held a deep and abiding affection had died
years earlier, and all that was left of [his mother] Annie Hoover was
her Bible. Hoover's capacity to feel deeply for other human beings
[was] interred with her."

Neither theory seems plausible. The idea that Hoover would conduct a homosexual courtship through letters he not only dictated to

a third party but also knew would be filed for posterity—and that he would do so in an era when having his homosexuality discovered would almost certainly have led to his dismissal from a job that was sacred to him—seems, at the very least, far-fetched. But so does the notion that Hoover was an unfeeling automaton. Surely he felt deep affection for Tolson—a trove of photographs discovered after Hoover's death includes tender photos Hoover took of Tolson sleeping. Perhaps Hoover found it difficult to express such affection, but that is not the same as being incapable of feeling it. From Hoover's letters, it is clear that he felt real affection for Melvin Purvis.

Hoover's mandate upon assuming the directorship was to remake the Bureau into an efficient investigative force. To do so he would need a clear vision of a new type of agent, and to his credit he had just such a vision. Hoover created an ideal that the men he hired would have to meet, and Melvin Purvis, as much as any other agent, embodied this ideal. "He was young, handsome, single, loyal, full of style and swagger, all of that," said Doris Lockerman. "It is not surprising that someone would have a crush on him. Many of us had crushes on him then."

However one interprets the letters, they demonstrate without a doubt that the relationship between Hoover and Purvis was unique. Hoover's feelings for Purvis certainly played a part in his decision to install him in the important Chicago position—indeed, to assign him to a task upon which Hoover's very future depended. Similarly, Purvis's feelings for Hoover—his faith in his incorruptibility and desire for his approval—allowed him to devote himself wholeheartedly to the director. They found, in each other, pieces missing from themselves. Purvis discovered his calling in Hoover's crusade against evil, and felt his deep sense of duty satisfied by Hoover's strict leadership. Thus did Hoover's fraternity of agents become Purvis's new family. At the same time, Hoover saw in Purvis the style and charm he lacked himself, and perceived a romantic, idealized extension of himself.

Both men benefited from the other's attention, and their personal friendship paved the way for their greatest professional success. But their relationship would be disrupted by a third man—a man who, so many decades later, remains linked to each of them. In this story of three men, the events of March 3, 1934, play a crucial role. What happened that day—what strange, improbable thing happened with a gun crudely carved from wood—set in motion the sweeping drama that would doom the delicate friendship between the director and one of his most loyal charges.

5

KIDNAPPERS AND CROOKS

June 1933

In Kansas City, Missouri, a war begins—with the rippling echo of gunshots, the shattering of glass, the splatter of blood, the scramble of feet. With the morbidly curious staring at a grisly tableau; with the unlucky dead strewn in gruesome repose.

It is Saturday, June 17, 1933. At the Union Station train depot, with its handsome granite facade and its bustling promenade, the Missouri Pacific locomotive steams into the station fifteen minutes behind schedule. It is quarter past seven on this hot summer morning. Aboard, hands cuffed in front, is Frank Nash, a bank robber and fugitive from the federal penitentiary in Leavenworth, Kansas. Nash has effected the easiest of escapes: Trusted enough to be named the deputy warden's personal handyman, he simply disappeared in the middle of running an errand. Now back in custody, he is being returned to Leavenworth, the first leg by train and the last thirty miles in a federal agent's black Chevrolet coupe, which is awaiting him in the Union Station parking lot.

A phalanx of officers, massed shoulder to shoulder, march Nash through the lobby, clearing away onlookers. The officers' eyes flit about, but nothing causes concern. Nash is whisked to the Chevrolet and begins to get in the back seat, but special agent Joe Lackey of the Bureau of Investigation orders him into the front. "That way," Lackey tells him, "we can all watch you."

No one sees the danger coming; no one notices the men darting between parked cars. Perhaps they hear someone yell, "Up! Up!" and see the glint of guns, but by then it is far too late. With one last command—"Let 'em have it!"—this hellish incident begins.

To the crackle of machine-gun fire, a Kansas City cop, Bill Grooms, crumples to the pavement. A spray of bullets through the sheet metal of the car leaves a police chief, Otto Reed, dead in the back seat. Nearly a minute's worth of heavy shooting and two more bodies are torn to shreds: another cop, Frank Hermanson, and a Bureau special agent, Ray Caffrey. In the front, a head explodes: Frank Nash, killed in an instant. "They're dead," says one of the gunmen. "They're all dead."

In all, five are dead, two are wounded, no one is caught. A clean getaway for the assassins. A mess of blood and glass and entangled bodies left behind. A brazen slaughter of lawmen, a flagrant ambush, a flouting of every commonly held principle of reason and decency. A massacre, pure and simple.

———

The Kansas City massacre, perhaps more than any other event, created the Federal Bureau of Investigation Americans know today. It remains a compelling and controversial crime. Historians can only speculate about the identity of all of the gunmen: Certainly the notorious Vern Miller was one of them, and most likely Charles Floyd—"Pretty Boy"—was another. Their intent was to liberate Frank Nash, who were it not for his last-second seat change—which put him in a position to be mistaken for one of his captors—might have indeed been freed. The cause of the carnage is also open to debate: Some say it was sheer savagery on the part of the shooters; others believe a sleep-deprived Joe Lackey, who accompanied Nash on the long train ride before putting him in the front seat of the Chevy, fumbled with a shotgun in the back of the car and accidentally killed Nash and two lawmen himself. What is clear is that the nation was stunned by the ruthlessness of the massacre, by the utter disregard for the authority of law. Yes, crime had been on the rise, with bank robberies and armed holdups and occasional shoot-outs between cops and fleeing bandits, encounters symptomatic of the

depression that forced so many men into bad choices. But none of it
had so jolted the country with a glimpse of its ugly underside. This
was not the first crime to captivate the nation—the kidnapping of
Charles Lindbergh's infant son in the spring of 1932, still unsolved
in summer 1933, had done that—but it was the first crime to truly
frighten the nation.

Within hours of the shooting, the special agents of the Bureau of
Investigation—who previously had not been officially permitted to
carry guns—were tossed weapons and ordered to learn how to use
them. "I cannot too strongly emphasize the imperative necessity of
concentrating upon this matter," Hoover said shortly after the gunfight, "without any let-up in the same until all parties are taken dead
or alive." The attorney general of the United States, Homer Cummings—who already had a plan in place to create a kind of national
super–police force to combat crime—invoked the massacre to push
through his agenda, and in early 1934 President Franklin Roosevelt
signed nine major anticrime bills into law. By federalizing such
crimes as bank robbery, extortion, and transporting stolen goods or
kidnap victims across state lines, Roosevelt bestowed on Hoover's
Bureau a broad and astonishing array of powers it would never relinquish. When Joe Lackey—who played dead in the back seat to
survive the massacre—recounted that the first flurry of bullets
meant "the war was on," he did not know how right he was. The
brief but deadly skirmish outside Union Station did indeed trigger a
war—not the kind of war the nation was accustomed to, with marching troops and bayonets and battles in far-off countries, but, instead,
a war on its own soil.

On the front line of this new war, as close to the action as anyone
and far closer than most, was young Melvin Purvis, who only eight
months earlier had assumed command of the Bureau's Chicago
office.

———

While history describes the Kansas City massacre as the opening
salvo of the war, it was another crime—one conducted without a single bullet being fired; indeed, with a fake gun—that defined the enemy for Purvis and Hoover. This other event truly held the nation's
attention, more so even than the slaughter outside Union Station.

The victims of the massacre, like its perpetrators, were faceless, impersonal, mourned and despised only in the abstract. This other crime produced both a hero and a villain the nation would come to know intimately—it instigated a conflict that would keep the nation spellbound for the next twelve months.

John Dillinger—shipped off to the Indiana State Reformatory at Pendleton in 1924 for mugging an elderly grocer—conceived a future for himself that was devoid of crime altogether. "We will be so happy when I can come home to you and chase your sorrows away," he wrote to his young wife Beryl from prison, "and it won't take any kids to keep me home with you always. For sweetheart I love you and all I want is to just be with you and make you happy." Such a virtuous scene of domesticity was not to be: Beryl divorced Dillinger in 1929, on the obvious grounds that he was imprisoned and thus not an ideal husband. Still, Dillinger held out hope for himself. "I know right from wrong," he wrote to his niece in 1929, "and I intend to do right when I get out."

Four years later, in 1933, he walked out of prison with five dollars in his pocket and his nine-year debt to society paid. The very day the twenty-nine-year-old emerged a free man, his father's second wife died of a stroke. He had lost his own mother as a boy; now another woman who might have assumed her role was gone. There would be no more hopeful letters from John Dillinger. Less than two months after his release he, along with two pals, held up a cashier at the tiny Commercial Bank of Daleville, Indiana. The bandits hustled out with more than $3,000. Three weeks later, Dillinger struck again, at the National Bank in Montpelier. This time the take was $6,700. That September, Dillinger held up the Massachusetts Avenue State Bank, instructing two terrified customers to keep their hands down, lest they clue passersby to the robbery in progress. The score: $21,000. It was an easy business, this bank robbing, and Dillinger was emboldened. In 1933 he returned to the grounds of his former prison and threw a heavy package over an outer wall. Inside the package were several guns and a box of bullets. His onetime fellow inmates—John Hamilton, Harry Pierpont, Charles Mackley—used the guns to subdue guards and walk out through the prison's front gate. The infamous Dillinger gang was born.

Almost as quickly, however, it was dealt a major blow. In September 1933 police grabbed Dillinger at a Dayton, Ohio, home and locked him behind bars. "I know I have been a big disappointment to you," Dillinger wrote his father. "If I had gotten off more leniently when I made my first mistake this would never have happened." He had not been in prison one full month when his prison pals repaid the favor they owed him, killing Sheriff Jesse Sarber at Ohio's Allen County Jail and springing Dillinger into the world again. After that, banks toppled like dominoes: The Central National Bank and Trust Company in Greencastle, Indiana, was hit for $20,000 in cash and more than $50,000 in securities. The American Bank and Trust Company in Racine, Wisconsin—$28,000. The First National Bank of East Chicago, Indiana, good for $20,000. In this last heist, Dillinger took four bullets to the chest, all of them flattened by his stolen bulletproof vest. Dillinger returned fire, and police officer William P. O'Malley, a husband and father, fell dead. "I've always felt bad about O'Malley getting killed," Dillinger would later tell his lawyer, but "he had it coming. He stood right in the way and kept throwing slugs at me. What else could I do?"

Police departments in Midwest cities upgraded to emergency status. Citizens were deputized, wanted fliers posted. Customers darted cautiously and quickly in and out of banks; the front doors and windows of houses were locked. People perceived a threat, something new and menacing. The forces of evil responsible for the Kansas City murders now had a face, and that face belonged to the handsome and smirking John Dillinger. No criminal had ever been like him, so bold, so unafraid of the law. He was both feared and—for his audacity—reluctantly admired.

Then, once again, a setback. A crackdown by police netted the ultimate prize: Fifteen officers found Dillinger entering a hideout in Tucson, Arizona. "What a laugh!" Dillinger snorted. "To be picked up by a bunch of hick cops." This time the authorities would take no chances. Bound in shackles and surrounded by guards, Dillinger flew to Chicago—his first time on an airplane—where more than 120 heavily armed officers waiting on the tarmac fell into a caravan that escorted the prisoner to a true fortress. On January 30, 1934, Dillinger arrived at what was considered an escape-proof prison— the Lake County Jail at Crown Point, Indiana.

It was an eventful passage and one that allowed Dillinger to shine. At Crown Point his cuffs came off, and suddenly reporters and lawmen alike were scrambling to get close to the famous outlaw.

Dillinger was a charmer, making jokes, smiling easily, scoffing at the prospect of winding up in the electric chair. Many people fell under his spell. A local prosecutor allowed himself to be photographed with Dillinger, who casually laid his elbow on the smiling fellow's shoulder. The chummy photo cost the prosecutor his job. Journalists, too, were impressed. "How long does it take you to go through a bank?" one reporter asked. Dillinger, his left lip curling upward into his well-known half-smile, said, "One minute and forty seconds flat." The *Chicago Daily News* would later observe, "His diction was amazing . . . his poise no less so . . . he rates in the eyes of calloused observers as the most amazing specimen of his kind ever seen outside of a wildly imaginative moving picture." He was not a hero, not in any sense of the word. But John Dillinger was clearly a star.

Yet his legend was only just taking shape. On Saturday, March 3, 1934, one month after Dillinger arrived at Crown Point, he proved there wasn't a prison built that could hold him. First a handyman named Sam Cahoon felt a gun shoved into his side as he walked down a corridor between two rows of cells. The man behind it was Dillinger. At his urging, Cahoon called a deputy, Ernest Blunk, and the warden, Lou Baker. They, too, became Dillinger's prisoners. Several guards were summoned and locked into jail cells. In all, thirty people were rounded up in cells, taken by Dillinger and only one another escapee. "See what I locked all of you monkeys up with?" Dillinger sneered on his way out of Crown Point, running his gun—fashioned from the tubular handle of a safety razor and a carved block of wood and blackened with shoe polish—across the bars of a cell. "Nothing but a little piece of wood." For good measure Dillinger robbed his captives of fifteen dollars.

And then he was out, free yet again. Dillinger stole a Ford from a garage fifty yards from the prison, ditched two prison officials he had taken as hostages, and drove toward Chicago. In his pocket was his fake gun. He was impressed with his own cunning and sensed the small prop held some significance. Later he would show it off to relatives, with whom he spent a weekend in Mooresville, Indiana, his hometown. "Johnnie, why do you take such risks coming here?" his father, John Dillinger Sr. asked when his son appeared at his farm late on April 5. "I wanted to see you folks again," Dillinger answered. "It's worth the risks." In fact agents did stake out the woods around the Mooresville farm, but Dillinger managed to slip away before they could close in. Photos appeared of Dillinger posing with his young nieces and proudly brandishing his wooden weapon. And so the legend grew.

Dillinger's brazen escape from Crown Point—much like the Kansas City massacre—provided another unsolvable mystery. Were prison officials bribed to make the escape possible? Did Dillinger whittle the gun himself from a washboard, or did his lawyer Louis Piquett arrange to have it smuggled into the prison for him? In the end, those details proved irrelevant; rather, his postescape activity was significant. Once he was safely away from the prison and cruising in his stolen Ford, Dillinger unknowingly crossed a figurative line. When he crossed the border from Indiana into Illinois, Dillinger probably had no idea he had violated the Dyer Act, which prohibited the transport of a stolen vehicle across a state line. But he had committed a federal crime, and thereafter the battle to end his freedom was joined. Federal forces had not been deployed to search for Dillinger after his first prison escape. But now that he had made a mockery of a superior jail, and triggered a slew of headlines and stories that touted his ingenuity, the federal government had every reason to get involved. For the first time, a federal warrant for his arrest was issued on March 7. Just that easily, John Dillinger became J. Edgar Hoover's problem.

And what a problem it was. In March 1934, Hoover's Bureau was unprepared to locate Dillinger. His existence had not been its concern, not until he drove across the state line. The Bureau had no network of informants, no place to turn for leads, no particular insight into his character. The day Dillinger escaped, an agitated Hoover called Melvin Purvis in Chicago. Purvis confirmed what Hoover already knew: Because Hoover had never instructed his agents to start a Dillinger file, they had no base of information to drawn on. The Bureau would have to start from scratch.

Hoover, under pressure from Washington to win the nascent war on crime, saw his greatest chance for success—and failure—in the sneering mug of John Dillinger. It would not do to capture dozens of lesser criminals; he would need to deliver the greatest gangster of them all. One of his very first startling moves was to pin the blame for the Bureau's slow start not on himself but on an agent he had never ordered to gather intelligence on Dillinger. "Last night I had the occasion to call Mr. Purvis at Chicago to inquire of him what steps had been taken in the Chicago office toward bringing about the apprehension of Dillinger," Hoover wrote in a memo to Harold Nathan just one day after Dillinger escaped, "and much to my surprise the Chicago office has done practically nothing in this matter." Hoover also scolded Purvis for not having informants and underworld connections he could turn to for help in pointing the Bureau in Dillinger's direction. The panicky scramble in Washington was surely obvious to everyone, but certainly Purvis felt the urgency more squarely than anyone else. As head of the Chicago office, it fell to him to win or lose this great new battle—a battle for which the Bureau was clearly unprepared. Overnight, Purvis's life changed dramatically. He now had one mission and one mission only—to get Dillinger, or else.

—————

Purvis had by no means been idle between the day he assumed control of the Chicago office in October 1932 and the day Dillinger broke out of Crown Point in March 1934. Those sixteen months were filled with danger, adventure, excitement, anguish, great successes, and difficult failures, and turned Purvis into a true crimefighter. He had spent his first five years in the Bureau interviewing businessmen and shuffling through the minutes of meetings, but his life changed once he got to Chicago. He moved from tax fraud and antitrust cases to take on a new and dangerous breed of crook. Now Purvis was matched against the kidnappers.

Along with bank vaults, freight trucks, and automobiles, wealthy businessmen became prime targets for America's Depression-era gangsters. The once-obscure crime of kidnapping quickly became a commonplace event. Many of the nation's most infamous kidnappings occurred on Purvis's watch in Chicago. It was an accident of timing that he became head of the office just as the city was becoming the flash point in the battle against desperadoes. "The date of my appointment . . . coincides roughly with the beginning of the federal government's intensive war on crime," he would later write. "Hell started popping immediately."

Purvis got his first taste of Chicago in January 1932 when Hoover assigned him to be the acting special-agent-in-charge—a sort of trial run to see how he held up under the pressure of big-city crime.

Purvis quickly proved he could act decisively amid chaos. In early 1932, Hoover assigned him to pursue gangsters Jimmy Keating and Tommy Holden, bank and payroll robbers with ties to Frank Nash, Fred Barker, and Alvin Karpis. His best leads, two women known to be associates of the gangsters, were nightclub entertainers—one at the Paramount Club, the other at the Minuet Club. Purvis rented a room adjacent to theirs at a Chicago hotel, and had agents listen to their conversations through the wall and monitor their comings and goings. When the women stepped out, agents searched their room. Purvis went in himself to retrieve fresh photos of Keating and Holden; with a camera borrowed from Northwestern University's crime-detection lab, he took pictures of the photos and circulated them among his agents. He also had agents tail the women to their nightclubs. One agent, pretending to be drunk, invaded every curtained booth at the Minuet Club in search of Keating or Holden. "He staggered from booth to booth, getting an eyeful at each entrance," Purvis wrote, "but one pugnacious individual seemed to resent the unexpected and apparently drunken entrance and gave him a black eye."

The Chicago office lacked the manpower for round-the-clock surveillance of the women, and one night they left their hotel when no agents were there. A hotel worker called the Chicago office to tip off Purvis; the women had remarked they were on their way to Milwaukee. "Mr. Purvis was immediately concerned, but was not stampeded," inspector Hugh Clegg later noted of the case. "He immediately requested all the men to be available, sent two agents to Milwaukee and took personal charge of the efforts during the course of the evening to find the women in question." Purvis, just recovering from a bad case of the flu, went out in a freezing rain with several agents to stake out a spot where the women were thought to be headed. At 3:30 A.M. agents located them and managed to resume their surveillance without blowing their cover. "That is another example of the fact that to [Purvis] the Bureau's interests come ahead of all personal inclinations," Clegg wrote, "as well as his personal welfare."

During his temporary Chicago stint in early 1932, Purvis also pleased Hoover by reorganizing the stenographic and clerical pool there. In April, Hoover moved Purvis out of Chicago and reappointed William "Skipper" McSwain—who had been called to Washington on special business—to run the office. "I am not exactly certain where I will send you," Hoover told Purvis. "Consequently, when McSwain returns to Chicago . . . you can proceed to Washington." Very few agents were summoned to headquarters to spend time with the director; Purvis had made the trip several times.

On May 31, 1932, Hoover assigned Purvis to head the field office in Birmingham, Alabama. Once again Purvis proved more than capable of running a Bureau field office. In July he not only supervised the capture of Edward Richard Norman, an escaped federal prisoner, but also exhibited deftness in his handling of the press—certainly a key part of any top agent's job. "The Bureau desires to express its commendation upon the intelligent and comprehensive manner in which you have handled the publicity incident to this case," Hoover wrote to Purvis on July 14. "The entire matter was managed by you in strict accordance with the Bureau's desires, views and policies."

It was in Birmingham that Purvis picked up one of the most important allies he would have in his career—his assistant, Doris Lockerman. Known then as Doris Rogers—the name of her first husband—she heard through friends the Bureau's Birmingham office was looking for a stenographer. "I applied for the job on the same day the place where I was working lowered salaries by 50 percent," she recalled. Doris's languid beauty was matched by a quick, dry wit, and she caught Purvis's attention immediately. "There was no doubt that Melvin and I liked each other right away," Doris recalled of their first meeting. "I had nothing but the kindest, warmest feelings for him and I think he felt the same way about me. I remember once he was too busy to dictate something and I said, 'Don't worry, I'll write it myself.' Melvin looked at me and said, 'You think you're smart, don't you?' And I said, 'Yes, I think I'm as smart as you.' And from that time on he was apt to turn many important things over to me. We were a nice little team."

In October 1932, Hoover finally gave Purvis the top slot in Chicago. Purvis replaced Skipper McSwain, who would soon leave the Bureau for private law practice. Great friends from their earlier time together in the field office, Purvis and McSwain became roommates in Chicago. It was a beneficial arrangement for both. Most special agents in Chicago either lived with their families or with other young agents, to save on rental costs. What little free time they had could not be spent hopping around town or dating women, because agents were prohibited from telling anyone what they did for a living. "They were awfully lonely most of the time," said Doris Lockerman. "What a thing it was to come to Chicago and have this amazing job and not be able to tell anyone about it. And so these poor young men wound up playing a lot of bridge and pinochle with each other. I don't think any of them ever had a legitimate date." Purvis, however, had the benefit of his handsome and outgoing friend, Skipper McSwain. "The two of them lived a far more social life than other agents," Lockerman noted. "When they did manage to go out together, Skipper could pull a woman aside privately and let her know that Melvin was head of the Chicago office. Skipper became a very good front for him."

Before he left Birmingham, Purvis asked Doris to come with him to Chicago to be his secretary. She had recently divorced her husband, and she had a small son to take care of, but the offer and the adventure it promised were impossible to resist, and she agreed. In November they moved into their new office on the nineteenth floor of the Bankers Building on West Adams Street in Chicago's downtown financial district. Across the street was the Federal Building, home to the U.S. Attorney from Chicago, the U.S. Marshal's Office, and other top federal officials. The building was "splendidly equipped and well-appointed," one memo noted, but the Bureau's office—which took up the entire floor—was decidedly ordinary. Visitors passed through a long hallway to the entrance, just past which sat Doris Lockerman as sentry. A small swinging gate by her desk led to the office behind her, occupied by Purvis. Along one side of the floor was the large bullpen, stuffed with more than 100 identical desks where the special agents manned their black telephones or sifted through their thick case files. Most days they would dictate new information to either Alice or Agnes Barber, twin sister stenographers who typed up every file with seven flimsy copies for eventual storage in one of several gray cabinets supervised by the file clerk, Helen Dunkel. A cheerful Polish office boy named Johnny Madala roamed the floor pitching in where he could and pestering Purvis for an official assignment. It might have been the office of an insurance company, a brokerage, or any other business, except for the total absence of personal touches. "No family photos on the desks, no paintings on the walls, nothing," said Lockerman. "It was all very plain, and it was all business all the time. There was never anything like a New Year's Eve party there, heavens no. What mattered was that the work was so interesting and important." Purvis's silver horse figurine, perched on his glass-top desk, was perhaps the only personal artifact on the floor.

In Chicago, Purvis confronted the kinds of grifters, con men, and crackpots he had not seen much of in Alabama or Oklahoma. Every day all sorts of people showed up at the office with tips and leads, most of them unfounded and many of them absurd. Early in his tenure as top agent, Purvis met with a jittery young man who claimed to have inside information about a hijacking ring. The man asked Purvis for a job, and Purvis explained he would have to apply in Washington.

"I'm afraid I can't," the man replied. "I've got a criminal record."

Then the fellow had a brainstorm. "Say," he said, "I know some men I can get to hijack a truckful of liquor. If I get them to do it and give you the dope so you can raid, will you give me a job?"

Purvis and his agents handled an array of urban crimes: hijacking, auto theft, extortion. Infiltrating criminal rings and catching perpetrators required a combination of sophisticated office work—fingerprinting, strategizing, profiling—and stealthy, dangerous fieldwork. Purvis himself often went on raids and stakeouts, though traditionally the special-agent-in-charge (SAC) was more likely to stay behind and coordinate efforts from the office. Similarly, a SAC usually did not interview suspects, since that would obligate him to appear at any subsequent trials, but Purvis often entered the interrogation room to form his own opinion of a suspect's innocence or guilt. When businessmen called the Bureau to report they had received demands for money from an extortionist, Purvis liked to meet with the victims himself. He was, by all accounts, a hands-on leader. At the same time, he was inexperienced in criminal matters. Unlike some of the grizzled veterans at the Bureau—men with two or three decades of police work or investigative experience behind them—Purvis had a mere five years of on-the-job training, and most of it in white-collar crime. He had no choice but to continue to learn the ropes as he went, and certainly it was less than smooth going in his early months in Chicago. Because the stakes were so much higher there, his mistakes would be amplified, just as his successes later would be exaggerated.

Kidnappings were by far his greatest challenge in his early months in Chicago. Two of his first big cases—the abductions of William Hamm and John Factor—would become bizarrely intertwined and would reveal, as much as anything, the limitations of a youthful crime-fighter in a city rife with crooks on either side of the law. "Purvis had to play ball with a lot of police officials who were crooked, and I don't think he always knew they were crooked," said Chicago historian and Dillinger expert Tom Smuysen. "I think he may have put too much stock in someone just because they wore a badge, and in Chicago that was a naive thing to do."

On June 15, 1933, William Hamm, chairman of the Hamm's Brewery in St. Paul, Minnesota, left work to get some lunch at his family's Tudor mansion on the hill above the brewery. A man he had never seen before hustled him by the elbow to the curb of the street, then pushed him inside a black Ford sedan that screeched to a stop. Hamm was hooded and forced to the floor of the Ford, which quickly disappeared into traffic. Later that afternoon Hamm's vice president of sales, William Dunn, answered his office phone. "We have Mr. Hamm," the caller said. "We want you to get one hundred thousand dollars in twenties, tens and fives."

Two weeks later, on July 1, 1933, the Bureau received notice that John Factor—a shady character more commonly known as Jake the Barber—had been kidnapped on his way home from a Chicago casino. Factor was wanted in Great Britain for defrauding investors of millions of dollars, and faced extradition to England; the U.S. Supreme Court was considering his case. For this reason many in Chicago believed the kidnapping was a hoax. "The underworld gossip was that his disappearance was a phony," Purvis would later write. "Factor, according to the story current, had kidnapped himself so that he would not be available should Washington grant extradition. . . . I did not credit these rumors." After eleven days a bearded and beaten Factor emerged from captivity; his family had secretly paid a $50,000 ransom. Purvis sat with Factor and listened to his tale. "Factor was still frightened when I talked to him," Purvis said. "He had been dealt with harshly, and I am sure that the story told by him of his sufferings was true."

By then Purvis had already settled on his suspects. "We assumed from the start, with no material evidence, that the Touhy gang was responsible," Purvis said. The Terrible Touhys, as the papers called them, were a gang of six brothers, the wayward sons of a Chicago police officer. One newspaper called them "one of the most vicious and dangerous mobs in the history of gang-ridden Chicago," and credited them with as many as thirty kidnappings. The leader of the gang was Roger Touhy—"the greatest single menace gangland ever offered America." Touhy was hardly that; for one thing, he never killed a single person. But he was a big-time bootlegger whose liquor and gambling businesses in Chicago's suburbs irritated mobster Al Capone. Touhy's involvement in a kidnapping was more than plausible, though Purvis admittedly had no evidence at first. Then he received a call from Dan Gilbert, the chief investigator for Chicago's state prosecutor. A former cop who answered to the nickname Tubbo, Gilbert had two stunning pieces of news for Purvis. First, he told him Roger Touhy was behind not only the Factor kidnapping but also the abduction of William Hamm, who had been released after a $10,000 ransom was paid. Gilbert even knew where Touhy was—the gangster and three pals had run their car into a telephone pole in Elkhorn, Wisconsin, where they were drinking and fishing for muskellunge. "A light mist was falling and I skidded off the road," Touhy later explained. "Nobody was hurt, but the pole broke off at the base and crashed to the ground. From the back seat [my companion] hollered, 'Timber!'"

Local police were not amused when they spotted guns in the back of the car: All four men wound up in jail. Purvis dispatched two agents to Elkhorn, and without waiting for a formal order of extradition, they rushed Touhy to Chicago. The agents led a handcuffed Touhy into Purvis's office and sat him in a leather chair in front of Purvis's desk. Purvis questioned him, but, Purvis later recalled, "Touhy wouldn't talk . . . when I asked a question, he laughed. When I demanded an answer, he laughed." Finally Purvis told Touhy he suspected him of kidnapping William Hamm. "What do you mean by ham, Mr. Purvis?" Touhy replied. "A ham sandwich? Or did I kidnap a ham steak?" Purvis said nothing but "looked at me in the tight-lipped, gimlet-eyed way that FBI men had," Touhy later said, "and which detective-actors on television have plagiarized."

Purvis ordered Touhy's handcuffs reinforced. Agents wrapped an escape-proof safety belt around his waist and attached the cuffs to it; another agent "held me on a chain like a dog on a leash," Touhy recalled in his autobiography. Touhy and his three cohorts were fingerprinted, photographed, and led into a room with a two-way mirror—"Judas glass," Touhy called it. On the other side of it, Factor identified William Sharkey, one of Touhy's associates, as one of his captors, though William Hamm, summoned to view the suspects, did not pick out Touhy. Nevertheless, based on other witness identifications, Purvis believed he had the culprit in both the Hamm and Factor kidnappings. He sent the Bureau's findings to prosecutors in St. Paul and Chicago, who tried Touhy for both crimes.

Purvis was stunned when a jury acquitted Touhy of kidnapping Hamm. The witnesses who picked out Touhy "were all reputable people but they were mistaken," Purvis would say. "Their inaccuracy was proven later when it was found that the Hamm kidnapping was a Barker-Karpis gang job." The possibly wrongful prosecution of Touhy and his associates had a tragic consequence. One night during the trial, William Sharkey fit a tie around his neck and hung himself in his cell at Ramsey County jail. "I wept," Touhy recalled. "Willie's life might not have amounted to much, but he shouldn't have been driven to ending it."

Still, Touhy and his two remaining codefendants faced conviction for abducting Jake the Barber. At trial Factor claimed to recognize all three men, even though he had earlier insisted he had been blindfolded during the entire ordeal. Outside the courtroom, Factor told an Associated Press reporter, "I wouldn't hurt a fly but I could take [Touhy's] throat and twist it until the blood came out. And I could drink the blood the way they tortured me." The first jury to hear the case could not reach a verdict; the jury in a second trial found the men guilty. All three were sentenced to ninety-nine years in prison. This time Touhy did not cry. This time he threw up. The Illinois Supreme Court upheld the sentences, and again Factor had his say. "It would have been a calamity," he declared, "if any legal technicality had upset the law's victory over these gangsters."

Purvis had been wrong in suspecting Touhy of kidnapping Hamm, but he was certain he had the right man in the Factor case. It would be twenty years before a federal judge ruled him wrong again. Touhy was still languishing in Illinois's Stateville Penitentiary when *Chicago Daily News* reporter John Patrick Lally began researching the Factor case. Judge John P. Barnes of the federal district court for northern Illinois was persuaded to consider the revised testimony of dozens of witnesses in the second Factor trial, and in 1954 he issued a ruling that cleared Touhy of any wrongdoing. "The court finds that John Factor was not kidnapped for ransom or otherwise on the night of June 30th and July 1st, 1933, although he was taken as a result of his own connivance," Barnes wrote. "Roger Touhy did not kidnap John Factor and, in fact, had no part in[ck] the alleged kidnapping. . . . Perjured testimony was knowingly used by the prosecutor to bring about Touhy's conviction." Furthermore, Barnes noted, "all the evidence establishes that the relationship between [Factor] and the prosecution was far more than the ordinary relationship between prosecuting witness and prosecutor"—in other words, Barnes contended, Factor and the prosecutors conspired to frame Touhy. The central figure in the setup was Captain Dan "Tubbo" Gilbert, the man who delivered Roger Touhy to Purvis in the first place.

Gilbert, as corrupt a figure as Chicago ever produced, was known as the richest cop in the world, though not by Melvin Purvis. He had been in charge of the Chicago office less than a year and did not know that Gilbert, while working with the state prosecutor's office, had never convicted a single member of Al Capone's crime syndicate—that he had, in fact, been an unofficial member. Because of that connection, Gilbert was determined to eliminate Roger Touhy, whose success in running liquor and gambling operations in Chicago made him a Capone-gang rival. "Touhy was not an acceptable person to Captain Gilbert," Judge Barnes determined. He "was an obstacle in the drive of the politico-criminal Capone syndicate to control and dominate the labor unions." Barnes's ruling paved the way for Touhy's release from prison in 1959. Then age sixty-one, he had served a quarter century behind bars for a crime he possibly did not commit.

His hard-fought freedom would prove short-lived. Only twenty-three days after being paroled, Touhy left the Press Club in downtown Chicago, where he had spent the evening discussing a book he was writing with Chicago *Sun-Times* reporter Ray Brennan. As he climbed the steps to his sister's home where he was staying, two men identified themselves as policemen and fired five shotgun blasts. The building's glass front door shattered, raining shards over the slumped body of Roger Touhy, who died a short while later at St. Anne's Hospital. "I am very broken up about it," John Factor told reporters after hearing of the murder. "I hope they get the killer."

In the weeks after his release, Factor claimed to be receiving demands for more money from his kidnappers, even after Touhy was
in jail. Purvis took control of the investigation. He tapped Factor's
telephone and listened in as a caller arranged for a money drop;
traces put on the calls allowed agents to rush to pay phones, though
they always arrived seconds too late to catch the caller. On August
12, 1933, a ransom delivery was arranged. Factor was instructed to
wrap stacks of money in newspaper and have a Western Union messenger take a green Checker taxi to a desolate road just outside
Chicago. Purvis conferred with Chicago police and devised a plan
for one officer to pose as the Western Union man and another as
the cab driver. A police chief believed the undercover cops should
not carry guns. "I disagreed," Purvis recalled, "and later, on the
morning of the pay-off, I told the policeman that he should by all
means take his weapon." Some thirty squad cars, with four officers
in each car, were arranged around the perimeter of the drop-off
site—a park on Twenty-second Street—to block every conceivable
exit. Dozens more federal agents joined the operation. The most
fanciful part of the plan was to have an airplane fly overhead to signal that the ransom had been picked up. Purvis secured an army
plane and army pilot and instructed him to "fly as low as possible,
and when the ransom transfer had been made . . . to rise and dip . . .
the police would know by the signal that the crooks were in flight."

When the time came for the ransom drop, Purvis stationed himself in the police chief's office. He chain-smoked cigarettes as he
waited for telephone calls from the scene. With 200 police officers
and Bureau agents poised to catch the kidnappers, he expected the
news to be good.

Instead, the kidnappers got away. Basil Banghart and Charles
"Icewagon" Connors screeched their car to a stop at the drop-off
point, seized a dummy package of money, and sped down
Mannheim Road. They met blockades at every turn but somehow
zigzagged their way to a stretch of woods. On foot they vanished into
the trees. The two men, Purvis would say, "were blessed with luck
that August afternoon." At least the army plane had dipped as
planned, cueing the frantic, failed chase.

———
—

There would be other setbacks in the Chicago office. The pursuit of desperate gangsters, Purvis learned, was a slippery business. In summer 1933, Purvis placed a Chicago apartment under surveillance to keep an eye on a nightclub waitress named Bobbie Moore. Purvis knew that Moore was friends with Vi Mathias, Vern Miller's girlfriend. At the time, Miller was one of the most wanted men in the nation, for his role in the bloody Kansas City massacre. Purvis's agents never spotted Mathias at the apartment, and the surveillance was dropped. That fall, Purvis tried tailing Bobbie Moore again. He tracked her to her new address at the Sherone Apartments on Sheridan Road. The building manager confirmed that Mathias had not only visited Moore but had moved into the building herself. Surely Miller could not be far behind.

Still, there was a problem—most of the agents in Chicago had no idea what Vern Miller looked like. Grainy photos were little help; besides, Miller would surely be wearing some sort of disguise. The Bureau needed someone who had actually laid eyes on Miller. Fortunately, they had such a person—Doris Lockerman. Purvis's personal secretary, a native of Huron, South Dakota, had indeed come across Vern Miller, who before he turned to a life of crime had been a well-respected sheriff in South Dakota. A Chicago special agent, Ed Notesteen, also knew Miller by sight and was assigned to the case. Because the Bureau was so understaffed, another unlikely person was recruited to help with the surveillance—Purvis's peppy young office boy, Johnny Madala, who despite having no college degree was eager to become a special agent. Now, he finally had his first real assignment.

Madala's job was to hide out in an apartment taken over by agents on the second floor, where Vi Mathias lived. His cover was John L. Malleck, a traveling auditor from Buffalo, New York. Hours of peering and snooping paid off when Madala spotted a man visiting Mathias and Moore during a Halloween party. He quickly called the Chicago office and said he thought he had seen Vern Miller. Next, Doris Lockerman and Notesteen wedged themselves inside a tiny, sweltering hallway cupboard that housed the building's dumbwaiter. By leaving the door open just a crack, Doris could see the back door of apartment 211, where agents suspected Miller was visiting Mathias. The two Bureau trackers set up a tall stool in the cramped space and watched the door for long hours. On November 1, 1933, the waiting ended. "I was practically nodding off in there when I heard the door open and saw a man step out," Lockerman recalled. "I knew right away this was Vern Miller."

Doris whispered to Notesteen that the man sneaking down the hallway with his fedora pulled down low was indeed Miller. Notesteen wasn't as sure. "That's Miller!" Doris whispered again. "It's Miller!" Apparently her whisper was too loud: "Miller heard me. He was on his way out of the apartment building anyway but suddenly he began to run." Several agents and police officers were aligned in and around the building, prepared to capture Miller should he flee. But a prearranged signal from an agent on the second floor was never seen, and in the chaos that ensued, Miller was able to hurtle down an emergency staircase and out a side entrance lobby door. Agents posted on the street had been looking for yet another signal—a shirt flapping from the window of the apartment staked out by Madala to signal that Miller was fleeing—and were not immediately sure the man shuffling out the side entrance was their target. Miller managed to reach his car and speed away as agents peppered it with gunfire. Incredibly, Miller escaped.

Purvis was not in charge of the failed raid; he was out of town on another assignment. Agent Ed Guinane supervised the stakeout and forgot to signal agents by waving a shirt out the second-floor window. Still, as head of the Chicago field office, the raid was Purvis's responsibility, and in Washington, Hoover was livid. Fortunately, Miller quickly ceased to be a problem for the Bureau. Not long after his improbable escape, he turned up in a drainage ditch at Cambridge and Harlow streets in Detroit. His naked body was wrapped in a blanket and bound tightly with all but twenty feet of a long clothesline. It was never determined which mobsters erased Miller.

If Purvis learned anything in his first year in Chicago, it was that stakeouts and surveillance were not an exact science. Calculating where to send which agents, and for how long, was perhaps his biggest challenge, and any decision he made had serious and possibly deadly consequences. He would learn this lesson again during the pursuit of Machine Gun Kelly, the handsome college dropout who in 1933 became yet another Public Enemy Number One.

On July 22, 1933, two men carrying guns interrupted a quiet bridge party on the screened porch of the handsome Oklahoma City brick mansion of Charles F. Urschel and his wife, Berenice. The intruders waved their guns at the couple and their guests, Walter Jarrett and his wife, and asked which of the men was Urschel. Neither of the well-dressed fellows seated in comfortable wicker chairs replied. "Well," said one of the assailants, "we will take them both." They did.

The gunmen released Walter Jarrett two hours later, after searching his wallet and relieving it of $50. But forty-three-year-old Urschel, a wealthy oilman, became the Bureau's next high-profile kidnapping to crack. Bureau policy was to delay undertaking pursuit of suspected kidnappers until the victim had been safely returned. Urschel's frazzled wife and relatives endured day after day of mailed instructions, ransom demands, and harrowing silences. Finally, directions were given for a drop-off of the $200,000 ransom, delivered in a tan leather Gladstone bag by a colleague of Urschel's, E. E. Kirkpatrick. He surrendered the bag to a man a half block from Kansas City's LaSalle Hotel; that pickup man was George "Machine Gun" Kelly. Nine days after he was abducted from his porch, an unshaven, bleary-eyed Urschel staggered home.

Investigation into Urschel's kidnapping was directed from the Bureau's Oklahoma City office. Though he had been blindfolded throughout his ordeal, Urschel had extraordinary recall of small but important details: the sound of chickens, cows, and hogs outside the kidnapper's hideout; the rattle of a well bucket being hoisted; the regular roar of planes passing overhead twice a day. These factors helped federal agents discover where he had been held: a ranch near Paradise, Texas. Agents arrested several members of Kelly's gang, but Kelly and his wife Kathryn—as well as most of the ransom money—remained at large.

Kelly's movement through the Midwest brought Purvis briefly into the case. As Kelly bounced from city to city, he kept in contact with associates through letters, some of which federal agents intercepted. One letter referred specifically to a bar in Chicago—the Michigan Tavern on South Michigan Avenue—where the Kellys could be reached by mail. An agent phoned Purvis with the information September 21. Purvis waited until the following day to send agents there; first he had them find and interview the mailman who delivered letters to the tavern, a tactic that yielded nothing. By the time the agents reached the tavern the afternoon of September 22, the Kellys—who had lunched there—were gone. In the weeks that followed, Purvis had to answer for his decisions. Why hadn't he sent agents to the tavern on the very day he received the tip? Purvis had no excuse. "This," Hoover would later say, "was a miserable piece of work." Luckily, Kelly's continued freedom did not come back to haunt the Bureau: A team of agents led by William Rorer, special-agent-in-charge of the Birmingham office, captured Kelly and his wife in a dawn raid on a bungalow in Memphis, Tennessee, on September 26. The Bureau would circulate the story that Kelly cried out, "Don't shoot, G-men, don't shoot!", effectively coining the popular reference to government agents. More likely it was his wife Kathryn who made the comment. Either way, few headlines would fail to use the nickname after that.

By his own admission, Purvis was relatively inexperienced when he reached Chicago, and his on-the-job schooling was intense and relentless. Case after case tested his resolve, and the simultaneous investigation of dozens of crimes continued unabated. Early 1934 brought him an encounter with one of the era's shrewdest gangsters, a former railroad engineer named Verne Sankey.

Fine-featured, well spoken, and elegant of manner, Sankey, age forty-two, had a list of five rich businessmen he intended to kidnap. One name on the list was Charles Boettcher II, a broker in Denver, Colorado. Sankey spent weeks trailing Boettcher until he had memorized his movements and routines. On February 12, 1933, Sankey waited patiently in Boettcher's driveway for his prey to return from a night at the theater. Sankey pushed a gun into Boettcher's back, rushed him into a sedan, and stuck a strip of adhesive tape across his eyes. Boettcher's startled and terrified wife clutched the kidnap note, politely presented to her by Sankey's associate, Gordon Alcorn. She watched the sedan disappear into the night, on its way to a remote ranch in Brule County, South Dakota—hundreds of miles northeast of Denver.

Boettcher's father Claude, an Episcopalian minister, agreed to pay the $60,000 ransom, but only after his son was released. Seventeen days after the abduction, Sankey let Boettcher go, trusting the clergyman to keep his word. On the day of the ransom drop, Sankey parked along a deserted road in Denver, where Boettcher's operatives were to drive by, wait for a signal, toss out the money, and keep going. Denver police decided to allow the drop to happen before swooping in on the kidnapper's car. Once Sankey had his money, though, he quickly abandoned his ride. Sankey ran into a shopping district and disappeared into the crowd. Denver police found nothing but an empty car.

Authorities in Denver figured out where Boettcher had been held, and placed police around Sankey's South Dakota ranch. Sankey spotted them through binoculars and was careful to stay away. Soon, Purvis got a tip that both Sankey and Alcorn were likely living in the Chicago area. The Bureau had entered the search for the man one newspaper called "America's No. 1 kidnapper."

The search lasted nearly a year. In Chicago, Sankey "pursued a careful course," Purvis would say. "He changed his ransom bills at ball parks and race tracks. He gambled in wheat and had extensive brokerage accounts. He lived quietly and with no ostentation." Purvis was also handicapped by knowing next to nothing about Sankey, who unlike nearly every other hoodlum was not part of a gang or connected in any way to Chicago's teeming underworld. He had never been arrested or served a single day in jail. "The typical criminal is dependent on his own kind for shelter and protection," Purvis said. But "the thieves, ex-convicts and gunmen who made Chicago their headquarters were not [Sankey's] friends."

Even so, Purvis made headway in the search for Sankey. Though the Bureau frowned on discussing active cases with the media, Purvis provided reporters with a few details of the manhunt. He hoped that a little publicity might produce an anonymous tip. Such a call came in, and Purvis was able to begin tracking Sankey's movements around Chicago. His agents came close to catching Sankey many times, raiding apartments where he had lived before departing to another safe haven. "Several times, as Sankey moved from place to place, they missed him by less than an hour," the *Chicago American* reported. "But agents under Purvis . . . kept on the trail." When Purvis raided yet another Chicago apartment in January 1934, his disappointment at not finding Sankey was tempered by a crucial tip: Tenants at the apartment remembered a man fitting Sankey's description who went by the name of W. E. Clark and who liked to get his hair cut at a barbershop on North Damen Avenue.

The shop's owner, John Mueller, confirmed for Purvis that Mr. Clark came in regularly for a shampoo, haircut, and scalp massage. By then, Purvis knew to marshal his forces quickly for important leads. Purvis assigned several agents to blanket the area of the

barbershop but to remain out of view. Some agents commandeered
an undertaker's store near the shop and set up round-the-clock surveillance, taking turns sleeping in coffins. Other agents moved into
the shop's back room. Purvis summoned Chicago police and devised a plan: They would wait for "Clark" to come in for his shave, allow the barber to lather him up, then swoop in for the arrest.

They wound up waiting ten days, far more than the well-groomed
Sankey had ever let pass between shaves. What Purvis didn't know
was that Sankey had recently undergone surgery to remove moles
from his face, leaving his skin too tender for a blade. The special
agents waited, in their chairs and coffins, until, on January 31, 1934,
the door to Mueller's shop swung open and in walked a grizzly Mr.
Clark. "He looked like a bird who had just come out of the wilderness," Mueller later told reporters. "His beard was a couple of inches
long." Sankey slumped in his usual chair and said, "Be pretty careful
with my face." Mueller's fellow barber, William Masser—briefed by
Purvis to lather up his customer prior to pressing a buzzer to signal
agents and police to move in—played his part perfectly, waiting until Sankey had his face covered by a hot towel before triggering the
raid. At the signal, six men rushed from the back room to Sankey's
chair, pinning his arms and legs. "We pushed the muzzles of our
guns against his bald head," one police sergeant recalled. "He
started up and we flung him back in the chair." John Mueller could
not resist commenting. "You're a cooked goose," he told his former
patron. Sankey's reply: "It's a hell of a way to treat a customer."

Agents hustled Sankey into the back room and stripped him of
every piece of clothing. They found no weapons, but in the lining of
his coat discovered a small box of gray poison pills. "Sankey seemed
to be dejected," Purvis told reporters on the scene. "He remarked
that he was pretty sorry he had not swallowed the pills." Purvis had a
handcuffed Sankey delivered to his office, where he kept him for
the next forty-eight hours, subjecting him to incessant interrogation. Sankey "seemed almost glad the pursuit was over," Purvis recalled. "He readily admitted his part in the Boettcher crime." But
that was not why Purvis detained Sankey for two days. He suspected
Sankey of another, bigger crime—the kidnapping of Charles Lindbergh's son.

When reporters got wind of the interrogation, they rushed to the
Bankers Building and waited in the entrance corridor for a bomb-

shell. Six armed policemen kept them company. Inside, Purvis allowed Sankey a quick snack but prevented him from sleeping even briefly. Outside, the press clamored for news and strained to hear the sounds of Sankey's raised voice. "Twenty-one hours, twenty-two hours, twenty-three hours passed," one reporter later wrote, "and the relentless grilling went on." Occasionally Purvis emerged with an update. "Sankey has not admitted any connection with the Lindbergh case," he announced early on. "But that doesn't mean a thing. We're keeping at him. Naturally, he would not admit this heinous crime until trapped." Inside his office, it was becoming clear to Purvis that Sankey was telling the truth. Pressed yet again to confess to the kidnapping, Sankey snapped. "I am a man," he screamed at Purvis. "I'd kidnap another man. I'd never touch a baby."

Finally, the interrogation ended—all Purvis had on Sankey was the Boettcher kidnapping, though it would be enough to put Sankey in jail for life. Purvis personally supervised the transfer of Sankey to Sioux Falls, South Dakota, where he was to be tried for the crime. Purvis arranged for a private car to be hooked to the end of a Milwaukee Railroad train; inside the car would be seven agents and officers surrounding a manacled Sankey. But just as Purvis was about to leave for the train station with Sankey, a prosecutor from St. Paul arrived at the Bankers Building and insisted on interviewing Sankey. Purvis phoned the station, fearing the train would leave without him. A railroad official assured him the train would wait and would leave only "when you personally give the signal." After finally arriving, Purvis climbed aboard the steaming locomotive, hung his body over one side, and waved his hand to signal the conductor to get under way. He smiled as the heavy wheels beneath him began to turn. "There was enough of the small boy in me," he would say, "to enjoy that brief sensation of omnipotence."

In Sioux Falls, Purvis handed Sankey over to a U.S. marshal. Hundreds of people turned out at the station to get a glimpse of the infamous kidnapper. At the South Dakota penitentiary, Sankey sat sullenly and silently through another thirty minutes of questioning. In Washington, Hoover and other top officials were ecstatic. Assistant U.S. Attorney General Keenan proudly declared, "This means the end of the man who is really America's Public Enemy No. 1."

It was an unequivocal victory for Purvis and his men, and it would reaffirm Hoover's faith in his protégé. Later Hoover would cite the

Sankey case as the reason for his continued confidence in Purvis. It did not matter that Sankey, true to his enigmatic character, found a way to beat the system before being tried. On February 8 he waited until two guards assigned to watch him in his cell walked a few feet away to find an aspirin. He quickly tied two neckties together and fashioned a sturdy noose. He stood on a chair and tied one end to a high bar in his cell; he slipped his head inside the other. Then Sankey wadded a handkerchief into a ball and stuffed it in his mouth, lest his cries alert his careless jailers. With that, the shrewdest of the gangsters kicked the chair out from beneath him and broke his own neck.

———

Purvis would not have much time to savor the praise he received for collaring Sankey. Just one month after the barbershop raid, John Dillinger escaped from the Crown Point jail. Kidnappers like George Kelly and Vern Sankey no longer were Purvis's top priority. Now the primary target was John Dillinger. Purvis, starting from scratch, produced not a single solid lead in the first month following Dillinger's escape. Hoover's confidence in him seemed to wane. "The Division is inclined to wonder concerning the intimate acquaintance on the part of your office with the actual developments in the Chicago district relative to the search for Dillinger," Hoover wrote in a letter to Purvis. The pressure was on to make some progress in the Dillinger case.

Finally, Purvis's legwork paid off. Despite Hoover's criticism that he lacked enough underworld contacts, Purvis did indeed have a network of informants. Since Dillinger's escape he had sent agents to various bars and apartments in Chicago to interview people who might have occasion to come into contact with the gangster. One such man was Larry Strong, who had once dated a woman known to have spent time with Dillinger. On April 9, Purvis received a phone call from someone with urgent information about Dillinger. The caller's identity is not clear from FBI records, but it was likely Larry Strong.

The tip concerned Dillinger's girlfriend—a striking woman named Evelyn "Billie" Frechette. The daughter of a full-blooded Chippewa Indian, she had met Dillinger in 1933 in a cabaret on

Chicago's North Side, and she claimed the two of them instantly fell in love. "I looked up and I saw a man at a table across the room looking at me," she later wrote. "He didn't look away when I looked up. He just stared at me and smiled just a little bit with the corner of his mouth. His eyes seemed to go all the way through me."

After Dillinger escaped from prison, he quickly hooked up with Frechette again. In early April he took her to spend a weekend with his family in Mooresville, a brazen and risky return to his hometown. The following Monday, Dillinger and Frechette were in Chicago searching for a safe place to stay. It was Frechette's idea to contact a man she knew and trusted—Larry Strong.

She met Strong at the U Tavern on State Street, and the two arranged to meet again that night at eight o'clock. Their rendezvous would be at a seedy corner tavern called the Tumble Inn, at the intersection of State and Austin streets. No sooner was the plan in place than Strong—or someone he enlisted to help—telephoned Purvis. At the Bankers Building, a team of twelve agents prepared for the raid. Purvis decided to lead the team and to be the first agent into the bar.

Dressed in a shabby outfit, Purvis arrived at the Tumble Inn at 8:00 P.M. He recognized Larry Strong, who was already dead drunk, but Frechette was not yet there. The remaining agents positioned themselves as inconspicuously as possible outside the tavern. They would wait for Purvis to exit the bar and signal them that Frechette was inside and Dillinger might be also.

Not much later, Frechette arrived with Dillinger, who parked his Ford near the corner of the street across from the bar. He had already circled the block to scan for agents, but Purvis's men were well hidden. Still, Frechette told him to stay in the car. "I'll go in," she said. "The last time you went in somewhere you were arrested." While Dillinger waited, Frechette entered the tavern and approached Strong at the bar. Purvis, sitting next to her, offered her a stool. She shook her head, and Purvis waited momentarily before standing up and walking outside. Purvis merely nodded to an agent, then reentered the tavern and, with the backup of several agents brandishing submachine guns, arrested both Frechette and Strong.

Purvis immediately sent two agents to search the basement. No Dillinger. Then he told them to see if the car that had dropped Frechette at the tavern was still there. Agent R. D. Brown, who had passed a parked car on the way into the bar, told Purvis he did not believe its driver was Dillinger. Another agent, R. G. Gillespie, who got close enough to write down the car's license plate number, agreed the man inside was not Dillinger. A third agent, J. J. Metcalfe, had seen Frechette step out of the Ford but could not identify its driver because the car was against a high curb and to see inside would have required Metcalfe to stoop very low, which could have aroused suspicion. Purvis and the three agents rushed outside, but the parked Ford was gone. The business of catching gangsters, Purvis was learning, required a great deal of luck.

Hoover did not come down hard on Purvis for the Frechette affair. After all, the capture of Dillinger's girlfriend was big news, and represented the sort of progress that the American public as well as Hoover's bosses were looking for. It was not long after the Tumble Inn episode that Hoover sent Purvis the encouraging handwritten promise that he would later work hard not to keep: "Keep a stiff upper lip and get Dillinger for me, and the world is yours."

Sitting in his Ford outside the Tumble Inn, Dillinger watched agents storm inside to arrest Evelyn Frechette. As he pulled away from the curb, he could see them bring her out in handcuffs. He had lost many women in his short life—his mother, his stepmother, his first wife—and now, it seemed, he was losing another. Alone in his stolen Ford, John Dillinger wept.

But Dillinger also vowed to avenge her arrest. In the days that followed, he contemplated breaking Frechette out of prison and punishing the men who put her there. One he marked for death was Melvin Purvis. Dillinger would get the chance to come face to face with Purvis—and to exact his revenge—much sooner than he had ever imagined, in a place as cold and desolate as the very end of the earth.

6

"THE MAN YOU WANT MOST IS UP HERE"

April 21, 1934

SPIDER LAKE, WISCONSIN

High in the north country, on a breath-frosting Saturday morning, a boy of eight tossed a baseball with two men. Emil Wanatka Jr. was the only son of the owner and proprietor of a two-story lodge in the woods of upper Wisconsin, on the shore of Little Star Lake, and the men playing catch with him were guests at the resort, part of a group of ten up for the weekend. The final blasts of a long, bad winter still iced the waters of Lake Superior thirty miles away, and Emil's father was happy to have such a crowd in an off-peak month. Even so, something about his guests troubled him. One of the men playfully lobbed the ball at his young son, but the other—short, feral, jittery, with squinty eyes and a constant frown—repeatedly threw it as hard as he could, relishing, it appeared, the crack it made in the child's tiny mitt. "He was throwing the ball too hard and my hand was hurting," said Emil Wanatka Jr., now seventy-eight. "So I quit and walked away."

It might have been insignificant, this boy's spoiled game of catch, were it not for the person who spoiled it. The man's casual cruelty— foreshadowing the imminent violence of that weekend and to be manifested again with far graver consequences—set in motion a series of events that had a profound and lasting effect on the Bureau. Events at the Little Bohemia Lodge, just south of the village of Manitowish along Highway 51, spurred changes in the agency that still resonate today. The raid that came to be known as the Battle of Little Bohemia also marked the darkest chapter in the career of Melvin Purvis, and one that he nearly did not survive. Many years would pass before Emil Jr. fully understood the significance of the bully's identity: Lester Gillis, more commonly known as Baby Face Nelson. The other man, the less menacing of the two, was John Dillinger.

They were not alone at the lodge. Also present were Dillinger associates Homer Van Meter, John Hamilton, Tommy Carroll, and Pat Reilly. These prized fugitives were "the largest aggregation of modern desperadoes ever bottled up in one place," Melvin Purvis would later say. "Never again would we have such a great opportunity as had been afforded us there." The Dillinger gang and their four molls chose a remote speck of a place deep in the raw woods of Wisconsin for their hideout, and yet they were still vulnerable, even there, to a tipster's maneuverings. An epic confrontation would have seemed inevitable. But what occurred at Little Bohemia was surreal, confusing, chaotic—a catastrophe of circumstance. Several unconnected events combined to undermine the efforts of federal agents, and to set the stage for tragedy: barking dogs, a loud car stereo, an agent's untimely remorse, and a devastating coincidence. In a wilderness lit only by headlights and muzzle blasts, Little Bohemia would haunt the Bureau and destroy two lives.

For Melvin Purvis in Chicago, the day of the raid, April 22, began serenely. It was a Sunday, and a rare day off for Purvis, who generally spent most weekends in the office or out in the field. Officially, a special agent was never off duty, not even on weekends. Agents signed out whenever they left the office and telephoned to report their location once they arrived at home. Even if they went across the street for a meal or a movie, they had to let the agent on duty know their whereabouts. It wasn't always easy for agents to access a telephone, but these were Hoover's rules and they had to be strictly followed. Still, this Sunday was quiet, and had the weather been nicer in Chicago, Purvis might have saddled up his stabled palomino for a ride in Lincoln Park. Instead, he was reading in his apartment when the telephone rang around one o'clock in the afternoon.

The caller was H.C.W. Laubenheimer, a U.S. marshal in Chicago. He had a message for Purvis from someone named Henry Voss, who claimed to have information about John Dillinger. Laubenheimer said Voss seemed credible and passed along his phone number to Purvis. Of course, Purvis had fielded hundreds of tips about Dillinger, the vast majority of which were worthless. With only sixty men at his command, he could pursue only a handful of leads and hope for the best. It was difficult to sort out the crackpots from the legitimate informants. In early April, Purvis had some of his men chase down leads that Dillinger was in Indiana, and he personally traveled to South Bend to search for the gangster. These missions proved fruitless. On April 18 federal agents raided the northern Michigan, Sault Sainte Marie home of Anna Steve, John Hamilton's sister, who had been spotted by neighbors harboring Hamilton and Dillinger the previous night. But the agents arrived too late and settled for arresting Steve, who spent three months in prison for her troubles. This was the pattern: Agents chased tips and followed leads, but Dillinger somehow always slipped away. Still, it seemed to Purvis that Dillinger was close at hand. Purvis quickly dialed Voss's phone number, to hear a tentative voice.

"The man you want most is up here," Voss said.

"You mean Dillinger?" Purvis pressed.

Voss was reluctant to repeat the name over a party line, but finally relented. "Six members of the Dillinger gang are at a resort called Little Bohemia," Voss said, "and John Dillinger is among them." He also said Dillinger would likely be at the lodge for at least another day. Could this be the tip that finally panned out? Purvis asked Voss if he had shared this information with anyone else—he hadn't—and asked for the name of the nearest airport, which was in Rhinelander, fifty miles south of Little Bohemia. Then he instructed Voss to wait for him on the tarmac. "Wear a handkerchief around your neck so I can identify you," Purvis told him.

Purvis at once called the Chicago office and ordered that every available agent be summoned. Then he telephoned Hoover in Washington and filled him in. Next he called the St. Paul office and spoke with Hugh Clegg, the Bureau's assistant director, who was in Minneapolis on other Dillinger business. The Mississippi-born Clegg, age thirty-five, was one of Hoover's favorite agents, much valued for his loyalty and his indiscriminately high opinion of Hoover's leadership. That loyalty, coupled with his unquestionable bravery, led to his promotion to assistant director in 1932, after only six years in the Bureau. Purvis reached him at 2:00 P.M. and relayed Hoover's instruction that Clegg fly as many agents as possible to Rhinelander immediately. Clegg chartered a Northwest Airways plane—at a cost of thirty-five cents a mile—and called around for a pilot. As soon as he found one, he and four agents sped to the airport; four other agents set out for Wisconsin by car.

Among Clegg's many challenges, one was immediate—he had no cars in Rhinelander. He asked about automobile lots in town and made his way to a nearby Ford dealership. In the sales office, he flashed his badge and asked the manager for cars. The manager refused to help if the agents were going after bootleggers. Liquor-law violators were considered only minor criminals in this part of the country, where bootlegged whiskey was indispensable during the long winters, and abetting in their capture would not be good for business. Clegg assured the manager they were not interested in bootleggers. Even so, the best the Ford manager could do was promise a couple of cars used by salesmen upon their return in two hours. Clegg was still haggling over the cars when he heard the throttle of an engine and saw Purvis's plane heading for ground.

In Chicago, Purvis chartered two cabin planes, one belonging to the actress Ann Harding, and instructed the pilots to have the planes warmed up and ready to go. He hurried to the Bankers Building and arrived with his tie and shoelaces still loose. Several agents were already there, some rubbing the sleep out of their eyes. The men collected Thompson machine guns and bulletproof vests for their urgent trip. An hour later Purvis and eleven agents departed Chicago's Municipal Airport for Rhinelander, a three-hour flight.

So far, there was only one plan: Get to Rhinelander, meet with Clegg, and make another plan. The agents knew nothing about the place they would be raiding or even about the surrounding terrain. Purvis had no guidance for his men, other than that they would be hunting for Dillinger. Voss's information that Dillinger would not leave the lodge until the following morning gave Purvis enough time to gather intelligence and formulate a strategy once he was on the ground. During the flight, Purvis and his fellow agents sat in silence.

The trip to Rhinelander left no nerve unrattled. Rough winter winds battered Purvis's plane for most of the ride, making even the pilot nauseous. The agents, backs rigid and breaths held, blanched as the cabin rocked in the sky. Braced against the turbulence, the agents pondered the peril of their impending mission. "The men in my plane were like soldiers awaiting the zero hour—and this was nothing less," Purvis later wrote. "Everyone knew that the venture would be no Sunday School picnic. Everyone knew that if there were six members of the Dillinger gang at Little Bohemia, they would not come out with their hands up."

The miserable plane ride was matched by a frightening landing. Just before dusk, Purvis's plane touched down at the Rhinelander airport, and immediately came the first bit of bad luck—the landing brakes on one wheel failed. The plane spun wildly around and its wing nearly scraped the ground, roughly tossing the already shaken men. Finally it chugged to a stop, and its passengers staggered out to the harsh greeting of the cuttingly cold winter air of northern Wisconsin.

Purvis bounded across the tarmac to meet with Clegg, whose plane had already arrived. By then, Clegg had debriefed Henry Voss, who was wearing, as instructed, a white handkerchief around his neck. Clegg got the story: Voss had come by his information through his sister-in-law, Nan, who was married to Emil Wanatka, owner of the Little Bohemia Lodge. Voss "stated that he had personally called at this inn on two or three occasions since Friday and had been informed by his daughter that a group of thugs was there, and she believed that John Dillinger was included among them," Clegg later wrote. Clegg showed Voss photos of Dillinger, but Voss had not seen anyone resembling him at the lodge. A photo of a flat-nosed Carroll, however, did get a response. Voss, it seemed, represented a real lead. "Although the identification of the gangsters for whom we were searching was not positive," Clegg would say, "the enthusiasm of Mr. Voss was of such a character that it was recognized that he was at least sincere." Clegg had Voss draw a diagram of the lodge and its surrounding cabins; the sketch provided critical information. "There was a lake to the rear of the house," Clegg learned from Voss, and "there was no means of escape by this lake." The agents would need to cover only three sides of the Little Bohemia Lodge.

Purvis and Clegg counted their men. Including the two of them, they were seventeen strong. At least four and preferably five cars would be needed. The consecutive descent of three charter planes

at the tiny Rhinelander airport drew a crowd of curious townspeople to the runway, and Purvis told them, perhaps unpersuasively,
that he and the others were members of a wedding party. He said
nothing about his men's grim faces.

It was around 6:00 P.M., and Purvis was happy to be on the
ground before dark. He was pleased that Clegg and his men had deployed so quickly to this remote outpost. Purvis and Clegg discussed
the other piece of crucial information relayed to them by Voss—that
the Wanatkas and their employees planned to hide in the lodge's
basement at 4:00 A.M. the following day, giving agents the chance to
stage a predawn raid without endangering them. This gave Purvis
nearly ten hours to get his men in position. He instructed agent R.
C. Suran to drive with Voss to Voss's home, two miles from Little Bohemia, to gather more information and scout a possible staging area
for the agents. After the two left, Purvis returned to unloading the
plane.

But only fifteen minutes later, Purvis was astounded to see Voss's
car screech up to the runway. Voss ran from the car shouting, "Mr.
Purvis!" Purvis told him to calm down and catch his breath. Voss
could not: He had bad news. On the outskirts of Rhinelander he
had spotted his wife in another car, going toward town. She was
rushing to find him with urgent information. Voss excitedly shared
it with Purvis: Dillinger had changed his plans. Now, he and his
gang would not be leaving Little Bohemia the following morning.
Instead, they would be leaving after dinner that very night.

Purvis was incredulous. "My first reaction," he would recall, "was
one of deep depression." Instead of ten hours to get into position,
now he had no time at all. While Dillinger and his men enjoyed a
warm and leisurely dinner before departing, Purvis and his agents
stood stranded on the airport runway, shivering hands stuffed in
pockets, without a single car to ferry them anywhere. It was 6:30
P.M. and nearly dark. Little Bohemia was at least an hour's drive
away. Purvis had lost the chance to survey the grounds of the lodge
and gather the details he needed to conduct a proper raid. Even if
he got the chance to confront Dillinger that night, he would be at a
great disadvantage. There would be no time to wait for the agents
hurrying to Rhinelander in cars, or to confer with Hoover in Washington about a strategy. For a moment, Purvis felt all hope was lost.
But only for a moment. Voss's bulletin electrified an already volatile

situation; it canceled any margin for error. There was no time to consider options; there was time only to make decisive moves. "The fever for action dissipated all other emotions," Purvis recalled. "We must get to Little Bohemia at once and trust to luck that we get there soon enough."

First, they needed cars. Purvis asked one of the curious townspeople on the runway for a ride to the Ford garage. Seventeen-year-old Isidor Tuchalsky drove Purvis and two other agents into town in his jet-black 1934 Ford Deluxe coupe. As he drove, he bragged about his "souped-up" car, claiming it could reach a speed of 103 miles an hour. He spoke proudly of its high-compression head and altered rear end. Purvis made careful note of this. At the dealership Purvis learned no cars would be available for at least another hour—far too late to do the agents any good. Purvis turned to his cocky chauffeur, known as Izzy. "I informed Mr. Tuchalsky that I would reimburse him in the amount of $15 for the use of his car that night," Purvis recalled. "He was hesitant about it, and it became necessary for me to advise that if he would not agree for me to use the car, it would be necessary for me to commandeer it. He agreed in a very friendly manner." That settled it—the agents now had one car, and a good one at that.

Still, they needed four more. Purvis ventured into Rhinelander and flashed his badge a few more times, rounding up four more cars, none nearly as impressive as Tuchalsky's coupe. But they would have to suffice; it was now dark and there was no time to spare. Purvis and his men drove back to the airport to pick up the other agents, and all seventeen reconvened inside the garage at the Ford dealership, where they could discreetly unpack and ready their weapons. They had the manager shut off the office lights before they loaded the hardware; each car was stocked with one machine gun, one rifle, and one shotgun. Purvis and Clegg huddled in the dark, drafty garage and hammered out their only plan. The five cars "would proceed with lights turned off to a point close enough to the house so that the surroundings could be clearly observed," Clegg wrote of that hurried meeting, "and immediately an organization would be arranged whereby the house could be surrounded and raided." The men designated to attack the front of the lodge— Purvis, Clegg, and four others—slipped on their twenty-four-pound steel vests, which they would wear for the next twelve hours. The other men were split into two groups, one to cover either side of the lodge. No coverage was needed for the back of the lodge, only 100 feet from the confining banks of Little Star Lake. Once the guns were loaded, the lead car, with Purvis driving, pulled off the Ford lot. The other cars followed at intervals, so as not to create a suspicious convoy. It was 7:30 P.M. Fifty miles separated the agents from Dillinger.

It would prove to be a long fifty miles. Highway 51, a straight shot up Wisconsin's belly, turned treacherous once it reached the fringes of the north woods. The roads, carved through stands of towering pines, were rutted and bumpy, difficult during the day and dangerous at night. No more than twenty miles into the trip, one of the commandeered cars stalled and clattered to a stop. Soon another car broke down. The eight displaced agents had to ride on the running boards of the operative cars, holding on with one hand and gripping their weapons with the other. The three good cars raced into the freezing night, subjecting the men on the running boards to bitter cold. Yet none of the drivers thought to slow down. "A great deal of distance was covered," Clegg would later say, "in a rather short period of time."

The remaining cars hung together long enough to bring Purvis and his men to the cusp of Spider Lake, two miles past which lay Little Bohemia. Purvis ordered the cars to stop and turn off their headlights. In ordinary times, this area surely would have struck Purvis as breathtaking country, with its rich forests, crystalline lakes, and mingled scents of cedar, balsam, and fir. Wisconsin's north woods was a rustic Shangri-la, different in beauty from Purvis's pastoral South but equally splendid and seductive. But in the dead of a moonless night, and under the pall of a treacherous mission, the north woods must have seemed a nightmarish setting—the very end of the earth. Only the hiss of night winds through the bare tops of trees broke the eerie silence. The agents stubbed out their cigarettes and took deep, painful breaths. The men balanced on running boards blew on their numbed fingertips. Finally, in total darkness, the cars restarted and felt their way along the last two miles of road. Purvis saw a single, dim light through dense trees about four hundred yards to the left of Highway 51. He instructed that two of the cars be arranged in a V-shape at the entrance to the lodge, blocking any exit. Then the cold and tired agents, all on foot, made their way over the slick layer of ice on the ground and through the arched, wooden roadside gate that bore two words: Little Bohemia.

———

Nine days earlier, in the deserted downtown business section of Warsaw, Indiana, at 1:15 in the morning, police officer Judd Pittenger, standing watch at the roadside, felt a sharp pain in his side. He turned and saw the tip of a Thompson submachine gun. "We want your bulletproof vests and we mean business," said one of two men who came up behind him on a street corner outside the Candy Kitchen. The speaker, Pittenger realized, was John Dillinger.

For the fifty-four-year-old Pittenger, instinct took over. He seized the barrel of Dillinger's gun and tried to wrestle it away. The second man, Homer Van Meter, poked his machine gun into Pittenger's back, then took Pittenger's pistol and bashed him in the head with it. "Don't hit me anymore," the officer pleaded, capitulating to the persuasive tactics of Dillinger and his crew. They marched Pittenger through an alley to the police station—where the gangster's picture was posted on the wall—and badgered him for the key to the weapons closet. "I have a couple of kids at home," Pittenger said in desperation. "That's the reason," Dillinger replied, "we don't want to kill you."

That was not reassurance for Pittenger, who bolted from the station while Van Meter gathered three Dunrite bulletproof vests. By the time a local posse could be formed, Dillinger and Van Meter had vanished. Roadblocks were set up, and hundreds of law officers roused from bed. None of this activity produced Dillinger. Dozens of tips and sightings were logged and pursued, but as usual most proved to be false leads. "Sometime one of those tips is going to be true," Melvin Purvis told the press around the time of the gangster's latest exasperating escape, "and then we're going to catch Dillinger. That time is going to be soon. We'll get him."

What else could Purvis say? Dillinger's elusiveness, and his ability to roam unimpeded from state to state in the course of committing crimes, had made him the most acclaimed desperado since Jesse James. His capture became a national obsession, inspiring an Indiana lottery based on the date of his arrest, a $5,000 reward from the Universal Newsreel Company, and even a street-vendor scam in

which an envelope purporting to contain photos of Dillinger—and
sold for fifty cents—turned out to be empty. "So," the vendor would
say, "he got away from you, too." Purvis received streams of letters
from citizens certain they knew how the gangster could be brought
to justice. "I have a good idea to get Dillinger . . . it's about machine
guns," wrote Paul Thompson of Ashland, Ohio, who proposed running a trip wire along the floor of a room and rigging it to four unmanned machine guns pointed at Dillinger's knees. "He will get his
feet tangled in it and it will set the guns off," Thompson explained,
though he offered no suggestions on how to get Dillinger into the
room in the first place.

The implication was that Hoover and his men were bungling the
job. Indeed, the battle of wills between Dillinger and his pursuers
was, at the time of his April 13 assault on officer Pittenger, an unde-
niably lopsided affair. It was simply easier for Dillinger to blend into
the fabric of America's heartland than it was for a few hundred men
to pinpoint the whereabouts of a single human being. Dillinger,
quick on his feet and careful always to keep moving, was inevitably a
few steps ahead of the men who had to wait for him to surface before they could track in his direction. There was no Bureau protocol
for hunting down gangsters like Dillinger, because there had never
been a gangster like him. Federal agents were essentially writing the
book as they chased him from state to state. Finding Dillinger was
like trying to shoot a fish in the ocean, not a barrel.

Purvis himself had allowed Dillinger to slip away when he raided
the Tumble Inn on April 9. But his arrest of Dillinger's girlfriend
Evelyn Frechette at the bar was a clear victory for the Bureau. It was
also the reason Dillinger traveled to Warsaw to steal the vests; he
needed them for a risky mission hatching in his head. Frechette, it
seemed, was the gangster's soft spot. At one point he told his lawyer,
Louis Piquett, that he planned to kill both Melvin Purvis and special
agent Reinecke, who had conducted the harsh interrogation of
Frechette. He even tracked down their home addresses. "We're going to be parked in front of their houses one of these nights and get
them before they get us," he told his lawyer. "That's all." Purvis, Piquett said, was merely following orders when he arrested Frechette.
"We'll leave Purvis out of it then," Dillinger replied, "but there's
nothing going to stop me from killing that son of a bitch Reinecke."

The other part of his plan was to break Frechette out of jail. This was the reason he needed bulletproof vests. He considered ambushing federal agents as they transported her to St. Paul to face criminal charges, and later cased the federal prison in Milan, Michigan, where she was eventually confined. Van Meter, for one, was not wild about the plan, but Dillinger would not give up the idea of liberating the woman he loved. First, however, he had to reassemble his gang, which had scattered after the St. Paul shoot-out three weeks earlier. Dillinger and his men had a way of gravitating toward each other after disruptive incidents, a process that usually took less than a month. Even the women in his gang knew how it worked. "The manner of doing so is to put feelers out around those hoodlums who are acquainted with the underworld," Pat Cherrington, who introduced Dillinger and Frechette, once explained to federal agents. "On some occasions it is necessary to travel two or three states, over a duration of two or three weeks, in order to make a connection." Sooner or later, Cherrington said, she knew "Dillinger, Hamilton and the crowd would contact these same parties who were to inform them where she was located." This network of shady contacts delivered Cherrington to a stunning convention of the Dillinger crew on April 19, a meeting held right in Purvis's backyard.

The place was Louis Cernocky's Crystal Ballroom in Fox River Grove, just outside Chicago. It was the same tavern where Dillinger had soaked his sorrows in whiskey the night he watched Frechette hauled away. The bar was known to the Bureau but was not under surveillance. Its location in a town of only 700 people would have made it difficult for agents to operate undercover. In addition, Cernocky had "a very close tie-in with the local officials," a Bureau report noted, and that provided him with protection against stakeouts. Even if it had been feasible to conduct surveillance of the bar, the Chicago office's limited manpower made it impossible to post agents indefinitely at every suspected mob hangout. Still, on April 19 such surveillance would have yielded an amazing sight— Dillinger and Van Meter were there, along with Hamilton, Carroll, and Nelson, as well as all their molls (minus, of course, Frechette). Nelson also brought along Pat Reilly, a small-time crook looking to join up with the big boys. The mood, for the first time in weeks, was light and friendly. Cernocky, unmistakable at 300 pounds, served

drinks and dinner and chatted easily with the men, particularly Nelson. The topic, understandably, was all the attention focused on the
gang after the St. Paul raid. The heat was on Dillinger too intensely
for him to attempt to rescue Frechette. The men needed a few days
in a safe haven, where they could stay out of sight, get some rest,
and plot their next move. Cernocky suggested a secluded resort that
would be perfect for the gang, and he handed Nelson a letter of reference that would ensure they were welcome. The place Cernocky
suggested was the Little Bohemia Lodge.

At seven o'clock the following morning, after a night spent
bunked on the second floor of Cernocky's tavern, Dillinger and his
men set out for Wisconsin in a four-car caravan. Dillinger, Hamilton, and Cherrington left first, in a Ford; a few minutes later, Nelson
and his wife, Helen Gillis, departed in a black 1934 Ford V-8 sedan
with Kentucky plates. After that, Carroll and his girl, Jean Cromp-
ton, took off in a new black Buick coupe with California plates, followed, finally, by Van Meter, his girlfriend, Maria Conforti, and
Reilly, in another Buick. Conforti had packed the winter clothes Van
Meter gave her money to buy, and she traveled with Rex, a small
black Boston bulldog, on her lap. The caravan comprised six men
and four women, a group that included five of the most wanted outlaws in the nation.

Baby Face Nelson got into trouble first. Two hours into the trip,
he ran a red light and collided with a Chevrolet coupe at the North
Leeds Cross Roads Junction in Arlington, Wisconsin, caving in the
Ford's left side and shattering the driver's side glass. Nelson kept his
temper in check and handed $83 to Keith Elworthy, manager of the
Midwest Canning Company, which owned the Chevy. He gave another $5 to the car's driver, John Delaney, who felt dizzy and had
double vision. Carroll pulled up behind Nelson and watched the incident unfold, careful to leave his motor running while he ducked
into Heidman's Tavern for three early morning beers. Finally, Nelson managed to start his battered car and drive it another fifteen
miles into Portage, Wisconsin, where he took it to A. R. Slinger's
garage and asked if he could store it there. Slinger "stepped into his
office a few feet away to obtain paper and pencil in order to write
down the instructions," he would later tell federal authorities.
"When he turned around, the young man was gone and he could

find no trace of his whereabouts." The stealthy Nelson and his wife were now on their way to Spider Lake in Carroll's car.

The three remaining cars would reach Little Bohemia by the evening of April 20, 1934. There to greet them was the lodge's colorful owner, Emil Wanatka. Burly and broad-faced, Wanatka left his native Bohemia to avoid army service in 1906, borrowing $18.20 from his mother for a seventeen-day voyage aboard the *Frederick de Grosse* ocean liner from Bremen, Germany, to New York City. "He came to this country with no money and he worked hard right from the start," said his son, Emil Jr. "He was a really tough guy." Wanatka took jobs as a baker, sailor, and even a prizefighter. He was working as a waiter in Racine, Wisconsin, when he met his future wife, Nan LaPorte, then employed as a nanny. Together they moved to Chicago and during Prohibition opened the Little Bohemia restaurant, which soon attracted sports celebrities like Jack Dempsey and Gene Tunney as well as its share of underworld figures. "That St. Valentine's Day Massacre—those were my daily customers!" Wanatka would later brag with a smile. The precise nature of Wanatka's relationship to the gangsters who frequented his bar is still unknown. He was once accused of murder, though ultimately the charges were dropped. "We always heard that he had killed a man," said Wanatka's niece, Ruth Dickerson Gardner, who fondly remembers her uncle and who today helps run the Birchwood Lodge, Voss's former resort two miles from Little Bohemia. "I asked my mother if he did and she said, 'Yes, but the man deserved it.'"

After Emil Jr. was born in 1926, the family left Chicago's mean streets for the serenity of the Wisconsin woods. Rugged, lusty land that once was home to the Ojibwa Indians, the Manitowish area is ethereally beautiful. "Nature has made a heaven," one local poet wrote, "in the land of the sportsman's dreams." In the nineteenth century, logging camps sprang up, filling the towns with all manner of lumberjacks, including Michigan jumpers (workers who bounced from one camp to another), jill pokers (lazy workers), swampers (men who trimmed leaves off fallen trees), and road monkeys (men who kept the paths in good condition). Fishing was another industry, and local guides made good livings packing box lunches of butter, potatoes, onion, and bacon for clients eager to troll the lakes for four-foot-long muskies. Resorts flourished in the summer, and in

1926, Wanatka bought a lodge on Little Star Lake, the deepest and clearest of ten interconnected lakes in the region. To a once-destitute immigrant like Wanatka, it must have seemed a truly magical place.

Wanatka, however, was relocating to a well-known gangster's lair. During Prohibition the remote reaches of upper Wisconsin were natural hiding grounds for bootleggers, who made frequent trips between Chicago and Canada to smuggle liquor. In the early 1920s, Al Capone often sequestered himself at a lodge in nearby Couderay. Wanatka christened his resort Little Bohemia, and named the road leading to it Nazdar Road—Czech for "welcome." Unfortunately, the two-story lodge burned down in 1931. Wanatka spent nearly $10,000 rebuilding it, incurring an enormous mortgage that would force him to stay open year-round. His was the only area resort to stay open during Wisconsin's brutal winters, and thus the only place to which a group of ten anxious Chicagoans could retreat in April for ice fishing, respite, and solitude.

One by one the cars pulled up to the empty lodge. Van Meter entered first and greeted Wanatka by name, settling in for a lunch of pork chops while Conforti's dog slurped a bowl of milk. Next came Nelson, who immediately aroused suspicion by handing Cernocky's letter of reference to Wanatka, then snatching it back and tearing it to pieces. Dillinger arrived last. They all bore one of the telltale signs of a gangster: heavy luggage, weighed down by guns. "There must be lead in this one," sixteen-year-old George Baszo,[TK] one of Wanatka's waiters, said while carrying a bag into the lodge. "What are these guys, hardware salesmen?" Still, Wanatka was less suspicious than he was happy for the business. His guests, he would later say, were "just like plain people. Everybody is jolly." They all entered Little Bohemia beneath a now-ironic greeting hand-painted on the archway in the wood-paneled foyer: "Through this door pass the best people in the world—my customers."

No doubt, Dillinger and his men relaxed a bit once they learned they were the only tenants at the lodge. They were careful to hide their cars in Wanatka's garage, and they kept their darting eyes on any deliverymen who appeared on the grounds. But for the most part, this stopover was to be a real vacation for the gang. For the next two days, they did little besides stroll the grounds, play cards, and eat generous meals. They made no telephone calls, took no visitors. Yet there was squabbling among them. At the center of it, not surprisingly, was the wild card, Nelson. Dillinger chose second-floor bedrooms for himself and the others but made sure Nelson was assigned the cabin a few dozen yards to the right of the lodge. "Who the hell does he think he is?" Nelson complained. The truth is that not a single person in Dillinger's gang liked or trusted Nelson. "They had a continuous fear around him," Pat Cherrington would tell federal agents. "All of them knew Nelson as a vicious character and one who loved blood, and had a great desire to kill anyone who got in his path." After bank robberies, Dillinger would steer an unwitting Nelson to the middle of a room, arrange his men around him, and allow Nelson to count off everyone's share, so fearful was he that Nelson would shoot them all and make off with the loot. None of the gangsters dared turn his back on Nelson for long. They kept him around because he was good at what he did. "It was often necessary to have him in on a job when they had one to perform," Cherrington said.

That Friday night, Nelson joined Dillinger and the others for a steak dinner and drinks in the lodge's unofficial barroom. Afterward, they played poker—a game that knocked down the first domino in what would be a tragic chain reaction. The men kept asking Wanatka to change five-, ten- and twenty-dollar bills for smaller denominations, and finally Dillinger invited him to sit in. Wanatka—who did not know the identity of his guests but was no stranger to the company of suspicious types—obliged. "The first hand there was thirty-four, maybe thirty-six dollars in the pot," Wanatka recalled. "I had a six and a king up. Dillinger had an eight and a king showing." Wanatka, who had two pair, reached for the pot, but Dillinger stopped him.

"Wait a minute, what you got?"

"I got kings and sixes."

"Too bad," said Dillinger, "I got kings and eights." As Dillinger scooped up his winnings, Wanatka got a look inside his jacket. What he saw changed everything. "Here are two forty-fives in shoulder holsters," he later recalled. "I got to thinking, 'Who could this be in dead winter with a couple of guns on?'" A moment later he saw that Nelson, too, was strapped. Wanatka excused himself, went to the kitchen, and picked up a *Chicago Tribune*. His worst fear was confirmed: A photo of Dillinger in the paper matched the man playing cards in his bar. Not much later he feigned sleepiness and quit the game. It struck him that the stone-faced Nelson did not say good night. In his bedroom he confided to his anxious wife that he thought one of their guests was John Dillinger. That night Nan Wanatka jumped whenever she heard their two collies, Shadow and Prince, barking on the grounds outside the lodge. "You can bet there wasn't much sleep," she would later say. "You lay on your back with your donkey's ears sticking way out." Dillinger didn't get a full night's rest, either; he and two other men worked three-hour shifts keeping watch overnight.

During breakfast the next morning, Wanatka pulled aside the man he knew only as Johnnie. "I took him into my little office and slammed the door," Wanatka recalled. "I looked him right in the eye and said, 'You're John Dillinger.'"

"You're not afraid, are you?" Dillinger replied.

"No," Wanatka said, "but everything I have to my name, including my family, is right here, and every policeman in America is looking for you." Dillinger, disarming as ever, placed his hand on Wanatka's shoulder. "Emil, all we want is to eat and rest for a few days," he said. "We'll pay you well and get out. There won't be any trouble."

The tension lessened, and Wanatka joined Dillinger and Van Meter for target practice outside the lodge. They took turns firing a .22 rifle at an empty gallon can of Bright Spot dill pickles set up on a snowbank 100 yards away. They also fired Van Meter's machine gun, its blasts echoing through the trees. The shooting unnerved Nan Wanatka. Then came the game of catch with Nan's young son Emil, a game Nelson wrecked with his intentionally hard throws. This was the last straw for Emil's mother. It was bad enough these rough men had invaded the lodge, but she would not allow her son to remain in harm's way. She hurriedly packed some of his clothes and announced she was taking him to her brother's house for his cousin's birthday party. She half expected someone to stop her from going, but there were no objections. "I remember Dillinger even gave me a quarter to buy ice cream," recalled Emil Wanatka Jr.

It was a careless mistake by the gangsters, for no sooner had Nan picked up her brother, Lloyd LaPorte, in Manitowish, two miles away, than she shared her terrible secret: Dillinger was at Little Bohemia. In the Manitowish home of her other brother, George LaPorte, where the birthday party was held, Nan huddled in the bedroom with George and her brother-in-law, John Voss. They, too, were told about Dillinger. Such news had never hit their little village, and Voss volunteered to break it right away. He suggested driving to Rhinelander, finding a secure phone line, and telephoning police in Chicago. George LaPorte had a better idea: He wanted to organize a posse of men and storm the lodge right away. "No," Voss told him, "wait until the federal men get here." But Nan Wanatka got cold feet. She wanted to talk to her husband first. The group agreed to postpone any action until the next morning. This was a fateful decision: Had Voss followed his instincts and alerted authorities immediately, Melvin Purvis and his men likely would have had enough time to surround the resort properly. As it was, Nan's brother Lloyd arranged to drop by the lodge the next morning to learn whatever plan had been devised.

Back at Little Bohemia, Emil Wanatka agreed they had no choice but to notify police. A letter was drafted to signal Voss he should make the call. It read:

> Henry—You can go to Rhinelander and call as planned. Not one word to anyone about it. Tell them to line up the highways. There will be more here tomorrow and don't let anyone know where you are going or why. We want to be protected by them as best as they can. Tell them that.

The trick would be to get the note to Voss undetected. This would not be easy, since Dillinger and his men had grown suspicious of their hosts. Suddenly they were eavesdropping on every conversation, scrutinizing every move, questioning every decision. Nelson, in particular, shadowed the Wanatkas, frowning as he followed them around. Nan Wanatka found a private moment to slip the note into a pack of Marvel cigarettes, which she planned to hand to her brother Lloyd. The next morning, Sunday, April 22, Nan awoke a jittery mess. She was so nervous she poured herself a shot of whiskey, even though she did not drink. Right on schedule, Lloyd LaPorte arrived; he had brought his mother with him to make himself less conspicuous. Out of one eye, he noticed Dillinger and Nelson in the lounge, looking his way. He tried to act as if nothing was out of the ordinary.

"Gee, I left my cigarettes at home," he said. "Have you got any, Nan?"

Nan Wanatka passed him the pack of Marvels without a word. She couldn't have spoken if she tried. Lloyd pulled a few cigarettes from the pack but did not hand it back. Instead he held it softly in his hand, and waited a few minutes before easing it into his pocket. Just then Emil Wanatka appeared and asked Lloyd to come to the bar. There, he told him to retrieve yet another pack of cigarettes from behind the flush box in the men's room. On that pack Wanatka had written the license plate numbers of the three cars in his garage. Lloyd LaPorte now had two packs of cigarettes, each a writ of execution should the gangsters discover them. Rather than leave right away, which might have raised a red flag, LaPorte returned to the kitchen and made small talk with his sister and mother. The tension was highly wearing for Nan Wanatka; it seemed she might faint at any moment. But LaPorte remained calm. Finally, he said his good-byes and strolled out the front door. Neither Dillinger nor Nelson looked his way. He got into his car and turned left onto Highway 51. Voss was waiting when LaPorte arrived to drive him to Rhinelander. About two hours later, Voss was on the telephone with Melvin Purvis. The word was out.

Yet even as Purvis learned of Dillinger's presence at Little Bohemia, the information he received was obsolete. At 10:00 A.M. that morning, three hours before Voss made his call, Dillinger began arranging to leave the lodge. First he settled his bill with Emil Wanatka. The rate Wanatka quoted was $4 a day per person. As usual Dillinger was generous; he paid the $120 bill and tipped another $110. This surprised Wanatka less than what Dillinger next told him: Instead of checking out the following day, he now planned to leave around six that evening. Little Bohemia had dollar-dinner specials on Sunday nights, and dozens of patrons would pass through the lodge throughout the evening of April 22. So much traffic surely made Dillinger nervous. He always knew when it was time to pack up and go, and this was the time. He had to wait for Reilly to come back from an overnight errand to St. Paul, but as soon as Reilly returned, they would be on their way. Dillinger asked Wanatka to serve the group one last steak dinner at 4:00 P.M.

It seemed this plan to get Dillinger would come up short, as all the others had. There was no way to get word to anyone that the gangsters were leaving early. Even if Voss had made it to Rhinelander and called authorities, what chance did federal agents have of making it to Little Bohemia by 6:00 P.M.? But two remarkable events occurred. First, Henry Voss's wife stopped by the lodge unannounced. She intended only to alert her sister Nan that her husband had indeed passed along the information about Dillinger, but now she was enlisted as a second courier. Nan took her sister by the arm and discreetly tugged her into the refrigerator room. "They're leaving as soon as Reilly gets back!" she blurted out. Somehow, Ruth Voss had to get to Rhinelander and deliver the update to her husband Henry, who could relay it to Purvis. The minute Ruth left, Nan downed another shot of whiskey. Years later she would blame the events of that weekend for her lingering health woes.

The other fateful twist came courtesy of Reilly, who arrived at the lodge on schedule, around dinnertime, but never got out of his car. Instead he scanned the grounds and wondered why there were no other automobiles in sight. Unaware that Dillinger had hidden the cars in the garage, Reilly guessed the gangster had either left already or been captured. Reilly panicked and drove off; his plan was to return after dark to snoop around. His mistake delayed Dillinger for several hours, giving Purvis more time than he believed he had.

While Purvis bounced in the choppy skies over Wisconsin, John Dillinger sliced into the steak Nan Wanatka prepared for him. Around the time Purvis touched down in Rhinelander, Dillinger was studying a road map in his second-floor room. As Purvis pulled his Ford coupe up to the lodge entrance, with headlights out, Dillinger was playing cards in the bar. A light snow fell over Little Bohemia. All was quiet.

———

Then the dogs barked. The collies, Shadow and Prince, who roamed the grounds and announced every visitor, yelped and howled when they sensed the presence of several men creeping toward the lodge. Purvis was shocked—Voss hadn't mentioned any dogs. It was around 10:00 P.M., and the agents had just left their cars at the entrance gate and were slowly advancing the 200 yards toward the lodge on foot. They had only two tactical advantages: nearly three times as many men as Dillinger, and the element of surprise.

Purvis was certain the sudden, incessant barking would have alerted Dillinger to their arrival. The agents' only choice was to rush to their positions and brace for a fight.

In fact, Dillinger hadn't even looked up from his card game. The collies had been barking all weekend, and by Sunday evening none of the gangsters gave them a second thought. But a far more critical development came at almost the same instant the dogs barked.

While scrambling toward the front driveway, Purvis saw someone leaving the lodge. It was more than one person—three men, then two more, five in all. There was only a single light source for hundreds of yards in any direction—a bright bulb burning over the resort's front door, nine feet up. In the wide half-circle cast by the light, "it was as brilliant there as at midday," Purvis would say. But anyone not in that glow was invisible. Purvis watched three of the men climb down from a porch and get into a 1933 Chevrolet coupe parked outside the lodge. The other two remained on the porch. The departing men had to be some of the gangsters trying to get away—who else would hurry to leave just when the collies began barking? He ordered agents to take their positions to the left of the house, while Clegg whispered to his group to circle around to the right. The three men in the car switched on the radio to full volume. A swing tune combined with the barking provided a surreal soundtrack for what was to come.

The Chevy, its headlights off, backed away from the lodge, lurched sharply to the left, then straightened up and headed for the agents in front. The driving was erratic, not normal. Purvis gripped his weapon tightly but said nothing. There was no time to confer with Clegg or make a plan; whatever happened now would be the result of instinct. The car kept coming, its headlights still off. The agents—Purvis and Clegg, plus Carter Baum and Jay C. Newman—aimed their weapons. The car radio continued to blare, the dogs to bark.

"Halt!" yelled Purvis. "We're federal officers!"

Clegg shouted, too: "Stop the car! Federal agents!" Baum and Newman screamed as well. The car kept coming.

"Fire!"

Twenty-eight bullets tore into the Chevy. Its body was ripped apart and its side window blown out. "It was just like a big windstorm," one of its occupants would later say. The two men who remained on the porch were screaming something, but their words were drowned in the din. Finally, the Chevy slammed to a stop, though its engine kept running. The driver-side door swung open and a man jumped out; he managed to dart into the darkness. Another man slipped out of the car and slumped to the ground. The third man remained inside the car. The agents relaxed their trigger fingers. Still the swing tune played at top volume as smoke and powder filled the air; still the dogs howled in the night. Then came the reckoning—was Dillinger one of these men?

He was not. Dillinger was safely inside the lodge, up and moving at the first crack of gunfire. Van Meter, Hamilton, Carroll, Nelson— all of them were roused by the shots into full getaway mode. But none of the five men who walked out of the lodge and prompted the shooting were gangsters. Two were resort employees, George Baszo and Frank Traube. The other three were patrons just finished with their dollar dinners and a few rounds of beer. Baszo and Traube were trying to convey that information with their useless yells—"Don't shoot! They are customers of ours!" The driver of the Chevy, the man who ran to the woods, was John Hoffman, age twenty-eight, an oil station attendant from Mercer, a neighboring town. He suffered a flesh wound above the right elbow and his face was cut by flying glass. The man who stumbled out of the car was John Morris, fifty-nine, a cook at the nearby Civilian Conservation Corps camp. He had a bullet pass through his right shoulder, just missing his lung, and another wound to his left kidney. These two were the lucky ones. The third man was Eugene Boisneau, thirty-five, a specialist at the CCC camp. He took three bullets: one in the left leg, one between the first and second cervical vertebrae, and one in the neck. He remained in the car, motionless. Purvis and his men did not yet know they had gunned down innocent civilians.

Then—more gunshots. "A bullet hit the ground a yard from my right foot, and two other bullets struck trees behind me," Purvis recalled. It was too dark to make out the quick-moving figure to his right; it seemed a mere shadow was firing at him. Purvis would learn only later that his attacker was Baby Face Nelson. Purvis turned and aimed his machine gun at the movement in the trees. He squeezed the trigger.

Nothing happened. The machine gun jammed.

Purvis dropped the tommy gun and reached for the automatic pistol in his pocket. By then the shadow was gone. There were more gunshots, this time from the second-floor windows of the lodge. Inspector Rorer, one of the three agents covering the left side of the lodge, had seen the silhouette of a man on the roof and yelled for him to halt. Shots were fired at him from one of the windows as the man on the roof jumped down on a snowbank behind the lodge. Rorer returned the fire and ran to the back, but stumbled in a deep drainage ditch. The sketch of Little Bohemia provided by Voss had failed to account for the ditch. Similarly, the agents assigned to the right side of the lodge were slowed by a barbed-wire fence, which had also been overlooked by Voss. Had his diagram included these two obstacles, federal agents surely would have reached the back of the lodge several seconds earlier. As it was, when Rorer got there he saw no movement in the thirty yards of woods between the building and the lake. No figures were discernible along the water's edge. There was no indication that anyone had escaped out the back of the lodge. Rorer returned to the front confident that at least some of the gangsters remained trapped inside.

Finally the shooting stopped. Overall, hundreds of bullets were fired in the span of a few seconds. The riddling of the Chevy, Purvis's encounter with Nelson, the exchange at the lodge—all of it happened in one chaotic burst. Purvis was still shaking when he focused again on the man slumped against the Chevy. He ordered one of the agents to bring a car and shine its headlights on the scene. "We're federal officers," another agent called out. "Identify yourself."

"I'm John," the man said.

"Hands up!" Purvis yelled. But the man could barely raise himself to his feet. Morris not only was shot but was drunk as well. He ignored the agent's instructions to come toward them slowly and instead ambled in the direction of the garage. There, he took a seat on the ground, produced a flask from his hip pocket, and threw back a long drink he richly deserved. His actions were slow, unthreatening; he moved as if in a dream. Soon he was back on his feet and ambling toward the lodge. "We continued to exhort him to come to us, but he did not do so and walked into the house," Clegg later recounted. "He offered no resistance, and orders were issued for no one to shoot at him unless he made some attempt to take the offensive." Purvis would have liked to tackle Morris, but the agents could not risk disclosing their places in the darkness. To move into the circle of light near the entrance was to become an easy target for anyone shooting from the lodge. Instead, Purvis watched the wounded Morris walk back into Little Bohemia, where he telephoned Alvin Koerner, owner of the Spider Lake Resort a mile and a half to the south. "I'm at Emil's," Morris said. "Somebody's held up the place." Then Morris collapsed.

Outside, headlights lit Purvis's back. He turned to see a car he did not recognize—it was Reilly, finally returning to the lodge. Danger, it seemed, came from every direction. Purvis ran toward the car with his pistol drawn, but Reilly quickly sped away. Purvis and Baum fired, taking out the radiator. This fourth round of shooting disturbed Purvis, whose fear of endangering agents in a cross fire seemed, at this moment, well founded. Unsure where his men were, he called for them to shout out their positions. Purvis needed to impose some sort of order on the situation. They also needed to identify the man still slumped in the running Chevy.

Purvis called to the man one last time, then aimed his pistol at the car while Rorer slithered toward it on his belly. Rorer reached into the front seat and put his fingers on the man's wrist. "I felt his right pulse," Rorer recalled. "It was semicold and indicated no heart beat . . . his right chest and shoulder were wet with blood. He was obviously dead." Rorer turned off the engine, finally stopping the loud music. Then he checked the man's wallet. This was Eugene Boisneau. Purvis was told the dead man was no gangster. The scope of the tragedy was just beginning to emerge.

Twenty-nine-year-old W. Carter Baum was tall and handsome. He was born in the nation's capital and had joined the Bureau four years before, in 1930. He was rugged and boyish and loved playing handball, and he made quick friends with everyone. He had a promising future and a wife and two baby daughters at home. Now he had taken an innocent life.

All of the agents were surprised to learn the dead man in the Chevy was a civilian, but none of them took the news as hard as Baum. He was dazed, disbelieving, in shock. He sat mournfully in one of the federal cars and cradled his still-warm machine gun in his lap. "I suppose I have killed an innocent man," another agent heard him say. "I can never shoot this gun again."

At least three other agents fired on the Chevy, and no one could say definitely that it was Baum's bullets that killed Boisneau. "Baum was close by me at the time and I saw him firing in the direction of the automobile," Purvis later said. "There were several other shots fired by other special agents and I am unable to state positively as to what bullets hit the car." Still, Baum immediately assumed responsibility for Boisneau's death. "He told me that night that he must have killed him," Newman later recalled. "He told me that he must have been the one who killed him as he was the only one who shot at him with a machine gun." Newman further explained that "Baum stood a little to the right and in front of me, and I did see him fire several times with the machine gun at the same time that the rest of us were firing. We were not using machine guns." Special agent K. R. McIntire remembered consoling a shaken Baum after the shooting. "He explained . . . that it would hurt him if he knew that he had killed an innocent man," McIntire said. "I told him the best way was to forget about it and to go about his business." But Baum's remorse seemed paralyzing, and agent Newman was worried about him. When Purvis told him to drive to Voss's lodge to telephone the local sheriff and fill him in about the raid, Newman asked to take Baum along, perhaps to get him away from the scene of the shooting. They left for the Birchwood Lodge in the Ford that Purvis had commandeered from Izzy Tuchalsky.

After that, things happened quickly. Along the way, Newman and Baum picked up a local constable, Carl Christensen, and enlisted him to help set up roadblocks. At Voss's lodge, Newman spoke with Koerner at his house. Koerner had a tip: There was a mysterious car parked outside his home, halfway between Voss's place and Little Bohemia. Newman and his companion left immediately to follow this lead. "We started out hell-a-whooping," Christensen later recounted. "I said, 'Go easy now, we're coming to the bridge and might meet somebody.'" They spotted a car on the side of the road, just where Koerner said it was. "Have your guns ready," Newman said. Baum, sitting between Newman and Christensen, clutched the machine gun in his lap.

The car was empty, so Newman maneuvered the Ford into Koerner's driveway, crunching gravel beneath its tires. Up ahead was another car, parked outside Koerner's home, with three men inside. Newman eased alongside it, believing perhaps that Koerner was at the wheel. "Who's in that car?" he asked. None of the three men answered. One of them jumped from the passenger side and came around to Newman's car. He had a gun in his hand and was yelling angrily. He was wild, crazed. This was the man who had sprung from the shadows and strafed the ground at Purvis's feet at Little Bohemia not long before: Baby Face Nelson.

Nelson liked shooting guns; he was not one to brandish a pistol idly. When he heard the gunfire at Little Bohemia, he had the easiest getaway of any of the gangsters. The only one not staying in the main lodge, he could have simply slipped out the back of his cabin and vanished into the woods. Instead, he came around front and fired wildly in the darkness. Only after he had emptied several rounds did he retreat into the forest and disappear.

Once his gun lust had been calmed, Nelson ran one mile south along the brushy lakeshore. He emerged at the first lighted home he saw, the cabin of George Lange and his wife. "Now don't get excited, I won't harm you," he told the terrified couple as he walked in, gun in hand. "But this is a matter of life and death. Do what I tell you and everything will be all right." To show his humanity, Nelson sat on their sofa, pocketed his gun, and gently petted the Lange's barking dog. He was not as civil to Mrs. Lange when she started crying. "Come on," he said, "shut up." The Lange's 1932 Chevrolet coupe, with George driving and his wife in back, got Nelson as far as Koerner's place before it stalled. Nelson had the couple knock on Koerner's door, then slipped in behind them when they walked in. At this point, he had four hostages.

Five more were on the way. When Nan Wanatka's brother, George LaPorte, who had wanted to organize a posse to smoke out Dillinger, heard about the shooting at Little Bohemia, he calmly retrieved his rifle from his home. He knew his sister Nan had already left the lodge for her safekeeping, but his brother-in-law Emil was still there. He summoned a friend, Carl Christiansen,[ck] got in his Ford, and drove to the lodge to see how they could help. The most pressing need was coats. LaPorte agreed to drive Emil and his two workers, Baszo and Traube, to Koerner's home to get warm clothes. At Koerner's, the four men ran from their car through the bracing cold to the door, which opened before they could knock. There to greet them was Nelson, who extended his hand not to shake theirs but to show them his automatic pistol.

Nelson waved his gun in a semicircle, covering all eight people he lined up in Koerner's living room. "I mean business," he told them, unnecessarily. He wanted a ride out of the north woods, to the town of Woodruff. LaPorte's car would do fine. "Are there any G-men in that car?" Nelson asked him, before ordering Emil Wanatka to do the driving. In the front seat Nelson stuck his gun in Wanatka's ribs. A turn of the ignition key and he would be on his way to safety. But there was a problem. "Jimmy," said Wanatka, using the name Nelson had given at the lodge, "I have no keys for this car." It was a crucial delay, because while Wanatka searched frantically for the keys, the car containing agents Newman and Baum appeared alongside them.

"Who's in that car?" Newman asked. No reply. "We had not come to a complete stop when a man jumped out of the front seat of LaPorte's car and pushed an automatic pistol through the open window of our car," remembered the constable Christensen, who was sitting beside Newman and Baum in the front seat. "Nelson said, 'I know who you are, a dirty goddamn bunch of cops.' And then: 'I know you have on bulletproof vests, so I will give it to you high and low.'"

Newman could not reach for his gun. Instead he leaned back in his seat, giving Baum a clearer shot at Nelson. This was Baum's moment of redemption. He had vowed never to fire his machine gun again, but now his life and the lives of others hung in the balance. It was no innocent man who was threatening to blow their heads off. This was Baby Face Nelson. But Baum did not raise his gun. Instead he also leaned back, as if to hide behind Newman. Baum's remorse at killing Boisneau was, it seemed, overriding his better instincts. Perhaps he would have raised his gun if given another moment. But there were no more moments.

Newman tried to grab Nelson's gun, then pushed his way out of the car. Nelson opened fire. The first bullet glanced above Newman's right eye, causing him to fall face first to the ground. Then it was Baum's turn. Nelson aimed his gun at Baum's neck but angled it downward. He knew what he was doing. The bullet sliced into Baum's neck just above his impenetrable steel vest and pierced his heart.

The big man staggered out of the car. Nelson was still shooting, indiscriminately now, firing in all directions. The headlights of Newman's Ford coupe lit the bloody scene. Baum walked a few steps and fell over a white single-rail fence, landing hard on his face. His machine gun, still in his hands, slipped from his grasp. At last he was free of it. With not a single person left standing, Nelson climbed into Newman's Ford and backed it down the driveway, spraying gravel against Koerner's house. Newman, bleeding from the head but conscious, fired seven shots after the escaping car; one of the bullets tore into Christensen's leg as he lay on the ground and played dead after being shot five times. The carnage was complete. In the eerie silence after the fusillade, Christensen heard a sickening sound. A gurgling, a gasping—it was Baum fighting for his last breaths.

———

The thirteen shots fired outside Koerner's home could be heard two miles away at Little Bohemia, where Purvis, who was still staking out the lodge, learned of the shoot-out. An hour or so earlier, he had been surprised when Wanatka, along with workers Baszo and Traube, suddenly walked out of the lodge with their hands up. The three had hidden in the basement during the shooting; Baszo and Traube crouched inside a coal pit. Purvis searched them and asked about the situation inside; Wanatka said he believed the gangsters were still upstairs. Purvis then allowed Wanatka to go to Koerner's house to get warm coats for himself and his workers. Now, an hour later, Wanatka was back, excited and breathing hard. At Koerner's, Wanatka had jumped from LaPorte's car and hidden in the woods as soon as Nelson took the pistol out of his ribs and turned it on agent Newman. He raced on foot from Koerner's house to Little Bohemia to report the news. Between gasps for air, he said, "All your men are dead." Purvis could make no sense of this brusque remark. Who was this man, and was this some sort of trap? Not recognizing him as the lodge's owner, Purvis asked Wanatka for his name and address. Then he asked him to spell Manitowish. Wanatka could not: "I never could," he would later say. Purvis, recoiling from the possibility that one or more of his agents had been killed, lashed out at the messenger. Wanatka, equally frustrated, answered back, "Who'd you come for, me or Dillinger?" Tensions could not have been higher; danger was everywhere. Purvis sent agents to check on Wanatka's story and resumed his surveillance of the lodge.

The desperate midnight hour came and went. The winds, already biting, whipped harder. Purvis had agents search the garage in front of the lodge; they discovered two cars fully packed with machine guns and luggage. No one knew if the gangsters were still inside the lodge. Another hour passed, then another. Before long dawn would break. The urgency gave way to nerve-racking tedium. Finally, the agents received the tear-gas canisters they had been waiting for. By then, sometime after 4:00 A.M., a posse of local men had gathered in the woods around the lodge. Purvis and Clegg marshaled them to serve as reinforcements, but talked them out of storming the lodge on their own. Purvis knew the time to raid Little Bohemia had come. He had the troops he needed, and the tear gas. If Dillinger was inside, more deaths were likely. Inspector Clegg gave the order to commence the raid.

Two agents drove quickly toward the lodge and skidded to a stop just outside; one of them aimed the tear-gas gun at a window and fired. The shell bounced harmlessly off a screen and fell to the ground. Another canister was fired. It, too, failed to penetrate the lodge. The canisters deployed and the stiff winds blew tear gas back at Purvis and the agents covering the lodge with their guns. Inside the lodge, nothing stirred. One agent, John T. McLaughlin, volunteered to run to the door of the lodge and throw a canister inside. It was an inspiring act of bravery. With smoke billowing inside, some of the posse members opened fire until Clegg told them to stop. When the shooting and the crackle of glass shards ceased, Purvis heard a voice. "We will come out," it said, "if you stop shooting."

"Come out and bring everyone with you with your hands up," Purvis yelled back.

The agents squinted to line up their guns with the lodge's front door. It opened slowly, letting out clouds of smoke. Finally, a figure—a woman. It was Helen Gillis, Nelson's wife. Next came Jean Delaney, and then Maria Conforti. Conforti had only one hand raised; in the other, she cradled her bulldog, Rex. That was all. No one else emerged. No Dillinger, no Van Meter, no Hamilton, no Carroll. Just three women and a puppy. Could this be a trap? Purvis accompanied five agents into the lodge to search for gangsters. The first floor, at least, was empty. The agents came out, their faces red and slick from the tear gas. After a breather, they reentered and searched the second floor: no gangsters. Then the cellar—again, no one. The lodge was empty. Dillinger was gone. All the gangsters were gone. The raid had failed. Purvis ran to the water pump and soaked his head in its spray, rubbing the tear gas from his eyes. He stood dejectedly outside the lodge as agents searched the grounds around the lake. His face registered confusion, exhaustion, pain. It was hard to make sense of it all. How could Dillinger have escaped again? How had the raid gone wrong?

It went wrong because the agents missed the embankment. The search of the grounds behind the lodge in the dawn light revealed something the agents had not known: The lakefront was actually nine or ten feet below the level of the lodge. After thirty yards the terrain dropped steeply down toward the lake, leading to a small stretch of sandy beach. In the dark of night, anyone straining to see the lake would not be able to discern this drop-off unless they knew about it. Certainly Rorer did not see it when he searched for silhouettes fleeing along the lake's edge right after the shoot-out. "The ground on which we were standing appeared almost on a level with the lake," he later said of his observations that night. "I conferred for some time with Clegg and Purvis and we were of the opinion that none of the occupants had then escaped." In fact, the embankment served as a wall that hid Dillinger from his pursuers. As soon as the shooting started, Dillinger jumped out a second-floor window and raced to the lake, slipping down the embankment and running north along the brushy sliver of beach between the lake and the woods. The diagram of Little Bohemia that Voss drew for Clegg accounted for neither the embankment nor the escape route along the lake's edge. Had Rorer known about the embankment, he might have gone all the way to the water and spotted the hustling figures of Dillinger, Hamilton, and Van Meter, all of whom made a clean getaway in the one direction Purvis believed was inaccessible to them. Voss, of course, could not be blamed for his lack of thoroughness. He likely believed that the tangled and sandy river's edge was not an adequate means of escape. He did not know how adept Dillinger and his men were at eluding capture. But Purvis knew this, knew it only too well. Dazed and exhausted, he prepared for what came next. Purvis and Clegg drove to Voss's lodge, two miles away. It was time to let Hoover know.

In Washington, Hoover received updates from Little Bohemia through the night. At 1:50 A.M. special agent Hardy, stationed by a phone in Rhinelander, called with news that the agents "think they have Dillinger surrounded." At 2:15 A.M. he called again to say "Dillinger is supposed to be surrounded at a place about 50 miles north of Rhinelander, Wisconsin, on Highway No. 51." Hardy added, "It is not certain [Dillinger] is still there," but Hoover could not suppress his elation: He passed word to the press that Dillinger was trapped. At 3:50 A.M. Hardy advised that agent Baum and a CCC camp worker had been killed. At 7:00 A.M. special agent Sam Cowley telephoned Hardy from Chicago for a progress report. "He advised me at that time that the three women with the Dillinger gang at the hotel had been taken into custody." Hoover now knew: Dillinger and his men had escaped.

Outside Koerner's house, three agents found the body of Baum behind the white fence. They gently picked him up and placed his heavy body on some hay. He was later put in the back of a truck and driven to a hospital at the CCC camp, where Dr. H.A.A. Oldfield pronounced him dead. Baum's two daughters, two-year-old Margaret and year-old Edith, would grow up fatherless. Purvis sent agent McIntire to accompany Baum's body on the Northwestern Railroad train from Eagle River, Wisconsin, to Chicago; from there, Baum's wife traveled with her husband's coffin on the Capitol Limited to Washington. Baum was eulogized at the Walter E. Humphrey funeral home and buried in Rock Creek Cemetery. At the time, he was only the fourth Bureau agent to be killed in an adversarial situation; his picture still hangs in the FBI's Hall of Fame. "That young special agent was my friend," Purvis later wrote. "I thought of his boyish ways and lovable character . . . I thought of that life being snuffed out by a gun in the hands of a ruthless and irresponsible killer."

Newman survived his wounds; so did Christensen. At Little Bohemia, federal agents confiscated the detritus of the Dillinger gang. They found a Winchester .351 automatic rifle, a Remington .22 automatic long rifle, a .38 Smith and Wesson double-action pistol, and a .38 Colt superautomatic, among several other weapons. They found the bulletproof vests that John Dillinger robbed from Judd Pittenger in Warsaw, Indiana. They found personal items: a twenty-four-tablet tin of McKesson's aspirin, packets of chocolate Ex-Lax, a jar of Burma shave cream, Dr. Lyon's tooth powder, a sterilized Linton gauze bandage. They found a large leather satchel, presumably used by Dillinger to carry money. They found six men's ties, several Springles undershirts, belts, socks, a Marlboro Warwick white dress shirt, ladies high heels, purses, and hats. Many of these items, after being catalogued, were returned to Emil Wanatka as compensation for the damage done to his lodge. They are on display there today.

After the raid Wanatka returned to Little Bohemia to find five windows on the left side of the lodge riddled with bullet holes. A back wall of that same room was pockmarked with about fifty small holes, not far from where his young son Emil Jr. had scratched his name in a panel of wood. Wanatka, nothing if not shrewd, chose not to repair the broken windows or shot-pocked wall; instead, he carefully preserved them, and to this day, the damage is visible to visitors at the lodge. Wanatka, struggling to pay a huge mortgage before the raid, would never worry about his finances again. In the years that followed, thousands of people traveled to Little Bohemia to see the place where Dillinger had yet again outfoxed federal agents. Wanatka's business boomed. In addition, rumors swirled that Dillinger left behind a large sum of money in his haste to escape into the night. The money never was found, and Emil Wanatka never claimed to have found it even though he admittedly searched very hard. "I never learned if he found the money or not," said his niece Ruth, who was well schooled in north-woods lore. "But I do know there's a loose rock in the back of Emil's fireplace that would have been a great place for someone to store a lot of loot."

A day after the Battle of Little Bohemia, Wanatka's son, Emil Jr., was finally allowed to return to his home. He could not comprehend what had happened there, though he knew something had. He heard the name Dillinger a lot, but it meant nothing to him. "I remember going back to the lodge and upstairs to my room," Emil Jr. said seventy years later. "I wasn't scared or anything. But then I sat on my bed and all of a sudden I started crying." Tears ran down his face and he didn't know why, so Emil went to the kitchen to ask his mother why he was crying. "I couldn't figure it out, but then they explained it to me," he says. "There was still tear gas in my room."

At daybreak on April 23, 1934, not long after the raid on Little Bohemia was complete, Melvin Purvis and Hugh Clegg retreated to Voss's lodge. Voss served breakfast, but Purvis could only push the food around his plate. Like the other agents, he was exhausted. He

had been up for more than twenty-four hours, and half that time he
was wearing a heavy steel vest. By then, reporters were flocking to
the town of Spider Lake to unearth and publish the story of the raid
gone wrong. At the Rhinelander airport, while waiting for his plane,
Purvis overheard people harshly criticizing him by name. Before
long two area residents circulated a petition demanding that Purvis
be suspended "pending an investigation of the irresponsible conduct of federal operatives on the night of April 22, in raiding the
John Dillinger gang hideout in such a stupid manner as to bring
about the deaths of two men and injury to four others, none of
whom were gangsters." The headlines and editorials were even
more brutal. "Urge Purvis Ouster," they cried. "Demand Purvis Quit
in Dillinger Fiasco." "Dillinger's success is not due to genius," one
columnist wrote, "but to the haziness or stupidity of those employed
to catch and keep him."

Without question, what happened at Little Bohemia was a disaster. Not only did all six of the gangsters get away, but three luckless
bystanders were shot, one fatally. Nelson's slaughter of Baum was a
horrific final twist. The raid remains a blight on the history of the
FBI, and surely one of its darkest hours. But it would not be right to
view the raid in terms of today's law-enforcement practices. To do so
would be a gross error of oversimplification and recklessly anachro-
nistic. Any analysis of Little Bohemia must give proper weight not
only to the terrible urgency of the situation but also to the primitive
state of law enforcement in the early 1930s. Purvis, Clegg, and their
men did not have the benefit of two-way radios, which would have
made coordinating their movements far easier. They could not avail
themselves of aerial surveillance or infrared binoculars or sophisticated intelligence-gathering equipment. To make a simple telephone call, they had to get in their cars and find a farmhouse or
cabin equipped with a line. Nor were Bureau agents trained in
SWAT-style tactics, which would not be introduced for several
decades. Raiding meant surrounding a place and barging in. The
Bureau did not have an established system for dealing with roaming
gangsters like John Dillinger, who were a modern phenomenon in
the early 1930s. There was no store of information and strategic insight to fall back on. Quite often Purvis and other agents-in-charge
had to make key decisions on the fly, with no protocol to guide
them. Further, the Bureau was a relatively small force equipped with

only a modest arsenal. Agents had been carrying weapons for only a few years before Little Bohemia. Hoover could not deploy hundreds of fully armed agents to a crime scene even if he wanted to. For Little Bohemia, the best he could muster was seventeen men. To criticize those men for their stupidity or sloppiness seems not only unduly harsh but also wrong. It would be more accurate to say that the most distinguishing feature of the raid was the bravery and dedication of those seventeen agents.

That is not to say that mistakes were not made. Why did Newman pull up so close to the parked car at Koerner's house, when he knew gangsters were on the loose in the area? Why didn't Purvis and Clegg contact at least one local police officer, not only to have him set up roadblocks but also to gain more intelligence about the lodge at Little Bohemia? "It might have been a different story if we had one local officer there," agent W. C. Ryan later testified at an inquest into the events. "A barbed-wire fence about fifty feet long . . . impeded our efforts to get to the rear of the resort. It appeared later that the boundaries of the resort cottages are divided by means of wire fences, which fact would possibly have been known to a local officer." Purvis and Clegg were criticized for not having a specific and effective plan for raiding the lodge, leading to the confusion and chaos of what followed. "When we got there we sort of circled around," Ryan also testified. "We had no particular orders as to where we would be."

Here, too, it is important to consider the incredible time pressure under which Purvis, Clegg, and the other agents were operating. After leaving Chicago, Purvis had always planned to meet with Clegg on the ground in Wisconsin, so that together they could devise a strategy. They expected to have at least ten hours to concoct a plan and get their men into position, but after learning that Dillinger was leaving immediately, they had next to no time at all to devise a plan. The agents had mere seconds to react, and could do little besides scramble wildly into position. "The situation arose so quickly it was almost impossible for orders to be given," agent K. R. McIntire testified at the same hearing. "Every agent [was] doing as he thought best, and which I think was wisely done by each agent." Darkness and confusion were Dillinger's allies.

At the very least, Purvis and Clegg did divide their troops into three distinct groups, each assigned to a section of the lodge. For instance, "the orders were that the men with bulletproof vests were to immediately rush to the front of the house," Ryan recalled. "These instructions were carried out I know, because two of the men in our car had vests on and they sat in the car all ready to get out first, which they did when we drove up." Though it commenced prematurely because of the awful coincidence of three men departing precisely as agents arrived—surely the pivotal bad break in the entire tragedy—once the initial chaos subsided, Purvis and Clegg, believing Dillinger was still in the lodge, resumed their leadership roles. "The agents were under control at all times, being directed by Mr. Clegg and Mr. Purvis, who told them where to stand and came around to see whether or not those orders were being followed," agent V. W. Peterson testified. Added agent L. D. Nichols, "I think [the raid] was carried off as well as could be under the circumstances."

Back in Chicago on April 23, Purvis ordered most of his agents to go home and get much-needed sleep. He and five other agents went straight to the Bankers Building to handle business regarding Little Bohemia. At the office he struggled to make sense of what happened, and played back every moment of the raid in his mind. "I could see that we had failed," he later wrote, "but I could not see that we had failed through our own fault, or how the attack could have been planned in the time available in any other way. Perhaps I was too close to the picture to see the fine points of it." The death of his friend Baum, in particular, weighed on him. At the Bankers Building, Purvis could see that his men were shell-shocked. They had lost one of their own; the war against crime was now a real war. "We've got more evidence to work on than we ever had before in hunting Dillinger," Purvis told reporters clustered in the foyer near the entrance of the office. "We'll have him before long." But at that moment, Purvis probably did not sound at all convincing.

He was also discouraged that, for the first time, Hoover's Bureau fell in the line of fire, drawing the derision of columnists, politicians, and irate citizens. The ugly headlines and calls for his resignation infuriated him, "not because of criticism directed against me personally, but because of unjustified criticism directed against the organization, which had not been at fault," Purvis wrote. In fact, Purvis had not been officially in command at Little Bohemia. The senior man on the ground was Clegg. "Mr. H. H. Clegg, Assistant Director, was in charge of this particular investigation, and not Mr.

Purvis," Hoover wrote in an April 26 memo to Attorney General Homer Cummings. But this distinction was lost on Purvis. He was top man at the Chicago office, headquarters for the hunt for Dillinger. He made as many decisions and gave as many orders at Little Bohemia as did Clegg. He was the Bureau's point person in its quest to eradicate the nation's public enemies, and he was prepared to accept the responsibility that this position entailed. Purvis went into his office and drafted a letter to Hoover.

Following the fiasco at Little Bohemia, Melvin Purvis resigned from the Bureau.

1

SURVEILLANCE

May 28, 1934
CHICAGO, ILLINOIS

The man lying shirtless on a rickety cot suddenly stopped breathing. His tongue curled down his throat and his eyes rolled back. His face turned a terrible shade of blue. John Dillinger was dying.

The nation's most hunted man had come to the end of his run, brought there not by federal agents but by an incompetent doctor. Only a month before, Dillinger had dodged the bullets that peppered his room at Little Bohemia, slipping out a back window and slinking along the lakefront and through the pitch-black pine forest until, a quarter mile from the lodge, he came upon Mitchell's Rest Lake Resort. Together with John Hamilton and Homer Van Meter, Dillinger knocked and entered under the guise of asking for water. But then Hamilton, without a word, ripped the telephone off the wall. The resort's owners, seventy-year-old Edward Mitchell and his frail wife, had heard gunshots in the distance a while before. They knew what sort of trouble had entered their home.

"You couldn't be Dillinger, could you?" Mitchell's wife, laid out on the sofa with the flu, asked.

"You couldn't have guessed better," replied Dillinger, who tenderly covered the woman with a blanket as soon as he learned she was sick. "Here you are, mother," he said. "We won't hurt you." For an outlaw, Edward Mitchell would later say, "Dillinger was a gentleman."

Fortunately for the Mitchells, neither their Model-T Ford nor a worker's truck parked in their yard would start, and so the damage they suffered at the hands of Dillinger was limited to a wrecked phone. The gangsters hijacked a 1930 V4 Model A from a nearby cabin, took its owner Robert Johnson hostage, and sped away from the Wisconsin woods that had nearly not released them alive. Dillinger would remain free for the rest of his life.

Yet his improbable escape from Little Bohemia, while burnishing his legend, also brightened the bull's-eye on his back. The federal raid, a failure in almost every sense, increased the attention the government and the public would now pay to Dillinger. Hoover's men had been embarrassed, and a special agent had been gunned down. Dillinger was now, in the words of his lawyer, Louis Piquett, "red hot." Dillinger knew this, and knew it would take something drastic to ensure his continued freedom. He would have to stage perhaps his greatest act of misdirection. Dillinger would have to escape his face.

Unlike many gangsters, Dillinger disliked wearing hats and glasses to hide his famous face. He often ignored the obvious peril of parading himself in public, a habit members of his entourage resented. "Goddamn that Dillinger," Helen Gillis, Baby Face Nelson's wife, complained while hiding in the basement of Little Bohemia during the shoot-out. "That fool never wears his glasses and always walks around in public where everybody can see him." Indeed Dillinger enjoyed flouting his ill-gotten celebrity. "He got a big kick out of filling station attendants asking him whether he had seen Dillinger," he told an Indiana homeowner he took hostage ten days after Little Bohemia. He "expressed the utmost contempt for local police departments, calling them 'a lot of clucks.'" At the same time, Dillinger held some measure of respect for Melvin Purvis and his men. "They were afraid of the 'Feds,'" the Indiana homeowner said Dillinger told him, "because of the fact that if a Federal Agent wanted an airplane he got one and if they wanted more men they got them and that the 'Feds' had all the money they needed to keep up the search."

For this reason, Dillinger decided on a new procedure known as plastic surgery. In late May 1934, he used his usual back channels to contact his lackey, Art O'Leary, and broach the idea. O'Leary quickly got in touch with Louis Piquett. Their first step was to find a

safe house for the operation. It was a reflection of Dillinger's popularity that people often approached Piquett to offer their homes as
hideouts for the gangster. Some were motivated by a taste for adventure; others by the lure of quick cash. Money led James Johnson
Probasco to volunteer his Chicago home on North Crawford Avenue as a haven for Dillinger. The sixty-six-year-old Probasco was a
washed-up hoodlum, his days as a burglar and a fence for stolen dia-
monds behind him. Now his dream was to buy the Green Log Tavern in Chicago, and harboring Dillinger seemed a fine way to fund
it. "I have to raise some money," he told Piquett, an old acquaintance. "If you see Dillinger, speak to him about me and tell him the
price is fifty dollars a day." Dillinger agreed to the plan but set the
rent at thirty-five dollars a day.

The next step was to get a doctor, and again Piquett would have
to troll the underworld to find one. The hard-luck character he
dredged up was a German-born physician and felon named Wilhelm Loeser. A veteran of both Northwestern University's medical
school and the U.S. penitentiary at Fort Leavenworth, Kansas—
where he served eighteen months for violating the Harrington Nar-
cotics Act—Loeser had developed a method of destroying
fingerprints with caustic soda. He obliterated his own prints "to prevent being picked up," he explained, after violating his parole by
traveling to Mexico. Piquett was intrigued. He paid Loeser $100 per
finger to eradicate the prints of one of his clients, and when that
went well, O'Leary and Piquett enlisted him for another, more important job. Without naming them at the time, "they stated that
John Dillinger and Homer Van Meter wanted their faces altered and
their fingerprints changed," Loeser, age fifty-eight, later told federal
agents. The men "would pay $5,000 [each] to have this work per-
formed." Piquett produced $500 as a deposit. Loeser—known to
everyone by his alias, Dr. Ralph Robeind—was in.

Dillinger moved into Probasco's home on May 27, 1934, and that
night gave O'Leary $3,000 toward the cost of the surgery. O'Leary
would get a third of the money; so would Piquett and Loeser. But
first they needed another medical professional to assist Loeser during the operation. O'Leary knew just the person: an acquaintance
named Harold Bernard Cassidy. Born in Wisconsin and trained in
medicine at the University of Illinois at Chicago, Cassidy, age thirty-
two, fell from grace by giving false testimony at a bank robber's trial.

That put him on the lam and made him vulnerable to O'Leary's advances. O'Leary called on him early on May 28 and counted off $600 in small bills. For that price Cassidy was now on board, too. He gathered gauze, adhesive tape, and iodine and showed up at Probasco's apartment at 7:30 in the evening of May 28.

Both Loeser and Cassidy instantly recognized their patient to be John Dillinger. But as Probasco's front door shut behind them, there was no turning back. Dillinger and the doctors went into the small bedroom to the left of the parlor. This was like no operating room they had ever known. A machine gun sat conspicuously in a bureau drawer; another poked from beneath the sheets of the bed. Bulletproof vests lay all about the house. The men went over the details of the surgery: Dillinger wanted a scar removed from between his nose and upper lip, three moles removed from his face, a bump in his nose flattened, and his famous chin dimple filled in. Dillinger took off his shirt and lay on a cot; Loeser asked him what sort of anesthetic he wanted. "Dillinger told him that he wanted to be put to sleep," Cassidy recalled. "I was selected to administer the anesthetic and I used ether."

Cassidy wrapped a towel around a small cone to form a mask and placed it over Dillinger's mouth. He tapped into a can of Squibb ether and began piping it in. Immediately something went wrong. Dillinger fought the gas, struggled, thrashed about. He had lied to Loeser about not having eaten; in fact, he had recently had two meals. Cassidy hurriedly fed his patient more and more ether. Still Dillinger resisted. Cassidy kept the ether flowing, emptying the entire can. But Dillinger's eyes widened, and the color in his face drained from pink to white to blue. His moaning and gurgling stopped, and his body quieted. Cassidy recoiled from the cot in horror. His back hit the wall and his mouth fell open. Loeser, in the bathroom scrubbing his hands, rushed out. "There was quite a commotion," O'Leary later said. "I heard some talk about Dillinger having passed on."

Unlike his assistant, Loeser did not panic. "Cassidy gave ether so recklessly and profusely to Dillinger that when I reentered the bedroom I saw that Dillinger was not breathing," he would say. "Cassidy stood helpless, wringing his hands." Loeser hurried to his bag and took out a hemostat, normally used to compress blood vessels to prevent hemorrhaging. He pried open Dillinger's mouth and fished out his curled-back tongue with the clamp, gripping it tightly and pulling back forcefully to free up Dillinger's windpipe. Dillinger's heart still was not beating. Loeser grasped Dillinger's elbows and pushed them hard into his ribs, trying to stimulate his heart. There was no response. Loeser pulled off the makeshift mask and breathed into Dillinger's mouth repeatedly until, suddenly, Dillinger gasped. His heart began to beat again. He coughed and gagged and breathed. It took several minutes for him to revive completely. But John Dillinger was alive.

Incredibly, the doctors decided to proceed with the surgery, this time using only local anesthetic. Dillinger was never fully unconscious during the procedure, and he moaned at every incision. Loeser cut away the moles and shaved away the scar. He sliced into the skin behind Dillinger's ears and removed tissue; he pulled his scalpel down Dillinger's nose and split it in half. He cut open the dimple on his chin and spackled it. He pulled the skin near his temples to lift Dillinger's face and eliminate lines and wrinkles. The grisly surgery took several hours; the sheets on the cot were soaked with blood and vomit. At the end of it, Loeser wrapped Dillinger's battered face in gauze. He had just altered perhaps the most famous face in the country.

Two days later, Loeser was summoned again to Probasco's house to tinker with the changes and to blast the bulbs of Dillinger's fingers with caustic soda. Morphine tablets took the place of anesthetic this time. Loeser then operated on Homer Van Meter, hammering away a hump in his nose and removing a portion of his lower lip to reduce its thickness. Loeser also scraped away a tattoo on Van Meter's arm. Not long after these procedures were done, O'Leary tracked down Loeser with bad news: Neither gangster was happy with the results. "Dillinger told me he thought his facial operation was 'the bunk,'" O'Leary said. "In his opinion it had not changed his facial appearance. He said he was going to call up Dr. Loeser and 'give him hell.'" Van Meter, Loeser recalled, "was greatly dissatisfied with the work done, inasmuch as the lower lip was only slightly altered and the bridge of the nose changed not at all." Loeser would later admit the work he performed was crude and sloppy. "The tip of Van Meter's nose would undoubtedly fill in as before," he said, "and the lower lip likewise fill out to its former size. Our efforts to remove the tattoo mark on Van Meter's arm were an absolute failure and undoubtedly resulted in a large scar in addition to the tattoo." After a third call-back to polish up his work, Loeser saw the dark side of his patients. Dillinger and Van Meter "walked up to me with submachine guns in their hands, which they pointed at me, and threatened to kill me if I divulged to anyone anything I had seen or done at this house," Loeser said. At almost the same instant, the doorbell rang in Probasco's house. The visitor was Baby Face Nelson. Loeser had seen enough. He refused to return to the house for a fourth time, despite O'Leary's warning that "I would soon be machine-gunned." Loeser wound up with $1,700 in tens and twenties for his trouble.

Dillinger, unhappy with his garish makeover, had nevertheless been transformed, literally and figuratively. His appearance may not have changed significantly, but his place in the popular culture surely had. Already infamous for his crime spree through America's heartland, Dillinger became, after Little Bohemia, something of a national obsession. Even before the escape, newsreels about his exploits drew more applause and cheering from moviegoers than clips that featured President Roosevelt or Charles Lindbergh. The press, bemoaned one columnist, "has built a halo of maudlin adoration about Dillinger." But Dillinger's defiance of the authorities at Little Bohemia significantly added to his aura. The futility of local and federal efforts to catch him bestowed folk-hero status on Dillinger. A nation desperate for direction and enamored of its new mechanisms of celebrity—syndicated newspapers, newsreels, on-the-scene radio shows—seized on Dillinger's pluck and guile as, if not admirable traits, then certainly fascinating ones. It was tempting to root for Dillinger as he crisscrossed from state to state, always a step or two ahead of the law. He became larger than life, a cartoon villain, "the arch-criminal of the age," according to the *San Francisco Chronicle*. A *Time* magazine graphic illustrating his paths of escape was labeled "Dillingerland," as if his pursuit were a national amusement. Even Will Rogers, the popular humorist, weighed in after Little Bohemia. "Well, they had John Dillinger surrounded and was all ready to shoot him when he come out," Rogers said. "But another bunch of folks came out ahead, so they just shot them instead. Dillinger is going to accidentally get with some innocent bystanders some time, then he will get shot."

None of this public hubbub went unnoticed in Washington. The embarrassment at Little Bohemia would have profound effects, both on the Bureau and on the entire apparatus of America's law-enforcement machine. Its impact reached all the way to the Oval Office. Dillinger, reborn, in a way, after nearly dying on the cot, was now reconfigured as a monstrous threat to the very fabric of democracy. On his capture, it seemed, hung nothing less than the future of the republic.

———

The mood on the nineteenth floor was grim. One by one Chicago's special agents arrived at the Bankers Building on the Monday after Little Bohemia to learn that one of their own was dead. They ran a phalanx of reporters in the outer hall, persistent men crushing forward for comment. They opened newspapers to read that their Bureau was a laughingstock; they heard their leader, Melvin Purvis, referred to as "stupid." It was a profoundly sobering week on the nineteenth floor.

Things were no less somber in Washington, where Attorney General Homer Cummings, the architect of the government's war on crime, lashed into his top commander, J. Edgar Hoover. "He was heard threatening to fire Hoover and just ripping into him in his office," Chicago historian Tom Smusyn recounted. "It was a bad mark on Hoover." With the *Evening Star* reporting that Dillinger's crime spree had thus far cost the government some $2 million—$1.5 million in law-enforcement funds and another half million in money stolen—Washington officials ratcheted up the rhetoric. "I don't know when or where we will get him, but we will get him," Assistant Attorney General Joseph Kleenan[ck] vowed in the days after Little Bohemia. "And you can say for me that I hope we get him under such circumstances that the government will not have to stand the expense of a trial." Cummings was even more succinct. "Shoot to kill," he proclaimed, "then count to ten."

The harshest criticism, however, came from within the Bureau itself. Werner Hanni, special-agent-in-charge of the St. Paul office, was one of the last agents on the scene at Little Bohemia, arriving well after Dillinger had escaped and Nelson had murdered Baum. But his May 1 memo to Clegg savaged the agents who had been present during the shooting. "From observations made of Little Bohemia," Hanni stated, "the description of the hideout given us by the guide proved to be accurate and correct, and there[ck] does not appear to exist any good reason whatsoever for Dillinger and his accomplices making a getaway." Further, Hanni continued, "It was quite evident that the raid was fully staged with a lack of organization, and a lack of knowledge and judgment cannot be concealed. The writer himself and those accompanying him en route to Bohemia proved to be tripped into a regular death trap."

The implication that those in charge of the raid had recklessly put their men in great danger incensed Hugh Clegg. He quickly alerted Hoover to the likely source of Hanni's displeasure—his feelings had been hurt. Though Hanni was in charge of the geographic territory that included northern Wisconsin and thus might have been called upon to lead the raid at Little Bohemia, Hoover selected Clegg, in the area on other business, to be in charge. Clegg, perhaps indelicately, gave Hanni no task more significant than dispensing equipment to departing agents. Another agent pulled Clegg aside and privately told him that "since it appeared that Dillinger might be caught, and as Mr. Hanni was in charge of the office covering the territory in which Rhinelander is located, that he might be 'hurt' or offended in some manner if he were not permitted to be present," Clegg explained. "I told Mr. Hanni if he cared to go he might do so, and he indicated that he would like to go." Hanni's fear of flying, however, forced him to travel north by car, ensuring he would not arrive at the lodge in time for the shooting.

Clegg also rejected the notion that he and Purvis had arrogantly neglected to contact local authorities in Wisconsin for their help. "There was, as heretofore pointed out, no opportunity," Clegg wrote, "and at the time an abundance of reasonable arguments against making telephone calls into an adjoining county, since our information did not trust this means of communication." In other words, the phone lines were not secure, and messages relayed on them could wind up in the wrong hands, a fact that Henry Voss had communicated to federal agents. The worst insult was Hanni's suggestion that Voss's sketch of the lodge gave Clegg and Purvis all the information they needed to stage an effective raid. Clegg found the original sketch and sent it to Hoover. Hurriedly drawn on lined, three-hole looseleaf paper, it accurately depicted the layout inside the lodge but did not include the drainage ditch to the left, the barbed wire on the right, or the embankment leading to the lake behind the lodge. It was, at best, a rough schematic that might have been helpful had agents gained earlier access to the lodge.

Hoover responded by ordering a thorough investigation of the events at Little Bohemia. He even instructed Assistant Director Harold Nathan to look into a bizarre allegation that on the night of the raid some special agents had mutinied against Purvis and Clegg and tied them up in a shack. Hoover asked Clyde Tolson to focus on Hanni's scathing memo. Hanni's complaints did not hold up under scrutiny. Before an investigation was complete, Hanni sent a second memo recanting his criticisms. "He makes particular reference to his . . . statement that he and those accompanying him en route to Little Bohemia proved to be trapped into a regular death trap," Clegg summarized. "He says that he did not intend to indicate any-thing except a physical situation that was entirely unavoidable." Hanni's initial comments, Tolson concluded with dismissive candor, "would appear to indicate a disordered and possibly hysterical state of mind on the part of Hanni when he wrote this memorandum. It may be that lack of sleep or other similar conditions existing at that time are reflected herein."

Hoover, under more pressure than he had ever faced as direc-tor—and, indeed, than he would ever face again—did not waver in the least. The tack he chose was to defend the performance of his agents, and he did so aggressively. Despite all the criticism, there were no specific suggestions that agents at Little Bohemia could have acted differently, beyond seeking the cooperation of local authori-ties. Their failure to do so reflected nothing so much as Hoover's own dislike of involving local officers in government business. In his office Hoover reviewed the petition to suspend Melvin Purvis, orga-nized by a local postmaster and signed by only a handful of people. Reporters had badgered Purvis about the petition and about the failed raid, but Purvis said nothing in his defense. "I never comment on things of that kind," was his only statement. Two days after the raid, Hoover took a phone call from Purvis and considered his offer to resign. "Mr. Purvis was greatly disturbed and wanted to assure me that he would be in perfect accord with any action I might desire to take affecting him personally," Hoover recalled of the conversation. Here was his chance to pin the entire fiasco on one man.

Hoover did not do so. He refused to accept Purvis's resignation. "I explained to him that while we are receiving criticism from many sources, we are still assured of one hundred percent cooperation from the Attorney General." Hoover also defended Purvis to Cummings, pointing out that Clegg had been in charge in Wisconsin. Hoover's final report on Little Bohemia attributed Dillinger's escape not to any negligence by either Clegg or Purvis but to "the extremely unfortunate incident whereby three drunken or at least drinking members of the Civilian Conservation Corps were in the Little Bohemia when our Agents arrived there and departed hastily, ignoring instructions to stop." Hoover did suggest that agents might have made an earlier attempt to discover if Dillinger was still in the lodge, though he did so "at the risk of second guessing." And he found no fault with any tactical decisions made by Clegg and Purvis. "It had been the plan of those in charge to have attempted to rush the house on arrival by the use of men wearing bulletproof vests," Hoover concluded. "This would, of course, have been dangerous, but it is my personal opinion that it would have been the correct plan."

Hoover had hired Purvis; had befriended him, groomed him, handed him the choicest assignment in the Bureau. Now, in Purvis's darkest hour, Hoover stood by him. Perhaps, as some have suggested, Hoover decided that with his own job on the line, it would be unwise to make scapegoats of men he himself had selected for the job. Perhaps his genuine admiration for Purvis and appreciation for his loyalty accounted for his quick defense of the agents. Perhaps it was a bit of both. Hoover also knew that no matter how hard he was on his men in private, they had to believe they had his support in public, or else they might not have been so willing to undertake dangerous missions. In any case, Hoover's only direct rebuke to Purvis came in a conversation about an informant on the evening of April 25, two days after the raid. "I impressed upon Mr. Purvis," Hoover recalled, "that I wanted less raiding and more confidential informants." That was all. Before long the petition to oust Purvis had been forgotten; so, too, were demands for his resignation in Chicago papers. Charles Delacy, editor of the Chicago magazine *Police 13-13*, disparaged these demands as a cheap political ploy. "Certain local congressmen, having recently waited for the opportunity to place a vote getter in Mr. Purvis' chair, have seized upon the Dillinger incident in Wisconsin as the means with which to accomplish their end," Delacy wrote in an item praising Hoover's support for Purvis. "Mr. Purvis' dismissal is doubtful. He is said to have the complete confidence of J. Edgar Hoover . . . for his work in the income tax prosecution of gangsters and for a more recent achievement—the capture of Verne Sankey, kidnapper."

Delacy was right: Purvis's job was safe. In addition to Hoover's backing, Purvis retained the allegiance of his men. Not a single agent under his command ever uttered a public condemnation of Purvis's leadership before or after Little Bohemia; nor, according to Doris Lockerman, did they do so in private. "Listen, these young fraternity men did not go around jangling love beads and saying, 'Oh, Melvin is wonderful, we love him,'" said Lockerman, who was friendly with most of the agents and dated several of them. "But they followed him into battle and they did so at great peril. These were all smart young lawyers with bright futures, and not one of them wanted to die for a mistake made by Melvin Purvis. They would not have tolerated it if he had been a bungler. I never heard one of them even [imply] that when a disaster occurred, it was Melvin's fault. Not in the slightest. He was respected and admired by all his men."

The major changes would be made not in Chicago but in Washington. A day after Little Bohemia, Attorney General Cummings sat before the House Judiciary Committee and implored President Roosevelt to push through the anticrime measures languishing in Congress. "If we had had an armored car up there in Wisconsin, our men could have driven right up to the house where Dillinger was," Cummings said. "The terrible tragedy would not have happened." Roosevelt, in a fireside radio chat in the week following the raid, addressed Dillinger's escape and called on Congress to pass Cummings's Twelve Point Crime Program. He summoned the head of the Judiciary Committee and made a personal appeal for quick action. In this way, the outrage over Little Bohemia fueled what would be a drastic and historic overhaul of the government's approach to fighting crime. One by one the crime laws passed, investing Hoover's Bureau with emergency powers it would never surrender. The new laws took crimes previously considered local offenses and placed them all under federal jurisdiction. Assaulting a government officer, kidnapping, inciting riots, smuggling arms, even robbing a nationally affiliated bank—all of these became federal crimes. One bill gave Hoover's agents the right to carry weapons and make arrests, something they had been forced to do without authority up to that point. It was a symbolic but important benediction.

These sweeping legal changes, in essence, created the modern FBI. Up until then Hoover's agents had acted in relative anonymity, known locally but not by the vast majority of Americans. Suddenly the country was aware of who they were—and aware of their incompetence in failing to capture the intrepid Dillinger. Yet at precisely the moment Hoover's agents entered the public consciousness, they became an entirely new and more effective fighting force. Though it had been happening slowly since the Kansas City massacre in 1932, the Bureau's men changed from primarily an investigative force into a combative one. They were now the "superpolice" that Cummings had envisioned. The murder of Carter Baum, it turned out, had more of an impact on the practice of law enforcement in the United States than any other killing of its kind.

All that remained, of course, was the capture of Dillinger. Hoover now had no excuses. The charming bandit from Indiana was officially a threat to national security. No greater menace existed. Dillinger's eradication was only one of many challenges confronting the Bureau, to be sure, but there is no question it was by far the top priority. Should Hoover fail to deliver Dillinger and deliver him quickly, it is hard to imagine how he could have kept his job. In the wake of Little Bohemia, he would no longer tolerate mistakes or even misfortune. Hoover decided to micromanage the hunt for Dillinger.

Melvin Purvis, deeply hurt over Carter Baum's death and still shaken by his harrowing night at Little Bohemia, spent his first day back from Wisconsin at the Bankers Building. He had not slept for more than thirty-six hours. He felt the weariness he felt after every raid, something he likened to "a drunkard's hangover." He had trouble eating for the next several days. Still, he had no choice but to carry on with the business of finding Dillinger. On the Tuesday after returning, he enlisted a new informant, an ex-convict from Joliet, paying him a $20 advance and promising $5 a day for his help in developing contacts that might lead to Dillinger. Purvis also monitored the cordon of police officers and sharpshooters established around the central states in the days following Little Bohemia. Despite the mobilization of small armies of searchers, no significant clues emerged. "We are still looking for him, but there have been no reports all day as to his whereabouts," Purvis admitted to the press on April 28. It was not the sort of update anyone wanted to hear. There was a palpable desperation within the Bureau. Hoover even proposed arresting Dillinger's father, but Assistant Attorney General Kennan[ck] nixed the idea. "Considering that Dillinger's father is involved in a natural sympathy that people have for blood relatives protecting their son . . . there would be bad public reaction to the institution for such prosecution," Kennan[ck] advised. "It would likewise cause many to believe that the authorities, failing to apprehend Dillinger, the real culprit, were attempting to give vent to their anger against those who would be expected to harbor him."

As always, Purvis spoke with Hoover at least once a day. No decision was too small to run past the director. On May 10 Purvis told Hoover about a phone call from a man claiming Dillinger and Van Meter, wearing bulletproof vests and carrying Thompson machine guns, barged into a home in Fort Wayne, Indiana, and spent two nights there. Purvis relayed his plan for setting a trap should the gangsters return. "Mr. Purvis felt that at least four Agents should be placed in this house," Hoover recorded in a memorandum. "But I suggested that he use only three. He will handle this lead in that manner." Just a day later Hoover reversed himself after speaking with Assistant Director Harold Nathan, who "suggested the advisability of placing four men in the house," Hoover noted. "I authorized Mr. Nathan to use four men instead of three."

Purvis knew he and his office would be under extra scrutiny by Washington. But he could not alter the basic apparatus of the Dillinger operation. Procedurally, nothing changed: Purvis continued to pursue informants, arrange for plants (or stakeouts) at known gangster spots, and field and follow hundreds of tips and leads concerning Dillinger. This latter task was the most tedious and time-consuming. Many of the tips, Purvis later explained, were valid, but "some were so-called spite tips coming from people who desired to embarrass someone else—their neighbor, perhaps, against whom they had a grudge. Some were from cranks who dreamed they had seen the gangster. Some were from fortune tellers who had received a vision and a message." The problem was that "there was no way of determining the veracity or the validity of the motives of the people bringing in information about Dillinger without a certain amount of investigative work." This proved enormously taxing on the limited resources of the Chicago office. Purvis had around fifteen agents assigned exclusively to the Dillinger case, and it fell to them to sift through more than 1,000 leads. Purvis addressed this disadvantage in his 1936 book. "If the number of cases received per month exceeds the number closed for the same period, the result is an unhealthy condition," he wrote. "This situation existed for many months in Chicago—all because of insufficient manpower."

Purvis was most concerned about the toll this workload took on his men. He knew many of them were exhausted, and the strain affected their work. Agents assigned to lengthy stakeouts were particularly vulnerable. "The mental and physical demands made upon them were stupendous," Purvis said. "Unending watching with constant alertness made frazzled nerves and tired bodies. The men on plants waiting for a criminal to come to a rendezvous or a visit to an old haunt could not be relieved of this nerve-wracking duty often enough—because all the other men who might have periodically exchanged places with them were also on plants or equally important work."

Purvis's secretary also was well aware of the tension. "These young men knew very well that every time they went out on a mission they were taking their lives in their hands," said Doris Lockerman as she recalled that difficult time. "They were always going into dark places, into speakeasies and alleyways, and they knew they could be shot at any moment. These men were not naive; they knew what their duty entailed. But after Little Bohemia I realized the mood in the office had changed. It was much more real now."

In subsequent weeks and under Hoover's increased scrutiny, Purvis's men showed the effects of this strain. An untimely run of botched assignments and bad luck began May 11 with a harmless but embarrassing incident: A Bureau Ford driven by Purvis was stolen from its overnight parking spot in front of his apartment. A baffled Purvis assured Hoover the doors and steering wheel had been locked. Eight days later, agents assigned by Purvis to tail Louis Piquett in Chicago allowed him to slip away after only a day. Dillinger's lawyer "knew he was under surveillance," Purvis telegraphed Hoover, "and succeeded losing agents who are now attempting to pick up [his] trail."

Then the three women seized at Little Bohemia returned to mock the Bureau once again. Helen Gillis, Jean Delaney, and Maria

Conforti, granted probation on May 26, sat for a debriefing at the Bankers Building before Purvis allowed them to go free. It was a foregone conclusion, for Purvis and the three women, that they would be shadowed. Six special agents, including Purvis's ace, Sam McKee, "were instructed to trail these women after their arrival here and to determine where they went and to cover the place where they went for an hour and a half after their arrival," Purvis later recorded. He also noted that twenty-four-hour coverage of the women was impossible because all the Chicago agents had to handle other important assignments as well.

The limited surveillance produced disastrous results. Two of the women, Gillis and Delaney, went directly to an apartment on South Marshfield Avenue that belonged to Baby Face Nelson's sister. A special agent convinced the operator of the filling station across the street to act as a lookout and notify the Bureau should Nelson stop by. The arrangement was not ideal, but with round-the-clock surveillance unavailable as an option, it would have to do. On May 27, Nelson appeared on South Marshfield Avenue and walked past the entrance to the apartment. He circled the block and walked past the entrance once more. Then he did it again, and again. On his fifth trip, convinced no federal agents were watching, Nelson went inside and spent an hour with his wife. Someone did see him—the filling station operator. Yet he did not call the Chicago office and only told an agent about Nelson's visit the following morning. Purvis was incredulous. On May 28 he drove to the filling station and, not finding the operator there, tracked him down at his home. Purvis wanted to know why he hadn't called. The station operator claimed the Bureau agent had failed to give him a telephone number; the operator also refused to allow Purvis to post an undercover agent at the filling station. The sight of Nelson had apparently spooked him. Later that day, Purvis called Hoover to relay the bad news. "According to Mr. Purvis, this address is difficult to cover," Hoover noted in a memorandum, "and he also mentioned the fact that he is greatly in need of Agents." Hoover asked Purvis for a complete report. He also ordered Sam Cowley, an inspector working the Dillinger case from his desk in Washington, to check up on the surveillance of the apartment on South Marshfield.

The more Hoover thought about it, though, the angrier he became. This marked the second time in five weeks that Baby Face Nelson had slipped through their fingers. On May 29 he sent Purvis a harshly critical letter. "I am becoming quite concerned over some of these developments in the Chicago district," he wrote. "We have had too many instances where surveillances have not been properly conducted, and where persons under surveillance have been able to avoid the same. It is imperative that every resource of this Division be utilized to bring about an apprehension, and an early apprehension, of the members of the Dillinger gang, and I cannot continue to tolerate action of investigators that permits leads to remain uncovered, or at least improperly covered." Hoover rejected Purvis's argument that he lacked the manpower to conduct proper surveillance, and implied Purvis and his men were simply not careful enough. Purvis had never before been accused of being careless; in fact, he was known for his thoroughness. It did not occur to Hoover that what he perceived as carelessness might in fact have been the inevitable result of stretching a small corps of men too thin. Hoover worked long hours and expected his agents to do the same. But Hoover spent those hours behind a desk, not in the field. Also, no one knew precisely what size force was needed to track Dillinger across the country effectively, simply because no one had ever had to deal with a roving gangster like him before. Purvis, in the field, believed more men were needed. Hoover, in Washington, did not. Hoover could have pulled agents from other offices and dispatched them to Chicago, but he declined to do so. At least for the time being, Purvis would have to make do with the resources in place. He pulled four agents off other assignments and had them watch the apartment on South Marshfield from a rented room across the street.

That very day, May 29, more bad news crossed Hoover's desk. He noticed a newswire announcing that Bessie Green, wife of slain gangster Eddie Green, was brought to Chicago by U.S. marshals to help federal agents in the Dillinger case. This information was, in theory, confidential. Hoover had Cowley call Purvis again to ask about the leak. Purvis told Cowley "he could not account for the source of the information but in his opinion it was concocted by the newspaper men." Hoover read Cowley's account of the phone call and wrote in the left margin, "Strange they should concoct the truth."

Hoover dictated another critical letter to Purvis, his second of the day. "It is particularly embarrassing to this office that confidential arrangements cannot be made to secure the assistance of a confi-

dential informant without this information reaching the daily
press," Hoover wrote. "I am advised . . . you were of the opinion that
it had been concocted by newspaper men. I cannot share this opinion with you." It was becoming apparent that while Hoover publicly
supported Purvis, he did not, as Charles Delacey reported, have
complete confidence in him. Hoover demanded Purvis try again to
trace the source of the leak. On June 1, Purvis wrote to Hoover
clearing all his agents of blame. But he admitted he might have
done something that caused the leak. A day after Bessie Green arrived in Chicago, Purvis learned she was complaining about her uncomfortable bed at the county jail. "In order to keep her in as good
spirits as possible I called the County Jail and requested that better
accommodations be afforded her if such was possible," Purvis recalled. "The inference might have been drawn by County Jail officials that she was assisting the Government." Purvis had shown a soft
spot for Dillinger's women before, as when he gave Evelyn Frechette
a break from her brutal interrogation. This was the Southern gentleman in him. But now his small act of kindness might have backfired.

By June 1, Hoover had another bone to pick with Purvis. A May
30 item in the Washington papers quoted Purvis as saying he believed Dillinger was already dead. Hoover wired Purvis for an explanation. "The statement that any interview whatever was had with me
is absolutely false," Purvis wired back. "I have issued no statement
and the whole story is an absolute fabrication and concoction." An
expanded version of the item ran in that evening's *Washington Star.*
A tip from an Indiana doctor who claimed to have treated Dillinger
for three serious wounds "added to the reports that Dillinger has
been buried in southern Indiana has convinced us that he really is
dead," the article quoted Purvis as saying. His agents, Purvis reported, were looking for Dillinger's grave in southern Indiana. The
next morning Hoover pressed Purvis to defend himself again. "I, of
course, understand that you did not make the direct statement,"
Hoover wrote, "but I would like to be advised as to whether you
made any statement to any person which would have been con-
strued in the manner it has been." Hoover was veering from insinu-
ation toward outright accusation: He did not believe Purvis had
made no official statement to the press. "I . . . desire to again state
that I have not made any statement from which any such story might
be concocted," Purvis replied. "Consistently in the past many weeks

I have not talked to members of the press when they called at this office or when they called on the telephone. The switchboard operator has been told . . . to state that I have no statement to make."
Reporters had pestered Purvis for comment about a remark by Attorney General Cummings, who said he believed Dillinger had died
from his wounds. Purvis insisted he gave the reporters nothing. "For
your further information," he told Hoover, "I would not have made
such a statement to the effect that John Dillinger is dead because,
primarily, I do not believe that he is dead."

Whether Hoover remained skeptical would not be recorded in
Bureau files, nor would any evidence surface about the source of
the quotes. But only a week later, on June 8, Sam Cowley informed
Hoover about a conversation he had with a reporter from the
Chicago News. Cowley said the reporter told him "that although he
personally is very friendly to Mr. Purvis, the press in Chicago have
determined to 'get Mr. Purvis if it is the last thing they do.'" It was
no secret the Chicago media found Purvis maddeningly tight-
lipped. The notion that the press could have targeted him, though
never proved, is not impossible to imagine.

The growing tension between Hoover and Purvis boiled over after yet another setback on May 31. That night, Purvis sent an informant with ties to Dillinger to the South Marshfield apartment to
try to learn of any plans Helen Gillis might have to meet Baby Face
Nelson again. The informant, a small-time thief on parole, arrived
at the apartment just as Gillis and Jean Delaney were leaving. From
an apartment across the street, four special agents watched the
scene unfold. The women spoke briefly with the informant, then
walked down the street and turned a corner. He hurried after them.
The agents, led by Ed Hollis, chose not to tail the women and risk
blowing the informant's chances of gaining their trust. It proved to
be the wrong decision. After fifteen minutes, Hollis and the agents
ran down to see why neither the women nor the informant had returned. They found him around the corner and learned from him
that Gillis had ducked into a movie theater. He assured the agents
he would steer her back to the apartment when she came out. But
Gillis never returned to the apartment. Both she and Delaney had
given Hollis the slip.

The best bait the Bureau had to lure some of Dillinger's gang to
Chicago had now vanished into the murky city. There was probably

no worse news to break to Hoover. Purvis phoned Washington with a report on June 2. This time Hoover sent Sam Cowley to Chicago to speak with Purvis in person. He arrived on the morning of June 3, a Sunday, and talked with Purvis at the office later that day. Purvis described the event as a miscommunication between himself and one of his men. "He specifically instructed Agent Hollis to keep [Gillis] under surveillance," Cowley relayed to Hoover, "although Mr. Hollis misunderstood the instructions." Cowley added, "He felt certain that [Gillis] could have been shadowed by the Agents without interfering with [the informant's] contact," and that "he felt that the Agents were too much inclined to take the informant's word at its face value."

Cowley's criticisms convinced Hoover something was amiss at the Bankers Building. "I asked Mr. Cowley to make a careful check of the entire personnel in the Chicago office and report to me upon same," Hoover later noted. Purvis stood up for each and every one of his agents. He knew mistakes had been made, but he believed they were honest mistakes and no indication of the caliber of men he had in the field. The gangsters they were chasing "were cunning people quite able to find shelter and harbor because the public felt more sympathy for them than for the banks that they robbed," said Doris Lockerman. "Trying to find them in a city as dense as Chicago without harming innocent people was an extremely delicate job. You would inevitably make ten mistakes for every one bull's-eye." The Chicago agents were overworked and exhausted, and Purvis had continued to ask Hoover for reinforcements. But still none had been sent. Instead Hoover sent Sam Cowley to find out what was wrong.

Hoover now had a confidant to serve as his ears and eyes in Chicago. For the director, it was a comfortable arrangement; it was less so for Purvis. "I telephoned Mr. Cowley at Chicago this afternoon and advised that I was of the opinion that the situation in Chicago would work out all right," Hoover noted in a June 8 memorandum, his first cheery assessment in several weeks. Though Cowley was essentially an administrator who spent the bulk of his time typing messages to Hoover, he had something Purvis had apparently lost: Hoover's trust. Not long after Cowley's arrival, Hoover decided to turn his inspection tour into a permanent assignment. "I had told Mr. Purvis that until we complete the Dillinger investigation,"

Hoover noted on June 8, "I wanted Mr. Cowley to take complete charge of the same." Incredibly, in that same memo, Hoover promised Cowley the extra men he had denied Purvis: "I told him if he needed more Agents, or anything else which would be of assistance, he can have them." Three weeks later Cowley had five extra men at his disposal.

Cowley would now oversee the Dillinger pursuit from inside the Bankers Building. This was not welcome news on the nineteenth floor. Cowley "was perceived as Hoover's lackey," said Lockerman. "He was an emissary from Washington, the boss's point man. We knew that he was coming for some undermining reason." The idea that Cowley could easily leave a desk job in Washington for the dangerous streets of Chicago struck none of the agents as realistic. "They knew which district attorneys could be trusted, and which ones were jealous of the Bureau," said Lockerman. "They knew which policemen could be trusted and which could not. They knew the territory, the nightclubs and the speakeasies and the hideouts, and Sam Cowley did not know these things. He knew what Hoover was thinking and what Hoover wanted, but how could he know what these agents knew from their experience day after day and night after night?" For this reason, Lockerman said, "The agents continued to view Melvin as their leader. They were not going to change their allegiance overnight from one leader to another, especially not to someone who was a stranger to them."

Even so, Purvis had been dealt a bad blow, and it showed. "He got quieter," said Lockerman. "He was always quiet, but now his face looked strained and he walked a little faster and he pulled his hat down a little tighter. He knew he was being undermined."

Cowley's June 3 arrival in Chicago, however, would not prove to be a watershed moment in the hunt for Dillinger. A far more significant development occurred only three days later in Washington. June 6 was the day John Dillinger unwittingly became a marked man in a way he never had been before.

8

THE BIOGRAPH THEATER

June 6, 1934

As notorious a criminal as Dillinger was in early 1934, he was not, to most citizens, a particularly valuable quarry. For a long time the largest reward for his capture was a paltry $25, and that was for stealing a car. But that would change. On June 6, 1934, the seventy-third Congress of the United States approved House Resolution 9370, more commonly known as the Federal Reward Bill. The resolution authorized the federal government to pay out as much as $25,000 for the capture of any criminal designated a public enemy. The bill was a direct response to the brazenness of Dillinger and other roving gangsters and to the futility of federal efforts to catch them. Attorney General Homer S. Cummings, acting on this new authority, issued a public statement on June 23. The reward for information leading to John Dillinger's arrest would now be $5,000. The reward for his capture would be $10,000. The government had just unleashed a new weapon in the war on crime—cash.

The new rewards were astonishing sums of money in 1934. The country remained in the vice grip of the Depression. In 1933, Americans had only 54 percent the income they had earned in 1920. More than 40 percent of all home mortgages were in default. More than a quarter of all households did not have a working wage earner. Long lines formed outside garbage dumpsters as people waited patiently to scavenge for bits of food. In 1934, 110 people in New York City died of starvation.

The prospect of receiving $10,000 was, to a poor and hopeless citizenry, close to unfathomable. Yet there it was, for the taking, a new and powerful incentive for ordinary people to help snare John Dillinger. For those who already had reason to trade on their association with Dillinger, the $10,000 was, perhaps, the final push to action. Cummings's reward more than offset Dillinger's romantic appeal, reducing him from a Robin Hood–style rogue to a target. If the race to get Dillinger was indeed a national amusement—a game tracked by newspapers and followed by all Americans—the reward for his capture dramatically raised the stakes. Now there was a third player, besides Dillinger and law enforcement. Now any citizen could, with a mere phone call, play the pivotal role.

The manager of the football team at the Utah Agricultural College receives a fine tribute in the 1923 edition of the school's yearbook, *The Buzzer.* Next to a photo of a squarely built man in a suit and tie, arms folded and unsmiling, runs a summary of his contributions. He "was on alert night and day during the football season looking after the interests of the team," it reads. He "was constantly on the job, willing to do all he could to make things pleasant for them and at the same time looking after all the details of team management in a competent and dependable manner."

This was Samuel Parkinson Cowley, who arrived at the Bankers Building with a reputation for the same competence and dependability he demonstrated in college. He was, without question, a capable manager and administrator at a time when Hoover's Bureau placed a premium on procedural efficiency. One of fifteen children—and the fifth of nine boys—he was born in Franklin, Idaho, and raised by Mormon parents in a plural marriage. He was only twelve when he was ordained a deacon, only fifteen when he became a teacher. At seventeen he was named an elder in the priesthood and spent the next four years on a church mission in Hawaii. The pursuit of a law degree from George Washington University Law School brought Cowley to Washington and, in 1929, into the Bureau. After some fieldwork in Salt Lake City, Detroit, and Chicago, he returned to the capital to supervise kidnapping cases. He drew Hoover's notice, and when inspector Hugh Clegg was elevated to

assistant director, a path was cleared for Cowley to become an inspector himself.

When Hoover dispatched Cowley to Chicago in July 1934, he did
not promote him over Melvin Purvis. There was no public announcement about the move, nor any internal memo recording a
formal change in the leadership structure in Chicago. This meant
that as special-agent-in-charge, Purvis continued to outrank Cowley.
Cowley himself never used language to suggest he was asked to take
over for Purvis. "I was instructed by J. Edgar Hoover to go to
Chicago and attach myself to the staff of Melvin H. Purvis, Chief of
the Division there," he told a reporter in October 1934. Nevertheless, Cowley did have Hoover's directive to oversee the nationwide
search for Dillinger. He had been unofficially designated the chief
of a special roving squad to get the gangster. Assigning him to the
Chicago office, however, was potentially problematic, and could
have created an appearance of authority that was uncomfortable for
both Purvis and Cowley. In fact, Cowley's arrival did not produce
dissension. By all accounts, Purvis was gracious and cooperative in
accepting Cowley's appearance in his office, even as he was surely
frustrated and displeased. Purvis never tried to cut Cowley out of
discussions or deals, and explained even to informants and suspects
that he had to confer with Cowley on all matters. In a 1935 plea for
clemency in front of the U.S. Parole Board, Wilhelm Loeser, the
doctor who performed facial surgery on Dillinger, described approaching Purvis to broker a deal to cooperate in exchange for leniency. Purvis told Loeser he had to bring in Cowley. According to
Loeser, "Anything Inspector Cowley did, and agreed to, he—Mr.
Purvis—would back up 100 percent."

The two men began their awkward collaboration with an early
June trip to Indiana to check on surveillance operations being run
out of the Indianapolis office. Then it was back to Chicago, where
the focus remained the same as in pre-Cowley days—securing good
informants. On June 2, Purvis fired Eddie Green, the informant he
selected to infiltrate Helen Gillis's South Marshfield Avenue apartment. It was Green's botching of that assignment that tipped the
scales and led Hoover to send Cowley to Chicago. By their nature,
all informants were somewhat scurrilous and less than completely
trustworthy. The trick was determining which of them told the truth
at least part of the time. Purvis believed he had good radar for their

reliability. When the Pinkerton Detective Agency tried to push one of their informants onto the Bureau, Purvis balked. "It is my opinion that the lead . . . is too indefinite," he advised Hoover on May 28, "and it is also my opinion that this [informant] is a four-flusher, and I do not believe that he is able to furnish any information of value."

Cowley now was involved in evaluating Purvis's informants. On June 11, Cowley terminated one of Purvis's underworld contacts, a man who claimed to know Baby Face Nelson. Purvis wasn't keen on cutting his informant loose. "He is not being reimbursed for any further services," Purvis assured Hoover in a June 18 letter. But "I have arranged with this informant to continue to keep his ear to the ground, and if he learns any valuable information he will communicate with this office." As he had before Cowley's arrival, Purvis frequently traveled to chase tips and meet personally with informants, usually on very short notice. During Cowley's first weeks in Chicago, Purvis rushed to meet one in Fort Wayne, Indiana—checking into the Anthony Hotel under the alias J. A. Stone—and also conferred with the chiefs of police and detectives in South Bend. Purvis also continued to receive the bulk of informant approaches, since his was the name known on the streets of gangland Chicago. "He was the person to contact in that city," said Doris Lockerman. "Everyone knew that. Nobody in Chicago ever heard of Sam Cowley."

On the face of it, the day-to-day workings at the Bankers Building did not change much. Cowley used Purvis's office when it was available, and set up elsewhere at other times. Before his arrival, Purvis had discussed any decisions about informants, tips, and surveillance with the agents working on the case; now, those discussions included Cowley as well. "Cowley did not come in and do anything differently," recalled Lockerman. "The agents were in constant contact with each other, as they always had been. All decisions were talked over with Hoover, all the time. No decisions were ever made by a single man." Still, Cowley's arrival created one significant change: Cowley seemed to relieve Purvis of some of the administrative burden in the Dillinger case. Cowley, not Purvis, had to write long memos to Hoover and had to brief several agents who arrived in Chicago June 27 for an update on the Dillinger search. Cowley also had to haggle with Washington over being reimbursed for vouchers he sent to headquarters.

Likewise, it was Cowley who heard from Hoover when something went wrong. He discovered quickly, as Purvis already knew, that deploying his limited resources was a tricky business, and that errors in judgment were inevitable. For instance, Cowley failed to order surveillance on Dillinger's lawyer, Louis Piquett, and also ordered his agents to stop shadowing Maria Conforti, one of the women seized at Little Bohemia. As a result of these oversights, Piquett was able to maintain constant contact with Dillinger through Art O'Leary, and Conforti easily slipped away to join Homer Van Meter. These were precisely the types of mistakes Cowley had been sent to Chicago to eliminate. Within three weeks of setting up shop in the Bankers Building, Cowley received a sharp admonishment from his boss over another leak of confidential information: an Associated Press dispatch that carried news about an interrogation of Pat Reilly. "It would seem that very definite instructions should be issued to Mr. Cowley and the other agents of the Chicago office that under no circumstances are they to discuss or disclose to a Probation Officer, or any other person, the details of investigative activity," Hoover wrote Cowley in a June 25 memorandum. "As I gather from the press reports, the information which has been printed to date has been substantially correct, and must necessarily have emanated, either directly or indirectly, from a member of our Division at Chicago."

As for Purvis, he was more cautious than usual after the uproar over his alleged "Dillinger is dead" remarks. When a rumor circulated that his agents had Dillinger surrounded in a Chicago hospital, Purvis slammed down the phone on nosy reporters and carefully advised Hoover of the matter. "I of course have made no comment to any member of the press," he disclaimed in a June 4 teletype. "I am merely giving this for your information."

The correspondence from Cowley's first seven weeks in Chicago shows that the operation to locate Dillinger progressed little under his watch. The agents assigned to the case continued to do their difficult work while tiptoeing around the hazards of Hoover's bureaucratic system. Hoover did make personnel changes after Little Bohemia: He transferred several agents with sharpshooting skills from southwestern bureaus to Chicago. Texan Charles Winstead arrived on May 12; Oklahoma-born Herman Hollis soon followed. Hoover also raided police departments for men adept with firearms, landing two members of the Oklahoma City department's pistol team, Jerry Campbell and Clarence Hunt. These were rough and rugged men, the antithesis of Hoover's new gentleman crime-fighter, but the debacle at Little Bohemia convinced Hoover he needed to bolster his Dillinger squad with experienced gunmen. Other than the new recruits, perhaps the only substantive progress was the Bureau's conclusion that, after Little Bohemia, Dillinger was being too hotly pursued to hide in a rural spot and thus was almost certainly stationed in a city, most likely Chicago. "He was able to live in one manner only, and that was as an inconspicuous, ordinary citizen in a middle class district," Cowley would later say. But in mid-July 1934, the Bureau still lacked solid leads and had no idea where their quarry was.

This would change, suddenly and dramatically, at 4:00 P.M. July 21, a Saturday. Purvis answered the telephone in his office at the Bankers Building and listened closely. The caller was Captain Timothy O'Neill of the East Chicago Police Department. He and fellow officer Martin Zarkovich had urgent information they wished to share with Purvis. The information was about John Dillinger.

———

Chicago is a city of ghosts—its dead seem not to vanish but to inhabit the mundane places where they fell. The curious still make their pilgrimages to these haunted places, though some bear no resemblance to the architecture of their past. Tourists, for instance, still canvass Chicago's North Clark Street in search of the parking garage where nine men were slaughtered in the St. Valentine's Day massacre in 1929, though nothing remains of the garage and the spot where they died is merely an empty lot. Still, people come. They come to hear the dead tell their tales.

On the night of May 24, 1934—a single day after the outlaws Bonnie and Clyde were finally gunned down—an unmarked black Ford was found stopped and facing east in the middle of Old Gary Road, a bleak stretch outside the town of East Chicago, Indiana. Inside the car, two men slumped in their seats. Their necks and faces were covered with blood and, on closer inspection, were full of holes. The men were Martin O'Brien and Lloyd Mulvhill, both detectives with the East Chicago police force. They were shot twelve times between them, at close range, with a Thompson machine gun. Their own weapons remained in their holsters, undischarged.

News of the slaughter quickly reached East Chicago detective Martin Zarkovich, a veteran officer assigned to the pursuit of John Dillinger. Zarkovich, a gruff and dark-skinned Yugoslavian immigrant, knew the ambush of O'Brien and Mulvhill bore the violent hallmarks of Dillinger's gang. But without eyewitnesses or any hard evidence, the crime proved difficult to crack. Years later it became clear Dillinger was indeed involved. On that May night, Dillinger drove a red delivery truck into East Chicago and parked it on Old Gary Road, an area known as a meeting ground for gangsters. Not much later the black unmarked Ford stopped alongside it, and one of the officers asked for identification. From the rear of the truck, Homer Van Meter slid open a door and fired on the detectives before they had any inkling of whom they had approached. The circumstances behind the killings, however, remain muddled to this day. Art O'Leary, Dillinger's crony, later claimed Dillinger told him the two detectives had been set up by someone in the East Chicago police department, to which Dillinger was paying protection money. "They were just trying to do their job and there's nothing wrong with that," Dillinger would say. "Their trouble was that they were getting to know too much." Surprised by the presence of the officers, who were sent unknowingly into a death trap, Dillinger and Van Meter had no choice but to resort to murder. "If we had given ourselves up," Dillinger said, "we both would have got the hot seat."

Nor has history reached a conclusion about Sergeant Zarkovich. One scenario holds that the murders of his fellow officers so incensed him that he vowed to step up his pursuit of Dillinger to avenge their deaths. Many more historians depict Zarkovich as despicably corrupt—and likely the person who, determined to stop their snooping into his illicit double-dealings with Dillinger, sent the unlucky detectives to their deaths. He had, after all, been convicted of taking payoffs in 1930, and some even suspected him of helping Dillinger escape from Crown Point in 1933. In either case, the murders gave Zarkovich a new incentive to see Dillinger not only captured but, ideally, silenced. Either Zarkovich was determined to kill the man who killed his colleagues, or he was desperate to destroy someone who, if taken alive, could implicate him. The brutal slaying of the two officers thrust Zarkovich from the fringes of the Dillinger drama into a starring role.

Seven weeks later, on July 12, a letter arrived at an apartment on North Halsted Street, in Chicago's Lincoln-Fullerton neighborhood. The letter bore the markings of the U.S. Immigration Service and was addressed to Mrs. Anna Sage. Inside were the results of Sage's appeal to reverse deportation proceedings and remain in the United States. The Romanian-born Sage had emigrated in 1909 and found her fortune running brothels in northwest Indiana and Chicago. She had weathered several raids and fines and had even twice been pardoned by the governor of Indiana, but now her luck was running out. Sage read the letter's stark pronouncement: Her appeals had been denied; there was a warrant for her deportation. It seemed all but certain that Sage would have to leave not only her adopted country but also her son Steve, born to her in the United States in 1910. For Sage to avoid this fate, she needed some kind of leverage. At the time, she had a rather remarkable houseguest. Staying with her was a man she later claimed to have been introduced to as Jimmy Lawrence, though she knew full well that his real name was John Dillinger.

———

In the span of just a few days in summer 1934, John Dillinger drove a truck in San Francisco, slept in a tourist camp in Iowa, changed a tire in New Mexico, took a drive in Virginia, and followed the Lewis Brothers circus in Ohio. That's what could be gleaned by someone poring through the hundreds of Dillinger sightings submitted to the Bureau in the days and weeks after Little Bohemia. Citizens could be forgiven for thinking Dillinger lurked around every corner. Reward posters featuring his likeness were shipped by the thousands from Washington to field offices in every corner of the country, then distributed to local banks and post offices. "Get Dillinger!" screamed the now iconic proclamation issued by the Illinois State Bureau of Criminal Identification and Investigation, a poster that featured Dillinger's smirking mug shot, notice of the $15,000 bounty, and the chilling coda "Get him dead or alive." The purpose of the sweeping campaign was to stamp his image in the minds of all Americans and to designate him the enemy of every citizen. Certainly it reinforced the public's perception of Dillinger as the craftiest and most feared villain of his time. Few people would have been persuaded by the assurances of Dillinger's lawyer, Louis Piquett, who told one Dillinger supporter his client "will rob no banks, but [intends] to travel in the path of righteousness . . . he told me that it was his intention to give the balance of his life in this world to God."

But on June 30, the master bank robber did strike again, in South Bend, Indiana. Dillinger, Van Meter, and Baby Face Nelson stormed the Merchants Bank on Michigan Street and made off with $28,000, but not before killing South Bend police officer Howard Wagner. After that, Dillinger disappeared again. Authorities had been chipping away at the Dillinger gang with the killing of Eddie Green, the arrest of Evelyn Frechette, and, on June 7, the shooting death of Tommy Carroll by a police officer in Waterloo, Iowa. But the big fish—Dillinger, Van Meter, Nelson—were nowhere near being hooked. It was Dillinger's genius to rob a bank in one state, flee into another, and sleep in a third, thus confounding local police and giving the impression that he could be literally anywhere. Dillinger was a phantom, elusive and ethereal, zigzagging across the heartland in a dizzying display of criminal hubris. In the early days of a scorching Chicago July, it seemed that catching Dillinger would depend less on the methods employed by his pursuers than on the likelihood that Dillinger would eventually make a mistake.

Eventually, he did. After surgically changing his features, and after giving his new face a test run in the South Bend bank robbery, Dillinger needed a new place to stay—he had been camped in Jimmy Probasco's home for too long. On July 4, 1934, he moved into the Chicago apartment of Anna Sage, and just as the Bureau predicted, he began living like an ordinary, inconspicuous citizen. Around this time, Dillinger told Maria Conforti "that he had been attending night clubs and other public places and as 'hot' as he was nobody recognized him," Conforti later confided to federal agents. Another Dillinger trick was to stroll by police cars and smile at the officers. "They had their chance then to take me," he told his pal Art O'Leary, referring to four officers who seemed to recognize him on a street, "but they didn't have the guts to go through with it." Indeed, Dillinger also attended a Chicago Cubs game, spent hours watching Sage's twenty-two-year-old son Steve play softball, and often went to the movies, among other outings. This was classic

Dillinger, brazenly flouting the authorities. Some might call it slop-piness—Dillinger letting down his guard. More likely it was the deep, dark streak of pessimism that ran through him. Like all gang-sters, he suspected his time on the earth would be short—that his death, most assuredly a violent one, was all but imminent. But until his time came, Dillinger would not live like a frightened and cower-ing fugitive. At the Cubs game, Dillinger noticed a man staring in-tently at him; clearly he had been recognized. Rather than leave, he later told O'Leary, he simply relaxed in his seat. "I figured it would attract too much attention if I got up and left," he said. "Anyway, it was too exciting a game to leave."

In retrospect, Dillinger's decision to live openly on Chicago's North Side almost seems like a death wish—after all, he was only a short car ride from Purvis's office in the Bankers Building. Certainly his calm and unhurried demeanor during his stay at Sage's apart-ment gave those who would betray him precisely what they needed: time—time to gather their nerves, time to carefully plot their moves. The Dillinger betrayed by Emil Wanatka at Little Bohemia was alert, on his toes, ready to scramble, suspicious of everyone. His hair-trigger reactions surely saved his life. The Dillinger who moved in with Anna Sage was a different man. Perhaps his many daring es-capes had led him to believe he was invincible. Perhaps it was the opposite, and he knew the end was near.

How Dillinger came to stay with Anna Sage is also unclear. Her history, however, suggests she was part of the same underworld in which Dillinger ran. In 1892 she was born Anna Cumpanas in the Romanian village of Komlos, though she claimed not to remember the town's name. Together with her husband Mike Chiolak, whom she married at seventeen, Sage boarded a German steamship for America and landed in Baltimore, Maryland. One day later they moved in with his sister in Chicago. Sage separated from Chiolak in 1915 and did not marry again until 1928. This second marriage, to Alexander Sage, ended within three years. "He stated that he was an advertising man," Sage later told federal agents. "After I married him he never did a day's work."

Sage, however, was fully capable of supporting herself. For a while she worked as a prostitute in East Chicago and even ran a brothel herself when its owner was arrested. In 1921 she bought an interest in the Kostur Hotel in Gary, Indiana. According to her version of events, the previous operator housed prostitutes in some of the rooms. He "had two girls in the hotel who were 'working,'" Sage later said. "I kept these two girls after we purchased an interest in the hotel." Thus did Sage open her first brothel, a rollicking place with a rough-and-tumble saloon in the basement known locally as the "Bucket of Blood." What kept Sage in business was her ability to foster connections with local police departments, almost certainly by extending them professional favors. One officer who became an intimate friend was Sgt. Martin Zarkovich of East Chicago. The two became so close that Zarkovich's wife filed for divorce and cited his relationship with Sage as a reason.

Sage returned to Chicago in 1933. A police raid of her apartment there produced enough evidence of her illicit dealings to persuade authorities to begin deportation proceedings. The specter of being shipped back to her small, steel-mill town in Romania hung over Sage as she took in her most controversial boarder. Sage's version has her friend Polly Hamilton, a fetching waitress who worked in the S&S Sandwich Shop in Chicago's Wilson Avenue district, introducing Sage to her new boyfriend, whom she called Jimmy Lawrence. "He kept his head down but I looked at him and got a glimpse of his profile and immediately recognized him as Dillinger," Sage later said of her freshly scarred visitor. "I asked him what was wrong with his face and he said he had been in an automobile accident. . . . I [told] Polly . . . that her boyfriend was John Dillinger. She did not admit it." This version of a Sage-Dillinger meeting is farfetched. For one thing, both knew many of the same underworld figures in East Chicago, which would make their accidental meeting in Chicago an incredible coincidence. "Whether or not [Dillinger] knew Anna Sage personally, he almost certainly was sent to her by their mutual friends, and it would have been she who introduced Dillinger to Polly instead of the other way around," C. Russell Girardin wrote in *Dillinger: The Untold Story*, a fine account of the Dillinger saga based on interviews with his lawyer, Louis Piquett.

It is clear that Sage, her son Steve, and Polly Hamilton moved into the North Halsted apartment July 1, 1934, and that three days later Dillinger joined them there. He stashed his arsenal of rifles and bulletproof vests in a locked closet. Life for this unlikely quartet was surprisingly normal—plenty of home-cooked meals, rides on a local roller coaster, even a double date with Dillinger, Hamilton,

Sage's son Steve, and his girlfriend. Perhaps the pleasant routines of an average life so appealed to Dillinger that he began plotting to quit the crime business altogether, for it was around this time that he began speaking of one last great score that would give him the means to flee his pursuers forever. "Van and I are going to pull off the biggest job of our lives," he told Art O'Leary. The boys were going to rob a train and walk away with millions. "We'll have enough to last us the rest of our lives," Dillinger said, "and right after it's over we're lamming it out of the country."

This last great score was not to be. John Dillinger ran out of time.

———

Heat seared the streets of Chicago on the afternoon of Saturday, July 21, when Melvin Purvis, at his desk, answered his telephone and arranged to meet Captain O'Neill and Sergeant Zarkovich, the Chicago police officers who "had 'real' information about Dillinger."

Two days earlier, on July 19, Sage had welcomed Zarkovich into her apartment. Dillinger was away for a few days—he was out of town planning a possible robbery—giving Sage the perfect opportunity to invite her old friend for a visit. Sage had nearly shared the news about her houseguest with her attorney. "I told him I wanted to see him about a very important matter and get his opinion," she would later say. "However, before going to his office I changed my mind . . . because I was afraid to trust anybody." But Zarkovich was not just anybody. According to Sage, she finally admitted to him that she was housing Dillinger around 3:00 P.M. that day. This set in motion the event Sage hoped would give her the leverage she needed to stay in the country. And Zarkovich had the best shot he would ever have to get Dillinger.

Zarkovich wasted little time. He brought in O'Neill, and together they laid out their trap. The two officers met Purvis at the Bankers Building about two hours after telephoning him on July 21. Purvis had already run the tip by Sam Cowley, who asked that they all meet in his room at the Great Northern Hotel. Purvis drove with the officers and took them up to Room 712. There, Purvis and Cowley learned of Anna Sage and of her promise to divulge where Dillinger would be on the evening of Sunday, July 22. O'Neill and Zarkovich had no interest in running the capture; they claimed they came to Purvis because they trusted him. "They were positive that the Division of Investigation . . . operates more secretly than any other organization and they felt that . . . there would be no possibility of any information as to any proposed plan for the apprehension of John Dillinger becoming known publicly," Purvis and Cowley later recounted in a joint affidavit. A plan was already in place for Anna Sage to meet personally with Purvis, and a two-car caravan—Purvis and Zarkovich in the lead car, Cowley and O'Neill following close behind—went directly from the hotel to a clandestine meeting place selected by Zarkovich: a dark, tree-shrouded street across from Children's Memorial Hospital on West Fullerton Street. Purvis parked in the shadows and waited for Anna Sage. A half hour passed. Finally, at 9:30, a woman turned the corner. "She walked past our car and down the street, seeming to survey the situation to determine that there was no trap set for her," Purvis said. "She returned and on a signal got into the car."

Sage knew Zarkovich would not betray her, but what about Purvis? "She seemed to be primarily interested in whether she should trust me," Purvis recalled. But in their few minutes together in the car, Purvis was persuasive. Unlike brusque, rugged street cops, Purvis had shown he was adept at courting and gaining the confidence of women in criminal gangs, and he had also shown uncommon tenderness toward them. He needed to convince Anna Sage, too, that she could trust him. Purvis drove her to a secluded spot along the banks of Lake Michigan and shut off the car. Sage poured out her story.

She had but two demands. The first was that she receive part of the reward for Dillinger's capture. "I told her I could not make any definite promise as to the exact amount," Purvis said, "but that I could guarantee that it would be very substantial. She was agreeable as far as the reward situation went." The other demand was more complicated: Sage told Purvis she was on the brink of being deported. If she delivered Dillinger, she wanted the Bureau to step in and stop the proceeding. From her demeanor, Purvis knew this was by far the more important of her two demands. Sage "had a great fear of deportation," Purvis would say. "She had reared a son in the United States. It was only natural that she should wish to stay here." Purvis was sympathetic but made no promises. It was, he explained,

beyond his authority to guarantee anything in an immigration matter. In years to come, there would be speculation about just what
Purvis promised Sage in that parked car. Did he guarantee that she
could stay in the country in exchange for her cooperation? Purvis
was emphatic that he made no such deal. "I informed her that I had
no authority to promise her that she would not be deported, and I
did not so promise," he declared in a statement issued after Sage's
identity was finally revealed to the public. "I did inform her, however, that I would bring to the attention of the appropriate officials
in Washington her actions in aiding the government . . . and that I
would recommend that some step be taken to prevent her deportation." Purvis told Sage he would do everything in his power to aid
her.

This was assurance enough for Sage. She told Purvis that Dillinger
planned to attend a movie the following evening, and that she
would be with him. Most likely they would see a show at the Marbro,
on West Madison Street, where they had gone in the past. Purvis
wrote his private phone number on a scrap of paper and handed it
to Sage. She agreed to call as soon as she was certain where Dillinger
wanted to go. One last detail remained. Sage agreed to wear an
orange skirt so agents could identify her.

The secret meeting disbanded. Purvis gave no serious thought to
raiding Sage's apartment and capturing Dillinger there. This was
against Sage's wishes, and he respected them. But Cowley later said
the Bureau did place an agent on North Halsted to watch for
Dillinger. Sage told Purvis that Dillinger was using the alias Jimmy
Lawrence and claiming to work at the Board of Trade. Purvis
checked to make sure no one by that name was employed by the
Board. Cowley contacted Hoover with details of the meeting, and
Hoover approved the plan to take Dillinger outside the Marbro.
"Promptly we surveyed that theater, made notes of the entrances,
exits and fire escapes," Purvis later wrote. Cowley himself traveled to
the theater to make sketches of the layout. It was the sort of plan-
ning and preparation Purvis wished he'd had time for at Little
Bohemia.

A restless night's sleep, and then Purvis and Cowley reconvened
at the Bankers Building on the morning of Sunday, July 22. One by
one the Chicago special agents were summoned to the office, many
of them forgoing their only day off. Most of the afternoon was

devoted to meticulous scrutiny of the details of Dillinger's capture. "Every bit of information in our possession was reviewed," said Purvis. "All possibilities were gone into, and plans were made to meet in the best manner possible any difficulties that might arise." Mainly Purvis and Cowley paced, waiting patiently for Sage's phone call. Purvis and his men were by now accustomed to the torment of inaction.

At 5:30 P.M. the telephone rattled and Purvis heard a familiar voice. "He's here, he's just come," whispered Sage, calling from a pay phone in a local store. "We will go to either the Biograph or the Marbro." That was all. Purvis put down the phone, stunned. No one had canvassed the Biograph. Special agents Earle Richmond and Jim Metcalfe immediately set out for North Lincoln Avenue, tasked with surveying vantage points and racing back to the office. The Biograph was a more problematic cover: Its rear exits opened up into a maze of back alleys. Purvis and Cowley had to rethink their deployment of agents. The assembled force—a mix of nineteen agents and five East Chicago police officers—had to be split up between both theaters.

The time came to try once more to get Dillinger. The agents were restless, ready to go and armed but, at Purvis's insistence, only with pistols; rifles and machine guns would endanger too many citizens. At 7:15 P.M. all the men crowded into Purvis's small office; sweat had already formed on many brows. Sergeant Zarkovich briefed the team on Dillinger's new appearance and on the two women who would be with him. Purvis spoke next. He had sent these men into dangerous situations before, and it was never something he did lightly. On this evening, though, there was an unusual gravity to the occasion. This mission had the feeling of a final showdown. Purvis rarely gave speeches to his agents, but tonight he felt one was in order. He stood among the gathered men and spoke in his soft voice:

> Gentlemen, you all know the character of John Dillinger. If he appears at either of the picture shows and we locate him and he effects his escape, it will be a disgrace to our bureau. It may be that Dillinger will be at the picture show with his women companions [but unarmed]. Yet he may appear there armed and with other members of his gang. There of course will be an undetermined element of danger in endeavoring to apprehend Dillinger. It is the

desire that he be taken alive, if possible, and without injury to any agent of the Bureau. Yet, gentlemen, this is the opportunity we have all been awaiting, and he must be taken. Do not unnecessarily endanger your own lives, and if Dillinger offers any resistance, each man will be for himself and it will be up to each of you to do whatever you think necessary to protect yourself in taking Dillinger.

At the end of the speech only four men left the Bankers Building. The rest of the agents were to wait for word that Dillinger had been spotted. Zarkovich and Winstead set off for the Marbro. Brown and Purvis drove to the Biograph.

———

Money—great stacks of crisp, new bills—littered the guest bed in Anna Sage's apartment. An odd criminal ritual was in progress. John Dillinger, in his sharp gray trousers and his white Kenilworth shirt, assembled his wealth in piles on his bed, both to make an accounting of it and to secure it in the safest place he knew. He neatly separated the five-, ten-, and twenty-dollar bills and counted each pile. He counted 200 five-dollar bills and rolled them into a tight wad, then wrapped it with a rubber band and slid it into his left pants pocket. He counted 100 ten-dollar bills and wrapped those too, placing the roll in his left hip pocket. The twenties—65 of them—were stuffed into his hand-tooled leather billfold, which was then placed in his right hip pocket. Miscellaneous ones, fives, and tens were folded and kept loosely in his right front pocket— Dillinger preferred not to wait for cashiers to break big bills when he made his purchases. Dillinger made note of the amounts in each denomination; together, it totaled $3,300. Sage, who watched the ritual while pretending to do other chores, once "asked Polly why Dillinger carried all that money on him," she later said to agents. "Polly told her he carried it so he could make a quick getaway if he had to."

His bounty counted and safely stashed, Dillinger was ready to go. Only after they left the apartment did he tell the women which movie they were going to see. Around 8:30, Dillinger, Sage, and Polly Hamilton began the short saunter to the Biograph. The theater was literally around the corner from Sage's apartment. They probably turned right onto North Lincoln Avenue and ambled on to a block of two-floor stores—the Goetz Country Club tavern, the National Tea Company—before reaching the Biograph roughly halfway up the block. Perhaps they took a shortcut and traveled through a back alley connecting Halsted Street to North Lincoln. Either way, they did not notice two men sitting in a car parked some sixty feet south of the theater's bright, blinking marquee, on a cobblestone street lined with steel trolley tracks. Ralph Brown and Melvin Purvis had been sitting there since 7:37, and they were anxious. Brown left the car every few minutes to telephone the Bankers Building for updates from the Marbro Theater. Purvis, for all the tips and leads he had followed—for all the hours he spent in the freezing woods of upper Wisconsin—had yet to lay an eye on Dillinger. He fought the urge to get out and scrutinize the arriving moviegoers, or even to tilt his head toward the crowd from inside the car. He tried just to sit still. "To have craned our necks as to observe in all directions would have aroused suspicion and might have frightened Dillinger," Purvis would say. "We had to sit in the front seat of the automobile facing the front." Purvis had already checked with the box office to find out the time of the next showing. The movie, *Manhattan Melodrama*, would begin at 8:30. That start time came and went, and still no Dillinger. A familiar dread seized Purvis. "We were discouraged," he later said. "We felt that this might be another failure."

Back at the Bankers Building, Sam Cowley stayed by the phone. He was to dispatch the agents as soon as he heard from a lookout at either theater.

At precisely 8:38 P.M. Purvis turned slightly in the car to see a startling sight—the very man whose likeness he had studied so intently. The man's hair was dyed dark black, and he wore a straw boater pulled low, but there was no mistaking it—this was John Dillinger. Anna Sage was there, in her orange skirt, and Polly Hamilton, too. But Purvis had eyes only for Dillinger. He watched as Dillinger—cool, casual, unhurried—paid ninety cents for three tickets. He was heartened that Dillinger wore no jacket because that meant he couldn't have many concealed weapons. He indulged, for a brief moment, the impulse to capture Dillinger with agent Brown, right there and then. "It might have been a simple thing for the two of us to take him," Purvis said. But what if something went wrong? "We would have been taking the chance of endangering the lives of several innocent bystanders. We knew his previous record, his utter ruthlessness and his entire disregard for human life. We let him go into the theater."

Purvis watched Dillinger disappear through the glass door to the right of the ticket seller's tiny booth. In an instant, he and Brown were out of the car. Brown ran to call Cowley. Purvis hustled to the box office and bought a ticket. There was a compulsion to follow Dillinger, to keep eye contact, to confirm his location—to pursue. Purvis passed through the ornate lobby and into the main auditorium. The cool of the theater—produced by giant fans blowing on blocks of ice—washed over Purvis, who was already bright with sweat. His thinking was simple: See where Dillinger sat; see if there were empty seats behind him. If so, three agents could take those seats. "One could pinion Dillinger's left arm, one his right, and the other his head," Purvis thought. But Dillinger had arrived too late and the lights were already down. The theater was packed with people. Purvis tried for a few seconds but could not locate Dillinger in the darkness. In fact Dillinger was sitting in the third row. Rather than walk the aisles peering and drawing attention, Purvis turned and left. The wait was not over—it had just begun.

On his way out Purvis checked with the ticket girl again. She told him the movie would last ninety-four minutes, but with newsreels the full show time was two hours and four minutes. Just a few moments later Purvis asked her for the times once more. Energy was coursing through him; he was jittery. He did not want to miss anything; he could not afford a mistake. Brown told Purvis he had phoned Cowley—the troops were on their way. But twenty long minutes passed and still Brown and Purvis were the only ones there. "I became extremely nervous," Purvis admitted—nervous enough to pester the ticket seller yet again. The relief of seeing his agents filing onto Lincoln Street nearly made him giddy. Purvis rushed to each one and shared the expected time of Dillinger's departure—10:35 P.M.

Cowley found Purvis and the two arranged their chessboard. They stationed agents McCarthy and Gillespie a few yards to the north of the theater, agents Hurt and Hollis to the right. The rest of the men—Welles, Lockerman, Richmond, Campbell, Metcalfe, Zimmer, Connor, Glynn, Suran, McGlaughlin, Ryan, Woltz, Sullivan—took positions in the alleys and across the street. When agent

Winstead arrived from the Marbro, he bolstered Hurt and Hollis to the south; thus the best shooters in the bunch blocked the direction Dillinger likely would go. Agent Brown remained in the car, should quick pursuit be required. The East Chicago officers—Zarkovich, O'Neill, and three others—spread out among the agents. Sam Cowley settled across the street from the Biograph, sixty feet from the entrance. "I was in a roving position and kept in touch with all agents in order to see that all points were being covered properly," he later recounted. Purvis—the only agent other than Cowley who knew what Anna Sage looked like—took the spot closest to the theater: a recessed doorway just ten steps to the left of the ticket booth. Purvis and the four men closest to the exit were to surround Dillinger as he left the theater. No one, however, was to act before Purvis gave two signals: a lit cigar would signify that Dillinger was spotted, and a wave of the hand was the cue to close in.

One procedural obligation remained—getting final orders from Hoover. In the library of his Seward Square home, Hoover took the call from Cowley and sanctioned the plan in place. "You have done well so far," Cowley said Hoover told him. "Give the men instructions to take Dillinger alive. But instruct them also to protect themselves, to take no chances. The life of one government agent is worth a million Dillingers." In coming days critics would charge that Hoover's and Purvis's exhortations to their agents that they take no chances with the trigger-happy Dillinger amounted to giving them orders to shoot to kill. Many Dillinger experts argue that Hoover was determined to exterminate the gangster as a way to convey the Bureau's superiority in the war on crime. But there is no record that any such order was ever given. If it had been, either Purvis or Brown could have put a bullet in Dillinger's head the minute he turned his back to buy a ticket.

Instead, a twenty-four-man force was ringed around the Biograph, armed and poised for the difficult business of capture. The challenge would be to stay alert for the length of the show. Purvis had suffered the twenty minutes it took for his men to arrive; now he would have to endure another two hours in the oppressive heat. But even the slightest concession to the elements, he felt, could be costly. "There was no way of knowing whether Dillinger would stay for the whole show," he later explained. "Some patron in the theater might arouse his suspicions, causing him to leave. . . . Our vigilance could not be relaxed even for a split second. I bit off the end of the cigar and nervously chewed on it."

The wait continued. Watches ticked with staggering slowness; restless agents checked and rechecked their weapons. Purvis had a hard time: He was parched, thirsty, anxious, frightened, weary, excited, all at once. He was not made of the same flinty stuff as the gangsters, and he knew it. He was a tightly wound, twitching bundle of wires. "Manhunting isn't a game," Purvis later wrote. "It's a grim and tragic affair. Manhunting is war, without quarter or kindness."

Still, here he was. Three months earlier, almost to the day, Purvis had been sure he had Dillinger cornered, but the bandit squirmed out of his trap. Now they were together again, and Purvis believed that all the work and worry, all the memos and meetings and sleepless nights, had led, inexorably, to this hour. "I knew that we could not let him escape this time," Purvis recalled of that interminable wait outside the theater. "We would never have another opportunity like this."

Nine o'clock. Nine-thirty. Ten. Ten-twenty. *Manhattan Melodrama* was deep into its closing reel. In minutes Dillinger would emerge. And then—what was happening? Bright headlights and a screamed command: "*Who the hell are you?*" One of Purvis's agents, Ray Suran, turned to see a riot gun pointed at his chest and a plainclothes policeman behind it. "*Show me your identification! What are you doing here?*" On Lincoln Avenue more Chicago detectives encircled the loitering agents, demanding identification. Purvis could not believe this. Neither he nor Cowley had notified the Chicago police department, not because of an oversight but quite by design. Just as at Little Bohemia, it was Hoover's policy to have his agents go it alone at the Biograph. The East Chicago officers were already aboard; they had, after all, delivered Sage to Purvis. But the benefit of alerting local police—and risking a crippling leak—was simply not there. The interests of secrecy and containment had also stopped Purvis and Cowley from bringing the manager of the Biograph into the fold. Both decisions now seemed to have backfired. The theater's engineer, taking a temperature reading on the street, had noticed the fidgety men positioned up and down the street and suspected an imminent robbery. He rushed to alert the manager, Charles Shapiro, who asked the ticket girl if she had seen anything suspicious. Indeed she had: a man who cased the lobby and asked repeatedly for show

times. Shapiro locked himself in his office and called the police.
They had arrived and were shaking down the agents for badges and
explanations.

The time was 10:30 P.M. The first moviegoers were beginning to
leave the Biograph.

Suran and the other agents explained their business and produced credentials. The plainclothes officers holstered their guns
but did not hurry to leave. Two more people came out of the theater. Purvis readied his match and matchbook. Some of his agents
were still busy with the Chicago cops. Purvis held fast to his spot
within the recessed doors. He would remember how his knees felt,
how they wobbled beneath him. Just then, just as these first few people were leaving, Purvis saw him—John Dillinger. He had watched
his movie and now here he was, sauntering out of the theater, almost carefree. Sage was with him, and Polly Hamilton. They could
have been any group of friends; the handsome Dillinger could have
been any working man. "I watched him as he moved slowly forward," Purvis recalled. "He looked into my eyes; surely he must have
seen something more than casual interest in them, but apparently
he didn't recognize me." Dillinger kept walking, past Purvis, south
toward Halsted. One hundred more steps and he would reach a
back alley. Purvis struck his match and lit his chewed cigar. The signal had been given.

Not everyone saw it, however. Some agents were not even facing
the theater because of the Chicago officers. Others had their view of
Purvis obscured by moviegoers. Purvis struck another match.
Dillinger was now halfway to the alley. Purvis fell in a few steps behind him. He was unsure any agent had seen him light his cigar, but
he waited before giving the second signal. There were too many
people around Dillinger, too many women and children. Rushing
him now would endanger them all. Purvis chose to wait precious
seconds to let the crowd diminish. Dillinger took more steps toward
the alley. He was only a few feet from Winstead, the sharpshooter. "I
knew right away," Winstead later recalled, "it was Dillinger." Behind
them Purvis felt he could wait no more. He waved his arm, and
waved it again. Still, he saw no agents. "My heart pounded," he
would say. "A slip might mean failure." Only then did he see his
agents closing in on Dillinger. Now, no matter which direction

Dillinger chose to flee, he would have an agent in his path. If he spun around and raced northward, the agent would be Purvis.

It happened in mere seconds. "Polly knew something was up," Winstead remembered. "She grabbed Dillinger by the shirt." Purvis noticed it, too: "I had seen the woman at his right tug at his shirt in a furtive sort of way as if to warn him that all was not well." Dillinger had been slow to sense danger, but now there was no question. He dropped into a slight crouch and moved his right hand to his pocket. A gunshot rang out, then another, then more—six in all. Startled citizens ran screaming. One woman collapsed to the ground.

Four bullets struck John Dillinger. Three did little damage; the fourth was devastating. It bore through the back of his neck, fractured his second cervical vertebra, crashed through his spinal cord and the right side of his brain, then exited through the lower lid of his right eye. Dillinger fell face first on the bricks at the entrance of the alley. Charles Winstead stood over him, holding the hot revolver that probably fired the crucial bullet. Purvis put away his own gun and came upon the fallen gangster. He knelt and took the Colt .38 handgun from Dillinger's grip. Purvis and Winstead turned him over and spoke to him, trying to coax the last bit of life from his crumpled body. But there was no spat curse, no final bravado. "I bent over him and spoke to him and tried to get him to talk," Purvis recalled. "But he was already dead."

As quickly as people had run from Dillinger when the shooting started, now they rushed to see what the shooting had wrought. The name of the nation's most famous outlaw sounded in the muggy night, electrifying the crowd. Later that night some would dip newspapers and handkerchiefs in Dillinger's blood. After the gunfire Sam Cowley rushed to call Hoover. A few agents helped keep space around the body. Purvis stood and stepped away from the scene. He was surprised to see the two buttons on his jacket were ripped away. "I had grabbed for my gun without thinking," he recalled. "I am frank to say that I do not know how it came into my hand."

One day after Dillinger's killing, a small woman in a pink summer dress arrived at the Bureau's headquarters in Washington and asked to speak with the director. Hoover did not hesitate to see her. The woman congratulated Hoover on the work of his agents. The death of Dillinger was a huge victory for the forces of good. But there was no joy in the woman's demeanor; her visit was somber and brief. This was the widowed wife of W. Carter Baum, the agent killed by Baby Face Nelson at Little Bohemia. She had come to take whatever small measure of solace there was in Dillinger's death. Not much later, Hoover declared Nelson the new Public Enemy Number One. "We're going to get that fellow," he told reporters. "Nobody can kill one of our men and get away with it."

That same day, July 23, 1934, Assistant Attorney General William Stanley had an idea. He knew Attorney General Cummings was traveling by train across the Midwest to visit prisons and publicize the government's war on crime. Why not have him stop in Chicago and congratulate an agent for getting Dillinger? Stanley sent a telegram to Cummings's drawing room aboard the Baltimore and Ohio number-seven train heading westward. "If this appeals to you," Stanley wrote Cummings, "I shall have him at the station and notify the papers." Cummings wired his reply. "Suggestion agreeable," he wrote. "You may arrange accordingly." Stanley quickly sent a memo to the Bureau. "Please ask Mr. Hoover to arrange to have newspaper men on hand when the Attorney General arrives in Chicago." Reporters and photographers were dispatched to the train station; the publicity stunt unfolded without a hitch.

William Stanley's little idea would have enormous repercussions. Part of the reason is that neither Stanley nor Cummings nor Hoover had any conception of how big the story of Dillinger's death would be. They could not have fathomed its impact on a nation starved for good news—could not have dreamed how it would, in its way, help restore the nation's faith in itself. There was no way Stanley could have foreseen the immense celebrity that would attach itself to those who played a part in ending Dillinger's spree of crime, and particularly to the man presented as the hero of the tale. Stanley simply crafted his scheme to boost the profile of the beleaguered Bureau. He did not recommend that Cummings congratulate Hoover. Nor did he suggest that Cummings shake hands with Cowley.

The agent he sent to the train station was Melvin Purvis.

9

PLEASURE AND COMMENDATION

July 26, 1934

In the last moments of his life—in the awful seconds it took him to fall nineteen stories to the unforgiving pavement—James Johnson Probasco might have thought of a dream that was to die with him: his wish to buy the Green Log Tavern in Chicago. He had lived a life of rough jobs and minor crimes, of work as a butcher, a trucker, a salesman, as the owner of a speakeasy, and as a fence for stolen jewels. He was no gangster, but he had run with gangsters, and he had played cards with John Dillinger. He never made much money, but he always found a way to work one angle or another. A garrulous fellow with a broad pug's grin, toward the end of his sixty-six years he went looking for a ticket—for a way out, a final score to set him up. Then he would buy the Green Log and drink beer with friends and hash over old times. He lucked into easy money when Dillinger picked his house as a hideout, the place where he had doctors reconfigure his famous face. In a way it was the crowning moment of Probasco's criminal life.

But everything changed on July 22 when Dillinger took a bullet to the neck. Within hours of the gangster's death, the same agents who trapped him on Lincoln Avenue began a sweeping roundup of his accomplices. Dillinger's scarred face provided confirmation that he had undergone plastic surgery, and at 10:30 A.M. on July 23 five special agents raided the modest two-floor cottage of Wilhelm Loeser, the doctor they suspected of performing the surgery. Peering through the windows of the house on Harvey Avenue, in Oak Park, Illinois, agents spotted an unfinished breakfast on the kitchen table. They broke down a side door and found Loeser standing halfway up the stairs, wearing only his pants and slippers. After lengthy questioning in a conference room at the Bankers Building, Loeser surrendered all the details of Dillinger's surgery.

That information led agents to another two-story frame building on North Crawford Avenue in Chicago. At 7:00 P.M. on July 25, agents staking out the home watched Probasco drive into his parking spot behind a Shell gasoline station. Two Bureau agents approached him from behind, but, alerted by the station attendant, Probasco hit the gas and sped off. No matter: An hour later an agent spotted Probasco's car and arrested him. Driven back to his home, Probasco watched agents collect damning evidence: a can of Squibb ether, three bottles of surgical cat gut, plenty of gauze bandages, and a .32-caliber Iver Johnson revolver. During the search Probasco almost seized a stove poker and nearly wrestled away an agent's gun. The old man would fight for the last of his freedom.

Probasco, too, was brought to the Bankers Building that night and put in the middle conference room, toward the rear of the nineteenth floor. This was where agents pressed suspects for information, sometimes in unpleasant fashion. "They would keep them there under bright lights for hours, sometimes as much as forty-eight hours," remembered Doris Lockerman. "There was questioning, questioning, questioning, under hot lights and being hungry, and being sleepy and scared to death. It was pretty heavy, and the agents were insistent. 'Tell us again what happened, and make it straight.' Most people were just worn out by this." Lockerman was at the office the next morning at 9:00 A.M. when special agent Morris Chaffetz relieved the agent who had watched Probasco all night. According to Sam Cowley, who supervised the interrogation (Melvin Purvis was away in Washington at the time), Chaffetz, a rookie agent, began the morning by taking Probasco's fingerprints. He left Probasco briefly to deliver the prints to the front of the office, but when he returned, the middle conference room was empty. A chair had been moved to the base of a window that opened onto a rear courtyard known as the Rookery. Chaffetz rushed to the window and looked down. "It was determined," a July 26 memorandum concluded, "that James Johnson Probasco had leaped from the window in the middle, rear conference room of the Chicago Division office and was instantly killed." Cowley did not even wait for agents to examine Probasco's badly mangled body to place his call to Hoover. He kept his cool and made sure his agents did, too. "We were all working at the time but we did not see it happen nor did we know it happened," Lockerman said. "But once it got out it was a terribly tense time at the office."

Hoover, for one, was furious—instead of basking in the glory of Dillinger's killing, he had to worry about a potentially damaging blunder. "Mr. Chaffetz walked out for a minute and the next thing they knew [Probasco] had jumped out the window," an incredulous Hoover recounted of his conversation with Cowley. "I remarked that this was extreme carelessness." Months earlier, another suspect, Boss McLaughlin, had complained to reporters that agents dangled him from that same conference room window. Not surprisingly, accusations soon surfaced that Probasco did not jump but perhaps was dangled or even pushed. Still, steps were taken to contain the possible damage. Cowley testified at a coroner's inquest that same afternoon, and he was relieved to relay to Hoover that the jurors ruled that Probasco committed suicide. Hoover and Cowley also quickly made Probasco's criminal record public, and announced they found a note in Probasco's home that indicated he was suicidal, though the note was not released and has not surfaced to this day. The local papers picked up the story but seemed satisfied that Probasco jumped of his own volition. "Dillinger Aide Leaps to Death," read a *Chicago Daily News* headline. "Dillinger's Host Dies in Leap," said the *Chicago American*. "I asked [Cowley] whether there was any indication that we were using rope wire on him when he jumped out of the window and Mr. Cowley stated there was not," Assistant Director Edward Tamm told Hoover in a July 26 memo. "I asked whether there were any references to McLaughlin's statement that he had been hung out of the window and Mr. Cowley stated there were none." Cowley suggested to Hoover that Chaffetz be suspended for two weeks, and recommended the same punishment for himself. "I stated I would suspend Chaffetz," Hoover told him, "but not Mr. Cowley."

Incredibly, a similar oversight occurred less than a month later. Federal agents were holding Probasco's girlfriend Margaret Doyle in her home, and she escaped to the bathroom and jumped from a third-floor window. Unlike her late boyfriend, she survived the fall. "I am terribly distressed," Hoover said in an August 17 memorandum. "This thing of people jumping out of windows is just going to be too bad for us."

In fact the backlash from both incidents was minimal; the press did not even learn of Doyle's leap for weeks. But Probasco's free fall to a messy death in the Rookery reflected the unforeseeable and often incomprehensible reaction to Dillinger's killing. Despite their months-long obsession with Dillinger, the Chicago agents were not conscious of the powerful forces his death would unleash, nor were they prepared for the sudden shift in the nation's collective consciousness that would transform the way they were perceived. They knew, of course, that they were involved in something big, just not how big. Perhaps Purvis sensed some small fraction if it when Doris Lockerman told him a day after Dillinger's death as he returned to the office that a man was there who wished to pay him $50 for his pants. "He had heard from a bystander that Dillinger's blood was on the cuff of the trousers, and he wanted them as a souvenir," Purvis recalled. "Needless to say he received neither the trousers nor a courteous response."

The hours and days after Dillinger's death were indeed a strange time. One great success of the operation was that no bystanders were inadvertently killed—a major concern after Little Bohemia. Another civilian death might have cemented the public's perception of the Bureau's agents as reckless. This time the worst consequences were two minor injuries suffered by women caught in the cross fire: A bullet struck Theresa Paulus in the right hip, and Etta Natalsky was hit in the left thigh. "I was about to move when I felt a sting in my leg," Natalsky later told reporters. "I said, 'I'm shot.' I started to drop to the sidewalk. My brother and my daughter caught me. . . . On the ground at the end of the alley was Dillinger. He was lying face down. His face was covered with blood." Both women recovered, and Purvis even later speculated that by asking for a live-in nurse, Natalsky took "full advantage of the circumstances surrounding her injury, and of the fact that the hospital and doctor bills are to be paid by the Division." Dillinger would incur no such expenses; his body lay in the alley for ten minutes until a police wagon arrived to take him away. The agents helped lift him onto a stretcher, and some rode along with police to Chicago's Alexian Brothers Hospital on Beldan Avenue. A swelling crowd there convinced police to have the doctor examine Dillinger in the wagon. At 10:55 P.M. Dr. Walter Prusaig searched for a pulse and declared, "This man is dead."

Through the night hundreds of people flocked to the spot where Dillinger fell. Radio reports kept the curious coming, though people saw only splotches of blood on the bricks. Sam Cowley had long since gathered Dillinger's shattered silver-rimmed glasses, his unwrapped cigar, and his straw boater hat. Cowley had not searched Dillinger's pockets, however, and by the time the body arrived at the Cook County Morgue, only $7.70 remained of his wealth. By most accounts, Dillinger rarely traveled with less than several thousand dollars stuffed in his pockets or in a money belt. According to Anna Sage, he began the evening carrying more than $3,000. Unless he incurred extraordinary expenses for refreshments at the Biograph, the greatest thief in the nation was himself victimized at the hour of his death. But by whom? The disposition of Dillinger's cash remains, to this day, a mystery, though there are a few tantalizing clues. An inquiry ordered by Hoover provided testimony from the agents who rode with the body to the morgue. Agent Daniel Sullivan recalled that, with Purvis watching, he examined Dillinger's body at the scene and "felt what appeared to be a roll of either money or paper in the right hand pants' pocket. [But] the contents of the pockets were not touched by . . . anyone." Not a single agent claimed to have seen anyone reach into Dillinger's pockets; everyone also insisted Dillinger's body was watched by at least one agent at all times. But special agent Murphy hinted at a possible scenario. At Alexian Brothers Hospital, both agents and uniformed police officers guarded the back of the wagon carrying Dillinger's body. At one point "I noticed two or three men come to the door of the patrol wagon, and asked to see Dillinger, stating they were police officers; they were in plain clothes," Murphy testified. "They were allowed to step inside of the patrol wagon to look at the features of Dillinger, and, to keep the crowds away . . . the door of the patrol was always closed." At the morgue, deputy coroner Jack Butler searched Dillinger's gray slacks and found a five-dollar bill, two single dollars, and a few coins, which he placed on the hard slab next to the body. No rubber-banded rolls, no hand-tooled billfold, and certainly no stacks of tens and twenties. Eventually East Chicago detective Glenn Stretch claimed he saw a fellow officer take the money from

Dillinger's pockets, though no charges were ever filed. The officer he implicated was none other than Martin Zarkovich.

However ignominiously Dillinger was treated in the patrol wagon, worse humiliations awaited him at the morgue, where he was the 116th corpse to be admitted that July. A horde of the morbid and the curious, drawn instinctively by news of Dillinger's death, was already swarming the grounds of the morgue, a dreary stone building with mesh wire over the windows. Agents transferred Dillinger's body onto a cart in the first-floor receiving room; there, agent Chaffetz took a set of fingerprints. Those prints were quickly dispatched to Washington, where—despite Dr. Loeser's best efforts—an agent of the Bureau's identification unit pegged them as identical to a set taken when Dillinger was jailed at Crown Point in 1933. "His fingers had been treated but the treatment had failed entirely," Purvis later told reporters. "It reassures us that talk of a new surgical 'disguise' is just bunk." At the morgue the receiving room grew tight with officers, agents, and other onlookers. To escape the crowd, Dr. Charles Parker wheeled the cart carrying Dillinger's body into an elevator and down to a basement examining room. Small, dank, and reeking of formaldehyde, that room, too, quickly filled to capacity. One police officer, Sgt. Frank Reynolds, shook the corpse's hand. In less than ideal conditions, and under the glare of dozens, Parker and deputy coroner Butler stripped and examined the body. Of particular interest to press people squeezed into the room was Dillinger's yellow-gold, jeweled Hamilton pocket watch, which had a tiny photo of Polly Hamilton tucked inside its lid. They asked to photograph the watch, but federal agents told Butler "not to allow the newspapers to take a photograph of this picture until Mr. Purvis had OKed same, regardless of the reporters' pleas," Murphy testified. Once he arrived, Purvis denied the reporters this permission, and ordered three agents to stay close to the body. But not even Purvis could prevent the coroner, Frank J. Walsh, from opening the morgue to the public the following day, July 23. More than 15,000 people passed through the basement to gape at the fallen gangster, his body naked except for a white sheet drawn to his chest, his brain already removed and placed in a jar of formaldehyde, his cold slab angled to give the crowd a better view. "None of the dignity of death was his," one reporter later observed.

An official inquest on July 23 ruled the death a justifiable homi-
cide, and the jurors even commended Hoover's agents "for their efficient participation in the occurrence as shown by the fact that
there was no further loss of life in the capture of a man of this type."
Frank Walsh remarked with some satisfaction that Dillinger's death
had cost the government only $6—one dollar for each juror. Surely
the gaunt old Quaker farmer awakened by a reporter that very day
in Mooresville, Indiana, would have found no humor in Walsh's
quip. The dazed, barefoot man was John Dillinger Sr., who blinked
the sleep from his eyes and said, "At last it has happened—the thing
I have prayed and prayed would not happen." Not much later Au-
drey Hamilton, Dillinger's sister and the woman who raised him, arrived at the farm. The sixty-nine-year-old father and his daughter
held each other and wept. The elder Dillinger accepted an offer
from Mooresville undertaker E. H. Harvey to ride with him in his
creaky gray hearse to collect the body, and the men, along with
Dillinger's half-brother Hubert, drove 225 miles to Chicago in blis-
tering heat. Dillinger Sr. stepped weakly from the car outside
Chicago's McCready Funeral Home on Sheridan Road, to be
greeted by hundreds of people who rushed the hearse they knew
would soon carry Dillinger. "I want a drink of water," Dillinger Sr.
gasped. "I feel faint." He could not even claim his son's body until
the following day, when the coroner finally released it. Dillinger
then was moved to the narrow embalming room in the back of Mc-
Cready's, and Harvey dressed the body. When Dillinger Sr. finally
saw his son for the first time in months, tears welled in his eyes. "My
boy," he said. "My boy." Later he was handed Dillinger's watch and
bloody shirt as well as $7.70.

———

Five thousand people remained massed around McCready's, waiting
for a glimpse of Dillinger. Police officers, sweating hard in the afternoon heat, muscled a path to the street so workers from the funeral
home could carry a brown wicker basket containing the body to
Harvey's hearse. Dillinger Sr. waved off several people who wished
to share with him the gruesome details of his son's killing. His heavy
sorrow surged into anger. "They shot him down in cold blood," he

told reporters. "He was surrounded by fifteen men, and that ain't fair. I'd rather have him shot than captured, though, and John would rather have had it that way." Chicago squad cars escorted the hearse along Route 41 toward Indiana; for part of the trip, Dillinger Sr. rode in the back with his dead son. Another mob had gathered in Moorseville to watch the casket be carried into the funeral home; another five thousand people filed past the body during a public viewing. On July 25 a motorcade carried Dillinger to the Crown Hill Cemetery. He was dressed in an ill-fitting gray herringbone suit and placed in a $165 octagonal plush casket. That afternoon the skies opened and rain soaked the mourners. As men took hold of shovels, the Rev. Charles Fillmore, who had baptized a young John Dillinger, intoned, "Yea, though I walk through the valley of the shadow of death." At 3:15 P.M. the earth took Dillinger. Funeral wreaths were shredded by those in search of souvenirs, some of whom were officers of the law.

Well east of Mooresville, another elderly man had a far different reaction when an Associated Press reporter tracked him down on July 23. He, too, appeared disoriented, but shed not a single tear. His son was "doing pretty good," a proud Melvin Purvis Sr., sixty-four, told the reporter invited into the family's Timmonsville home. Young Melvin, he added, was "a kind of quiet boy. He didn't go in at all for cop and robber games and cowboy and Indian, and that sort of thing when he was a child—not at all, as I remember. He began all this justice work seven years ago. He just went up there to Washington and got a small job at it and climbed himself to where he is."

It was a neat synopsis of the unlikely adventure of Melvin Purvis, who was now, a mere seven years after stumbling into his line of work—and quite literally overnight—the most famous law officer in the country. The death of Dillinger, the nation's archcriminal, sparked a frenzy of press coverage, a blizzard of bold, blaring headlines, not only in Chicago but in every major city as well as in countries across the globe. It seemed not a single soul was oblivious to what happened at the Biograph, nor was anyone without an opinion of its significance. No less a figure than Adolph Hitler, the rising German dictator, expressed an interest in the story, in the Berlin paper *Vodkische Beobachter*. "The Chicago chief of police shot him like a mad dog in a public street, filling him full of holes, as a sieve, without regard to bystanders," Hitler was quoted as saying. "Does a land where such things happen still deserve to be called a country where law rules? Without court procedure, without a single question, the man was shot into the great beyond."

This collective absorption in the story produced a tidal surge of interest that was well beyond anyone's understanding or control. Accustomed as they were to the attention of local beat reporters, Purvis and his agents were not prepared for the intense reaction to Dillinger's death. "I don't think anyone was," said Richard Gid Powers, a professor of American culture and the author of several stellar books about the FBI, including *Secrecy and Power: The Life of J. Edgar Hoover.* "No one anticipated the incredible enthusiasm with which the story was greeted. People were just kind of in awe of what was happening." Doris Lockerman recalled that "all of us who worked with Melvin Purvis were amazed that law enforcement at that level was so interesting to people. Today, when we have so many pseudo- and quasi-idols, it is very hard to remember that back then it was an exceptional thing for someone to be that recognizable, to be universally exciting in the eyes of the world. And it amazed all of us. But this was a very unique time in the public's awareness of the clash between law and order. The war on crime was the biggest story there was."

In July 1934, America remained staggered by the Depression and starved for any morsel of encouraging news. "The United States had been on a losing streak for so long," said Powers. "It had a government that was finally trying to do something, and that was a relief, but the public also wanted some results. And it turns out, in a way that nobody could have foreseen, the war on crime produced just such dramatic results. And these results symbolized just what the country needed: It needed to know it had a government that was not only committed to action but that furthermore could actually succeed."

The collective yearning of the nation invested the killing of Dillinger with an importance far beyond what the elimination of a single gangster actually signified. Hoover, Purvis, and everyone else underestimated people's desperation for some jolt of reassuring news. It is not an exaggeration to say the Bureau's success in stopping Dillinger helped to restore the nation's faith in its government and, indeed, in itself. Today, the public latches onto stories purely for entertainment, but in the early 1930s, the impulse that impelled such shifts in mass consciousness was far more complex. A weary and impoverished nation absorbed the death of Dillinger as a bracing ray of hope.

Some of this euphoria quite naturally found its way to Washington. Hoover praised both Purvis and Cowley by telephone shortly after Dillinger was killed, and the next day dispatched official letters of congratulation. His letter to Purvis, sent special delivery by air mail and addressed "Dear Melvin," is appreciative and generous.

> I wanted to write and repeat to you my expressions of pleasure and commendation which I tried to convey to you last night. The shooting and killing of John Dillinger by Agents of your office under your admirable direction and planning are but another example of your ability and capacity as a leader and an executive. I am particularly pleased, because it again confirms the faith and confidence which I have always had in you. While the expressions of the public are most laudatory, you and I both know how fickle such may be, but I did want you to know that my appreciation of the success with which your efforts have met in this case is lasting and makes me most proud of you.
>
> The gratification with which the Attorney General received the news when I spoke with him just before he took the train for the West would have indeed pleased you if you could have heard his expressions. He and Mr. Stanley, the Assistant to the Attorney General, have both been so patient and helpful in their attitude of confidence and support, that I was glad that the Division could "get" Dillinger and "get" him itself. This would not have been accomplished had it not been for your unlimited and never-ending persistence, effective planning and intelligence, and I did want you to know how much I appreciate it.

A week later Hoover wrote a warm and complimentary letter to Melvin Purvis Sr. in Timmonsville.

> I did want to write and to convey to you my great pride in having associated with me in this Division your son. Of course, I know how proud you are of him, and in fact how proud the whole community must be of what he has accomplished in the field of law enforcement. His courageous and fearless act of last Sunday night is but

another indication of that sterling qualification of character which is so marked in him. His tireless energy and high personal standards have won the confidence of all who have come into relationship with him. Executive capacity far beyond such as is usual at his age has placed him in positions of responsibility which he has always filled with credit. An unvarying courtesy which has never sacrificed principle for the sake of advantage has won him the respect and confidence of a wide circle of friends, such as many a man of far more mature attainments might envy. His work has done much to contribute to the success of the Division of Investigation, in which he is recognized as one of its most capable executives.

I know that it would have done your heart good to have heard the very high praise and commendation paid to him by the Attorney General of the United States. A few days ago [your son] was here in Washington with me, and while he received much in the way of public applause and recognition, he conducted himself with that simple modesty which is so characteristic of his makeup. Of course, I feel proud of him for what he has done in the Chicago district. Not only in the John Dillinger case, but in many other of the more important criminal cases, he has proved himself to be worthy of the confidence and responsibility imposed on him. During the period of time when he was subjected to much unfair criticism and attack, he carried on like a true soldier and finally came through to a success-ful conclusion, fully justifying all of the faith and confidence which had been imposed on him. I am proud of him, not only because he is one of our capable executives, but because I can call him a friend, for he has been one of my closest and dearest friends.

I wanted you to know personally how much I thought of him, for I believe that it might make you feel also a little happier, if that is possible, in this hour of his success.

The letters may not be as intimate and informal as Hoover's ear-lier correspondence with agent Purvis, but neither are they standard-issue commendations. Hoover was effusive in his praise for his protégé, missing no opportunity to cite in glowing terms not only his work on the Dillinger case but also his overall character. It is tempt-ing to regard the two letters as genuine expressions of the satisfac-tion and pride Hoover felt for Purvis in the hour of their greatest mutual success. Yet gauging Hoover's sincerity requires comparing another letter he crafted that same week. Hoover, of course, sent an official letter of commendation to Sam Cowley as well as to Purvis. But he also sent Cowley a private letter about the Dillinger killing. "To you," it read, "must go the major portion of the credit." That single line presaged the Bureau's official version of events at the Biograph, a version that would take shape in the months after Dillinger's death and that would endure for the next several decades.

Regardless of Hoover's private estimation of Cowley's role in Dillinger's death, newspaper editors were not interested in the burly, low-key Mormon. Local and national reporters were much more familiar with the stylish Melvin Purvis. After all, he was the agent they knew to be in charge of the Chicago office, the agent who had presided over several key arrests and raids. It is hardly surprising that when word of the Dillinger shooting reached city news desks, reporters focused their attention on Purvis. The outer foyer at the Bureau's Chicago office filled up in the predawn hours on January 23, and Purvis—normally reticent and quite capable of brushing past the media horde without a word—on this day entertained reporters in his office. To have completely ignored the clamor for comment on the day of the Bureau's most shining victory, and at a time when the Bureau's image was badly in need of burnishing, perhaps did not seem to him to be a viable option. On a personal level, Purvis surely felt some measure of redemption. Only three months after the killing of a civilian and the murder of Carter Baum at Little Bohemia, he had played a part in ridding the nation of the scourge that set the fiasco in motion. He had helped pierce the very heart of the deadliest criminal gang in the land. The pride he felt is manifest in the almost giddy narrative he provided to reporters in the days after Dillinger's death. "It was a good job the surgeons did but I knew him the minute I saw him," the *New York Times* quoted Purvis as saying. "You couldn't miss him if you had studied that face as much as I have." And later: "Dillinger gave one hunted look about him and attempted to run up an alley. . . . As his hand came up with the gun in it, several shots were fired by my men before he could fire. He dropped, fatally wounded. I had hoped to take him alive but I was afraid that he would resist to the last."

Purvis did seem to place himself at the center of the narrative, but he was also quick to credit his men for their bravery and decisiveness. "Melvin Purvis did have a certain amount of dramatic in-

stinct," recalled Doris Lockerman. "He knew there was drama in
what he did. All the men realized that, too. I think they all basked a
little bit in their heroism. They had always known they were a cut
above the gumshoe, the street cop, but now they were feeling that
they were an elite, and Melvin Purvis epitomized the elite of that
elite. There were no other Special Agents in Charge who had quite
the dash he had." Even so, she said, there was no real change in
Purvis's demeanor after Dillinger's death—no arrogance, no grandstanding. Nor was the relationship between Purvis and his men any
different. "Privately he might have rather enjoyed the attention, but
he would never have let anyone in the office know it," Lockerman
said. "You see, he was no hero to us. He was just the boss, just one of
the people who were all working together on the same thing. We
were not all kneeling to Melvin Purvis."

In the end, it did not much matter how Purvis chose to tell his
story; the media hardly needed his cooperation to anoint him the
hero of the hour. "He Got His Man," the *Chicago Daily Times* declared beneath a picture of Purvis in a late July 23 edition. The *New
York Evening Journal* headlined a series of Dillinger photos "Underworld Melodrama—in Three Scenes (A U.S. Production Directed by
Melvin Purvis)." The *Chicago Herald and Examiner* ran a story entitled
"Purvis Is New Type of Sleuth; Soft Spoken, but Gangs Fear Him." It
read, "A slight, sharp-featured young southerner of 32 yesterday received the praise of a nation as the nemesis of America's Public Enemy No. 1." An editorial in the same paper declared, "With Purvis
and his splendid men the taking of Dillinger was all in a day's work
. . . the organization, which the indomitable young Mr. Purvis per-
sonifies as Chicago chief, is one of the greatest criminal hunting
agencies in the world." One newspaper even referred to Purvis as
the "Chief of the Federal Bureau of Investigation."

Then came the request from the U.S. Attorney General's Office to
send Purvis to meet Homer Cummings at the train station. The re-
sulting photograph—a towering Cummings in a white suit and white
fedora stiffly shaking hands with Purvis, youthful enough to be mistaken for Cummings's son—appeared everywhere. It ran in *Time*
magazine with the caption "Melvin Purvis and Friend." Despite the
fact that he had been summoned for the photograph by the attorney
general, and had proceeded only with Hoover's blessing, Purvis
would be blamed for what the photo accomplished—it essentially cut

Hoover out of the story. Whatever credit did not fall into Purvis's lap found its way to the office of Homer Cummings, the visible and media-savvy attorney general.

Hoover, as painfully image-conscious as any public figure, enjoyed very little of that first heady rush of media attention. This was the first serious disruption of the system he had rigidly put in place at the Bureau, a system designed to depict his agents as anonymous and uniform and to ensure that any credit due the Bureau flowed directly to him. "Dillinger's killing changed that significantly," noted Richard Gid Powers. "Now it was one of Hoover's men who was the public face of the Bureau, and it was one of his men who the country looked upon as essentially the leader of the war on crime. And this ran counter to Hoover's idea of professionalism, which to him meant that he had independence while everyone else had to follow his orders everyday. In his mind he wanted all of his men to be rule-followers. And suddenly Purvis, because of his celebrity status, could, to a certain extent, call his own shots."

In hindsight, it seems inevitable that Purvis would be portrayed as the drama's protagonist. Hoover's formula for fostering the idea of a collective victory clashed with the needs of both the public and the media. An organizational victory is simply not as compelling as an individual one. People always gravitate toward the individual hero; their appeal engages us in deep and irresistible ways. Thus did Purvis become a unifying image for the nation to celebrate, at a time when it was desperately in need of just such an image. Purvis was both a hero and a completely accessible figure. He was not abnormally tall or muscular; he was short and slender. He spoke in a soft voice and admitted to often being afraid. Despite his aristocratic leanings, he was someone the average American could easily identify with. "The public believes in heroes and villains and it always will," said Powers. "In the time of Dillinger the public wanted an action hero and Purvis fit the bill perfectly. He was good looking, he dressed sharply, he had a career in Chicago that put him in a glamorous light. He was the real deal and he became the action hero the American public wanted."

Watching Purvis ascend to hero status in the span of just a few days was, for Hoover, surely difficult. The very qualities that attracted him to Purvis years before—his Southern charm, his handsome appearance, his crisp demeanor—were now facilitating Purvis's assumption of a role that Hoover had long coveted. At the same time, those qualities highlighted why Hoover, a less appealing figure than Purvis, could not very well assume that role himself. "If Purvis could have done his work anonymously, Hoover would have loved that," said Lockerman. "He would have loved the results without the publicity. But he wound up with a hero who was much more charming than himself. And that's really what Hoover was jealous of."

There was little Hoover could do to stem the tide, though he tried. "I do not believe in talking for broadcast purposes on such a case," Hoover declared a day after the shooting, in declining to provide either himself or Purvis for an NBC radio show. "The way we feel is that the job is done, we have other work to do, and we want to 'lower the curtain.'" That same day Hoover had Assistant Director Ed Tamm impress this policy upon Purvis. "I told [Cowley] that you wanted him, as well as Mr. Purvis, to know that the broadcasting company and the Movietone people had been pestering you in an effort to have either you or Mr. Purvis broadcast concerning the Dillinger case and to take a Movietone, and that you absolutely refused to authorize such a broadcast or any Movietones," Tamm recorded in a July 23 memorandum. "You do not, under any circumstances, want any newsreel or broadcast made."

Hoover realized that the public's fascination with the Dillinger case would not be soon exhausted. There would be steady demand for stories and reports about various facets of the entire case. As a result, reporters working the story would zealously seek new angles and fresh insight, and this, Hoover decided, was something he alone would provide. By parceling out access to the inner workings of the Bureau—memos, methods, statistics—Hoover was able to control the tenor of these follow-up stories. The information he disseminated stressed the Bureau's organizational strengths while diminishing the impact of its individual agents. "Hoover gave reporters pretty much a complete package that offered a new way of looking at the story," noted Powers. "This package eliminated the role of Anna Sage and even of Melvin Purvis, and explained that because of the scientific prowess of the organization, the FBI would have caught Dillinger sooner or later." This was a fallacy. Nearly every major Bureau case up to that point had been solved because of the contributions of an informant. No amount of scientific sleuthing could have delivered Dillinger to the Bureau as neatly as did Anna Sage's betrayal. Yet to acknowledge that would have been to admit that the Bureau's war on crime was dependent on informants, an acknowledgment Hoover was unwilling to make. He might have suggested that because his agents were so adept at cultivating informants, because they had such strong reputations for integrity and bravery, they were able to use good old-fashioned police work to produce exceptional results. But this rationale would give too much credit to individual agents. Hoover insisted the focus be on the Bureau's cutting-edge scientific methods and streamlined organizational system—structures that he had introduced.

A few days after Dillinger's death, Hoover had Clyde Tolson feed information about the Bureau's hiring practices to *New York Times* reporter Hal H. Smith. Smith's complimentary July 29 article was not about Purvis or Dillinger but rather about the Bureau as a whole. It was accompanied by a single image: a photograph of Hoover. The article demonstrated Hoover's ability to co-opt reporters and use them to control the story. "I have looked with growing admiration upon the work that you, your assistants and agents have been doing," Smith gushed in response to Hoover's note of praise for the article. "Please thank Mr. Tolson for his valuable assistance."

Hoover's note to Smith was not uncommon: He made a point of tracking down the authors of profiles flattering to the Bureau and sending them personal letters of thanks. In this way Hoover identified friendly reporters and kept them well-stocked with inside information. It is a measure of the importance Hoover placed on these thank-you notes that on July 31 he berated Tolson for not composing them quickly enough. "There have been a number of very excellent editorials and articles written about the Division and its work in connection with the John Dillinger case," Hoover wrote in a memorandum. "I have seen practically no letters drafted for my signature, expressing appreciation for these articles. It would seem to me that common courtesy would demand that we acknowledge favorable publicity when we receive the same."

Hoover had another tactical weapon: Sam Cowley. As his emissary in the Chicago office and the only rival to Purvis's authority, Cowley was the sole agent Hoover could use to draw attention away from Purvis. He believed Cowley was not receiving his share of the credit for Dillinger's killing, and he knew Cowley could be counted on to deliver the company line. Pushing Cowley to the front of the story would enhance his organization-first formula. Five days after Dillinger's death, Cowley advised Hoover he wished to cooperate with Jack DeWitt of *American Detective Magazine*, which intended to run an article about the Bureau. Cowley "wanted to know if it would be all right to give Mr. DeWitt a photograph of the Director, as a well as of Mr. Purvis," Hoover recorded. "I told Mr. Cowley that this would be all right, and that he should also include his photograph; that if he didn't give him all three, he shouldn't give any." But Hoover didn't stop there. He persuaded DeWitt that Cowley was the unsung hero of the Dillinger affair, and allowed Cowley to sit for an in-depth interview for the story. "Please do not go reticent on me and boil out yourself as you appear in this story," DeWitt wrote to Cowley after the interview, by way of asking him to approve the finished article. "I am assured at Washington that you deserve far more credit in this case than I can give you with my poor ability." Hoover authorized the article in spite of the protests of inspector W.H.D. Lester. "I am of the opinion that this is a very dangerous precedent to set and I believe that articles such as this, especially when they appear in any detective magazine, will prove detrimental and will result in adverse criticism of the Division," Lester wrote in an August 7 letter. But Hoover would not be dissuaded. The article ran and opened precisely this way:

> "One man alone is responsible for the end of John Dillinger, and that man is J. Edgar Hoover, Director, Division of Investigation, U.S. Department of Justice," began Samuel P. Cowley, Department of Justice agent, when I told him that he had been named to me in Washington as the Government's specially assigned "Dillinger man," in the hunt which ended when the notorious outlaw died like a dog in an alley.

Hoover, Cowley continued, "built up the organization which functioned like a well-trained army until Dillinger was caught . . . he directed the maneuvers necessary in tracing and cornering the man . . . J. Edgar Hoover's orders were carried out to the letter." Billed as "the official Government account of the trailing and death of John Dillinger," the article reflected, in its closing lines, the essence of Hoover's formula. "It is J. Edgar Hoover's intention to make a pariah of every public enemy," DeWitt wrote. "It is the sworn duty of every man in his department to help him to the utmost of [his] ability to that end." DeWitt's Hoover-devised access to Cowley seems to have seduced the author into delivering Hoover's message, and certainly left him smitten with the Bureau and its director. "May I take the honor and pleasure of another call on you when I have nothing but motives of pure friendship to bring me," DeWitt wrote to Cowley after finishing the article, "and a desire to hear more about this man in Washington who has fired you with his squareness—and has set fire to me through you."

An August 1 Associated Press article read as if it had been written by the director himself. Headlined "Hard Work—Not Heroics—in Life of Federal Operatives," the article reported that "Some investigators, due to their positions as leaders of squads or because of individual feats in the capturing of notorious criminals, may be thrust temporarily into the limelight . . . [but] it is the policy of the division of investigation to have no recognized 'aces' or 'big shots.'" The article did say that Hoover was "particularly pleased at the vindication of Agent Melvin H. Purvis, who had been severely criticized by some outsiders." But, it quickly added, "Hoover is anxious now that the noise and tumult die down in order that the men may return to their work in relative obscurity."

Beyond these largely successful attempts to spin the Dillinger story, Hoover exploited Cowley's continued presence in Chicago. Through Cowley he was able to monitor and regulate Purvis's dealings with the press. A day after the arrest of Harold Cassidy, the second doctor involved in Dillinger's facial surgery, Hoover phoned Cowley to discuss the release of the news. "I inquired who gave out the press statement at Chicago," Hoover recorded in a September 1 memorandum. "Mr. Cowley stated that Mr. Purvis gave out the statement, though he, Mr. Cowley, was present at the time . . . I told him I felt he should be at the Commissioner's office, and should make whatever appearance or statement found to be necessary." Hoover strove to keep Cowley out in front of the story, even though FBI files suggest that the taciturn Cowley was less interested in, and likely less adept at, dealing with the media than was Purvis.

Hoover remained threatened by Purvis's close relationship with reporters, or at least the ease of his rapport with them. On September 3 he had Ed Tamm investigate a leak of information about Anna Sage that he blamed on Purvis. "I asked whether there was a possibility that Mr. Purvis had given out this information and Mr. Cowley

stated no," Tamm said. "I told Mr. Cowley that the Director wants
him to indicate to Mr. Purvis that he should shut off the steam on
this thing and don't give anything out like this." Tamm again noted
Cowley's assurance that the leak was not from him or anyone in
Chicago, but he also warned Cowley that Purvis "should be very
careful in this regard."

Despite Hoover's concerns about Purvis's chattiness with the media, Purvis did not much change his approach to the press in the
weeks following Dillinger's death. After the initial wave of interviews, Purvis generally resumed his normal reticence. He did not,
for instance, cooperate with any reporter for a full-length magazine
article, as did Cowley with *American Detective.* On August 7, Walter
Winchell, the *New York Daily Mirror* gossip writer and the most influential columnist in the country, stopped in Chicago on his way from
Los Angeles to New York. He visited the Bankers Building and met
with Purvis, pestering him for inside information about the
Dillinger case. "Mr. Winchell asked questions which had been asked
repeatedly by other newspaper men, particularly concerning the
source of the tip, and the identity of the person, or persons, who
fired the shots, and I of course declined to discuss any of these matters with him," Purvis related to Hoover on August 9. Winchell later
complained about the meeting to Hoover, with whom he was close.
"In Chicago my paper's editor there assigned me to try and 'break'
Purvis with a story on the late John D.," Winchell wrote to Hoover.
"But Purvis wouldn't budge with any worthy comment and my re-
portorial prestige, as it is called, suffered no little."

Such assurances were not enough to satisfy Hoover. He continued to rely on Cowley to keep tabs on Purvis. Although he had originally sent Cowley to Chicago to focus solely on Dillinger, he now
saw an advantage in broadening this mandate. In a September 6
letter, Hoover granted Cowley wide-ranging stewardship over
Chicago's big cases. "In addition to the supervision of the Dillinger
case I desire that you personally assume control and direction over
all investigation of the [Edward George] Bremer kidnapping case,"
Hoover began, referring to the crime that brought Alvin Karpis and
members of the Barker gang into the Bureau's orbit. "I desire that
you also assume personal supervision of all angles of the Kansas City
Massacre case," Hoover continued, adding Pretty Boy Floyd to Cowley's mix. Furthermore, "I desire that you continue in Chicago in

your present capacity of supervision of all remaining angles of the Dillinger case"—which meant, of course, tracking down Baby Face Nelson. Hoover also gave Cowley authority over field offices associated with these cases, essentially entrusting him with the supervision of the entire Midwest. But once again Hoover did not accompany these new marching orders with any official statement or redesignation of personnel. "I told [Cowley] that I am not sending a copy of this letter to either St. Paul or Kansas City for the reason that I feared if I did this, there would be even less work performed in these two districts," Hoover explained.

Cowley, for one, seemed stunned by his broad new powers. His arrangement in Chicago was awkward, to be sure, but he and Purvis had found a way to make it work. There was, if not a friendship between them, at least a healthy respect, as well as the inevitable collegiality that develops over long weeks spent in the same bunker. Now Cowley was being ordered to usurp Purvis's authority in the matter of Pretty Boy Floyd, a case he had not worked. "Mr. Cowley suggested that Mr. Purvis be furnished with a copy of the letter [about the change]," Hoover recorded in a September 5 memorandum, "since up to date he, Mr. Cowley, had had no supervision over the Kansas City Massacre case. I told him I would see that Mr. Purvis receives a copy of this letter, and the letter will be phrased to indicate that he, Mr. Cowley, is on special assignment from Washington, operating out of Chicago." The director was pushing Cowley to play a larger and more visible role in the ongoing war on crime—in effect, to act as Hoover's surrogate. Hoover's blunt efforts to direct attention away from Purvis and toward Cowley would have profound and unexpected consequences for both men.

This move by Hoover further corroded his relationship with Purvis, which had been strained since early 1934, when the pressure of seizing Dillinger weighed heavily on Hoover, and he began to question Purvis's capability. Still, not all civility was lost. Hoover quickly approved raises for both Purvis and Cowley; he bumped Purvis from $5,600 a year to $5,800. Purvis responded by trying to rekindle their old camaraderie, inviting Hoover in late August to visit him in Chicago on his way to an American Bar Association meeting in Milwaukee. "Hope you will be able to stay in Chicago a few days," Purvis wired. "Bill McSwain is a member of the Union

League Club here and is making arrangements so that you and your party will have the entire courtesies of the club if you so desire . . . Mac and I both believe you would enjoy it." Hoover's response was cordial: "I received your telegram and want to let you know how grateful I am to Mac and you for your thoughtfulness . . . I will probably be in Chicago only a few hours passing through en route to Milwaukee, so it will hardly be worth while for Mac to make these arrangements." Around the same time, Hoover sent Purvis a section of the London *Evening Standard* that featured photos of Purvis and Dillinger, another unsubtle jibe at Purvis's celebrity. Purvis responded, "You state you thought I would enjoy receiving this item which appeared in the paper, but if you realized how fatigued I became at examining my own physiognomy when I shave in the morning, you would understand that the observance of my photograph must not be the most pleasant occupation. Let's hope that all of the photographic cuts have now become worn out." On July 28, Purvis received a letter from Hoover requesting he sign copies of a photograph showing Hoover greeting Purvis at Washington's Union Station after Dillinger's death. "It appears necessary to have the photographic unit work overtime to supply the demands of your 'public' for copies of your picture," Hoover wrote. "What is this power?" At the bottom of the letter, Hoover drew an arrow from this last question and, in his own hand, added, "P.S. The fact, Mel, is that Miss Gandy actually prepared this letter, so her question nonplussed me." If Hoover's secretary did indeed script this remark, it was, coincidentally, quite similar to earlier observations Hoover made along the same lines. Certainly he could have struck the comment had he wished.

Yet these friendly letters were outnumbered by the barrage of criticisms and procedural admonishments Purvis received in the weeks after Dillinger's killing. Just two days after saluting Purvis's "capacity as a leader and an executive," Hoover sent him another letter, this one curt and addressed "Dear Sir."

> Your attention is called to previous requests by the Division for three photographs of yourself . . . will you please give this matter your immediate attention so that the photographs may be available for the Division files?

Hoover also complained about getting a busy signal on Purvis's unlisted telephone at the Bankers Building. "In order that there will be no misunderstanding in the future, I wish to state that the unlisted telephone located in your office should not be used for any other purpose than communicating between Washington and the field office," Hoover scolded in a September 12 letter. In another instance, he chastised Purvis for venturing out of Chicago without submitting a leave slip. Purvis appeared exasperated. "I did not depart from Chicago," he replied in an August 23 letter, "and I have no sufficient explanation to offer for my failure to submit these slips. I regret that this matter was overlooked by me." Hoover swooped into the Bankers Building for a personal inspection of the office in late August. What he found there displeased him. "I was surprised to note that not only was the cabinet containing [firearms] unlocked, but that the room in which the cabinet was located was unlocked, and at the time I visited the room there was no one in the room," Hoover wrote on September 4. Hoover's concern, apparently, was that gangsters would somehow gain entry to the unlocked cabinet: "I cannot emphasize too strongly my insistence that the proper precaution be taken by you in the proper safeguarding of this equipment in order to avoid any theft thereof or seizure thereof by elements of the underworld."

Perhaps the most bizarre admonishment arrived on September 13.

In the telephone conversations with you at Chicago from Washington, I have had considerable difficulty in distinctly understanding you. I do not know whether it is due to any technical difficulty with your telephone, or whether it is due to the fact that you do not speak loudly enough to be heard. I have had the phone checked here, and found that our phone is technically satisfactory. I would suggest that you have your phone checked because this condition has existed over a rather long period. It might also be desirable for you to speak in a little louder tone of voice in your conversations over the long distance.

Purvis's typically formal reply implies that he wondered why Hoover did not simply ask him to raise his voice during their conversations: "In accordance with your suggestion, I am having the telephones checked to determine if there is anything wrong here. I recall two occasions when Mrs. Kelly or Miss Gandy have requested me to talk louder, and I have done so. I will endeavor to see what the difficulty is and to correct it at once." Of course, these petty critiques, mixed in with complimentary letters, represented classic Hoover. He was as quick to condemn as he was to commend. To have earned Hoover's professional and even personal admiration, as Purvis seemed to have done, provided little long-term immunity from his wrath. Hoover's greeting—Mel, Mr. Purvis, Sir—varied with his mood, or more precisely with his current impression of Purvis's efficiency. This practice, however, was not reserved for Purvis; nearly every agent was at the mercy of Hoover's whimsical judgments. "It's like the old fight films from the 1920s and '30s: 'He's down, he's up, he's down, he's up, he's down again!'" said Joe Koletar, an FBI special agent from 1969 to 1994. During his tenure Koletar worked in the Bureau's personnel section and had occasion to review the files of many agents, including Melvin Purvis's. "The Bureau was very small back then and Hoover probably knew every agent personally," Koletar noted. "And in the space of just a year you could see from the personnel files that an agent had been demoted and then promoted, demoted and promoted, over and over. He would do something to irritate Hoover, then he would do something that Hoover liked and he would be back in his graces. And Purvis was one of those agents who was up and down a few times in his career."

Another source of tension was the Bureau's handling of Anna Sage. The bullet that ended Dillinger's life did not close the Dillinger case; many loose ends remained. There were the allegations that Sgt. Martin Zarkovich, who helped deliver Dillinger to the Bureau, had known Dillinger and had been aware of his whereabouts for weeks. The implication was that Zarkovich used Purvis to have Dillinger killed. "Zarkovich put Dillinger on the spot in order that they might gain possession of Dillinger's wealth," Matt Leach of the Indiana State Police advised the Bureau, claiming an informant had implicated Zarkovich. Purvis assured Hoover that "neither Captain O'Neill nor Zarkovich indicated at any time that they had any particular desire to have Dillinger killed. As a matter of fact both Mr. Cowley and I remember their contemplated plans as to where they would have Dillinger held when he was caught." Cowley told Hoover he believed Leach's accusations were "a frame-up," and Hoover agreed the Indiana police were "jealous because they didn't get [Dillinger] themselves." In any case, Hoover saw no advantage in pursuing the allegations, and on July 31 he sent both Zarkovich and O'Neill letters expressing his gratitude for their cooperation.

This letter meant both men remained eligible to earn a share of the reward for Dillinger's capture, which was set at $10,000. Purvis acknowledged the officers were responsible for setting Dillinger's killing in motion, and O'Neill, for one, was grateful not to have been ignored by the Bureau. "Permit me also to express my appreciation of the unselfish attitude assumed by your Mr. Purvis," O'Neill wrote to Hoover in response to Hoover's letter of commendation. "In cases as spectacular as this there is the temptation to let none of the credit of achievement get away. My hat [is] off to Mr. Purvis." Yet Purvis did not believe either officer deserved a share of the $10,000; what had they done except bring Anna Sage to him? "Purvis suggested that they not be given any part of the reward," Hoover noted in a July 30 memorandum, "since they rendered little assistance." In the end, however, Purvis agreed with Cowley to give the men a share, and O'Neill and Zarkovich received $2,125 each. Three other East Chicago officers were awarded $250 each.

That left $5,000, earmarked for Anna Sage. On Lincoln Avenue the night of the killing, Sage had drifted discreetly away from Dillinger lest she get in the way of a federal bullet. When the first shot shattered the quiet, she hurried with Polly Hamilton to the corner; then the two women hiked up their skirts and ran. Sage went straight to her apartment and immediately changed out of her soon-to-be famous outfit. Perhaps unwisely, she returned to the Biograph later that night, but all that remained of the man she betrayed were his bloodstains. Sage's biggest fear was that her identity would be revealed, inviting retribution from Dillinger's cohorts. She, too, had been unprepared for the extraordinary reaction to Dillinger's killing. Terrified that she would soon be discovered, she turned to the one man she felt she could trust: Purvis. On July 23 she had Zarkovich drive her to the Bankers Building, where she intended to ask for protection. But Cowley took the meeting, not Purvis, and later told Hoover that Sage was "most hysterical . . . she is upset over the fact that the East Chicago people got themselves in the papers, and . . . she believes that this in itself is enough to put her on the spot." Cowley could not help Sage until he conferred with Hoover, and in the meantime she spent another frightening night in her apartment. Meanwhile, Purvis took O'Neill and Zarkovich to lunch in Chicago and persuaded them not to divulge any more details about the shooting that might help reporters identify Sage.

But then Chicago detectives showed up to arrest Sage in her apartment. She fished out the scrap of paper with the phone number Purvis had given her and frantically called him. The detectives took her to the Sheffield precinct house and questioned her there for hours; reporters soon had enough information to write about a mysterious female informant dubbed the Lady in Red. Cowley succeeded in wresting Sage from the Chicago police and ordered two agents to drive her and Polly Hamilton—summoned to the Bankers Building by Sage—to the safety of a nondescript hotel in Detroit. They remained there while Cowley, Purvis, and Hoover hashed out the matter of Sage's two demands. Fulfilling Purvis's first promise— that Sage would receive a substantial reward—would be the easy part. Hoover agreed to give her $5,000, though he scoffed at her request to hurry the payment; it was not until October that Cowley personally presented Sage with $5,000 in cash.

The question of staying her deportation was far trickier. Purvis played the part of Sage's counsel and tried to fashion a deal that could work. It did not help that Sage wanted to return to Chicago, where she risked being arrested again or uncovered by reporters. Very quickly, Hoover was becoming annoyed with the woman most responsible for his Bureau's greatest success. "If they want to take the chance of being 'put on the spot' it is up to them," Hoover told Purvis. "If the informant insists upon returning to Chicago when we advise against it, I [see] no reason why we should concern ourselves about her." Hoover also indicated he would not be willing to fight very hard to keep Sage in the United States. "She will not help the immigration situation by returning to Chicago now," he told Purvis, "because the immigration authorities will probably deport her before we have all the 'kinks ironed out.'"

Purvis, on the other hand, was adamant that his promise to Sage be honored. He had given his word that the Bureau would do its best to help her. Much later, after Sage's identity became public, Purvis issued a strong public statement in support of her campaign to stop the deportation.

Certainly the service which she performed for the government and,
for that matter, for the people of this country in aiding in ridding the
country of this menace should not be belittled. She did furnish the
information which led to Dillinger's capture, and I for one am not
ungrateful, and I sincerely believe that some step should be taken,
whatever that step might necessarily be, to prevent her deportation.
She desires to remain in the United States, and as a part of her reward for having furnished the information referred to, I believe that
she should be allowed to do so.

It was, in many ways, a courageous statement for such a highly regarded law officer to make. Sage was a prostitute, a brothel owner, a
swindler. There was absolutely nothing to gain from taking up her
cause. Yet here was Purvis championing her as a patriot and insisting
she was more than worthy of citizenship.

In mid-August, it looked as if a deal might be reached. The Department of Labor agreed to hold her deportation warrant in
abeyance for three months, provided Sage leave Chicago and stay
clear of the law. "If she is out of Chicago by that time, they will not
forward [the warrant] any place else; [but] if she is there and is
picked up, she will go head over heels out of the country," Ed Tamm
recorded in an August 16 memorandum. Cowley took the terms to
Sage and reported to Hoover that "she is very excited and wants to
get out of town but says she is broke." Cowley lent Sage $100, and
soon she was on a bus to Los Angeles.

Sage vanished for a while, but both she and her troubles quickly
resurfaced. Perhaps her mistake was returning to Chicago, which
she eventually did, though it does not appear she ran afoul of the
law again. In any case, Indiana officials renewed their efforts to have
her deported for her past transgressions. When she had to fight
again to stay in the country in late 1935, neither Purvis nor Cowley
was in a position to help her in any way. Hoover, by then more powerful than ever thanks in large part to Anna Sage, let every opportunity to assist her slip by. Sage petitioned Indiana Governor McNutt
for a pardon, but he, too, declined to help. Federal judge John
Barnes presided over a deportation hearing in October 1935 and
heard supportive testimony from Sage's old friend, Martin
Zarkovich. But the assurances Purvis had given Sage carried no legal
weight. On January 22, 1936, the U.S. Court of Appeals denied

Sage's petition to stay in the country. Three months later she was put on a train to Ellis Island and from there escorted onto the steamship *President Harding*. She died in Romania, of liver failure, in 1947.

———

Purvis had vowed to do everything in his power to prevent Sage from being deported, but once he was no longer able to help her, the only other Bureau man who could have done anything— Hoover—looked the other way. Purvis never publicly condemned Hoover for the broken promise, but since he made no secret of his strong support for Sage, it has long been speculated that Sage's deportation was, for Purvis, the final straw that shattered his friendship with Hoover. In fact, by the time the *Harding* disappeared over the Atlantic horizon, Purvis already had a host of reasons to suspect that Hoover was not, in any sense of the word, a friend.

The reckoning wrought by Sage's tip continued in the weeks after Dillinger's death. Federal agents picked up Louis Piquett, his crafty lawyer, on August 31; he was sent to prison for harboring a fugitive. Wilhelm Loeser, the doctor who saved Dillinger's life before trying surgery to alter the gangster's face, was returned to federal prison on existing drug charges. On August 23 police in St. Paul gunned down Homer Van Meter; he died, just as his friend Dillinger had, in an alley. "His trigger finger was a split-second slow and the blazing fire from a police machine gun felled him as he fled," eulogized the *Washington Post*. "Dillinger must have been born under an evil star," Purvis would later say. "Those whose lives touched his either went to prison, died ignominiously by electrocution, committed suicide or were killed by law-enforcement officers."

Other menaces remained. In Washington, Hoover had gathered an array of Dillinger artifacts—a white plaster death mask made at the Cook County morgue, Dillinger's straw boater, his shattered silver-rimmed glasses, his unsmoked La Corona–Belvedere cigar—and arranged them in display cases in the anteroom to his office. But by the time the displays were ready for viewing, Hoover was already hunting new game. He still seethed at the thought that Baby Face Nelson was free, but in summer 1934 he demoted Nelson on his list of villains. It was time, he believed, that the Bureau find and bring to justice a killer who had eluded capture for more than a year. Thus it was that Pretty Boy Floyd became Public Enemy Number One.

In the Bankers Building, Purvis worked his cases. He was famous now, and with fame came attention both desired and destructive. Three days after Dillinger's killing, Purvis received a letter containing a death threat; it was signed by Dillinger's pal, John Hamilton. Four days after that, a Louisville broadcaster came over the radio late at night to announce that Purvis had been killed. An Associated Press reporter called Washington for confirmation and also called the Chicago coroner's office. Finally he dialed Purvis's unlisted home telephone number. A groggy Purvis answered and assured the reporter that he was, indeed, still alive.

Surely Purvis was beginning to suspect during this period that he faced threats not only from outside the Bureau but from within as well. "Purvis was not stupid," said Doris Lockerman. "He was not unaware. We had the feeling that he knew everything that was going on around him all the time, but that he was trying to rise above it. He was behaving like a gentleman. He was trying to maintain the proper respect and hoping that Hoover would come to his senses and realize he was being petty. But he knew. Melvin Purvis would not have been the top FBI man had he not been very perceptive."

Soon another gangster episode would once again thrust Purvis into the spotlight, which in turn only made the bulls-eye on his back more visible. But in the scorching summer of 1934, he had—in addition to Hoover's increasing animus—the goodwill of a nation that believed itself in his debt. Purvis received more than 400 letters congratulating him for snagging Dillinger. He heard from politicians and from ordinary people, from movie producers and from CEOs. He heard from women who, smitten with his good looks, offered to reward him for his valor in person; he heard from Walter Winchell, who said, "I told you that you would wind up getting the glory." Reading the notes, he must have felt enormous pride, until he came to one particular letter, which likely evoked a different emotion. "My dear Melvin," it began. "I know you will get and have gotten a great many letters and you no doubt will think that here is just another one of congratulations . . . Well, my boy, we are all proud of you and I know that you feel relieved and feel that you have truly accomplished something worthwhile. I hope that you will never have to go through with two such hours again." The letter, from a married woman in Baltimore, continued, "You are a celebrity now and I want to tell you—whether you believe it or not—that I am very happy for you . . . Melvin, I hope you will be careful—you have such a hazardous job."

The letter, which today is buried among hundreds of others in Purvis's personnel file, bore a familiar signature: *Rosanne.*

10

PRETTY BOY

October 20, 1934
WELLSVILLE, OHIO

Something evil came to Wellsville in the dead of night. It came to the hill where young Ducky Fryman lived with his family. Ducky's real name was Harold but nobody called him that, because they could always find him wading in the nearby Ohio River. On the morning of October 20, Ducky had finished his main chore—rummaging for dry branches and sumac plants his father could use for kindling wood—and was idly kicking stones, trying to kill the long morning hours. He could not have known that in moments something would occur to electrify the sleepy town of Wellsville.

Down the hill, Ducky's father Joseph worked his small strip of garden between the railroad tracks and the two-lane road that separated his home from the river. An early frost had killed some of the vegetables he relied on to feed his four sons and four daughters. Before the Depression ravaged Wellsville, Joe Fryman worked the assembly line at the American Sheet and Tin Plate Company. But like most people in town, he watched his job disappear. To provide for his family, he grew tomatoes, corn, squash, peppers, and potatoes; his wife Emily, barely five feet and not quite 100 pounds, canned enough for the cold winter months. By this October morning, most of the garden's bounty had already been harvested, but there were still a few runty tomatoes and peppers glazed over by the frost, which Joe tenderly picked and placed in a basket.

Joe's young son-in-law David O'Hanlon stopped by to help Joe haul a load of coal. It was common practice in Wellsville to get coal from McLain's brickyard, now closed, in the part of town called Silver Switch. For years freight cars dumped coal into huge piles at the brickyard, where it was used to fire the kilns that forged the brick. But now the yard was shuttered, and people like Joe made "secret requisitions," sneaking into the yard and skimming coal off the pile to use to heat their homes. A watchman at the brickyard, spying a truck pulling up or a man pushing a wheelbarrow, always looked the other way.

Joe Fryman himself never hesitated to help others when he could. He always ran food out to the transients who camped along the river hills on their way from town to town. The hoboes would rest a day or two, scrounge for meals, and move on after leaving behind some kind of marker—a scratched message in a tree, perhaps—to let the next set of vagabonds know they could find a meal there. Joe Fryman never chased any rovers away from his property, but once they were gone, he'd make a point of going to their campsite and clearing away any signal or marker left behind.

Helping ragged hoboes was one thing. But the two men in suits he spotted on the hill that bright fall morning did not look like itinerants. They were too well-dressed, and too carefree in the way they lounged on blankets, as if they were picnicking. Joe's gut told him something wasn't right. They were on property owned by Lon Israel, an old widower too frail and weak to scatter the men by himself. Joe was not a physically imposing man—he was balding and a wiry five feet eight inches—but he was as tough as the sheets of steel he used to pound. He was known to hoist heavy railroad ties, one on each shoulder, and march up hills without breaking stride. His instinct now was to confront the strangers on the hill. Under the guise of inspecting some pear trees near the clearing for frost damage, Joe and his son-in-law approached the two men up near Israel's home.

He found one of the men, the taller, broader of the two, sitting on the grass a few feet away from the other. Keeping track of both their movements was tricky. Joe asked the men their business. "We are out here taking pictures," the taller one replied, explaining how they were driving with their girlfriends and got lost. Their women would soon return from a trip into town, and then they would be on their way. The men were friendly enough, thought Joe, but where was the camera if they were taking pictures? "Do you live right down there?" the tall one asked Joe, pointing to his house. The question was menacing enough for Joe to lie and say he lived elsewhere. Well then, the stranger said, ending the small talk, "If you see a couple of girls down there on the street, tell them to come on up, we're waiting on them."

As Joe returned to his house, he encountered Lon Israel returning from the Frail convenience store. Israel had to cross Joe's property to get to the store, and he liked to stop on his way back to share a few words with his friend. He was perturbed to hear Joe tell him two mysterious fellows were loitering on his property. "Sounds fishy to me," said Israel, who trudged back to the store and asked its proprietor, Mary Frail, to use her phone—the only one for miles—to telephone the police.

That is how Sheriff John Fultz, Wellsville's chief law-enforcement official, learned that two strange men had spooked townsfolk near Silver Switch. Ten years on the job and privy to crime bulletins from most of the Midwest and the eastern seaboard, Fultz knew of the special circumstances that might endanger his town. The tip about the strangers carried far more significance for him than Joe Fryman or Lon Israel could have imagined. Fultz turned to two men idling away the morning at the station and told them to come along. Of the three, only Fultz was armed.

Ducky Fryman watched unnoticed from a few hundred feet away as the three groups of men—his father and Lon Israel, Fultz and his two tagalongs, and the two strangers on the hill—converged in the clearing behind Israel's home just past noon. Ducky heard popping sounds, cracks, so many he couldn't count. He heard crisp ricochets behind him, heard missiles whiz past his face. The bullets came so close they snapped the air around Ducky's ears, small sonic booms he would hear again years later as a grown man fighting in the Pacific during World War II. This day, Ducky heard his father yelling, "Get in the house, get in the house!" But Ducky did not move. In a matter of seconds the shooting was over and the men were dispersed. Ducky watched the taller stranger ditch something beneath a rabbit hutch and run for the woods—the very woods from which Ducky had gathered his family's kindling. "And then he was gone," recalled Fryman, now eighty-three. "He just slipped into the trees and disappeared."

The man loosed upon Wellsville was tall, with broad shoulders, a dark blue suit, no tie, no hat. He was a man who had robbed at least forty banks, and maybe as many as sixty; a man who had already picked out his gravesite, a plot his mother tended to keep it ready for when the time came; a man with ten fingers but only six fingerprints, the identifying ridges on the tips of four fingers sandpapered off; a man in possession of a green gold Verithin Gruen watch with an even ten notches carved in its crystal face, one for each of the ten men he had shot to death.

In the hours after this man vanished into the Wellsville woods, fathers across the area took their old shotguns from closets and cupboards and told their frightened wives to lock the doors and windows. A posse of men, more than 200, set out in groups of two and three to comb the tangled forests and scan for glimpses of flesh or clothing between the clusters of trees. It fell to these ordinary citizens, hastily deputized by Sheriff Fultz, to find this man before further mayhem came to their town. It would be three more days before any of them could be sure that the man they were chasing, the monster in their midst, was, in fact, Public Enemy Number One—Pretty Boy Floyd.

The telephone rang just as Melvin Purvis finished a late Sunday morning breakfast in his hotel suite. He had checked into Cincinnati's Alms Hotel under an assumed name, Mr. Marshall, an alias he used to keep reporters off his trail. Since the Dillinger killing, the press had taken to following Purvis and reporting, bulletin-style, on his comings and goings. Secret missions, they called them, meaning only that they did not know his plans. Part of the reason the press chased Purvis so intently was that he shared so little of himself with them. "Dealing with the public, Purvis is a clam personified," the *Cincinnati Enquirer* lamented. "The ubiquitous reply he has to all questions is, 'Sorry, Colonel, I have no comment to make.'"

Yet Purvis's reticence only fanned the public's interest in him. Hoover, intent on saving publicity for himself, would have to take covert steps to lower his agent's profile. One such step was to pull him off the Robinson kidnapping, a case Purvis had been working hard to solve. Thomas H. Robinson had kidnapped Alice Stoll in

Louisville on Wednesday, October 10, and Purvis had flown to Cincinnati on the strength of reports that placed the fleeing Robinson in the area. He had followed the fugitive's trail across three states, and felt he was one lucky break away from capturing him. Purvis had even driven Robinson's abandoned Ford sedan, key evidence in the case, from Cincinnati to Louisville, where he testified before a grand jury about his involvement in the pursuit of Robinson.

After testifying, Purvis called Hoover, who told him that publicity about his whereabouts was hurting the Bureau's efforts to find Robinson. Purvis felt that he and his crew had been trying hard to keep their movements under wraps and had, by and large, succeeded. But Hoover was adamant and told Purvis to quit the case immediately. Purvis did as he was told and packed up for Chicago.

He got as far as Indianapolis before his stubbornness took hold. Purvis and his men—Sam McKee, Bud Hopton, and John Connor, the so-called Chicago Wrecking Crew—bristled at Hoover's directive to give up on Robinson just as the hunt was heating up. Their dull desks back in Chicago did not beckon. In Indianapolis, Purvis telephoned Hoover with an idea. "I believed a plan could be worked out which would allow our operation to be more secret," he later explained. "We could set up headquarters in a hotel in the outlying section of Cincinnati and operate separately from the Cincinnati office."

Hoover agreed to let Purvis continue on the case. Purvis and his agents returned to Cincinnati and booked rooms at the Alms Hotel. They arrived late on the afternoon of Saturday October 20, went to bed early, and slept late into the morning. Around noon the telephone rang, and everything changed.

The call was from H. D. Harris, acting special-agent-in-charge of the Cincinnati office. Harris had information about a gunfight in Wellsville, Ohio, and about a Sheriff John Fultz who claimed to have captured Adam Richetti. Richetti, among the most wanted men in the country, was Pretty Boy Floyd's running pal and an accomplished bank robber in his own right. Harris further reported that Fultz had wounded a second man before he vanished in the woods. Purvis did not need to be told that this second man was most likely Floyd.

Harris's call to Purvis triggered a swift and massive mobilization of federal manpower. Purvis called Washington and told Hoover his plans: He was dropping the Robinson case to concentrate on Floyd.

Hoover had no choice but to dispatch Purvis on yet another dramatic manhunt he knew would make headlines across the country. Purvis and his men checked out of the Alms and headed for the Cincinnati airport. On little notice, Purvis managed to book a small plane for the short ride across Ohio. He spent most of the trip staring silently out the window at the Ohio forests below. Purvis felt a familiar mix of adrenaline and dread. There was nothing about these urgent searches that excited him or struck him as glamorous; for him, they were necessary but terrifying parts of the job.

The flight was uneventful until its last minutes. Their destination, the tiny Wellsville airport, was closed for repairs, its landing strip too decrepit to be used. The pilot advised they continue to Pittsburgh, forty miles to the east. Purvis balked; he had no intention of wasting an hour driving backward from Pittsburgh. He would cede nothing to Floyd in their looming battle, certainly not the advantage of yet another hour's head start. Purvis insisted that the pilot land in Wellsville. The pilot argued against it but Purvis held firm. The plane banked steeply and nosed downward toward the airstrip, which was littered with construction equipment. The landing lights were not working at all in the dusk. No one spoke as the plane made its sharp descent and finally touched ground at 6:30 in the evening, bouncing along the jagged strip, throttling forcefully back, skidding off the end of the runway before, at last, stopping "on a dime," Purvis later recalled. The ashen pilot switched off the power and finally took a breath.

————

Three days earlier, Charlie Floyd, foot pressed hard on the gas pedal of his blue Ford sedan, didn't see the telephone pole until he ran into it. Neither did his scrawny sidekick, Adam Richetti, asleep in the back seat, or the two sad-faced women with them, sisters Rose and Beulah Baird. Their late-night ride along the Ohio River on the way to Kansas City, begun several hours earlier in Buffalo, had been bumpy but quiet, until in the heavy morning fog Floyd lost his bearings for an instant and swerved headfirst into a pole along Route 7. The crash sounded worse than it was. Floyd and his passengers were banged up but not seriously hurt. The two-year-old V-8 Ford, purchased three days earlier with $350 of Floyd's stolen money, sustained serious front-end damage. Its fender and hood were badly mangled, but with a little straightening out, Floyd figured, it should be able to get them to their destination. The groggy men shook off their stiffness and surveyed the lonely landscape. On the run from federal agents, they were suddenly stuck in the remote town of Wellsville, Ohio.

This was not the first time that car trouble had landed them in a tight spot. On June 16, 1933, fresh from robbing the Farmers and Merchant Bank of Mexico in Missouri and making off with $1,628, Floyd and Richetti had driven their Pontiac coupe into Bitzer's Garage in Bolivar, Missouri, so that Richetti's brother Joe, a mechanic there, could fix a damaged fender. The boys had banged up the Pontiac driving it through a set of locked garage doors while stealing it from an Oklahoma schoolteacher. It was their bad luck that Sheriff Jack Killingsworth of Polk County pulled into the garage shortly after they did, to gas up his cruiser and catch up with his friend Ernest Bitzer. Richetti recognized the plainclothes sheriff and rashly yanked a machine gun from the Pontiac. Floyd had no choice but to train his two .45s on the six people in the garage and hold them at bay while Richetti moved their arsenal of weapons into his brother's car. "This is life and death with us," Floyd, polite as ever, explained to his captives. "We have to do it; they would kill us if they could." Later, Sheriff Killingsworth remarked on how impressed he was with Floyd's courtly manner. "I saw right away, he was a right nice fellow," he told reporters. "He would kill a man, but not unless he had to."

Floyd did not have to kill anyone that day. Once Richetti had filled up the car, Floyd let five of the hostages go; he ordered the sixth, Killingsworth, into the back of the new getaway car. The gangsters drove to Deepwater, Missouri, and forced the sheriff to flag down a brand-new Pontiac. They made it their new getaway car, and its driver, Walter Griffith, their new hostage. They finally let both men go in Kansas City late that night. The next day, June 17, 1933, Floyd and Richetti played their parts in the Kansas City massacre, killing four law enforcement officers.

They spent the next eighteen months on the run, the most wanted criminals in the country besides John Dillinger. Those were hard, melancholy months for Floyd, who could not shake his deep feelings of dread and doom. "How would you like to be hunted day and night?" he complained to Killingsworth during the abduction. "Sooner or later I'll go down full of lead." Floyd saw himself as a victim of his zealous pursuers. "I am not as bad as they say I am," he wrote in a typically morose letter to an Ohio newspaper not long after the Kansas City massacre. "They just wouldn't leave me alone after I got out."

Indeed, Floyd was never considered as depraved and ruthless as Baby Face Nelson or Clyde Barrow, the ten killings to his credit notwithstanding. Many who knew him could not be shaken from their view that Floyd was more mischievous than murderous, a good-natured clod caught up in unfortunate circumstances. One of seven kids raised by a moonshining cotton farmer in the lush Cookson Hills of eastern Oklahoma, he earned his nickname by showing up at a poker game with slicked-back hair and a sporty new suit. Driven to become something other than a farmer, he traded five gallons of homemade whiskey for a pearl-handled pistol and used it to steal $11,929 from a St. Louis bank. Perhaps the most romantic aspect of his legend is that while looting many banks, Floyd also ripped up loan and mortgage papers, in theory returning to citizens the money stolen from them by an uncaring government. Floyd was also, in his way, a family man. Married at twenty to Ruby Hargraves, he once presented their young son Jack with a heavy sack stuffed with coins. "When you want to take your friends out for ice cream," Jack recalled his father saying, "go right ahead."

Floyd's chief talent, though, was evading capture. To Hoover, Floyd's remarkable slipperiness was worse than galling—it was embarrassing. After the Kansas City massacre, Floyd and Richetti disappeared so thoroughly the Justice Department never had a single solid lead as to their whereabouts. The nation's newspapers even stopped writing about their favorite fugitive. Hoover did entertain reports that Floyd, through intermediaries, was trying to work out a deal to surrender. Hoover even acceded in principle to Floyd's main demand—that he not be put to death. But the director quickly tired of negotiating with someone he considered a multiple murderer, and instead began talking tough. "Orders are out to kill Floyd on sight," he would declare. "If we once catch up with him, we won't take any chance of his surrendering."

The government's increasing interest in him flushed Floyd out of his hiding spots in crime-ridden Cleveland and Detroit, the cities in which he burrowed after the Kansas City murders. In September 1933, he and Richetti figured their best move was to leave Ohio for Buffalo, New York, a city with no significant underworld and thus far less federal scrutiny. They would not weather the harsh Buffalo winter alone. Before setting off, Floyd called on Juanita Baird, his long-time moll, in Toledo, instructing her and her sister Rose, visiting from Kansas City, to pack their bags. "Charlie said that we were going with them; they did not say where," Rose later remembered. "We knew better than to ask questions."

Juanita, in particular, knew that being with Floyd involved a good deal of sacrifice. Homely and heavy-lidded, with a flat nose and a mole on the right cheek of her broad squat face, she met Floyd at her sister's house in 1929 when he was an ex-con making his living dealing dice in a Kansas City pool hall. Back then, Floyd had far more style than money. They married only weeks after meeting and moved to Colorado, but relocated frequently as Floyd's career as a bank robber took shape. In 1931, in a street-corner gun battle with police, Juanita took a bullet to the head. She survived, and she and Rose spent the next ten months in jail.

The new sacrifice for Juanita involved leaving her family in Toledo to hide out with Floyd and his unpleasant friend. Floyd, at least, could be fun and charming, but his pal, known as Eddie, was quiet, surly, strange. "He always sat around with his head down, saying nothing, which aggravated us," Rose later told federal agents. "During the time that we were in Buffalo, we barely got along." Floyd rented a five-room, second-floor apartment on 18th Street, under the name George Sanders. The dreary apartment, number 821, was their home for the next twelve months.

Little happened in Buffalo, which was just how the gangsters wanted it. Mostly, they sat around playing cards, rarely leaving the apartment. Occasionally, kids from the neighborhood knocked and asked for food, and once a fellow tenant and his wife stopped by, but otherwise Floyd took not a single visitor in the entire year. No mail arrived, no telegrams, no packages; the apartment did not even have a telephone. This was a place to hide, to wait, to cease to exist. In that way it was a sort of prison, and their lives in frigid Buffalo were a sort of penance. It might have gone on this way for many more months had Floyd not opened a newspaper one day in Octo-

ber 1934 and read about his indictment for his role in the Kansas
City massacre. Richetti's picture was in the paper, too. Out of sight
and mind for so long, they would now be big news again, tacked up
on every police blotter in the country. Juanita remembered the men
exchanging grave looks. The sisters knew enough to realize they
would have to pack again.

Shortly after reading the article, Floyd gave Juanita a wad of
money and told her to buy a car. She stopped by the Niagara Motor
Company and, using the name Byrl West, paid $350 for a blue Ford
coupe with Dunlop balloon tires and New York plates. "Charlie
asked us if we wanted to go home," remembered Rose. "We were all
more or less homesick but Juanita and I were the only ones that
mentioned that we would like to go home." Three days later they
were packed and gone, heading for Kansas City by way of Ohio.

Then came the early morning wreck in Wellsville, stranding them
on the banks of the Ohio River. Floyd reached into the banged-up
Ford and pulled his Thompson submachine gun from between the
two front seats. The plan was to have Juanita walk to town, find a
garage, and have a tow truck sent, while the men hid in the woods
until the car was fixed. Rose would wait in the car for her sister to return. The wet river fog had not yet lifted when Floyd and Richetti
clambered several hundred feet up the steep, wooded hill along
Route 7 and found a small clearing on a slope. They put down their
blankets near two big rocks and started a small twig fire to warm up.
Above them, the morning sky brightened; below, just past the highway and the railroad tracks, the lazy Ohio River ran indifferently, as
if this were the ordinary start to any ordinary day.

———

Sheriff John Fultz, more powerful in Wellsville than even its mayor,
was nothing if not decisive. After getting Lon Israel's call, he ges-
tured to the two men chatting with him at the police station,
William Irwin and Grover Potts, and dragged them into history.
"Come on, boys," he said, "go with me."

The three men climbed into a police cruiser and sped toward Silver Switch, Irwin and Grover unarmed and unaware of what was
happening. The sheriff, on the other hand, had an idea that this

might not be a routine nuisance call. A day earlier, reports had crossed his desk that two men had robbed the People's National Bank of Tiltonville, Ohio, thirty miles south of Wellsville.

A short, sturdy fellow with a pointy nose and flat, thin lips that curled at the edges into a winking smile, Fultz was an outsized personality in Wellsville, known for his generosity and sureness. The son of a riverboat pilot from West Virginia, he also had steered riverboats up and down the Allegheny and Ohio rivers in his early twenties, before a series of mild winters kept the water level low and grounded the boats. His brother William went to work for the railroads, but the extroverted Fultz turned to law enforcement, certainly a more social occupation. Rising to the rank of lieutenant, he was named Wellsville's chief of police and became the law in town. Besides him, the force consisted of one and occasionally two other officers; Fultz's decisions were final and he answered to no one. Wellsville citizens were fine with that and turned to Fultz as a kind of benevolent problem solver. He was the town's fixer, its go-to guy. His nephew Fred Fultz, now eight-five, recalled getting into a scrape with another teenager and winding up in front of his uncle. "The juvenile officer wanted to get me in trouble for beating this kid up, but I kept telling my uncle I didn't do it," Fred said. "Well, he had the juvenile officer over for dinner that night, and the problem went away just like that."

A man most himself in the approving gaze of others, Fultz never missed a chance to burnish his legacy. The call from Lon Israel stirred the protector in him. He drove into Wellsville on Kountz Avenue and stopped near the closed-down brickyard, ditching his car along the road and working his way up the hill on foot, Irwin and Potts beside him. They collected Israel in his front yard and set back down the hill to find the strangers. The confident Fultz, however, never reckoned that the surrounding trees and scraggly bushes put him at a disadvantage against his prey. This, after all, was Floyd's element; they did not call him the "Phantom of the Ozarks" for nothing. He proved immensely gifted at traversing the thickest of woods, on foot and even in a car. So many times he had been all but captured by small armies of police, only to slip their grasp and vanish again inside a forest. Here on a wooded hill in Wellsville, he would not likely be taken by surprise.

Indeed, it was Fultz and his men who were in for a jolt. They had walked only twenty-five feet when, quick as a heartbeat, Floyd sidled out from behind a tall clump of bushes. No rustling, no tip-off—suddenly, just there. "What do you want?" he demanded, stepping forward and producing a .45-caliber pistol. "Stick 'em up."

Fultz did not realize he was standing toe to toe with Pretty Boy Floyd. He had seen his likeness on wanted posters but did not link the expressionless photos with this scowling, square-jawed face. Still, by most accounts, Fultz's actions in the next moments were either incredibly courageous or quite foolish. For starters, he neither stopped nor raised his arms. "We have no business sticking them up," he told Floyd as he kept walking toward him. "We are just going down to the brickyard to work." Floyd wasn't buying it. He noticed Fultz move his hands toward his belt line. "Don't do that, I will shoot you," he ordered. "Fellow," said Fultz, "you don't need to think we are crazy."

Cocky as ever, Fultz kept walking toward the stranger. "I walked right into the gun and he held the gun against my stomach," is how Fultz remembered it. "I thought he would try to frisk me and I would get a chance to hit him." But Floyd merely backed up a step and allowed the men to pass. They continued down the hill, and Floyd fell in step behind them, gun still raised. "Now don't run or I will shoot you," he warned. "There's nobody going to run," said Fultz.

They marched single file for several yards, Fultz reaching for his belt again, Floyd threatening to fire. Fultz could not get far enough away from Floyd to make his move. In between them, Israel, Potts, and Irwin quietly followed Fultz's lead. They did not know that Floyd was steering them all into a trap. Near the bottom of a path, Fultz spotted Adam Richetti, lying leisurely on a blanket and propped up on his left elbow. "Hello, buddy," Fultz said, "you seem to be taking it pretty easy." Richetti smirked.

Fultz and his ragtag squad were pinned between the strangers. Floyd did not allow them time to figure a way out. "Don't let them kid you, he's an officer," Floyd yelled to his partner. "Shoot him."

Richetti bolted up, showed a pistol in his right hand, and fired at Fultz. The sheriff did not immediately return Richetti's fire; instead he shot back up the hill at Floyd. Floyd used Potts, Irwin, and Israel as shields and lobbed shots down the hill. Richetti emptied his gun at Fultz and stopped to reload; Fultz squeezed off three shots at Richetti before he ran out of bullets. Floyd finally emptied his .45 and ran to the blankets. He calmly reached beneath one and retrieved his prize: a stolen Thompson submachine gun, fully loaded. Floyd gripped its trigger and opened fire.

Luckily for Fultz, the gun jammed. Floyd got off only one shot, which lodged just beneath a second-floor windowsill on the side of Lon Israel's house. By then Israel had scrambled away and ducked into his home, where he dug out two double-barrel, twelve-gauge shotguns and gave them to Irwin and Potts. The newly armed men rejoined the shoot-out; Floyd, firing back with his revolver, hit Potts in the left shoulder. This was the opening Floyd needed. As Potts went down and Irwin ran for cover behind Israel's house, Floyd slipped away. While Fultz was busy loading two shells and chasing the fleeing Richetti down the hill, Floyd ran the other way, up the hill and toward the woods. He ditched the Tommy gun beneath a rabbit hutch and made for the tree line. "I ran around to the other corner of the house to throw me closer," Irwin remembered, "but when I got around I couldn't see anything of him." Floyd had disappeared.

Richetti, meanwhile, had trapped himself between his pursuers and the Ohio River. His only hope was to play every gangster's trump card—the willingness to slaughter civilians, something officers of the law took pains to avoid happening. Richetti hopped a fence and made for a one-story house near the bottom of the hill. Seconds before he got there, its owner, Irma La Russi, fastened the back lock. Richetti pounded on the door and heard a bullet explode in the wood only feet from his head. He turned to see Fultz running at him, gun blazing. Richetti quickly surrendered, even though it likely meant the end of his freedom, perhaps his life. "For God's sake, don't shoot me, don't kill me, I am done," Fultz recalled him pleading. The sheriff obliged, frisked his captive's pockets and sleeves, and ordered him to put his hands on his head. He marched him back to the road and turned him over to a deputy who had just arrived. Fultz had been grazed in the ankle and Floyd had escaped, but that was okay. The sheriff had a feeling he might have landed a very big fish indeed, and he was right.

———
—

Charlie Floyd had ditched his trusty Tommy gun but still had two fully loaded pistols as he ran a jagged path through the woods. Both guns were Model 11, U.S. Army issue Colt .45s, their serial numbers filed off. Floyd had also rigged one to shoot automatically—to empty the full magazine with a single squeeze on the trigger. He must have felt he had a decent chance to get away clean. There were acres of woods to hide in, far too many for Wellsville's puny police force to comb thoroughly. He could hold his breath ten feet from a pursuer and go unnoticed in the scraggy brush. If he could commandeer a car and get on the roads, he might even be able to clear out of Wellsville before the authorities set up roadblocks. And if he could get on the highway, he could make it to Youngstown, Ohio, just a short ride to the south, and there his underworld contacts would squirrel him away. Floyd surely knew the hour after the gunfight represented his best chance at cheating the law yet again.

Not long after fleeing, he came out of the woods, ruffled and dirty, on a hill above the Peterson place. In its open garage, two teenagers, Theodore and William Peterson, were working on a Ford with their friend George MacMillen. Floyd approached the boys and, all smiles, asked for a lift to Youngstown. "I will give you $10 if you fellows would be interested enough to drive me," he said.

The Peterson boys were interested and loaded Floyd into the Ford. But before they took off, their mother called down from the house. The brothers were due across the river at 1:00 P.M. on another errand, she reminded them, so they couldn't be wasting time driving to Youngstown. That, thought George MacMillen, was a lucky break for him. He led Floyd to his Model-T Ford and revved it up. He did not think it strange when Floyd instructed him to stay off the main highways and stick to side roads.

But then Floyd said, "I suppose you know who I am." MacMillen said he did not. "I am Floyd, Pretty Boy Floyd. The radios are flashing it all over the country. The papers are full of it." To drive the point home, Floyd pulled back his jacket and revealed one of his guns.

MacMillen understood. As he drove, his mind raced to hatch a plan to shed this menacing stranger. Chugging his Ford up the steep final stretch of Baum Road, he tugged on the choke and announced the car was out of gas. Floyd believed him. MacMillen idled the car and allowed it to drift backward into a ditch beside the road. Floyd got out and pushed, but the Ford was going nowhere. The burden of

Floyd's escape now shifted from MacMillen to another man—the owner of the greenhouse near where the Ford had stopped.

He was George Baum, a short, German-born father to two young girls. When he was younger, he made pottery, as so many men in clay-rich Wellsville did. But his doctors told him the pottery dust was bad for his health, and Baum took that as a signal to indulge his life-long fondness for flowers. In the greenhouse he built behind his home along Route 45, he raised snapdragons, lilies, and carnations, which he sold in Pittsburgh and in a little shop in Wellsville. That October morning, Baum's pet dog Curly roamed the dry grounds around the greenhouse while Baum, then sixty-five, loaded flowers into his tan 1929 Nash sedan. He noticed Floyd and MacMillen approach and stopped his work. "How about getting some gas, I will pay you for it," Floyd asked politely. Baum said he had no gas to give. "How about draining some out of your car?" Floyd responded. Baum said he wasn't able to siphon gas out of his car, and anyway he had no hose. Floyd then "thought he would like to have Mr. Baum to take him to a gas station," MacMillen recalled. "I thought that was a good idea . . . thought maybe we could notify police." Neither MacMillen nor Baum liked the looks of the stranger, but neither realized, as MacMillen later put it, "he was as bad an actor as he is. He seemed very nice and polite." Baum agreed to drive Floyd to get gas.

The three men were not in Baum's Nash for long before Floyd, from the back seat, stuck the larger of his two .45s between the men up front. "Old man, I have a surprise for you," he told Baum. "Just keep driving." With Floyd barking directions, Baum drove west on Township Line Road, picked up Route 45, and headed to Lisbon, one town over from Wellsville. From there it would not have been difficult for Floyd to get on Route 30 and disappear. The Nash got to within 100 yards of the Lisbon-Wellsville border, but that was it.

Floyd had John Fultz to thank for the setback. The sheriff had the foresight to contact police in Lisbon and ask for roadblocks on the three passage points between the towns. Without those roadblocks, Floyd would have been long gone. Charley Patterson of the Lisbon police department was lunching at the Hostetter[ck] Hotel when the Wellsville fire chief drove up and described the gunfight at Silver Switch. Patterson climbed on the fire truck's running board and held on as it raced to the city building. There, he teamed with Columbiana County deputy sheriff George Hayes. The Lisbon police department had a few more recruits than the Wellsville force, but it was no more sophisticated; its officers had to buy their own guns and hope the county could afford ammunition. Both Hayes and Patterson were fully armed that day—Patterson with a light sawed-off shotgun—when they drove together to the railroad crossing at the edge of Lisbon. There, they began stopping cars.

They had stopped about a dozen when Baum's Nash rolled toward the bridge over the creek that separated Lisbon from Wellsville. Just beyond the bridge was the roadblock. Seeing the police, Floyd ordered Baum to turn left off Route 45 and onto a dirt road that ran past a mill and over the railroad tracks. Sitting in the back, Floyd raised up from his crouch for a moment to steal a look out the window. It was a costly mistake. "When the car turned to the left to go down into the mill I saw what I thought was a head bob up and down in the rear," remembered George Hayes. "I told Patterson to watch where the car went." As luck would have it, boxcars were stopped on the railroad track, blocking any passage. Baum had no choice but to turn around and get back on Route 45. Hayes and Patterson watched the Nash reappear and drive away from them. They were sufficiently suspicious to abandon their roadblock. The chase was on.

With four or five cars between them and Baum's car, Hayes and Patterson followed the Nash onto Route 30. They tailed patiently until it jumped off the highway and onto an undulating dirt stretch aptly known as Roller-Coaster Road. Hayes hit his horn to warn traffic away and set off after the Nash.

Floyd heard the horn and knew he was in trouble. He ordered Baum to step on it, and the old man pushed the Nash as fast as it could go. The car hurtled up and down the steep slopes of Roller-Coaster Road. Baum accelerated with such force that the accelerator stuck, and George MacMillen had to help him release it. But then, surprisingly, the Nash slowed down and pulled over.

It was MacMillen's recollection that Baum stopped the car on his own so that he and MacMillen could make a break for it. Baum later told his daughters he stopped on Floyd's orders to see if the speeding car behind them might pass. Either way, as soon as the car stopped, Floyd shot out the back window and fired toward the advancing police. One bullet crashed through Hayes's windshield and zinged between the two cops. That was their cue to leap from their car and return fire. They could not have known that the two men advancing toward them with their hands raised—Baum and MacMillen—were good citizens, not gangsters. Five of their bullets hit Baum's Nash; years later children would delight in sticking their fingers through the holes. One slug hit Baum in the right leg.

Meanwhile, Floyd used his two prisoners as shields and made a break for the trees. He rolled under a roadside fence and slipped easily into the woods; he was gone before Hayes and Patterson finished shooting. Somehow he had eluded authorities yet again. Hayes ordered Patterson to pursue Floyd while he warned nearby farmers to lock up their cars. Before long, the biggest manhunt Ohio had ever seen was under way.

Night fell, and with it came a hard rain. Half the men combing the woods gave up, with no sign of Floyd to report. On that miserable night, Floyd's pal Richetti sat in a dry, warm jail cell in Wellsville; the Baird sisters, Rose and Juanita, heard about the shoot-out while waiting at the garage and left for Kansas City in the fixed-up Ford by themselves. Floyd would remain among the elms and sycamores for the next two days. Now and then he would emerge, and citizens would spot the strange, hatless man sprinting here or walking there. But they got only fleeting glimpses. It would take some measure of luck and skill to lay a hand on him.

———

The world came to Wellsville over the next two days, or so it seemed. Necks craned to see airplanes buzzing in low, their engines throbbing in the sky like thunder. Federal agents from Pittsburgh, Chicago, Detroit, Cincinnati, Kansas City, and even Birmingham arrived in speeding automobiles at all hours, day and night. Packs of reporters and photographers descended on this dot of a town that didn't even have its own hotel. So many urgent telephone calls were placed between Wellsville and Washington that people trying to get through on ordinary business could not penetrate the jammed switchboards. Before the end of the weekend, the nation's top officials could pick out Wellsville on a map and describe its steel and pottery industries as well.

The highest-ranking official on the ground was Melvin Purvis. Ray B. Long, the county sheriff who first alerted the feds to Richetti's capture, met Purvis and his men at the airport and drove them to the Wellsville police station. On the way he briefed them on the situation: Sheriff John Fultz, Purvis learned, was not at all happy federal agents were on the way.

Bracing for an unwelcome reception, Purvis marched into police headquarters and announced himself as Mr. Marshall. What he saw at the station astonished him. Sheriff Fultz's ground-floor office swarmed with people, both men and women—with townsfolk, friends, relatives, even reporters. In Chicago, Purvis confined the beat reporters to the front hall of the office. Purvis knew immediately he would not be able to control the situation—the man in charge was Fultz.

Fultz had captured Richetti around noon on October 20 and locked him in the largest of the three holding cells at the station. He pushed his prisoner hard to come clean about his identity and that of his running pal. But Richetti did not budge: His name was Richard Zamboni and he was traveling with a fellow named Joe Warren, a gambler he met in Tupelo. The ninety-eight dollars in his pocket, Richetti insisted, were poker winnings. In Fultz's version of events, he never believed Richetti's lies. A day after the capture, Fultz consulted a small booklet featuring photos of the nation's top criminals and recognized both Richetti and Floyd. But Sheriff Long told Purvis he was the one who first identified Richetti on October 21 when he spotted Fultz interviewing a prisoner. He recognized the man as Adam Richetti from photos Justice agents had sent him. Long told Fultz he had captured a wanted federal fugitive, and only then did Fultz confirm it by consulting the photo book. Once he knew his captive's identity, Fultz took two self-serving steps: He warned Long not to alert federal agents, and he summoned reporters to the station. Apparently, Fultz had no plans to advise the Justice Department about his single-handed capture of Richetti. He let the entire day of the capture, October 20, pass without notifying Washington, and his prize catch was well into his second day in custody before Long made his call. Long "telephoned the information as to the apprehension to the Cincinnati Office at his own expense and much against the wishes of the Chief of Police," the special-agent-in-charge in Cincinnati, E. J. Connelley, explained to Hoover in a dispatch two days later.

When Purvis walked into the station a few hours after Long's call, Fultz's media circus was in full swing. The sheriff had repeatedly trotted Richetti out for photos with different officers and posed for several himself, his satisfied grin not dissimilar to Richetti's defiant smirk. Purvis pulled Fultz aside and asked for a rundown on the capture. The highlight of Fultz's account was his insistence that he shot Floyd in the stomach, and that Floyd was most likely dead.

Purvis asked to let his agents speak with Richetti in private. Fultz agreed. Purvis told agents Sam McKee and Herman Hollis to conduct the interview in Richetti's cell while he continued debriefing Fultz. The agents encountered a jittery but stubborn prisoner. Richetti kept asking why the agents were interested in him. He insisted the man he was traveling with was not Charlie Floyd, that he had not seen Floyd since they kidnapped Sheriff Killingsworth in Missouri nearly two years before. McKee and Hollis asked Richetti to voluntarily sign a waiver releasing him to their care. He balked at first but finally consented—provided Sheriff Fultz agreed to release him.

In the office, Fultz and Purvis agreed on little. They proposed strategies to locate Floyd, but Fultz casually dismissed Purvis's ideas. Purvis learned that heavy rains had driven away half the men who had been combing the woods for Floyd, and that nightfall was effectively ending the search altogether. He suggested encircling the fourteen miles of road around the woods by parking cars every thousand yards or so. Fultz shrugged off the notion that the woods could be surrounded. What about a plane dropping flares to light up the forest? No pilots with knowledge of the area were available. Then came word that if the agents wanted to take Richetti, they had to go through Fultz. Purvis had had enough. He told Fultz the Department of Justice intended to prosecute Richetti for his role in the Kansas City massacre. It was imperative Fultz deliver up Richetti immediately so that agents could get him away from reporters and take him to a secure location in nearby Cincinnati. Purvis explained that with a prisoner like Richetti, the Bureau needed three or four days of intense questioning in a controlled environment to build a case. Would Fultz get Richetti to sign a waiver of release?

He would not. Fultz asked if Purvis had any official indictment or warrant relating to Richetti, but Purvis had flown directly from Cincinnati without one. Fultz said he couldn't very well take Purvis's word for it that Richetti was a federal fugitive. Besides, Fultz had an open-and-shut case against Richetti for assault with a deadly weapon.

"Richetti tried to take my life," Fultz asserted. "He shot one of my citizens and he nicked me; therefore I feel that we have a right to take
care of our case." Purvis countered that the penalties Richetti faced
in the Kansas City affair far outweighed whatever sentence he would
receive in Wellsville. Fultz didn't budge. Never mind that Richetti
would likely serve a mere thirteen years for shooting at him. He'd be
damned if he would just hand over his prisoner to anyone.

Purvis kept pushing for Richetti's release, to no avail. Fultz called
in reinforcements: Wellsville's mayor, W. H. Daugherty,[ck] county
prosecutor John Lafferty, and assistant prosecutor William Springer.
Purvis again recited the charges against Richetti, but the Wellsville
men sided with Fultz and grew only more determined. The sheriff
told Purvis that if he returned with a proper indictment, he might—
might—consider releasing Richetti.

The provisional concession hardly satisfied Purvis, who was accustomed to getting his way, right away. He told Fultz he wanted to interview Richetti again, but Fultz, sensing he had prevailed in their
first skirmish, said he hadn't eaten yet and was hungry. He was going
out for a bite now, but he would return to the station around 10:30
that night. If Purvis came back then, he could interview Richetti.

Purvis left rankled and empty-handed. He did not like the plan in
place to capture Floyd, which to his thinking was no plan at all. He
was frustrated that his special-agent status carried so little weight
with Fultz, who was behaving as if he had reeled in a 500-pound
marlin on a fishing trip. Purvis was also bothered that he had to use
his alias, Mr. Marshall. Would revealing his true identity have cowed
the cocky Fultz into cooperation?

Purvis and his team of three drove six miles to the Travelers Hotel
in the neighboring town of East Liverpool. It was the only decent
hotel in the area, and the only one large enough to accommodate
the coming influx of federal agents. Situated on the cobblestone ex-
panse of Fourth Street, the four-story building had 100 small, spare
rooms that were rented primarily to itinerant salesmen, who paid
three dollars for a night's lodging, or five dollars for one of the
larger suites. Located halfway between New York City and Chicago,
the hotel got its share of traffic in all seasons. Across the street was
the well-known Ceramic Theater, which on Sundays hosted top jazz
musicians who couldn't play in Pittsburgh because of blue laws.
Purvis booked several rooms and picked for himself number 320, a

two-windowed corner room that looked out on Fourth Street. That room became the headquarters for the quickly mobilizing effort to snare Pretty Boy Floyd.

Nearly nonstop for the next two days, armed agents hustled in and out to chase down leads, while phone calls lit up the hotel's small lobby switchboard. The owner, a garrulous redhead named Sarah Edmondson, had never seen such a flurry of activity, and sought to involve herself in the excitement. She took over the switchboard and helped pass urgent calls along to Purvis, and she offered the second-floor conference room as a command post for gathering agents. Edmondson even fielded the many calls from Hoover. The director was so determined to be kept apprised that he insisted Purvis post an agent in Room 320 around the clock to take his calls.

Purvis called Hoover as soon as he settled in his room. He filled him in on Fultz's grandstanding, and Hoover made his dissatisfaction clear: "We do not want to let Floyd get away because of any dumbness on the part of the police chief," he said. Purvis told his boss he would need an indictment to spring Richetti, and Hoover arranged to have Sheriff Thomas Bash of Kansas City swear out a murder warrant and fly to Wellsville with special agent Sam Cowley. Hoover also made it clear who was in charge of operations in Wellsville, and that was Purvis. In later years he would suggest that Cowley, who arrived the next day, October 22, was actually the agent who ran the hunt for Floyd. But on the evening of October 21, Hoover was unequivocal. The orders were for all agents arriving in town to report to Purvis at the Travelers Hotel. "I told Mr. Purvis that Richetti should be moved quietly and by our agents," he said in a memo typed up at 7:35 that night, "and that then he, Mr. Purvis, would be free to take charge of the hunt."

Purvis did so with his usual thoroughness. In all, nineteen agents from six different bureaus streamed in through the night; seven from Detroit, four from Cincinnati, three each from Pittsburgh and Chicago, one from St. Louis, and another from Birmingham. Purvis divided the agents into squads of three or four and dispatched two teams to raid the homes of Adam Richetti's sister, Minnie Shustek, and brother, David Richetti, who lived in the area of nearby Dillonvale, Ohio. Purvis could not be sure that the man who fled into the woods was Charlie Floyd. All he had to go on was Sheriff Fultz's identification based on a photo. Richetti may have been traveling with a relative; if so, the agents sent to Dillonvale would find out.

Purvis assigned another squad to interview potential witnesses at local hospitals, car companies, and train depots. If Floyd was indeed shot, as Fultz insisted, there would be a trail of blood somewhere. Three more squads took off for the highway along the woods where Floyd disappeared. Purvis saw no need to waste an agent by sending one to babysit Richetti; Fultz had the station surrounded with his new deputies, all armed against any gangsters wishing to break out their cohort. Preparing to respond quickly to solid leads, Purvis lined up rifles and shotguns against the walls in room 320 so agents could grab them and go.

The rain was still drenching Wellsville when, at 10:30 that night, Purvis sent agents McKee and Hollis back to police headquarters to interview Richetti again. When they arrived, Fultz was nowhere to be found. A half hour later, Fultz appeared but raced past the agents to the mayor's private office. He instructed a deputy not to let in any visitors unless they were newspapermen. McKee and Hollis waited outside the mayor's office as reporters and photographers filed past them. They tried several times to get in, but were refused every time. Fultz kept them waiting for more than three hours, until 2:15 in the morning.

By then, two more agents had shown up, and Fultz finally allowed them all into the office. He refused, however, to discuss the matter of releasing Richetti to their custody; instead, he rehashed the heroic details of the gunfight and capture. McKee insisted, as Purvis had, that the agents needed to interview Richetti in private, away from reporters. Fultz announced he was tired and said, "Hell, I'm going to bed."

Agent Hollis fumed. He reminded Fultz of his promise to allow them to reinterview Richetti. Grudgingly, Fultz took the agents into his private office and had Richetti brought in. At the same time, he ushered in a few police officers and several men in plainclothes Hollis suspected were reporters. Clearly, this would be a perfunctory fulfillment of Fultz's promise. The agents could not be expected to discuss sensitive government matters in such a setting, but they had little choice. They began their second interview of Richetti.

It went nearly as poorly as the first. Richetti continued to insist he hadn't seen Floyd in months, that the man with him in Wellsville was a gambler named Joe Warren. He said he hitchhiked his way into town on a truck and was minding his own business when Fultz showed up. Richetti did admit to carrying a .45-caliber automatic and confirmed the Tommy gun belonged to his partner. He also confessed to kidnapping Sheriff Killingsworth with Floyd a year earlier, but rationalized that he was dead drunk when he did it. There was no indication Richetti would cooperate with the federal agents anytime soon, or that he would move off his position of needing Fultz's blessing to sign a waiver. McKee and Hollis wrapped up their dismal interview.

Fultz was not entirely uncooperative. He repeatedly told the agents he believed the badly wounded Floyd was likely hiding out in one of the houses along a certain stretch of Route 45. He had not been able to search them himself, he explained, because he did not have enough time. It was an astonishing statement considering he had just spent three hours repeating his story to reporters and posing for pictures with his prisoner. In the context of Fultz's conduct over the next few days, it seems likely his tip to the agents was intended to throw them off Floyd's trail, increasing the chances that one of his own men would make the capture. The agents, however, were not impressed by the tip. By then, they fully realized Fultz was milking his moment in history at the expense of federal efforts to find Floyd.

McKee and Hollis reported to Purvis about their failed evening. The government's first day in Wellsville was all but over, with nearly nothing to show for it. Purvis knew that most of the 200 men who had earlier combed the woods had given up and gone home. The few men still searching, though, were a cause for concern. They were not trained law officers; they were sons and fathers and even grandfathers moved by the excitement of the day. Purvis feared that in the wet, dark forest, one of them, in their zeal, would fire at a moving figure and hit another searcher. Purvis would have preferred to hunt for Floyd around the clock; to shut down for several hours was to cede a great deal to the master escaper. The men in the woods were not under his command, and their safety was not his responsibility. Nevertheless, Purvis arranged to have the search halted at 2:00 A.M. and the men sent home. Only a ring of officers around the forest was maintained.

Late that night, he also made the decision to abandon his alias. In the search for Floyd he would once again be Melvin Purvis, special-agent-in-charge.

11

CONKLE'S FARM

October 22, 1934
WELLSVILLE, OHIO

The business of hunting Charlie Floyd resumed at daybreak October 22, a blustery Monday. Floyd had been on the run for nearly two days; Melvin Purvis had been in Wellsville for twelve hours. Purvis slept little that night and worried about the Floyd search. The legend that surrounded Pretty Boy, after all, was built on stories of ordinary folks helping the blue-collar bandit escape. John Steinbeck referred to Floyd's mythic appeal in his Depression classic *The Grapes of Wrath*. "When Floyd was loose an' goin' wild, law said we got to give him up," his character Pa Joad says. "An' nobody give him up. Sometimes a fella got to sift the law."

Even so, Purvis had a suspicion that Floyd was still close by. Although wresting Richetti from Sheriff Fultz was important, it was not Purvis's top priority—that was to catch Floyd. One way or another, the government was going to get its hands on Richetti; the only question was when. Floyd, on the other hand, was on the verge of showing up Hoover and his men once more. They might never have as good a chance to nab him again.

At dawn, Purvis telephoned Hoover to fill him in. Purvis had sent a man to the Wellsville airport to meet Sam Cowley, who was flying in with Kansas City Sheriff Thomas Bash, a warrant for Richetti's arrest their precious cargo. But at 7:00 A.M., a small chartered plane circled the shabby landing field and kept going. Cowley, no doubt, was not as inclined to risk the rough landing Purvis had chosen. Hoover was anxious that Cowley present the warrant to Fultz and finally gain custody of Richetti. The idea that someone he viewed as a country-bumpkin cop could outsmart the Department of Justice's best and brightest agents infuriated Hoover. It did not help matters that the morning's newspapers carried stories about Sheriff Fultz's heroic shoot-out with Floyd and his defiance of federal agents. The stories described the high drama of Fultz shooting Floyd in the stomach, though by then Purvis was reasonably sure that if Floyd had been hit at all, it was a minor flesh wound. The *East Liverpool Review* ran a statement Purvis made late on October 21. It was his only official comment to the press. "Tonight I made a formal demand upon the chief of police of Wellsville for custody of Richetti," Purvis said. "He refused to turn over the prisoner."

Purvis wished he had not made the comment. The last thing he wanted was for the Richetti matter to turn into a personal showdown with Fultz. He told Hoover in their morning conversation that when Cowley and Bash finally arrived, he did not plan to accompany them to the Wellsville police station. He was not backing down or dodging confrontation; this was a practical decision. Purvis believed Cowley would have better luck without him there. A night had passed since Fultz and Purvis stared each other down; now, perhaps, the sheriff would realize he had nothing further to gain by keeping Richetti. Fultz had already defied the Bureau's top man; now he could hold his head high as he handed the prisoner over to a different agent. Hoover disagreed with Purvis's thinking and told him he expected him to go with Cowley and Bash. In the end, Purvis did as he thought best and stayed behind, sending an agent he trusted, Herman Hollis, to accompany Cowley.

Instead, at eight that morning, Purvis and other agents drove to Wellsville to reinterview James Baum, the florist who unwittingly helped Floyd escape. Lisbon police officers had shot Baum in the leg, their bullets intended for a fleeing Floyd. When the officers took off after Floyd, they told Baum to stay by the road and wait for them, wounded leg and all. A bystander who witnessed the shootout came back with iodine and applied it to Baum's bloody calf. Baum eventually drove himself to town and was treated by his physician. The town of Lisbon never reimbursed Baum for his medical expenses.

Department of Justice agents were swarming his front porch. Some agents treated Baum's young daughter Aletha and other friends and relatives to an artillery display, showing off the machine guns and demonstrating, without firing, how quickly they could be deployed. Purvis met with Baum in his bedroom, where Baum had his bandaged leg propped up. Purvis had follow-up questions about his encounter with Floyd, but he was mainly interested in warning the Baums to steer clear of reporters. The family was inundated with requests for interviews, and Purvis explained that keeping a low profile would be their best option. "They didn't know how many friends Floyd might have nearby and would want revenge," Baum's daughter Aletha remembered years later. Purvis arranged for an agent to stay with the Baums for the rest of the day.

A few miles away, at the Wellsville police station, Sheriff Fultz's infuriating stalling continued. Cowley and Bash arrived at the station shortly before noon and presented their warrants to Fultz and Mayor Daugherty.[ck] Bash had a warrant charging Richetti with murdering five men; Cowley had another for a motor vehicle theft violation. Hoover told his agents he wanted them to "bunco" Fultz, to wield with a heavy hand the ungodly power of the federal government and thus cower Fultz into releasing Richetti. Cowley officially restated the government's demand that Adam Richetti be turned over to their custody so that he could be tried for the murder of a federal officer. "I understand now when these warrants were made out, the purpose of them, and their full force," Mayor Daugherty[ck] responded with dutiful solemnity. He did not, however, agree to let Richetti go. Taking the warrants with them and offering no explanation, the mayor and Fultz abruptly left the office. A few unnerving minutes later, Daugherty[ck] returned alone and introduced a new obstacle: He was starting an investigation—into what he did not say—and would not have an answer for them until the investigation was complete. The most he would divulge was that he was seeking legal counsel on the matter of the warrants. He told Cowley to come back in two hours.

Cowley walked out empty-handed, just as Purvis had the night before. This Fultz fellow would not be pushed around. Hoover was willing to call in the big guns, specifically the governor of Ohio and the United States attorney general. These were drastic steps he preferred not to take, however. They would amount to an embarrassing concession that the Department of Justice had been stymied by a small-town sheriff. On the other hand, allowing Richetti to remain in Fultz's control was its own black eye for Hoover. A second front in the government's assault on Wellsville had now been opened, with Fultz nearly as big a concern as Pretty Boy Floyd.

Purvis, meanwhile, had returned to the Travelers, where he paced his corner room. For long stretches he was the only agent there. Tips came in from citizens claiming to have spotted Floyd, some of them promising, none fruitful. Purvis sent out his squads to chase down leads and waited for reports they telephoned back to his room. He knew it was wise to stay by the phone, both to be able to take Hoover's calls and to avoid being caught across town if a solid tip came in. Still, he found it difficult to stay in the room while dispatching his men one after the other. He felt the familiar clenching of his insides. "There were men who served with me who never knew the emotion of fear," he later wrote. "They belonged to the glory company of history, those joyous daredevils who, from time immemorial, have been vainly waiting for a commander to order a charge on the gateways of hell. I admire them, but my nervous system is not built that way." Yet the more he waited, idle, the more he wanted to grab a weapon and go after Floyd.

Shortly after 1:00 P.M. on October 22, the phone in room 320 rang. Purvis answered and, for the most part, listened. Then he tucked his .38-caliber detective's special revolver in his waist and summoned the switchboard to dial Hoover in Washington. When he hung up with Hoover, Purvis sprinted out of the Travelers, leaving the phone at his headquarters unmanned.

———

Charlie Floyd was wet, fatigued, sore, and hungry, but his major problem may have been that he had no hat. These days a man roaming the woods in a felt-rimmed fedora would seem strange, but in 1934 the opposite was true. Every description of Floyd circulated to reporters, citizens, and police included the salient detail that he wore no hat. Particularly in the driving rain that drenched eastern Ohio that weekend, Floyd's unadorned head was a dead giveaway.

He could not get his hands on a hat, but he could fix the growling in his stomach. Floyd could spend weeks in the woods without starving, feeding on hickory nuts and pears and apples and vegetables swiped from gardens. But trudging over the steep bluffs and craggy cliffs of the Columbiana County wilderness raised an appetite, and Floyd wanted a full meal. He had no doubt he could get one from friendly strangers, and he did not feel the risk was too great if he left the sanctuary of the woods. Several people reported seeing a hatless fellow wandering their property or coming up on a nearby road that weekend, but the sight of him was not necessarily alarming. This was the Depression, and it was not uncommon to have bedraggled men appear on front porches asking for food.

Around 12:30 P.M. on October 22, Floyd picked a farmhouse and dusted off his suit. He had covered several miles on foot in almost twenty-four hours, moving east from Lisbon and steering clear of Wellsville. Now he found himself just north of East Liverpool, only a few miles from the Travelers Hotel. He approached the farm's owner, Robert Robison, and was invited to come in and wash up. Robison's daughter, Mabel Wilson, fixed Floyd a sandwich and served him a plate of ginger cookies. Not the finest meal, perhaps, but better than nuts and berries. Floyd ate the sandwich and stuffed some cookies in his pockets.

He thanked his hosts and returned to the woods, but less than three hours later he was hungry again. Floyd walked along Sprucedale Road, which climbed steeply to a peak on which sat two simple farmhouses. One belonged to Mildred Conkle and her husband Frank. At ten minutes to three Floyd walked past that farmhouse and continued to the next, a fifty-acre spread about 100 yards farther down Sprucedale Road. Its owner, Mildred's sister Ellen, had bread baking in the oven, and perhaps it was the sweet aroma that drew Floyd to the back door. Hearing a knock, Ellen Conkle, a widow who lived alone and was cleaning her smokehouse, looked to see a scruffy figure covered with thistles and pine needles. The man's blue suit and white shirt were smeared with dirt, his black oxford shoes scuffed and dull. His square face was dark with stubble. Ellen Conkle thought that with a nice shave, the man would be good-looking. She opened her back door and let him in.

Floyd said he was lost and asked for something to eat. He was hunting with his brother, he said, and somehow they got separated. Conkle wondered who would think to wear a suit in the woods. "What are you hunting?" she inquired. Floyd's answer: squirrels.

That didn't sound right either; no one hunted squirrels that late in the day in ebbing sunlight. "The truth is I've been drinking," Floyd finally said, but Conkle didn't believe his third lie, either. "I could see that he looked wild, but he did not seem to have been drinking," she later told a reporter. "He was a very pleasant man to talk to."

In other times, such suspicions might have been enough to make her send him away. But these were tough times, and Conkle asked the stranger what he wanted to eat. "Meat," said Floyd. "I'm hungry for meat." Conkle unpacked spareribs from her smokehouse to serve with potatoes, rice pudding, bread, and coffee.

While she cooked, Floyd washed up, then rested in the back-porch rocker and read a copy of the Sunday *East Liverpool Review*. Conkle hadn't read it yet, and anyway she never bothered with the front-page stories on thugs and gangsters. That was lucky for Floyd, since he was the star of the paper. He read about the gunfight in Wellsville, Richetti's capture, his own daring escape, the posse in the woods. He read how Melvin Purvis vowed to bring Pretty Boy Floyd to justice. "He seemed a little nervous" after that, Conkle remembered. "But I didn't think much of it." Floyd tore through the food she gave him: several thick slices of fresh bread, the hot ribs, all the potatoes, every-thing but the pudding, which he did not touch. "Fit for a king" he pronounced the meal, and pulled a dollar bill from the roll in his pocket. Conkle did not want to take it, but Floyd left the dollar for her. Ellen Conkle would keep that dollar for years to come.

Floyd was not finished asking for favors. He needed a ride to Youngstown, but Conkle could not do it. At the same time, she did not want the stranger lurking in the area that night. Her brother, Stewart Dyke, was husking corn out in the fields with his wife Flo-rence, and they would soon return. Floyd could wait outside, by Dyke's Model-A Ford, and see if they might take him. Floyd lingered a moment. He nodded sheepishly at Ellen Conkle. "I look like a wild man," he finally said. "I feel just that way." Conkle smiled and said nothing, and then Floyd was gone.

Stewart Dyke's car was parked beside a corncrib. Floyd slid into the driver's seat and spied the keys in the ignition. When Dyke came in from the fields a few minutes later, at 4:00 P.M., he saw the stranger in his car, trying to turn it on. "Your sister said you would take me to the bus line," Floyd explained. Dyke was too busy with chores to do it, but he did agree to ferry Floyd to the bus depot one town over in Clarkson. Dyke's wife Florence was not happy to hear that; she didn't like the looks of Floyd and disliked the idea of riding with him even more. She went so far as to snatch the keys out of the car. It took a little reassuring to get her in the car with Floyd for the short ride to Clarkson.

By then the autumn sky was darkening, the sun starting to dip behind the distant hills. Charlie Floyd was washed and well fed. These pinstriped government agents, these rabid local sheriffs, they burned to gun him down and claim his riddled body as a prize. But the ordinary people—the farmers and railroad workers, the widows and mechanics—were always there for him. There in the near twilight of a cool fall day, it must have seemed to Charlie Floyd that his freedom was worth fighting for, and that with just a little more luck, he might be all right.

———

Some of the agents Melvin Purvis assigned to patrol the highways north of Wellsville stopped to interview a farmer around 1:00 P.M. This was turning into a busy day for the farmer, Robert Robison, who already had hosted an unannounced visitor a little earlier. The assigned agents identified themselves to Robison and showed him a glossy black-and-white photograph. Robison recognized the face— this was the man he had fed a sandwich not thirty minutes earlier. Robison confirmed the man had asked for a ride to Youngstown. He also confirmed the man did not have a hat.

The agents hurriedly left the farm and found a telephone. Cliff Risler, the senior agent, dialed the Travelers Hotel. Purvis picked up and learned that Floyd had left Robison's farm on foot and was most likely still in the vicinity of the Bell schoolhouse, east of Highway 7. Federal agents had not been this close to Pretty Boy Floyd in eighteen months. Purvis alerted Hoover and mobilized the last available squad.

Purvis kept this last squad grounded at the hotel for just such urgent tips. These were his most dependable men, handpicked for guts and skill: Sam McKee and Bud Hopton, crack agents in the Chicago office and Purvis's partners in the Chicago Wrecking Crew, and David Hall, a top man from the Detroit office. Hall and Purvis packed revolvers; McKee and Hopton carried machine guns. The last squad got into Hopton's 1933 Chevrolet and sped to the school-house. They arrived in less than ten minutes.

Purvis conferred with the agents there and found a farmhouse to make two calls. The first was to the police department in Youngstown, Ohio. Purvis—burned when he did not contact local police in the Little Bohemia case—briefed them on Floyd's movements and asked for patrols and roadblocks. Next, Purvis called the Travelers and reached agent Hollis, who had returned from Wellsville police headquarters. Purvis told Hollis to call the East Liverpool police chief and request as many men as could be spared to search for Floyd.

East Liverpool Police Chief H. J. McDermott, a cop for more than thirty of his fifty-three years, took Hollis's call shortly before 3:00 P.M. and sounded the town's police siren. Moments later the chief handed guns from the weapons closet to patrolman Glenn Montgomery and desk sergeant Herman Roth. When officer Chester Smith showed up, McDermott gave him the choice of a revolver or sawed-off shotgun. A decorated World War I veteran and an ace marksman, Smith chose neither. Instead, he selected a 32-20 Winchester rifle. "If we run into him, he's going to be running," Smith reasoned. "Those pistols won't be worth a damn." McDermott said, "All right, let's go," and the Liverpool squad, in the chief's 1934 Chevy, joined the hunt for Floyd.

A short while later they caught up with Purvis and his men along Route 7, and McDermott honked his horn. Purvis got out, identified himself, and told the officers he believed Floyd was somewhere in the woods along Route 7, moving toward Youngstown. Purvis's plan was to circle around and head him off. The federal men did not know the roads, so Purvis invited the officers to cruise with them. He told them to take the lead, and his squad would follow.

The eight men drove from farm to farm, getting out to question people and searching every shed. They walked up muddy hills and across clover patches, shotguns cocked, pistols gripped, hats pulled low. For the most part, the grim posse walked without speaking, not in bunches but spread apart to make less inviting targets. More than once they saw a lone figure on a faraway hill, their pulses quickening as they gave chase, only to greet a startled farmer or hobo. The men wondered if Floyd might be watching them from the woods, invisible as ever and poised to strike.

Their first stop, down in a valley named Echo Dell, was the Levi Hickman farm. Purvis questioned Hickman and learned the village constable had just been by with warnings about Floyd. Next they drove to Jim Anderson's spread on the Sprucedale/Clarkson Road. Purvis and Montgomery walked 200 yards across a field to question Anderson, who was working his plow. Yes, Anderson had seen a stocky man without a hat walking on the road two hours earlier. Now there was no question Pretty Boy Floyd was within the government's grasp. Finding him in the brush and brambles would be another matter.

Purvis issued orders to search every abandoned home and barn. Purvis went alone into one dark barn, kicking up the straw on its main floor before climbing the straight wooden ladder to its loft. He was all but convinced the barn was empty when he heard a rustling below. Purvis slowly drew his gun and held his breath. The rustling continued. Purvis felt the nerves come alive in his body. Then he heard the unmistakable sound of climbing. Someone was coming up the ladder.

Purvis aimed his revolver at the opening to the loft and moved not so much as an inch. A second later he saw the top of a head appear. He held his fire but prepared to shoot. He watched hard as a man came through the opening. Instantly, he recognized the face: It was Sam McKee. Purvis let out a long breath and holstered his gun, full of relief. "True, we were looking for Floyd and hoped to find him," he would later admit with typical candor, "but somehow I dreaded the encounter. Floyd was a killer; I knew he wasn't to be taken alive." Purvis stepped out of the barn and breathed deeply of the clean autumn air. The landscape was oddly serene, just as he had left it. But everything seemed more vivid. "Strange," Purvis later remarked, "that Death should stalk in that beautiful spot."

The search continued. At one farm Purvis took off his hat as he questioned a woman standing on her front porch. Behind him he could hear the huffing and kicking of a charging ram. Purvis shooed the ram away and resumed his questioning, but the animal was as dogged as he was and charged a handful of times. Purvis finally admitted defeat and moved along.

The men had grown tried and hungry and stopped at an orchard for pears and apples. The intensity of their search slackened just for a moment. The officers kidded Purvis about his brush with the ram, and they watched a search plane fly over them, low to the line of the trees. The afternoon light was draining away, and Purvis knew that soon darkness would send them all home. He could not bear the thought of giving Floyd yet another twelve hours to escape. A feeling of futility descended. It seemed a remote possibility indeed that they would turn a corner or crest a hill and come upon Pretty Boy Floyd. Still, they had not lost all hope yet, nor was all the daylight gone. The men stuffed their pockets with fruit and got on their way.

The two-car caravan rolled up Sprucedale Road, climbing 300 feet to the top of a hill. At the peak sat two simple farmhouses. One of them belonged to Ellen Conkle.

———

Trouble—that's what Stewart Dyke thought; this is going to be trouble. He had just offered Floyd a ride in his Model-A Ford, as much to get rid of him as to help him out. Now he looked up to see a police cruiser pulling into the driveway. The instant he saw the car, Dyke connected the dots. "I knew something was going to happen; I didn't know what," he later said. "I had a stranger, and I knew their business, so I figured the worst was yet to come."

Dyke saw the officer's Chevy before Floyd did. It was in the driveway now, less than thirty yards away. But Dyke's Ford was still largely obscured by the corncrib, a crumbling wooden thing roughly ten feet wide and raised a foot off the ground. Dyke guessed his best move was to come out from behind it, into plain view. He put the Ford in reverse and slowly backed up three or four feet.

Patrolman Glenn Montgomery—Curly to his friends—was the first law officer to spot Charlie Floyd. In the back seat as his chief pulled into Ellen Conkle's driveway, he felt his heart seize. "I noticed standing in back of the machine that was parked on the opposite side of the corncrib this Charles 'Pretty Boy' Floyd," Montgomery recalled at the official inquest, "standing there without a hat on." When Floyd climbed into the back seat of Dyke's Ford, Montgomery yelled at his boss to stop driving. Just then, Purvis and his men turned into the rocky driveway and stopped, blocking any exit. Purvis saw the man in the car and thought, *That's him, that's Floyd.* The agents got out and lined up with the officers in a half circle. Behind the corncrib, Stewart Dyke calmly backed his car into the open. Charlie Floyd turned to his left and saw what must have been a terrifying sight—two cars, eight men, weapons trained on him. "Drive behind that building," he barked, nodding toward the corncrib and pulling out one of his .45s. "They are looking for me."

Slowly, the Ford rolled back behind the corncrib. Stewart Dyke had to think fast: He did not want to be trapped when the shooting started. He pushed the car door open and said, "Get out, you son of a bitch." Floyd "obeyed me just the same as if he intended to," Dyke later said. "I don't know whether he intended to or not." Gun in his right hand, Floyd scrambled behind the corncrib. Purvis peered beneath the crib and watched Floyd's trousered legs as he ran back and forth three or four times. The agents and officers approached the corncrib, rifles and revolvers drawn.

"Floyd," Purvis yelled, "come to the road. If you don't, we will shoot."

Trapped behind the corncrib, Floyd had several options. He could have commandeered the Ford and made a break for it through the fields. He might have tried to pick off the lawmen one by one. He could have taken a hostage and played out his drama that way. But Floyd's instincts steered him away from those choices. He was never quick on the draw, never in a hurry to fire on anyone. Nor was he keen on using the people who helped him as human shields. Floyd was an escaper. And so, Charlie Floyd ran.

He bolted from behind the crib and took off for the woods. They loomed less than 200 yards to the west, behind the farm. Floyd would have to run uphill about half that distance. Then, if he made the ridge of the hill, he would dip out of sight and have just a few dozen yards to go. Once inside the woods, gnarled with vines and cut through by cliffs, Floyd would be uncatchable. All that lay between him and the forest was a field of clover. Charlie Floyd ran for his life.

Behind him, Melvin Purvis yelled again: "Halt!" The other agents and officers yelled to Floyd, too. The gangster knew better than to run in a straight line, fixing himself inside some agent's scope. "He ran with a swinging kind of half-turning motion, as though he was trying to dodge or sideslip any shots," said Montgomery. Floyd looked over his right shoulder to survey his pursuers. He might at the same time have squeezed off a shot or two. That, at least, would have scattered the men and bought him precious seconds. For some reason, though, Floyd did not fire his weapon. He simply ran, in his strange, jerky fashion, gaining scant distance, perhaps sixty yards, before, in the loudest voice a soft-spoken Southerner could muster, Melvin Purvis gave his fateful order.

"*Let him have it!*"

Then the shooting began. Nearly a hundred shots tore through the quiet sky in a matter of seconds. Mildred Conkle would report that her ears rang for a week. Floyd heard the blasts and stopped for the barest of instants before resuming his zig-zag sprint. Purvis had ordered Hall, armed with a pistol, to drop to the ground, giving McKee and Hopton good, clean shots with their machine guns. A few feet away, Chester Smith, the best marksman of the group, lowered himself to one knee and raised his Winchester to shoulder height. "Everybody, the eight men, I think, were all firing at the same time," remembered Montgomery. Purvis, no mean shot, leveled his detective's revolver and emptied all six cylinders. "It was funny there were so many to shoot him," Mildred Conkle remarked to reporters the following day. "It looked like a bunch of hunters after a rabbit." Or, as Stewart Dyke put it, "They was mowing the grass and weeds."

It was a few minutes after four the afternoon of Monday, October 22, when the first bullet hit Charlie Floyd. It tore through the tendons and bones of his right arm with a force that spun him around. Another, more devastating bullet bored through his back and shattered the eighth rib on his left side, deflecting downward in his body through his diaphragm, stomach, and small intestine. Yet another slug passed between two right ribs and ravaged his kidney and pancreas. Blood from severed arteries flooded Floyd's body. He ran on a few steps and then fell to the ground, landing on his left side. He had made it to the crest of the hill after all, only to slump in a heap behind it.

Yet Floyd was not through; he struggled to turn to his right and perhaps stagger to his feet. He still had his rigged .45 automatic in his right hand, its hammer cocked, but the damage to his arm was too severe for him to squeeze the trigger. The agents and officers had stopped shooting and were advancing cautiously up the hill. When Floyd saw them he tried to raise his gun and aim it at the officers—the last criminal act of his life. Officer Montgomery grabbed Floyd's hand while Sergeant Roth reached into Floyd's belt and pulled out his second .45. The officers handcuffed Floyd as Mont-

gomery asked his name. Floyd gave the name Murphy. Montgomery
asked again. And, again, "Murphy." Then Melvin Purvis stood over
the bloodied fugitive. They were two of the most famous men in
America, in a time before television made fame a cheap and instant
thing. Both were thirty years old, both handsome and polite, both
lived lonely, abnormal lives dictated largely by the actions of the
other. One existed simply to elude capture, one was devoted to the
job of capturing him. They met, finally, in this place, a raw and random stretch of farmland. "You are," Purvis said, "Pretty Boy Floyd."
The raspy reply, through a wounded smirk: "I am Charles Arthur
Floyd."

There was no telephone on Ellen Conkle's farm, so Purvis and
agent Hall climbed into the Chevy to go find one. At the same time,
agent Sam McKee pressed the dying Floyd to own up to his role in
the Kansas City massacre. "To hell with Union Station," Floyd spat.
"I ain't telling you nothing." Then, "Fuck you." Floyd was "very defiant," Herman Roth remembered. "Very sneering answers. Half
sneering smile on his face." Though it hardly seemed necessary,
Chief McDermott asked him, "How bad are you hurt?" Floyd said,
"I'm through. You have got me twice."

A gangster to the end, he asked the Liverpool officers, "Who the
hell tipped you off?" And then, "Where's Eddie?" the nickname for
his faithful running buddy, Adam Richetti. His very last words were,
"I'm going." Charlie Floyd died on the spot where he fell at 4:25
P.M., fifteen minutes after three bullets cut him down.

Police Chief McDermott ordered Smith and Roth to carry Floyd's
body to a grassy spot under an apple tree close to the road. In Clarkson, Purvis dialed Washington and delivered the best news possible—Floyd was shot and no agents had been killed. Hoover
arranged for an ambulance while Purvis raced back to the Conkle
farm. By the time he got there, Floyd was already dead. Chester
Smith recalled that Purvis asked him for Floyd's two fully loaded
.45s. Smith refused, and Purvis flatly ordered him to surrender the
weapons. "The look he gave me," Smith would say, "was like he
could kill me right there because I contradicted him." Purvis later
wrapped up the guns and took them with him to Chicago; Smith

had to settle for the fifty rounds of live ammunition he rummaged from Floyd's pockets.

The officers loaded Floyd's body in the back of Purvis's car, propped it between Smith and Montgomery, and took it to the Sturgis Funeral Home in East Liverpool. Floyd's hands remained cuffed during the ride; Chief McDermott recalled that Purvis insisted they stay on. The Chevy pulled into the funeral home's cobblestone driveway and descended to the garage, which led directly into a cramped basement embalming room. With Floyd laid out on a coroner's slab, Sam McKee inked his fingertips, retrieving the six good prints and the four smudged ones. The prints were driven to the Pittsburgh airport and loaded on a plane bound for Washington. The next day, the discernible ridges precisely matched those on Charlie Floyd's federal fingerprint card.

At the funeral home, Purvis took a call from Hoover. Purvis assured the director that Public Enemy Number One was dead. The autopsy was not performed until 11:00 P.M. by two local doctors, Roy Costello and Edward Miskall. The death certificate would list Floyd's occupation as "bandit." As Floyd had feared, he did indeed become a trophy for the men who bagged him. After coroners cut off his blue suit, the officers divided it into small swatches they handed out as keepsakes. Then a coroner fastened a metal brace beneath Floyd's chin to prop up his limp head and drew a cloth up his naked torso on the slanted table that held him. Thus made presentable, Floyd posed for dozens of photographs, with grinning officers holding shotguns aligned behind him. Word that Floyd had been shot in the nearby hills quickly spread through East Liverpool, and by 8:30 that evening thousands of people were massed on the narrow street outside the funeral home. Obligingly, McDermott opened the parlor to them. As many as 10,000 people filed through the small first-floor sitting room to the right of the home's staircase. They were not allowed to study Floyd's blank, stubbly face for long; the line moved so quickly that roughly fifty people passed by the body every minute. The morbid procession lasted nearly three hours, the crowds so unruly they collapsed the porch railing and trampled rows of shrubbery.

Purvis was not around to see the spectacle; he returned to Room 320 at the Travelers Hotel. Aware that the killing of Floyd would generate worldwide publicity, he called for an immediate inquest into the shooting. At 10:00 P.M., he welcomed the coroner, E. R. Sturgis, and county prosecutor, Ed Lafferty, to his room. A stenographer, Myra McCormick, was hastily summoned. Exhausted, Purvis asked Sam McKee to run through the day's events for their sworn statement; Purvis sat next to him and sleepily nodded his assent. When McKee was finished, Sturgis told Purvis he planned to hold his own inquiry into Floyd's death, even though it was not required by Ohio state law. Purvis would get word of his findings in a few days.

In Washington, Hoover could barely contain his glee upon hearing of Floyd's demise. He quickly telephoned Attorney General Cummings with a report; one account had Hoover rushing to the seventh floor of the historic Justice building to deliver the news in person. Already conscious of the need to shape the public's perception of the killing, he informed Cummings that his agents were solely responsible for Floyd's death. Hoover also cheerfully fielded calls from reporters across the country. At 4:40 P.M., less than a half hour after Floyd died, Hoover spoke with a reporter from the *Chicago Daily News* and passed along the statement he had crafted with Cummings: "Department of Justice Agents a few moments ago shot and mortally wounded Charles 'Pretty Boy' Floyd." The East Liverpool officers had already been excised from Hoover's history.

Putting his own spin on events almost as they were happening meant somehow silencing his agents in Ohio, and this Hoover quickly set out to do. When he called Purvis at the Sturgis home a little over an hour after Floyd died, he ordered him to disperse most of the agents there and to get himself out of the state as soon as possible. Hoover had not restricted Purvis from talking to reporters a day after Dillinger's killing, and that decision had backfired on him. He had resolved not to repeat the mistake. With Floyd's body still warm, Hoover commenced his efforts to make Melvin Purvis invisible. "I told Mr. Purvis . . . I thought he should go on into Chicago and lay low for a couple of days," Hoover recorded in an October 22 memo. "Purvis advised that he had his picture taken, that he had been receiving inquiries from newspapers, whereupon I instructed him to tell the newspapers all statements would have to come from Washington." Hoover spoke with Sam Cowley, his eyes and ears in Chicago, later that evening. "Mr. Cowley is to remain [in Wellsville] with a few men to clean up the odds and ends," he said of their conversation. "Mr. Purvis is also to leave tonight and the curtain pulled down on the publicity there."

Purvis did as he was told. He packed his few belongings and left the electrified town of East Liverpool. He did not know it, but from that day forward, the hunter became the hunted.

———

For others, primarily J. Edgar Hoover, the days after Floyd's death were a heady and hectic time. Americans could not get their fill of stories about gunfights and gangsters, and this was the biggest, most charismatic criminal since Dillinger. Had they happened today, the events in Wellsville would have triggered round-the-clock coverage on CNN and every other news network. As it was, it seemed every newspaper and magazine wanted a piece of the Floyd story—and of Melvin Purvis.

When word got out that Purvis had been present at Pretty Boy's killing, he was touted as Floyd's slayer before any details were made public. The headlines played up Purvis's reputation as nemesis of the nation's top crooks. "Panic for Gangdom," screamed one. "And Again Melvin Purvis Triumphs," went another. The press did not need access to Purvis to write these stories. His selection as protagonist was preordained by the rigid rules of media—that heroism must have a face, preferably a handsome one. As for Purvis, he strained to buttress the notion that Hoover was the real hero, just as Cowley had done in his interviews with reporters in the weeks after Dillinger's death. "The search was directed by J. Edgar Hoover, director of the department, from Washington, and I have been in constant contact with him by telephone and telegraph," Purvis told reporters in Ohio. "Mr. Hoover has been particularly anxious as have we all to bring about the apprehension of this and other similar hoodlums."

Nor did Purvis say or do anything to elevate himself over the other agents. Surrounded by reporters as he left the Sturgis Funeral Home, he announced, "The hunt is over, Floyd is dead." When pressed on exactly who had killed Floyd, Purvis said, "We all did." He made no effort to determine if one of the six shots he fired felled Floyd; as in the Dillinger case, Purvis did not permit the slugs retrieved from Floyd's body to be matched against his agent's guns.

He deeply believed that no one agent should claim a greater share of credit nor shoulder a greater burden of guilt than any other. He based his protocol on what was followed in military executions. "Some of the rifles are loaded with blank cartridges, and some of them are loaded with real cartridges. Thus, no member of the punitive party ever has blood guilt on his soul," Purvis wrote in 1935. "No one will ever know, so far as I am concerned, who sent Dillinger and Floyd to their eternal rewards." Purvis believed such discretion should be part of his agents' code of conduct. But he also felt he was sparing his men unnecessary anguish down the line. "Most of us were young fellows," he remarked of the Dillinger shooting in 1959. "We had a feeling there was no great honor in taking part in killing a man."

Many years later, the identity of the agent who fatally shot Dillinger would become known. But only five shots were fired at Dillinger. The matter of which of the ninety-three bullets fired at Floyd hit their mark is far less clear. Chester Smith, without question the best marksman in the group, quickly claimed credit for the first bullet that struck Floyd in the arm and slowed him down, as well as for the next one that dropped him to the ground. "I didn't intend to kill him, didn't want to," he boasted in 1979. "When I draw a bead on something, I get it." Nearly sixty years later, Bud Hopton, one of the agents who accompanied Purvis that October afternoon, said that he and agent Sam McKee had fired the fatal shots. "When he ran across a field, Sam and I just cut down on him with a submachine gun," he recalled. "We dropped him and then the police came running down there."

The most controversial claim came in 1979, when Chester Smith stepped forward with what he called the true facts of Floyd's killing. His stunning assertions, headlined "Blasting a G-Man Myth" in *Time* magazine, had Melvin Purvis summarily ordering the execution of a wounded and defenseless Floyd. In this version, Smith winged Floyd and was standing over him when Purvis ran up. "Back away from that man, I want to talk to him," Purvis allegedly ordered. After Floyd refused to answer a question about his role in the Kansas City massacre, Purvis commanded an agent to "Fire into him!" Smith claimed agent Herman Hollis blasted Floyd once in the chest. Purvis's explanation: "Mr. Hoover, my boss, told me to bring him in dead." The official version of events, therefore, was a massive cover-up.

Smith spoke out, he said, because all the other lawmen at the shooting were now dead and could no longer be harmed by the truth. In fact, one lawman, Bud Hopton, was still alive and vehemently refuted Smith's claim of a cover-up. To be sure, there were many holes in Smith's story. For one thing, Smith was known as, at best, a bender of the truth. "People took everything he said with a grain of salt," said Tim Brooks of the East Liverpool Historical Society, a respected scholar on the subject of Floyd's death. "He spun many, many tales over the years that just had people shaking their heads." The biggest hole in his 1979 version of events had to do with Herman Hollis, the agent Smith said executed Floyd. Hollis was in Ohio as part of the force assigned to the case, but he never got near Ellen Conkle's farm. Another problem: Smith's own memories of the shooting kept changing. In the version he shared with *Time,* Hollis fired a revolver. He told another newspaper that Hollis used a Tommy gun.

In addition, it is highly unlikely that such a sweeping cover-up could have been arranged in such a short time. Convincing the four East Liverpool officers to synchronize their stories and lie under oath at the official inquest two days later, and to perpetuate those lies in every account they provided reporters over the next weeks and months, is far-fetched enough. Purvis would also have needed to draw witnesses Ellen and Mildred Conkle into his subterfuge. Both spoke with reporters in the days following Floyd's death and giddily basked in their brush with celebrity, betraying not the slightest hint that they were harboring sinister secrets about what really happened.

If there was a cover-up, it certainly fooled East Liverpool coroner E. R. Sturgis, who interviewed thirteen of the drama's principal players, separately and under oath, on October 23 and 24. He sent his findings to Purvis on October 25, and Purvis telegraphed them to Washington. "After a complete hearing of the known facts regarding the activities of Charles 'Pretty Boy' Floyd from Saturday, October 20th, to Monday, October 22nd," wrote Sturgis, "I find that he was justly shot to death by a combined force of Agents of the Department of Justice and officers of the East Liverpool Police Department while making an armed attempt to escape."

In a way, cornering Floyd on the Conkle farm proved a less rigorous exercise than gaining custody of Adam Richetti. Once Purvis left East Liverpool, Cowley took over the department's efforts to free Floyd's sidekick from Sheriff Fultz's clutches, with, at least initially, a similar lack of success. Hoover dispatched two assistant U.S. attorneys to Ohio on October 22, but even they could not persuade Fultz to release his prisoner. At a conference the next day, Fultz once again reneged on a promise to hand over Richetti. Instead, he arraigned him on charges of carrying a concealed weapon and fined him a whopping $75. The sheriff went so far as to transfer Richetti from a cell at the Wellsville police station to a more secure prison in nearby Lisbon. There, Fultz twice trotted out Richetti to preen him before curious townsfolk and groups of baffled school children.

Fultz coupled his defiance with a thorough trashing of Melvin Purvis. He described to reporters how Purvis had insulted him by using a fake name, how the condescending agent made haughty demands and tried to intimidate the sheriff's men, how he ran with information Fultz provided but refused to share his own intelligence. "Mr. Purvis and his men walked out and would not cooperate with us, and instead went to another city after we had given full details of the case," Fultz said in a statement. "He was captured only a short distance away from where we had mentioned." The local papers featured editorials blasting Purvis; one paper referred to Fultz as the "Little David" chief of police who brought the government's top man to his knees. None of that sat well with Hoover, but there was little he could do. Fultz held Adam Richetti for eight days, before finally releasing him to federal agents. A Kansas City jury found the reedy, sad-sack gangster guilty of murder on June 17, 1935, two years to the day after the slaughter at Union Station. He died in a Missouri gas chamber, screaming and gasping, just after midnight October 7, 1938.

Then there were Floyd's two .45s; Hoover coveted them. "I want those guns for ballistics examination," he told Cowley a day after Floyd's death. "I am almost as much interested in that as in gaining custody of Richetti." Linking the guns to the Kansas City massacre was surely Hoover's primary interest, but it was not his only one. Hoover already had Dillinger's pistol on display outside his office in Washington; Floyd's hardware was next. "The Director desires that the two Floyd guns be placed in the exhibit cases in the reception room," stated an October 26 memo to special agent Thomas Baughman, who supervised the ballistics examination. Purvis took care of securing the guns for Hoover, and on November 1 Floyd's .45-caliber

Colt automatic pistol took its place in a glass box outside Hoover's office. The other gun was locked away; one trophy, Hoover apparently decided, was enough.

In the handful of gritty river towns in eastern Ohio that attested to the doomed path of Pretty Boy Floyd, the days slowly resumed their sleepy rhythms. For many, though, life was never the same. The indomitable Sheriff John Fultz was cut off from receiving federal bulletins and charged with interfering with a federal investigation. His constituency, though, saw the hero in him, as it always had. Chester Smith, the patrolman who drew Floyd in his scope on the Conkle farm, parlayed his prominent role in the killing into a promotion to captain. Lon Israel, the Wellsville widower who made the telephone call that sealed Floyd's fate, took to wearing a long overcoat wherever he went. Beneath it he hid what he called his sticks—two loaded shotguns.

Little Ducky Fryman, the boy caught in a hail of Floyd's bullets, lived a boy's life no more. One of his chores was to ferry a bucket of milk the mile from his sister's house to his family's home. The quickest route was through the woods—the very woods into which the ephemeral Floyd had slipped. After that weekend, Ducky Fryman never cut through the woods again.

Charlie Floyd finally made it home to Salisaw, Oklahoma, in a cloth-lined, unfinished pine box. His mother, Mamie Floyd, heard of her son's death the evening it happened and sent a telegram to Police Chief McDermott. "If he has been killed," she wrote, "turn body over to reliable undertaker and forbid any pictures being taken of him and bar the public." It is unlikely her wishes would have been heeded even if the telegram had arrived in time. When East Liverpool was finally through with Floyd, they loaded his coffin onto a Pennsylvania railroad baggage car bound for Pittsburgh. Three days later, at the Salisaw train station, his nine-year-old son Jack heard the distant wail of a train whistle, which meant that his father, for whom he had waited all night, was nearly there. It was 2:00 A.M. when the boy watched relatives and family friends cluster around the train as the coffin was gently unloaded. "For years," Jack Dempsy Floyd said in 1992, "every time I head a train whistle it reminded me of that sad night."

More than 20,000 people attended the funeral of Pretty Boy Floyd in Akins, Oklahoma. A preacher spoke of the evils of crime, but the real message was abundantly clear. To many downtrodden souls in a depressed nation, Charlie Floyd was, indeed, a hero.

In Chicago, Melvin Purvis returned to his apartment close to the lakefront in the city's near North Side. Streetcars clanged along trolley tracks, and delivery trucks choked the narrow, teeming streets, but in Purvis's apartment, all was strangely still. Hoover spoke with him the morning of October 24 and instructed him to stay away from the Bankers Building. Hoover explained the disappearance of his most famous agent, at one of the crowning moments of his career, by passing around a story that Purvis was ill. He "is not feeling so well this morning," Hoover stated in an October 24 memo. "I told him to remain at home for a couple of days." In the end Hoover kept Purvis away from the office for one full week.

So it was that Melvin Purvis spent October 24, his first full day back from Ohio, in forced seclusion in his apartment. He had one visitor, Harry E. Wild, a clerk for the Division of Investigation who stopped by in the afternoon to pick up Floyd's two guns. Otherwise it was quiet, as if nothing extraordinary had happened.

October 24 was Purvis's birthday. He was thirty-one years old.

12

WHEN THE FALL IS ALL THERE IS

February 1935

One last drink before a life in jail—where was the harm in that? Volney Davis—captured, shackled, all out of luck—asked this small mercy of two special agents escorting him from Kansas City, where he was picked up on a stakeout of his Pontiac sedan, to Chicago, where he would be interrogated about his many crimes. A wiry 123 pounds, with beady eyes and a vertical scar above his right eyebrow, Davis was not a big fish, but neither was he a nobody. He had housed Dillinger after Little Bohemia; had buried Dillinger's running pal John Hamilton; had been part of the crew that killed a policeman while robbing the Stockyards National Bank in St. Paul; had played a role in the bloody kidnapping of St. Paul businessman Edward Bremer. He was a top soldier in the notorious Barker-Karpis gang, and some said he was its meanest member. Like any good gangster, Davis had served a stint in prison, scraped off part of his fingerprints, and crisscrossed the country with his gun moll in tow. He "had that maddening restlessness so common to the professional hoodlum," Melvin Purvis once remarked. "Sometimes, he told me, he would climb into an automobile in the middle of the night and ride and ride with no particular destination or purpose in mind. His only object was to put miles between himself and the place he had been."

The endless roads finally led him to Kansas City on February 6, 1935. Acting on a tip, five special agents staked out spots at the United Motor Service garage on McGee Street at 7:30 that morning, and were waiting for Davis when he arrived for his car around 12:30. Davis, in a brown suit and blue overcoat, peered through a window before entering, on the lookout for feds, but he did not look hard enough. Agent V. F. Trainor approached quietly from behind and announced the arrest; Davis, armed with a .32-caliber automatic, surrendered without a fight. The agents persuaded him to sign a waiver of removal and whisked him to the Kansas City airport, where the only aircraft available for the three-hour flight to Chicago was a small cabin plane that held three passengers and a single pilot. Trainor and special agent Thomas Stakem locked Davis in handcuffs and leg irons and wedged him into the plane for the afternoon flight. But the pilot flew into a storm and lost his course in the threatening clouds. It was all he could do to bring them down in a cornfield near Yorkville, Illinois, ten miles south of Aurora.

The agents and their quarry hitched a ride to town with a farmer so that they could call Melvin Purvis to make new plans for bringing in Davis. They found the nearest place with a phone, the Vaiding Hotel and Barroom, and freed Davis from his cuffs and irons. Once inside, Trainor slipped into a phone booth, while Stakem and Davis took seats at the bar. Stakem needed a drink to calm his nerves after the shaky ride, and what sort of man would he have been had he not allowed his prisoner to have one, too? Out of decency, Stakem let Davis drink one last cold stein of beer.

Davis immediately smashed his stein into Stakem's face and jumped headfirst through a closed window onto a concrete walkway. Stunned, Stakem drew his gun from his hip holster and staggered to the window; Trainor heard the crash of glass and ran outside. Both agents fired shots, but they were aiming at nothing more than a shadow in the dark.

It was an inauspicious beginning to the year for the Bureau—and for Trainor and Stakem, both of whom were fired for letting Davis escape. Still, the blunder was not as damaging as it might have been. Hoover's army of agents had built up a sound reserve of goodwill and could be forgiven the occasional mistake. By late October 1934, they had rid the nation of two of its three big gangsters—Dillinger, cornered outside the Biograph, and Floyd, trapped on Conkle's farm. In November 1934, only a single fugitive with a federal price on his head continued to roam the land—Baby Face Nelson, the man who killed one agent at Little Bohemia and nearly picked off Melvin Purvis, too. With Floyd's death in Ohio, Nelson became the new Public Enemy Number One.

———

Purvis received the usual commendation from Hoover for his work in the Floyd case. "The successful termination of the hunt for Floyd was I know, in large part, due to the splendid work performance by you in directing the activities of the Division in Ohio," Hoover wrote on October 23. "The courage and efficiency of the representatives of the Division will I know prove to be of great value in the work which we are all attempting to do in connection with the current warfare against the criminal element." At the same time, however, Hoover imposed a one-week furlough to keep Purvis away from work lest he once again siphon off all the glory and attention. In the end, though, it hardly mattered that Hoover sequestered Purvis. It made little difference that Hoover dismissed dozens of requests for interviews with Purvis as well as pleas for photos and biographical details. The American public had long since anointed Melvin Purvis its hero crime-fighter, and no containment strategy could hope to change the nation's mind. "That Mild Little Fellow—It's Purvis, Deadly to Gangsters," the *Chicago Tribune* declared in a headline following Floyd's death. "If you saw him in a hotel lobby, you might say he was a young college instructor," the article began. "But that would be before you learned his name was Purvis—Melvin Purvis." "Purvis, with Soft Southern Drawl, Has Become 'Poison' for Criminals," announced another headline. "Purvis marked another notch in his gun—the death of Pretty Boy Floyd," went the story. "A normally mild-mannered southerner who 'sees red' when dealing with criminals today became the most dangerous nemesis of the desperado." The press Purvis received after Floyd's death personalized him in a way Hoover had never anticipated. The dramatic shooting in East Liverpool merely sealed Purvis's fate: He was now a full-blown star.

On October 26, four days after the Floyd shooting, famed gossip columnist Louella Parsons announced in the *Washington Herald* that Paramount Pictures planned to make a movie of Purvis's life. It would be called *Federal Dick* and star George Raft and, as Purvis, Cary Grant. Parsons claimed the movie had the full blessing of the Department of Justice. Not surprisingly, Hoover seethed at the news. He ordered J.E.P. Dunn, his top agent in Los Angeles, to grill Paramount's West Coast studio chief, Emanuel Cohen. The investigation determined there were no concrete plans for a movie, and that a writer had merely been retained to bat around ideas. Hoover called Purvis at home and demanded to know whether Purvis was as appalled by the rumor as he was. Purvis promised that he was. "We agreed that it was the most outrageous thing we had ever heard of," Hoover said of his conversation with Purvis. "Both Purvis and myself view the whole idea with absolute horror and disgust."

Purvis's assurances, much like his imposed exile, did little to calm Hoover. The media continued to romanticize Purvis. "With Melvin Purvis, youthful sleuth of the Department of Justice, as the boogey man of gangland," read one newspaper item, "the wives of gangsters now put their babies to sleep with the warning: 'Grab some shuteye, mug, or I'll tip off Melvin Purvis.'" Hoover had wished for an agent who could capture the biggest gangsters for him; he had never bargained for an agent so suited to capturing the public's fancy.

FBI records show that in the weeks after the killing of Floyd, Hoover ceased to maintain anything but a pretense of friendship with Purvis. In the days after Purvis denied Hoover a second chance at glory, Hoover systematically began to neutralize his most famous agent.

Hoover's maneuverings were not subtle. Media requests for access to Purvis and for photos of him were routinely denied. When Vera Connelley of the *New York Herald Tribune* asked for material on Purvis—"she desires intimate details—something to make an interesting more or less personal story," Clyde Tolson recounted in a memo—Hoover stated flatly that he "did not want anything given." When Norma Abrams of the *New York Daily News* asked to interview Purvis, she was furnished only with "his date of appointment to the Service and the colleges he attended, as such matters are public information," a memo noted—though Hoover did add "it would be perfectly all right if Miss Abrams wanted material on the Division as a whole." Hoover also sent Purvis a pointed letter outlining what he called "the official policy" of the Bureau regarding the attention of journalists. "There is a growing tendency upon the part of the press to indulge in somewhat melodramatic descriptions of the Division's work," Hoover wrote. "This tendency, aside from the lack of good taste involved, is harmful to the prestige of the Division and may militate against the successful consummation of the work under its jurisdiction. It is believed that this tendency should be discouraged by you whenever possible."

Hoover's effort to diminish Purvis's publicity reached its height on November 16, when Henry Suydam—a publicist hired by the Department of Justice to help shape its image and designated special assistant to the U.S. attorney general—wrote to Hoover requesting that he assist the Associated Press in preparing an advance obituary of Melvin Purvis. "Attached is the material that the AP is going to put into its morgue of Mr. Purvis," Suydam wrote. "Would it be possible to have it checked?" To Suydam's surprise, Hoover refused even to peruse the AP's reporting for inaccuracies. Suydam—one of the primary forces behind the Bureau's public relations victories of the 1930s—appeared incensed by Hoover's decision. "I cannot help but feel that the Department's relations with the Associated Press are being unnecessarily prejudiced," he wrote in a harsh memo to Hoover on November 21. "In view of the fact that Mr. Purvis at the time of the Dillinger killing was ordered to Washington by the Department, was interviewed and photographed in the Attorney General's office posing with the Acting Attorney General and the Director of the Division of Investigation, it seems to me somewhat paradoxical for the Department now to refuse even to check a biographical sketch of him not to be used except in the event of his death. The data desired cannot result in any present prominence for Mr. Purvis. I feel that this attitude is one that puts the Department and the Division of Investigation in a false position, and for no substantial reason."

Hoover answered to no one in the Bureau, but he did take orders from the attorney general. An angry note from Suydam, who had Cummings's ear, could not be ignored. Hoover grudgingly read over the biography and provided Suydam with additional details about Purvis. But he made his reluctance clear. "I well appreciate the fact that in Mr. Purvis' case there has already been much publicity concerning him, and some of the publicity which surrounded the killing of John Dillinger was at least affected through the cooperation of myself and other officials," Hoover wrote in a forceful memo to Suydam. "I think that a mistake was made, however, and should there arise another similar case, it will be my very strong recommendation that no individual be singled out to receive the public commendation or to be dramatized as the man responsible for the death or capture of a notorious desperado." Hoover then listed his reasons for this sudden reworking of the Bureau's media policy. First, "such publicity naturally circumscribes the usefulness of the employee in the service for the future. As a result of the publicity which Mr. Purvis has received, we cannot use him on cases where his services would be very useful because his identity could not be kept secret." There was, of course, no evidence to support this reasoning. By the time he took to the hills of Ohio to chase Pretty Boy Floyd, Purvis was already nationally known as Dillinger's slayer. His leadership of the force that cornered Floyd was not compromised in any way by his fame; indeed, he might have received more cooperation from local authorities had he used his own name instead of an alias when he arrived in East Liverpool. Certainly some restraint in dealing with the press was advisable for Purvis. But to make him essentially invisible seemed less in the interest of the Bureau—which was benefiting from the nation's fascination with and support of its star agent—than in the interest of Hoover and Hoover alone.

The director's two-page letter to Suydam listed another reason for his Purvis blackout. "No one employee of this Division can ever be responsible for the successful termination of any case," he wrote. "Our system of operation is such that through cooperative efforts a case is broken. This, of course, is well known with[ck] the service, and consequently, when publicity is given to one man as being the so-called 'hero' of a situation, it is likely to engender jealousies which would be harmful to the morale and esprit de corps of this Division. In the past there have been no such jealousies existing within the Division, and I am particularly desirous of avoiding any such feelings." In retrospect, there is astonishing irony in this statement. Thousands of pages of FBI records reveal no trace of bad feelings between Purvis and the agents under his command. There is no evidence any of them resented Purvis's fame. Yet these same files are rife with examples of Hoover's consuming envy of the attention that flowed to Purvis in the wake of the demise of Dillinger and Floyd.

Hoover knew that distancing Purvis from reporters was not enough. He also had to keep him away from gangsters like Dillinger and Floyd. This would be nearly impossible as long as his reputation as a giant-killer endured. Purvis could not, after all, be sick and housebound forever; sooner or later he would get the chance to put another notch on his belt. "Hoover understood that for his FBI formula of teamwork and science to be accepted by the public, Melvin Purvis could not be in the picture anymore," noted Richard Gid Powers. "He knew it meant that he had to eliminate Purvis." FBI files indicate that because firing Purvis was not an option, Hoover chose instead to depict him as a careless and ineffective leader.

On November 17, 1934—three weeks after Floyd's death and Louella Parsons's movie rumor—Hoover dispatched inspector James S. Egan to Chicago. His orders were to carry out a white-glove inspection of the Chicago office. Such inspections were standard protocol under Hoover. "They would come in with a white handkerchief and check the insides of drawers for dust," remembered Doris Lockerman. "It was ridiculous and some of the inspectors knew it. We would smile the whole time they were doing this, and they knew we were laughing at them, and they were laughing, too, but they had to do it anyway." Egan's inspection, however, was no laughing matter. Purvis's troubles began on the very first day of the inspection, when Egan sat checking his wristwatch until Purvis arrived at the office at 9:50 A.M. To compound his lateness, Purvis failed to jot down his time of arrival in the daily log. "It is felt that an Agent in Charge should be at his office between 8:30 and 8:45 every morning in order to lay out the work and direct the efforts of the others who report at or about 9:00," Egan wrote. In fact, Purvis was often out late at night on stakeouts, and just as often handled Bureau business on the way into the office. Egan also noticed that some of the stenographers "had not settled down to work until about 9:15. This is very important . . . a full and complete explanation is desired."

Egan maintained this scrutiny for ten days. At the end of his stay, he produced a thoroughly damning document that portrayed Purvis as unfit to lead the office. "This entire report reflects unfavorably on [Purvis]," Egan said in his summary. "This Agent in Charge has not been exercising proper supervision over his office . . . he is extremely temperamental, egotistical . . . he had been giving more time to his own personal interests and to his social activities than he had been giving to the office which he represents." Hoover did not wait for the report to be issued—he telephoned Egan midway through the inspection, on November 23. "I have a pretty good picture of this office," Egan told him. "Want me to high spot it?"

Hoover said he did. "The road work box is all out of kilter," Egan began. "The ticklers we found dating back as far as June had never been taken out of the file . . . dirty underwear and shirts, and so forth, in some of those cell rooms, and I think they belong to the Agents . . . fruit in the desks and one of the stenographers smoking . . . dirty dishes were found behind a radiator in the storeroom." Egan initially put the blame for the state of the Chicago office on two agents who were acting as supervisors. But Hoover had another take on it. "Those things you have mentioned, though, Jim, they are really the responsibility of Purvis," Hoover said. "He can't alibi that on the ground that he hasn't got enough men."

"Well," replied Egan, "that's what I was going to say."

"It's the lack of proper supervision on the part of Purvis," Hoover continued.

"It is absolutely, positively lack of supervision and thought in the management of the office as I can see it," Egan said. "I think these conditions are pretty rotten."

"Well, I think they are very bad," said Hoover. "Yes, very, very bad . . . . I want you to set [Purvis] down. I'd go down the line—1, 2, 3. It seems to me that he hasn't measured up to what we've been expecting him to do."

The report itself was a laundry list of violations. A scouring of office files allowed Egan to find 232 instances of "undue delay in handling cases," his most serious charge. The rest of his findings had to do with the administration and physical condition of the office. "The desks, file cases and cabinets have been maintained in a terribly lax manner," he wrote. In the stenographer's room, Egan noted a "Postal Guide of July of 1931, which appears to be the latest Postal Guide in this office." He even recorded that Sam Cowley—Hoover's handpicked man in Chicago—had improperly stuffed an original code telegram in his desk drawer. The wardrobe cabinets used by the agents and stenographers came under particular fire, containing as they did stray straw and felt hats, a soiled shirt, and old newspapers. Egan cited twenty-five incoming communications not stamped as received, seventeen unacknowledged letters, five improperly posted assignment cards, three improperly indexed cases, two wanted notices not properly posted, and "a number of dirty dishes on a window sill behind the file cabinet." In all, the report listed more than 100 transgressions.

Egan's conclusion gave Hoover a blueprint for the removal of Purvis from Chicago. "This Agent in Charge . . . has been leaving the work to others who have not been properly trained or who have not had sufficient interest therein to do the same properly," Egan wrote. "It is believed that after a period of approximately ninety days this office should again be inspected and if the conditions have not improved and the office is not in first-class shape, this Agent in Charge should be placed in a smaller office where he would have to do the work himself." Purvis defended himself to Hoover in person, before he even saw Egan's final report. In Washington on another matter during the time of Egan's inspection, Purvis anticipated its negative findings and issued "the stock reply—namely, that he didn't have enough men," Hoover later told Egan. "I didn't make any comments, because I realized that where the cases have been delayed and all that sort of thing, that may be true. But those things that you have mentioned are not the result of any shortage of men."

Hoover clearly believed that Purvis was a poor administrator. In fact, Purvis freely admitted that administration was not his strong suit. He explained to Egan that he had little time for clerical matters, that he was too busy following leads and organizing raids. It is true that Purvis often behaved more like just another agent than the agent-in-charge, which inevitably led to a certain laxity in the running of his office. Purvis did not set out any rules to govern the appearance of desks or wardrobes. He often signed letters and memos without proofing them for accuracy, and he frequently fell behind on paperwork. He believed his job was to find and capture criminals, not to make sure tickler files were right side up. Yet in a Bureau headed by a man who prized organization and efficiency, Purvis's lack of attention to detail was glaring. Hoover placed great faith in the power of orderly and systematic effort, of rules and regulations and protocol. It was undeviating attention to procedure, he believed, that led to successful casework. However chaotic an agent's life became, he was still expected to be in the office on time and keep a tidy desk. Hoover was sure this was possible; Purvis was not.

Just over a month after Pretty Boy Floyd's death, Egan's exhaustive report became part of Purvis's personnel file, effectively putting him on notice. Yet Purvis had far graver concerns than dirty plates and soiled hats. On the very day James Egan completed his inspection—Tuesday, November 27, 1934—an urgent message reached the Chicago office.

———

George Nelson knew instantly something was wrong. Instinctively he fingered the trigger of the automatic he held in his lap. The man on the front porch, squinting in the sun, would get the bullet if it came to that. Nelson had just driven his brand-new black Ford V-8 sedan, stolen a day earlier from a dealership, down the gravel road that led to the Lake Como Inn in Lake Geneva, Wisconsin. He stopped it a few yards from a house alongside the inn. His wife, Helen Gillis, was in the passenger seat, and in the back his pal John Chase clutched a Colt rifle. They were looking for a friendly face—Hobart Hermanson, the man who owned the inn and had helped them hide out in the past. Nelson had no particular reason to be at Hermanson's, but neither did he have to be anywhere else, and a visit to the inn seemed a good way to kill time. But then the stranger appeared on the porch, and Nelson gripped his gun. He asked through the car window if Hermanson was there. No, the stranger replied, he was not. Nelson calmly turned the Ford around. "Sure as hell that's a G-man," he said as he drove away, "and we caught him with his pants down."

Nelson was right. The man on the porch was Jim Metcalfe, a special agent from the Chicago office. Metcalfe had his suspicions, too. He suspected the man he had squinted to see through the glare of the windshield was the very man he had spent three weeks staking out the inn to find. He telephoned Chicago.

George "Baby Face" Nelson—real name Lester Gillis—was no ordinary gangster, not even when compared to the most ruthless criminals of his time. Dillinger was to some extent a gentleman bandit, more pleased by his fame than by the thrill of lawlessness; Floyd was a reluctant hoodlum, wracked with regret and self-pity. But Baby Face was a different breed—he was pure evil. "Nelson liked killing for killing's sake," observed Purvis. "He was diabolical in appearance and grinned when he killed. Because of his brutality, his sadistic delight in the sheer joy of killing, he stands in a class by himself."

Nelson was twenty-five but had the features of a child, hence his ironic nickname. Most photos show him frowning, his face scrunched and sour, his expression, as one FBI bulletin noted, "sharp and stern." He looked like nothing so much as an overgrown schoolyard bully. Raised in Chicago's seedy Tenderloin district, the seventh child of Belgian parents, he grew up in harsh poverty and learned quickly to fend for himself. Always undersized—he barely topped five feet four inches as an adult—young Lester "was a plenty tough kid," an early acquaintance once said. "Hell, he had to be, a banty rooster like him, living in that neighborhood where if you weren't tough you got cut up good. He knew how to use a shiv and a bicycle chain—a gun, too." At age twelve he began stealing and stripping automobiles. "He stole a lot of stuff and was fast and slick at boosting cars," the acquaintance recalled. "He got caught because he stole too much."

Nelson was thirteen when he drew two years at the St. Charles School for Boys for auto larceny. The same crime netted him another two years there at age fifteen. It made no difference that the house officer in his dorm described him as "one of the best boys ever in that cottage." By then, there was no turning back. The underworld contacts he made at St. Charles paved the way for his criminal career. After leaving the school he was part of a tire-theft racket that thrived on Chicago's South Side; he operated a still in Evanston, Illinois, until the man he hired to cook the mash stole most of the alcohol; he switched to armed holdups once the bootlegging business dried up. He joined a gang that robbed a bank in Hillside, Illinois, in 1930, and recklessly spent his haul on things like a $350 watch for his new wife, Helen, a Polish salesgirl also from the Tenderloin. His next job—the heist of a small jewelry shop just off Michigan Avenue—was doomed from the start; its owner slipped out back and summoned police. Lester Gillis was booked under his alias, George Nelson, assigned prisoner number 5437, and sent to the Illinois State Penitentiary in Joliet.

It could not hold him. A guard transporting him in a taxicab from a courthouse back to Joliet was stunned to feel a revolver poking his ribs; he dutifully unlocked Nelson's handcuffs and watched him drive away. In 1933 Nelson hooked up with the Dillinger gang, and as its most ruthless member, he eventually became its torpedo, or machine-gunner. The alliance of gangsters was an uneasy one: Dillinger and Nelson neither liked nor trusted each other. One source of bad blood was Nelson's envy of Dillinger's renown. Melvin Purvis recalled receiving a report that "Nelson and Dillinger jealously compared their ratings in the 'Wanted' circulars issued by the Federal Bureau of Investigation, and that Nelson was once morose and sullen because a larger reward was offered for Dillinger than for himself." Stubborn, defiant, petulant, Nelson could not accept being anyone's lackey, and after nearly coming to blows with Dillinger at Little Bohemia over the sleeping arrangements, he would never again be part of someone else's gang.

After escaping Little Bohemia and slaying special agent Baum, Nelson leisurely crisscrossed the country, driving back and forth between Illinois and California. Together with his wife Helen and his pal Johnny Chase—a holdover from the Dillinger gang—he spent several weeks in Nevada and California, hiking up mountains, staying in tourist camps, and visiting old mines. On one trip back to Chicago, a police cruiser pulled Nelson over for speeding. The gangster's car was packed with guns and ammunition. But Nelson stayed calm, and the police officer saw no need to search the car. Nelson paid a five-dollar fine and went on his way.

While Nelson vacationed, Hoover and his men struggled to pin him down. By October 1934 they knew he was spending time on the West Coast. That month agents from the San Francisco office grilled a woman named Sally Backman, who was known to be the girlfriend of Johnny Chase and who had been spotted and arrested in Sausalito, California. Questioned through the night at the San Francisco Bureau office, Backman finally provided a detailed account of Nelson's travels in Nevada and California.

In Washington, Hoover seized on the leads and put Sam Cowley on a plane to Los Angeles. Cowley's orders were to spend one day each in the Los Angeles and San Francisco offices to make sure these crucial leads were being properly followed. "The Director feels that [the agent-in-charge of the San Francisco office] does not have the experience necessary to put the proper punch into this matter," E. A. Tamm advised Cowley in a conversation on October 12. "The Director would like to have [your] reaction to the whole setup as to what is going on down there."

Sally Backman's confession included another tantalizing clue: a town in Wisconsin where Nelson had said he planned to spend the winter. Backman could not recall the name of the town, even though she had spent time there, and so she was flown to Chicago to see if her memory could be jogged. Special agent Charles Winstead—the man whose bullet killed Dillinger—drove Backman through several small Wisconsin towns until they found one she remembered: Lake Geneva, site of the Lake Como Inn. The inn's owner, Hobart Hermanson, confessed to harboring Nelson in the past and cleared the way for Winstead and two other agents to set up a stakeout at the inn in early November 1934.

With traps set everywhere for him—in garages out West, in bars in the Midwest, in his favorite Wisconsin inn—Nelson would have done well to avoid his previous haunts. Still, he steered inexorably toward the places he knew best. He returned to Illinois on November 25 to assemble a new gang for a train robbery he envisioned. On November 27, Nelson, his wife, and Johnny Chase drove to the Lake Como Inn, where they hoped to visit with Hermanson.

Instead they found agent Metcalfe on the porch. While speeding away from the inn, they passed another car, this one driven by another special agent, Colin McRae. Though McRae saw Nelson only fleetingly, the rookie agent was quicker to recognize him than Metcalfe had been; he turned his head and made note of the Ford's license plate. Back at the inn, Metcalfe called the Chicago office. Baby Face Nelson was in town.

At 2:45 P.M. on November 27, Sam Cowley answered the ringing telephone at the Bureau office in the Bankers Building, to be told that Nelson was headed toward the Chicago suburbs. This was not some sketchy tip; this was a confirmed sighting by two Bureau agents. Cowley would need every available man to follow this lead. He quickly sent the only two agents in the office out to patrol Highway 12, which Nelson was likely using. He also dispatched two other agents who were working a phone tap. Finally, he asked Ed Hollis— who with Purvis and Winstead had surrounded Dillinger at the Biograph—to join the hunt as well. Rather than stay behind to coordinate, as he had done when agents were dispersed to downtown Chicago to find Dillinger, Cowley decided to arm himself and go after Nelson with Hollis.

Cowley's next step was critical. Before leaving the Bankers Building, he stopped by Purvis's office and filled him in on the lead. Purvis shot up from his chair and said, "Let's go." But Cowley declined the help.

"It won't be necessary," he said. "Hollis and I are just going to cruise around and see if we can spot the car on the highway. When we get set, I'll phone you."

Then Cowley was gone. Perhaps it was that Hoover had given him secret orders to keep Purvis away from situations in which he could make more headlines, though certainly no such orders appear anywhere in FBI files. Perhaps it was that Sam Cowley—so long the desk-bound bureaucrat—felt he needed to do something to live up to Hoover's estimation of him, to personally kill or capture a gangster without Purvis around to get the glory. Whatever the reason, though he desperately needed as many men as he could find to follow the lead—and though Purvis was far more experienced in conducting raids and seizing criminals—Cowley elected not to have Purvis join the chase for Nelson. Cowley did not even call Washington with the tip and asked Purvis not to do so either. He gathered a submachine gun and slid into a Bureau Hudson, setting off in search of Baby Face Nelson.

Out on the black asphalt of Highway 12, confrontations loomed. Nelson's Ford sedan drove past a Ford coupe stopped by the side of the road. The coupe held special agents Bill Ryan and Tom Mc-Dade, sent to search for Nelson by Cowley and both apprised of Nelson's license plate number. The agents looked back and were startled to see that very plate on the speeding sedan. This small movement—spinning in their seats to read the plate—had not been sufficiently discreet, however. Nelson, peering in the rearview mirror, caught it and assumed the worst.

"What the hell is this?" he asked. "Let's see who those birds are."

A strange automotive ballet ensued—Ryan and McDade made a U-turn to pursue Nelson, but only seconds later Nelson made his own U-turn and drove back toward the agents. When he passed them he made another U-turn across the grassy median—now he was chasing the agents. Nelson did not lay back: He drove alongside the coupe and waved his pistol at the agents.

"Pull over," Nelson ordered them, as if he were the law. With their roles reversed, the agents sped away. Next, Nelson pushed Helen down to the floor, hit the accelerator, and ordered Chase to "let them have it." Just as at Little Bohemia—where instead of fleeing he had stayed behind to fire at Purvis—Nelson seemed eager to engage his foe in battle. In the back seat, Johnny Chase hesitated; he wasn't as convinced as Nelson that the men were agents. Nelson, confident in his instincts, held the wheel with his right hand and stuck his pistol out the window with his left, shooting at the coupe. Ryan returned the fire, squeezing off seven shots.

"What in the hell are you going to do, sit there?" Nelson yelled at Chase. "Can't you see they are shooting at us?" Chase aimed his rifle at the coupe and fired through the windshield of Nelson's car. Helen Gillis, kneeling on the floor beneath the passenger seat, felt shards of glass rain on her head. "The next thing I heard," she later told agents, "is my husband saying they must have hit the motor; we are losing speed." Nelson's sputtering Ford fell behind the fleeing coupe.

Ryan and McDade radioed reports of the shoot-out to Purvis in Chicago. From the office Purvis coordinated efforts to send local lawmen to the chase area. Soon he received another report, this one from Hollis and Cowley. They had just passed Nelson's bullet-scarred car on the highway and had made a U-turn to give chase. Nelson glanced in his rearview mirror and noticed Cowley's Hudson spinning around to follow him. He stepped hard on the gas but to no avail; the Hudson gained steadily until it was only a few hundred feet away. Farther ahead Ryan and McDade pulled over and hid in the roadside grass, hoping to ambush Nelson; in the Hudson, Hollis and Cowley readied their guns as they gained even more on Nelson; and in the leaking, listing Ford sedan, Baby Face Nelson grasped for some idea on how to escape the fast-advancing law.

It happened in only a few seconds. Nelson gripped tight on the wheel and spun it hard to the right, taking the Ford onto a dirt road beside the highway outside Barrington, Illinois. "We came to a sudden stop," remembered Helen Gillis. "I stepped out of the car and ran into a field along the roadway and laid down." Just as Helen

Gillis was ducking for cover, Ed Hollis was following Nelson onto the dirt road, barely decelerating as his car made its sharp turn off the highway. His disadvantage was not knowing that Nelson had by then slammed on his brakes. Expecting the chase to continue, he saw Nelson's parked car far too late, and only hit his own brakes after passing it. The Hudson screeched and spun to a stop fifty yards past Nelson and Chase, who were already out of their car and poised to shoot. Hollis and Cowley had driven into a trap.

The agents had no choice but to step from their car and fight back. Before they even opened their doors, Nelson and Chase were firing on the car. "The great heroism of these two officers cannot be fully realized," Purvis would later say. "When they jumped out of their car they faced almost certain death, but they had a duty to perform." Cowley—who like many agents had neglected to qualify on the Bureau's pistol range, as he was required to do—aimed his submachine gun and pulled the trigger. Hollis pointed his Winchester and did the same. In the twilight of the day, the flash of their guns lit up the sky, and the horrible racket of bullet blasts and bursting glass brought several bystanders out of two nearby filling stations. They watched frozen as four men fought a brief but deadly duel. Nelson was relentless; when his Monitor 30.06 rifle jammed, he grabbed another bolt-action rifle and brazenly abandoned the cover of his car. He walked toward Hollis and Cowley, firing as he went.

Just as suddenly as it had started, the shooting stopped. Chase remained behind his car, and Nelson was near Cowley's Hudson, but they were the only two left standing. Ed Hollis lay slumped near a telephone pole he had tried to hide behind; one of Nelson's bullets caught him in the forehead. Sam Cowley was in a ditch by the side of the road, bleeding badly from his stomach and chest. Nelson, rifle still in hand, claimed the agents' Hudson as his own, driving it to Chase and commanding, "Throw those guns in here and let's be going." Before Chase could climb in himself, Nelson told him, "You better drive." It was then Chase realized Nelson had been shot.

At the Bankers Building, every phone line lit up with calls from witnesses to the carnage. Purvis took a call from the Stanford, Illinois, police chief and learned there had been a shooting. The news was catastrophic: Sam Cowley was alive but badly wounded, and Ed Hollis was dead. Purvis asked another agent to phone Washington with the grim report. Meanwhile he and three other agents grabbed weapons and ran to a waiting Hudson. As Purvis drove, he flicked on the car's siren. They were not rushing after Nelson; dozens of other agents and police officers were doing that. Purvis was headed to the hospital to see Cowley.

A car salesman who happened by the scene of the shooting had driven the wounded Cowley to Sherman Hospital in Elgin, Illinois. When Purvis arrived, he learned Cowley had been anesthetized and wheeled into the operating room. Purvis went in to see him. The seriousness of Cowley's stomach injury was obvious. "He had a small bullet wound on one side and a large gaping wound on the opposite side where the bullet had left his body," Purvis recalled. "I looked upon his torn body [and] feared that I would never talk to him again." Cowley had shown great courage and character that afternoon. The first man to find him sprawled in the ditch, state trooper William Gallagher, heard Cowley gasp, "We are Federal men. Take care of my partner first." To agents Ryan and McDade, he said, "Did they get Hollis? Help him, forget me." Now, at the hospital, he awoke briefly from his pained sleep and saw Purvis.

"Hello, Melvin," he said quietly, "I am glad you are here."

"Rest quiet," Purvis said, "and you will be all right."

As the doctors came to take him from the operating room, Cowley gazed at Purvis and delivered his final report: "I emptied my gun at them."

————

After Cowley's operation, Purvis called Hoover from the hospital at 7:50 P.M. The news was disheartening. Doctors gave Cowley only a one-in-twenty-five chance to survive. He was hemorrhaging badly and peritonitis was likely to set in. Hoover asked about Cowley's wife, Lavon, who had not yet arrived at the hospital, and instructed Purvis to give her special attention. He also impressed on Purvis the importance of using every resource available to track down Nelson that night. But Hoover was also concerned about controlling the publicity that was sure to follow the shoot-out in Barrington. He gave Purvis clear and explicit instructions. "I advised Mr. Purvis that he should remain at the hospital until Mrs. Cowley had arrived, and then he should proceed to Chicago, leaving an Agent or two at the hospital," Hoover recorded in a November 27 memorandum. "I ad-

vised him that no statements should be issued to the press; that if
necessary, he should establish some headquarters outside of the office as the newspaper men would be covering the office." Hoover
could not keep Purvis away from Cowley's bedside, nor could he
pull him off the hunt for Nelson—not without another agent in
place to direct the search. But Hoover could and did take steps to
limit Purvis's exposure to the press.

Nor did Hoover want Purvis to continue running things in
Chicago. Shortly after learning of the shooting, Hoover called inspector Hugh Clegg in Pittsburgh and had him board a 7:30 P.M.
plane for Chicago to "take charge of the entire situation." He also
summoned Assistant Director Harold Nathan from Tucson, as well
as agent-in-charge Earl Connelley of the Cincinnati office. None of
the three was likely to reach Chicago before midnight, which meant
that for the moment Purvis was the ranking agent at the scene. But
that was just for the moment. Even in this time of crisis and tragedy,
Hoover did not neglect to address the threat he felt from Purvis.

At the hospital Purvis waited to see Lavon Cowley. News of the
shooting was reaching Cowley's relatives in different ways. Hoover
himself discussed the matter with two of Cowley's siblings, telling his
brother Joe that Cowley "had a chance to pull through," something
he knew was not likely. In Salt Lake City, Cowley's mother Luella
had a premonition during a meeting of the Seventeenth Ward Relief Society. "I am frightened," she said. "I feel like someone in my
family is dying." Not much later a neighbor told her she had heard
about the shooting on the radio. Cowley's wife was notified by the
Chicago office and picked up by agents in a battered Chevrolet, the
only available car. The agents brought their wives with them to con-
sole her. Finally she arrived at Sherman Hospital, clutching her
seven-month-old son. "I shall never forget the tightening in my
heart when I saw her," Purvis recalled.

Surely Purvis knew by then that Cowley would not make it. The
.45-caliber bullet that tore through his stomach and intestines had
simply done too much damage. A bulletproof vest would have saved
him, but Cowley found them too heavy, as did Purvis and most of
the agents. Cowley was defenseless against the rampaging, sure-
shooting Nelson. Purvis had been lucky at Little Bohemia—it had
been dark and Nelson's bullets missed him by inches. But in broad
daylight Cowley had been an easy target. Purvis watched Cowley's

wife cry as she stood by her husband's hospital bed. This, he knew, was the blackest hour in the Bureau's short history.

Then Purvis saw a reporter.

Hoover had warned him to issue no statements to the press. He had explicitly ordered that he should avoid reporters at any cost. Now Elgar Brown of the *Chicago American* was asking for a comment. Purvis might have brushed him off. He might have said nothing and walked out of the hospital, as Hoover had demanded. He might have, if he was inclined to talk, made a simple statement about Cowley's bravery. But Purvis had a different role to fill. In anointing him a national hero, the press had come to expect a certain behavior from Purvis, a certain dramatic flair that fit their image of him as a fearless crime-fighter. At Sherman Hospital, Purvis played his part once more.

"If it's the last thing I do, I'll get Baby Face Nelson—dead or alive," Purvis said to Brown. "Nelson ought to know he hasn't a chance at eventual escape."

This speech to Elgar Brown—this vow to avenge Sam Cowley at his deathbed—would turn out to be a defining moment, both for Melvin Purvis and for J. Edgar Hoover.

———

Elgar Brown had his story—the man who got Dillinger and Pretty Boy Floyd had sworn an oath to bring down Baby Face Nelson. The *Chicago American* ran the story the following day. After speaking with Brown, Purvis left the hospital and returned to the Chicago office—against Hoover's wishes—to coordinate the search for Nelson from there. At 1:00 A.M. came word from agents at the hospital. There was no official prognosis, but one agent overhead Cowley's doctors say they did not expect him to see the morning. As soon as he heard this, Purvis threw on his coat and rushed back to Sherman Hospital—again, against Hoover's wishes. At 2:17 A.M., Sam Cowley died from his gunshot wounds. Purvis was there.

Cowley was the third man from his office to die within six months, all of them at the hands of Baby Face Nelson.

The next few days were bleak. The body of special agent Hollis was taken to a Chicago funeral parlor to prepare it for the trip back to his native Iowa. Hollis's wife and young son had stopped by the

Chicago office the afternoon Hollis was shot, to meet him for a planned dinner that night. His wife's face went blank at hearing the incomprehensible news. The day after the bloody battle, Hollis's wife and two special agents accompanied his body on an overnight trip to Des Moines, where another special agent met the somber group at dawn. Hollis's body lay in state in the Iowa Capitol Building. After the funeral his widow received $5,000 from the Department of Justice for her loss.

At Sherman Hospital, Lavon Cowley sagged to the floor when her husband died, shaking so much that doctors gave her a sedative. She, too, accompanied her husband's body on its long trip home to Salt Lake City. There, it lay in state at the Utah Capitol Building, through which thousands passed to pay respects. In days to come, the car salesman who drove Cowley to the hospital would write a letter to his widow telling her that Cowley "proved to me that an ideal, self-sacrificing American really did exist." Harold Nathan, in his funeral eulogy to Cowley, told the gathered mourners that "Sam Cowley was one of the simplest men I ever knew . . . His was simplicity of the saints, seers and heroes of the ages, the simplicity of true worth, of true dignity, of true honor. We, of the Division, are very proud of him. As generations of new agents come into our service, they will be told of the life and death of Sam Cowley."

Hoover also spoke at the funeral. Cowley, he said, "was brave enough to be scrupulously honest in little things as well as big things. He didn't accept the easy way out, a half-truth, a white lie, or a turned head. . . . That's the kind of courage that can carry a man proudly from the cradle to the grave." Yet it was in a citation sent to Cowley's widow that Hoover delivered a message he had been long eager to express. The citation honoring Cowley was a clear and pointed rebuke of the prevailing wisdom regarding Melvin Purvis's role in the war on crime. "Sam Cowley . . . deserves the credit for perfecting the arrangements that resulted in the location and killing of John Dillinger," Hoover stated. "Sam's command was supreme in the Chicago region; all members of the Chicago office were cognizant of his overall plan. It was he who mapped the campaign, working from a secret office with unlisted telephones, and it was this campaign which led to Dillinger's death. . . . It was due to Sam's modesty that the general public did not know the true facts concerning the downfall of our most publicized ruffian of recent years. . . . 'I'd just rather stay in the dark as I've been doing,' Sam had told me over the telephone."

On November 29, Philip Sadowski, an undertaker in Niles Center, Illinois, thirty miles from Chicago, took a call from someone claiming to know where a body could be found. Sadowski alerted Axel Stolberg, the chief of police, who in turn called the Bureau's Chicago office. Not long after noon, with curious bystanders surrounding the scene, searchers found a body in the weeds in a ditch on the corner of Long and Niles streets. The body was naked and wrapped in a blanket. A white handkerchief, now red, was wedged into a deep wound in the abdomen, and a money belt, also caked in blood, was discarded nearby. In Chicago, Purvis sent two agents to lift fingerprints.

Several hours earlier, Johnny Chase had driven Baby Face Nelson, badly wounded in the shoot-out, to the Chicago suburb of Wilmette. There, Nelson found an old friend, Father Coughlin, who declined to harbor the fugitive but agreed to direct him to a place where the group would be safe. Suspicious to the end, Nelson went instead to the home of Ray Henderson, who had connections to the Chicago underworld. Henderson helped Chase carry Nelson into a bedroom. There was no doctor to help the dying gangster, so Chase tore up a bedsheet and wrapped the pieces around Nelson's wounds, while attempting to stop the bleeding with a handkerchief. "Don't leave me now," Nelson said to his friend in a hoarse whisper. But Chase left to dump the Hudson they had stolen from Hollis and Cowley.

That left only Helen Gillis to tend to her husband. "It's getting dark," he said to her as he grew weaker and weaker. "Say goodbye to mother." His last sound was a harsh, guttural exhalation, at 7:35 P M. With that, Baby Face Nelson was gone. When Chase returned, he helped Helen Gillis wrap her husband's body in a blanket and drag it into an old sedan. They drove around Chicago in the dead of night, looking for the most lonesome place they could find. On the edge of a neglected cemetery, ringed with high and shielding weeds, they dropped Nelson's body to the dirt.

An autopsy showed Nelson died from seventeen wounds caused by bullets from the guns of Ed Hollis and Sam Cowley. The most ravaging wound was to his abdomen, through which a .45-caliber bullet had passed. That bullet was fired by Sam Cowley.

Although another Public Enemy Number One had been killed, it came at a high price for the Bureau. And even though Purvis had not been at the shooting, he would pay a price, too. By 9:30 the morning after the shoot-out, Hoover had learned of Purvis's vow to avenge Cowley's death. Hoover was furious. "I stated very emphatically that I am displeased with the publicity," he told Hugh Clegg on November 28. "I do not want to send Mr. Purvis out of Chicago unless absolutely necessary, but I may have to in order to take care of the publicity situation." Purvis, he went on, "exercises poor judgment in appearing publicly, putting him in a position to be quoted by newspapermen." Clegg, who stood shoulder to shoulder with Purvis in the dark forest at Little Bohemia, tried his best to convince Hoover that Purvis was still useful to the Bureau. He told Hoover that Purvis was anxious to help in the search for Nelson, but Hoover ordered Clegg to keep him away from the action. "He will be of little value because of the fact that he is so well known," Hoover declared. Clegg suggested Purvis work out of a back room at the main Chicago office. Hoover said, "This would not be advisable." Finally Clegg said Purvis could accompany the body of Ed Hollis to Des Moines, where he was unlikely to be besieged by reporters. Once again Hoover rejected the idea. "Mr. Purvis is not to accompany raiding parties," Hoover ordered. "He is not to come to the office; should not accompany the bodies of either Mr. Cowley or Mr. Hollis to their homes, and is to remain in the background generally . . . he should remain at home until such time as we can work out something for him to do."

In Chicago, Hugh Clegg was instructed to offer no explanation to reporters curious about Purvis's absence at such a critical time. "Inform the press that Mr. Purvis is still Special Agent in Charge," he told Clegg, "but the instant investigation is being conducted under [your] supervision." Inevitably rumors circulated that Clegg had replaced Purvis in Chicago, and that Purvis would not return from his mysterious exile. Hoover denied them but refused to clarify why Purvis was missing.

Hoover next moved to isolate Purvis even further. He had long contemplated establishing a secret, second office in Chicago, out of which his special Dillinger squad could operate free from the pesky reporters hovering in the hall near Purvis's office. Now he acted swiftly to make it happen. Hoover arranged to have Earl Connelley find rooms outside the Bankers Building and set up the secret office. By December 4, Connelley had rented an office two blocks away, in Room 1026 of the New York Life Insurance Building, for $100 a month. He installed three unlisted telephone numbers and secured a post office box for mail. The secret office was up and running by December 6.

Hoover then officially stripped Purvis of his command of the Chicago office. He placed Earl Connelley in charge not only of the Dillinger case—which included finding Johnny Chase and Helen Gillis—but also of the Kansas City massacre case and the Karpis–Barker gang. These were the three biggest and most pressing cases in Chicago. "Purvis will handle all other matters arising in the Chicago district," Hoover instructed in a memorandum. "Purvis should [also] be under orders to promptly comply with Mr. Connelley's requests." Yet all of these orders were confidential: The outside world knew nothing of Purvis's de facto demotion. On occasion one of Purvis's contacts would call him with information about some facet of the Dillinger case, or request his help in pursuing a lead. His instincts were to do whatever he could to lend a hand. On December 20, Hoover felt the need to restate his orders, and instructed that a letter be sent to Purvis "so that he will understand that he is not to have anything to do with the [Dillinger] case," Hoover wrote.

Purvis received the letter on December 23, 1934. "Please advise the Division by return mail whether these instructions are clearly understood by you," Hoover wrote. Certainly Purvis understood fully that he was no longer in charge of any case of any consequence, and that he likely never would be again. "He was bewildered," recalled Doris Lockerman. "He was bewildered that he could do as good a job as he had done, for as long as he had done it, at great sacrifice of time and effort, and still be treated badly. I think he couldn't believe that it was happening." Hoover's swift neutralization of Purvis, in the wake of his vow to avenge Cowley, "really hurt him," she said. "We could see a change in his attitude, and we all could tell that he was losing grace. There's no doubt that he sensed it, and that he knew something was happening that he was powerless to stop."

On Christmas Eve, Purvis traveled to South Carolina to spend the holiday with his family. On December 29, only five days after Purvis received the letter from Hoover confirming his demotion, *Literary Digest* published an issue listing the ten outstanding personalities of 1934, based on a poll of 240 newspapers across the country. Hitler made the list; so did Mussolini. The highest-ranking American was the president, Franklin Roosevelt. The second most famous man in the country, according to the *Digest*, was Melvin Purvis.

J. Edgar Hoover did not make the list.

———

Purvis began 1935 as a seriously compromised agent-in-charge. He still had his title and the loyalty of his men but very little else. He remained the nominal head of the Chicago office, and as such was inevitably exposed to major crimes and meaningful casework. On January 8, 1935, dozens of agents from the Chicago office staked out two apartments in an effort to find Dock Barker, the patriarch of the notorious Barker-Karpis kidnapping gang. A telephone tap had led agents to the two addresses—the Surf Lane Apartments on Chicago's North Side and another apartment on Pine Grove Avenue, fourteen blocks away. Purvis and Earl Connelley, in charge of the roving squad of agents then stationed in Chicago, suspected that Barker—using the alias Mr. Esser—was hiding out at the Surf Lane Apartments.

Twelve special agents surrounded the apartments, blocking every exit. At 6:30 P.M. on January 8, a man matching the description of Mr. Esser walked through the apartment's courtyard and into the street. The agents moved in and grabbed Dock Barker, who had slipped on a patch of ice as he tried to get away. As they patted him down, they were surprised to find he was unarmed. "Where's your gun?" one agent asked. "Home," Barker replied, "and ain't that a hell of a place for it?"

Purvis got his crack at Barker at the Bankers Building. Hoover was desperate to find out where the rest of the gang was hiding out, and he gave orders to lean on Barker hard. Still, "he sat in a chair, his jaw clenched, and he looked straight ahead," Purvis recalled. "His eyes told the story of an innate savagery." Purvis's interrogation produced nothing, nor did the efforts of other agents brought in to question Barker. Fortunately, a second raid that night netted another gang member, Byron Bolton. He surrendered valuable information about the gang, and in particular about its hideaway in Florida. All the agents had to do, Bolton told them, was find a lake with a big alligator in it named Old Joe. Connelley, in charge of the Florida expedition, never did locate Old Joe, but thanks to a map found among Barker's things, he did pinpoint the hideaway house in Oklawaha, Florida. A furious shoot-out there on January 15, 1935, left both Ma Barker and her son Fred Barker dead.

Around the time that these raids were conducted, Hoover had begun to saddle Purvis with a series of demeaning assignments. First, Hoover assigned Purvis the task of interviewing prospective candidates for the Bureau, a job normally reserved for inspectors and not agents in the field. In early January 1935, Hoover ordered Purvis to St. Paul to meet with applicants, which not only kept him away from sensitive work but also removed him from Chicago. At the same time, Hoover used the damning criticisms in inspector Egan's report as justification to analyze Purvis's every move. The scrutiny began with Purvis's return from his Christmas break. "A search of the records of the Division fails to disclose an application blank for recent leave of absence from Mr. Purvis," Hoover's cohort, Clyde Tolson, reported to the director on January 3. "His leave expired at 1:00 P.M. on December 31st [but] he did not report to the Chicago office . . . [he] remained at his home where he took care of some official work." Hoover accepted the explanation that Purvis had not been instructed that his orders were to depart for St. Paul that day. But he also pointedly noted that "in view of the inclination of Mr. Purvis to be somewhat careless in carrying out specific instructions . . . we should be most particular in the instructions which we issue to him in order that there can be no excuse for his failure to comply with what our wishes are."

For the next five months, Hoover continued to saddle Purvis with busywork and random assignments. On January 7 he ordered him to sift through stacks of files relating to thirty-eight war-risk insurance cases dating to December 1933. In late January he summoned Purvis to Washington for a five-week assignment. "Bring warm clothing," Hoover advised—the job placed Purvis on an outdoor rifle range in the dead of winter. Hoover also stuffed Purvis's personnel file with a series of critiques regarding largely insignificant matters. "You have been requested no less than four times to submit a photograph of yourself to the Bureau," Hoover complained in a February

23 letter. "I can see no reason why this request was not complied with weeks ago." On March 13, Hoover blasted Purvis for scoring poorly on a routine efficiency test and ordered him to study his rules manual. On March 25, he harangued Purvis for sending a gun to an outside lab for a ballistics test; a few days later he blamed Purvis for a leak of information to the *Chicago American;* not long after that a simple clerical error—four missing pages from a job application sent to Washington—provoked another stern letter. On May 12 Purvis was chastised for granting one of his men four days' leave without consulting headquarters: "Section No. 90 of the Manual of Rules and Regulations [states that] Agents in Charge may grant leave for not more than two days."

Another complaint stemmed from an accusation that agents in Chicago could not get in to see him "except by appointment," noted a Bureau report. "You have to take matters up through the switchboard operator if you desire to see the Agent in Charge." Purvis explained that Assistant Director Nathan, acting on orders from Hoover himself, had instructed him to limit the hours that agents could meet with him in the interest of efficiency. Even so, Purvis denied he was ever unavailable to agents who needed his attention. "If I was told that the Agents could not see him when they wanted to see him, it was a lie," an inspector noted that Purvis told him. Further, Purvis said he believed "he had enemies in the office"—the only way he could explain the accusation. Purvis asked for the names of the agents who complained; Hoover did not provide them. There is no hard evidence that Hoover used agents as spies or that he planted someone in Chicago. Yet "everyone knew there was a mole working in the office," said Lockerman. "We just did not know who it was. Once the agents realized this the trust and fellowship that had developed among them was undermined." Former FBI agent William Turner said, "We had this saying in the Bureau: 'Every office has it's submarine, so just watch for the periscopes.'"

On March 8, Clyde Tolson took a call from a tabloid editor, Louis Ruppel, and listened as Ruppel relayed a rumor he had heard. "Mr. Purvis went to a party some time ago at Chicago, became intoxicated and waved a gun at persons at a party," Ruppel reported. "It might prove very embarrassing to [Hoover] if [he] continued to endorse Mr. Purvis." Ruppel could not provide any details about the incident or vouch for the person who told him about it. Still, Tolson took the sketchy rumor straight to Hoover. On March 9, Hoover asked Purvis to defend himself. "The story is an unmitigated and unadulterated lie and the person responsible for same is a liar," Purvis replied. Despite this denial, Hoover was not inclined to give Purvis the benefit of the doubt. He ordered Pop Nathan to go back to Ruppel and press him for the informant's name. Again, Ruppel could not provide it. Even so, Hoover was happy to have Ruppel dig around for more information damaging to Purvis. "I expressed the Director's pleasure at the desire of Mr. Ruppel to cooperate," Nathan noted, "and said that we would be glad to receive any additional information at any time."

In those contentious early months of 1935, Purvis continued to receive praise from outside the Bureau. Hoover learned that both the mayor of Chicago and the police commissioner "admired the efficiency" displayed by the Chicago office, and had singled out Purvis for providing "wonderful cooperation," according to a Bureau report. The U.S. attorney in Chicago also lauded Purvis for helping to prosecute cases. In March, Hoover was informed that the men in the Chicago office were unhappy with agent D. M. Ladd, the man Hoover picked to supervise raids in place of Purvis. "The special agents of the office, in connection with the conduct of raids, have been kept waiting in the Chicago office until time for the raids," Hoover noted in a March 12 letter. "Previously, it was the practice of Mr. Purvis, when raids were to be conducted, to permit the special agents to go to their homes where they would be advised by telephone of the time and plans for such raids . . . [the agents] are somewhat resentful of being required to remain at the office . . . for long periods of time."

The strongest endorsement of Purvis came from Hugh Clegg, who had supported him in the tense days following Cowley's death. This time Clegg was tasked with evaluating Purvis at a conference of agents-in-charge in April 1935. By then Purvis was in his fifth month of restricted duty, and he had already received countless reprimands from Washington. Even so, Clegg noted, "I feel in all sincerity that he is intensely loyal to the Director and to the Bureau. His high personal regard for the Director continues unabated in spite of what he probably feels to be some sort of punitive administrative action which has been taken in his case." If he had a leadership flaw, Clegg said, it was that he was too protective of his men. "He has participated in a considerable number of raids and I believe is somewhat too much inclined to personally participate in some of the investigative activities of this character rather than to delegate the leadership to others," Clegg wrote. "I think he does this intentionally with fear that the men participating with him in these raids will feel he is not bearing his share of the danger."

Despite this flaw, Clegg continued in his evaluation, "the same spontaneous activities which lead him into difficulties and occasional criticism are likewise the same qualities that contribute to 'make the breaks' in cases and force them to a successful conclusion." It was true Purvis chafed under the strict regulations imposed by Washington, Clegg said in summary, but his loyalty to Hoover compelled him to keep trying to accommodate those rules. "I believe that he has in the past and will continue in the future to demonstrate that he can and does learn rather important, but to him, heartbreaking lessons," Clegg said, "which eventually contribute to making him even better qualified."

Clegg's high estimation of Purvis, much like the other testaments to his ability, did not impress Hoover. Bureau files from early 1935 indicate he was intractable in his belief that Purvis was no longer useful to him. "It was apparent to everyone that Purvis was targeted," said Lockerman. "Everyone believed he was singled out for punishment and exclusion. Personally I felt he was dying inside at the time. He knew he was being railroaded." One of the last indignities came on May 3, 1935, when—despite knowing that Purvis already worked six days a week—Hoover demanded more. "Changes have been made with regard to certain of the Special Agents in Charge interviewing and examining applicants throughout the country," Hoover advised Purvis. "Effective immediately it is my desire that the applicants pending in the Chicago District be interviewed and examined by you and that Sundays and holidays be utilized for this work so that it will not interfere with the regular functions of the Chicago office."

Despite being stripped of authority over the biggest cases, Purvis still found himself involved in important and dangerous manhunts. He was not allowed anywhere near the search for the new Public Enemy Number One—Alvin "Creepy" Karpis, a leader of the Barker-Karpis gang—but there were other fugitives on the loose in Chicago, and in June 1935 one of them surfaced long enough to draw attention. On June 1, at 2:25 P.M., Purvis took a telephone call from two special agents who had received an urgent tip from a Chicago office informant. Purvis learned that Volney Davis—the gangster who smashed an agent with his beer mug to gain his freedom—had come out of hiding.

Purvis knew how to mobilize quickly for such pursuits. He ordered Martin and Williams to the home of the informant, where they were to keep an eye out for Davis and wait for backup. He also dispatched six agents to cover Anne's Beauty Parlor on West Madison Street, where the informant said Davis had promised to take her. Then Purvis ran to his car, turned on the siren, and raced toward the informant's address, shutting off his siren a few blocks from her indistinct brick house in a new Chicago development.

Before Purvis arrived, agents noticed a Ford V-8 coupe with Georgia plates drive past the home and make a U-turn at the corner. The driver parked in front of the informant's house and went inside. The agents knew immediately this was Volney Davis. A few minutes later, at 3:05 P.M., Purvis and several other agents pulled up on the street. Purvis had Martin get in his car and park it behind Davis's Ford; he told him to be ready to ram the Ford should Davis try to drive away. Purvis sent agents Williams and Chaffetz to the rear of the house to block Davis from slipping out a back door, and he put agent Cassidy to the south of the front doorway. Purvis and agent Suran took the spots nearest to the front door. None of the agents, Purvis recalled, was adequately hidden. "There was no real concealment for us," he later wrote. "I [was] sheltered slightly by a sort of brick alcove or chimney, but in plain view of anyone who came to the window."

Once the house was well surrounded, Purvis and his men could only wait. "The wait seemed interminable—years, ages," Purvis said. "As a matter of fact, it was about twenty minutes." At one point three people walked by and stopped to stare at Purvis and his men. Purvis was afraid Davis would glance out the window and see these people gawking. Without speaking, he took out his badge and showed it to the bystanders, waving them away with his arm. To his relief they kept walking, and the stakeout continued. Still, Purvis had been rattled. "I am quite willing to admit that I was frightened as we waited," Purvis said. "Volney Davis, we knew, was a desperate man. He would be delighted to shoot it out."

Purvis's anxiety was such that he began to doubt Davis was even in the house, despite being told by two agents that he was. The slow seconds ticked by in the still heat of the afternoon, as the agents kept their hands near their guns and their eyes on the unmoving door. Finally, at 3:20 P.M., it budged. Purvis had ordered the agents not to leave their positions until the suspect was clear of the house and near his car, and so no one moved as Davis walked unknowingly to the sidewalk and approached his parked Ford. At the last second Purvis gave a signal, and the agents moved in. Purvis yelled for Davis to put his hands up.

Davis kept walking. He reached his car and opened the door, but before he could get in Purvis and Suran were on him. They lunged at Davis "and reached him almost simultaneously," Purvis recalled. "The force of the impact of our two bodies bowled him over." Davis collapsed to the sidewalk, stunned, and Suran ordered him to his feet. The fugitive did not move quickly enough, so Purvis and Suran grabbed him by the arms. Davis flailed to get them free, and in the struggle hit Suran's gun, which shot a round into the car. It was sheer luck that neither Suran nor Purvis was hit. "I'll get up, I'll get up," Davis protested, but by then three other agents were there to push him against the car and force his hands into cuffs.

Purvis had agent Chaffetz search Davis's Ford; inside Chaffetz found a loaded Colt .38 automatic pistol and two loaded .380-caliber clips. Purvis told agent Martin to drive the Ford to the Clark–Van Buren garage to have it checked for fingerprints. Purvis put his handcuffed prisoner in the back of his car and drove him to the Chicago office. At the Bankers Building he whisked him to the nineteenth floor in the freight elevator, and swore the elevator operator to silence. In the late afternoon he took a call from Hoover. "I instructed Mr. Purvis . . . to keep Davis handcuffed at all times and to keep the apprehension confidential," Hoover recorded in a memorandum. "I discussed with Mr. Purvis the removal of Davis to St. Paul . . . he should be removed to St. Paul by plane after dark tonight." Purvis told Hoover he wanted to keep Davis in Chicago so that he could personally interrogate him. Normally, Purvis had other agents grill suspects, to avoid being called as a witness at a trial. But because Purvis's duties in Chicago had been severely curtailed, he chose to sit with Davis and question him for hours. "I asked him why he had taken his life in his hands to escape after the plane was forced down," Purvis recalled. "He shrugged his shoulders and grinned. 'Don't you think freedom is worth it?' he asked." Purvis got Davis to sign a waiver of removal and provide a full and detailed account of his criminal activities dating back to the early 1920s.

Perhaps Purvis knew the Davis case would be his last hurrah. Hoover, as usual, kept a close watch on the publicity connected to the arrest. "If he receives any inquiries about Davis he will say he knows nothing about it," Hoover recounted of his conversation with Purvis that afternoon. Three hours later, after residents who heard the accidental shot at the scene had notified the press, Hoover ordered Purvis not to talk about Davis to the reporters gathered outside his office. To ensure Purvis did not have a chance to speak to reporters, Hoover once again ordered him to disappear the minute he put Davis on a plane to St. Paul.

One day after the arrest, on June 2, Purvis and several agents escorted Davis to the Chicago municipal airport. Davis was manacled to two agents and pushed aboard the chartered, trimotored Stinson plane before a reporter at the airport could see his face. Purvis, coming up behind the hustling agents, smiled at the reporter and said, "I'm going out for some air." Purvis watched the plane—bound for Minnesota—take off at 8:00 P.M. After that he went to his apartment. He did not talk with reporters about Davis's capture or otherwise acknowledge his role in the arrest. Instead, Hoover had an agent in Tacoma, Washington, break the news to the press on June 3.

Purvis was not done with the case, however. As was his custom, he tried to make sure the informant who set up Davis was taken care of. The woman was distraught because her family had learned of her association with Davis, and now they were being hounded by relentless reporters. Purvis offered to move her and her family to another location until things quieted down, but the woman said her family would never allow it. Purvis arranged for the woman's father to come to the Chicago office, where he sat with him and explained that his daughter had acted valiantly and performed an important service.

Volney Davis was charged with conspiracy to kidnap Edward Bremer and arraigned before a federal judge in St. Paul at 10:00 A.M. on June 3. Some in the courtroom were surprised to hear Davis plead guilty, although he was told he had the right to plead not guilty and go to trial. Once again, Davis merely shrugged.

"Aw, hell, I might as well [plead guilty]," he said. "You can't get away from those G-men."

———

Hoover sent no letter of commendation to Purvis for his role in capturing Volney Davis. By then he had already decided Purvis's fate. On April 4, 1935, Hoover sent Clyde Tolson a memorandum outlining the details of a proposed shake-up. Hoover listed fifteen agents-in-charge who were to be transferred to new field offices. Most of them were being promoted from smaller to larger offices. There was one glaring exception: Special-agent-in-charge Melvin Purvis was to be transferred from Chicago to Charlotte, North Carolina.

Purvis sat for one more indignity from Hoover. In late June 1935, Purvis approved the use of a car to help officers from the Bureau of Prisons transport a convict named Jacob Berman to Alcatraz prison. Hoover demanded an explanation and said, "The Bureau does not feel that you should have used a Bureau car for this purpose." As he had dozens of times before, Purvis dictated a conciliatory letter to Hoover. "I understood . . . the Attorney General was very interested in this matter," he explained on July 2. "I therefore was of the opinion that it would be wise to assist them as much as possible."

Several days before he composed that letter, Purvis asked his brother-in-law, William Lee Davidson, to come to Chicago for a meeting. They discussed the sorts of jobs Purvis could get were he to leave the Bureau. "You know, he was just bruised to pieces by then," said Doris Lockerman. "He was embittered by all the rejection and criticism and innuendo." After only eight and a half years in the Bureau, he had been ruined by forces he could hardly comprehend. "You can think of it in terms of vast, seismic movements of public opinion and government policy," noted Richard Gid Powers, "and Melvin Purvis is caught in the gears of all that in a way that he doesn't know what is happening to him."

On July 10, 1935—just two weeks short of the one-year anniversary of the death of John Dillinger—Purvis sat at his glass-topped desk and composed a brief telegram to J. Edgar Hoover. "I hereby

tender my resignation as Special Agent in Charge of the Chicago office of the Federal Bureau of Investigation, to become effective as of
the close of business Friday, July twelfth," Purvis wrote. "The Bureau
in whose service I have enjoyed the associations of so many fine men
will always have my sincere best wishes."

Hoover had the resignation on his desk by midmorning July 10.
This time he was only too happy to accept it.

13

HOOVER THE HERO

July 1935

Melvin Purvis cleaned out his office in the Bankers Building on the morning of July 12, 1935. He packed his few belongings, including his favorite horse figurine, and shook hands with agents who shuffled in to wish him well. The mood on the nineteenth floor was glum. "For the longest time Purvis didn't want to believe what was happening, and so he hung on hoping it would change," recalled Doris Lockerman. "But by the end he knew he had to believe it. He had no choice but to go."

The Bureau made no formal announcement about the resignation. Still, reporters picked up on the news and rushed to the Bankers Building with photographers in tow. They were not allowed in to see Purvis, and settled for snapping his picture from the foyer. When Purvis finally left the office, surrendering a command he had held since his appointment on October 25, 1932, he refused to answer questions or comment on suggestions that he and Hoover were feuding. He walked briskly through the media gauntlet. The beat reporters stayed on his heels and kept pushing. Down on the street Purvis insisted his reasons for quitting were "purely personal," and denied a rumor he had a job lined up with New York City's vice squad. Still the reporters pushed. Hadn't Hoover driven him out? Was Hoover jealous of Purvis's fame? Wouldn't Purvis, now that he was free of him, say something derogatory about Hoover? Finally Purvis stopped. "Frankly," he said, "I'm glad to be out of here." It

was the closest he ever came to publicly voicing displeasure with
Hoover.

The resignation of the Bureau's star agent made headlines across
the country. On July 12 reporters reached Hoover in Atlantic City,
where he was attending a convention of the International Association of Chiefs of Police, and asked for his side of things. Hoover
would say only that Purvis had been replaced by special agent D. M.
Ladd, and that there had been no disharmony between them. And
that was it. Hoover even called Henry Suydam and told him not to
provide reporters with any information about Purvis, not even the
number of years he had served in the Bureau. Hoover wanted a total blackout; he believed the matter would simply go away. "There is
no comment that can be made," Hoover said, "as there is nothing
to say."

Here Hoover badly miscalculated the nation's interest in Purvis.
The newspapers would not allow such a celebrity simply to slip out
of view, and the Bureau's silence served only to fuel speculation that
a feud with Hoover was the reason Purvis quit. For years afterward,
it would be rumored the resignation had something to do with the
solving of the Roy Frisch case, which was announced to the press on
the very day Purvis left his job. In fact the announcement was
Hoover's crude attempt to divert the headline writers. Roy Frisch, a
forty-one-year-old Reno banker whose naked body was dumped in a
shallow grave near a mine shaft outside Reno, had been killed by
Baby Face Nelson. Purvis felt that any announcement about cracking the Frisch case should come out of Chicago. But Hoover forbade Purvis from talking to the press, citing a desire for secrecy
until agents searching the Nevada desert located the body. Yet
Hoover himself did not wait until Frisch was found to break the
story. When reporters contacted him on July 12, Hoover personally
announced that the mystery of Frisch's disappearance had been
solved, and that agents were searching for the corpse.

Hoover's announcement was not the reason Purvis resigned—he
had long since made the decision to walk away. He did not clarify his
precise reasons—not then, and not in the years to come. Shortly after leaving, he agreed to be filmed for a newsreel that appeared in
theaters less than a week after his departure, but he was no more
forthcoming than before. "For the past few years I have been leading somewhat of a hectic life," he said. "But now I'm going to find a

pipe which will hold a pound of tobacco and get on somebody's front porch and rest a while." Even so, the squad he left behind at the Bankers Building had no doubts why Purvis left. "We all knew the reason," said Lockerman. "There was no other reason other than the fact that Hoover wanted him to be a failure. Every agent saw it coming, saw it the first day it began. It was as plain as if it had been written."

Purvis's evasive answers and Hoover's silence did not satisfy the press. Reporters knew there was more to the story. Purvis's resignation, and that of another agent in New York, "strengthen the rumor that a revolt is brewing in the Department of Justice," wrote the *Philadelphia Record*'s Cecil Pennyfeather in his July 15, 1935, column. "Many agents are said to be dissatisfied with the leadership of J. Edgar Hoover, and other resignations are expected." The Associated Press reported, "Although officials declined to comment on reports of dissension, an authoritative source said privately friction between Hoover and Purvis was known to exist." At the same time, columnists delivered glowing tributes to Purvis. "Few men have left public life with a brighter record for integrity and efficiency than Melvin Purvis," the Denver *Rocky Mountain News* declared in an item headlined "A Loss to Uncle Sam." "The whole country will wish him the best of luck—and will wish, also, that some way could have been found to retain a little bit longer the services of so accomplished a sleuth." NBC broadcaster Lowell Thomas on July 12 told his radio listeners, "The G-men have lost one of their biggest G's—not big physically but in reputation. Melvin Purvis, the man who shot Dillinger, is called Shorty, so today the Department of Justice is short of Shorty."

In ensuing days, Hoover gradually realized that although he was rid of Purvis, he would not soon be rid of his reputation. The mystery behind why so dedicated an agent would simply step down—at such a young age and at the height of the Bureau's successes—only added to Purvis's mystique. Surely Hoover realized that pushing Purvis out the door was a tactical blunder—that at least while Purvis was with the Bureau, Hoover could limit the agent's exposure to the press. Purvis, however, now was free to talk to the media all he wished. The combination of flattering testimonials to Purvis and rumors the Bureau was in turmoil perhaps alerted Hoover that forcing Purvis out was only a first step, and that next he would need to tackle Purvis's heroic image. Indeed, Hoover's animus toward Purvis did not end when Purvis walked out of the Bankers Building.

On the day of Lowell Thomas's broadcast, Hoover phoned Purvis and asked him to explain his resignation. Purvis said he had no definite plans but did have several proposals he wished to pursue, including the prospect of working with a law firm in Chicago. Then Hoover asked "if there was any situation in the service which had caused him to submit his resignation." Purvis's answer was telling.

"I don't know of anything," he said, "that you don't know about the whole situation."

This was good enough for Hoover, who immediately accepted the resignation. News of it blindsided Attorney General Cummings, who got the information from reporters. Cummings called the Bureau for an explanation and got none. On July 12, Hoover called Purvis a second time. Under pressure to answer satisfactorily as to why Purvis resigned, Hoover was determined to put the matter to rest. "I said there had been inquiries to the effect that Mr. Purvis had been dismissed, that he was dissatisfied," Hoover recalled of the conversation. "I told Mr. Purvis my reply [to reporters] had been . . . that the resignation was entirely voluntary, that there was no element of discord between the Bureau and Mr. Purvis." Hoover tried to enlist Purvis to help him save face: The "Washington papers have been playing up the story of the resignation, and I thought the rumors ought to be stopped if possible as they were not good for him or for the Bureau," Hoover said. "Mr. Purvis thanked me for calling."

A short time later, Hoover returned a call from Joseph Q. Riznik, a reporter for the *New York American*, and engaged in pure spin control. "I wanted him to know the circumstances surrounding the resignation of Mr. Purvis. . . . [It] was entirely voluntary on the part of Mr. Purvis and there was not the slightest basis for any impression of any lack of harmony or dissatisfaction upon his part," Hoover said. "I told Mr. Riznik I would like him to put over as strongly as he could the true circumstances surrounding the resignation . . . and to put to rest any rumors to the effect that he was dismissed or that he resigned because of any dissatisfaction." A personal call from the director was something of an honor for any reporter, and Hoover knew this. No less an ally than Walter Winchell, the noted columnist and staunch Hoover supporter, volunteered to help. "I was thinking of doing a brief piece about why I suspect Purvis resigned," he wrote to Hoover in late July. "Men who get $2,900 per annum and win fame become restless for money." The campaign to conceal the feud between Hoover and Purvis—and to depict the resignation as a crass grab for profit—was under way.

Hoover's tactic worked, and it became Bureau gospel that Purvis resigned in order to cash in on his fame. Some books on Hoover date his dislike of Purvis to these months after the resignation, but Hoover turned against him more than a year before Purvis quit. Hoover himself fed *New Yorker* reporter Jack Alexander the suggestion that his disapproval of Purvis stemmed from Purvis's many post-Bureau endeavors. "Hoover encourages his men, especially those with families, to accept promising offers from the outside and sends them on their way with his benison," Alexander wrote in 1937. "With one exception, he is enthusiastic about his graduates. The exception is Melvin Purvis, who won nationwide publicity when he led the party that ambushed John Dillinger." Purvis's perpetuation of his celebrity, fanned by several endorsement deals that played up his hero status, "leaves the Director cold," Alexander wrote.

During the postresignation days, Hoover became consumed with worry about what Purvis would do. Would Purvis speak poorly of Hoover to the press, promoting himself as the top G-man at the director's expense? Would he come clean about the feud between them, revealing Hoover to be a petty and vindictive leader? Would he take sole credit for tracking Dillinger and Floyd, exploding Hoover's carefully constructed fiction that the Bureau succeeded because of the scientific advancements he instituted? If Hoover could not keep tabs on Purvis as thoroughly as he did while Purvis was with the Bureau, he could use the stealthy agents at his disposal to keep tabs on Purvis for him. And so, just days after Purvis resigned, Hoover began systematically gathering intelligence about every major public move his former protégé made. This practice did not continue for weeks or months or even years; it continued until Melvin Purvis was dead.

———

In leaving the Bureau, Purvis left a world where his celebrity was suppressed to enter one where it was high currency. Freed from the yoke of Hoover's strict press controls, he saw his fame blossom into something quite rare. The press kept close watch on his comings and goings, putting news of his appearances—"Former Ace 'G' Man in City"—on the front page. Even Walter Winchell dropped tidbits about Purvis into his columns. Though Hoover would later achieve a more enduring celebrity, Purvis was the first—and only—field agent to become truly famous.

Purvis did not seek this spotlight while he was at the Bureau, but once it found him after his departure from the agency, he was not uncomfortable in the glare. In October 1935 a federal judge in Louisville summoned Purvis to testify in the trial of the kidnappers of Alice Stoll, a case Purvis had helped crack while in the Bureau. In the predawn hours of October 9, Purvis boarded the Pennsylvania train from Chicago to Louisville, and prepared to shave to be ready for his 7:10 A.M. arrival. Local reporters invaded his Pullman car before he had finished lathering. Still, he was jovial; there would be no Hoover to call him on the carpet for his comments. "I was at my home in Chicago all day yesterday and I promised to come down here as soon as the marshal telephoned me," he casually told reporters as he finished shaving. As for his next move, he said, "I have several things in view. None of them is definite yet and I can't talk about them."

During this time, Purvis was a man full of plans. First to line up for his services were publishers, who wanted the inside scoop on Dillinger and Floyd. "It is possible that I will not be entirely without something to do," Purvis wrote to his sister Mary Beth, by way of describing his many meetings with magazine editors. He finally agreed to write a series of articles about his Bureau days for *Redbook* magazine. The Associated Press broke the story just four days after Purvis resigned. "I felt it would help a lot if the public better understood the real facts of criminal detection . . . and had a real appreciation of the firm determination of the government to run the criminals to earth, even if it takes a lifetime to do," Purvis said of his decision to write for *Redbook*. "Somewhere along the line an idea may shine through that may lead to a better understanding of the crime problem and eventually to a better curb on crime."

Purvis used his interview with the AP to clarify his one and only negative remark about Hoover—"Frankly I am glad to be out of here." Purvis "intimated that he had desired for some time to put into print his experiences in the war on crime," went the AP story.

"It was in that connection, he stated, that he was glad to get out." Thus did Purvis continue to try to repair the damaged bridge to his former mentor.

In late 1935, Purvis began expanding his *Redbook* articles into a book. "Right now I'm writing my memoirs of my career as a G-man," he told reporters. "I hope they're modest." *American Agent* appeared in 1936 and cost $2.75. Its subhead was the publisher's marketing tool, and Purvis surely knew it would rankle in Washington: *The Inside Story of America's Most Famous Man-Hunting Organization*, stated the cover, *Told by the Greatest of Its Operatives*. Purvis received a modest advance and delivered chapters on Pretty Boy Floyd, Volney Davis, and Roger Touhy. John Dillinger rated three chapters. "The career of Melvin Purvis has been blazoned on the front pages of the nation's press from the time he took over the Chicago office," read the dust jacket. "A young man, with a soft Southern drawl and cold black eyes, he accomplished more in three years of ridding the Midwest murder belt of major criminals than the whole police force had done in many years." The text inside was far more modest, as was his preference. "Melvin Purvis makes sensational statements because he is dealing with sensational facts," a *New York Times* review of the book explained. "But his manner of writing is not sensational. His book is quietly presented, carefully thought out, informative, exciting, challenging—and excellent."

October 1935 brought Purvis something of a high-society coming-out party—an evening at the 21 Club in New York City. He and his sister Mary Beth, who came up from South Carolina to stay with her brother, were the guests of Harry Evans, editor of *Family Circle* magazine. Evans met Purvis in the Southampton home of Mr. and Mrs. Charles E. Merrill, its publishers, and invited him and Mary Beth to dinner at 21, the infamous former speakeasy on West Fifty-second Street. Purvis accepted. It was an impressive score for Evans. "Motion picture stars are, of course, accustomed to being introduced around as celebrities," he wrote of the dinner at the 21 Club. "It isn't often that you can reverse this situation. I mean that it's difficult to find a person you can introduce to a movie star and have the movie star think *he* is meeting a celebrity. This happened the other night at 21."

Joan Crawford and her new husband Franchot Tone dined at a table not far from Purvis's. Richard Barthelmess, a veteran Hollywood star, stopped by to say hello, to the delight of Mary Beth. Then came actor Chester Morris, who had played a character based on Purvis in *Public Hero No. 1*. Evans saw the moment and seized it, taking Morris by the arm and dragging him to his table. "There's a man over here you've wanted to meet for a long time," he told him. When Morris saw Purvis, he acted like a starstruck fan. "Good heavens, you're Melvin Purvis," he blurted. "Know you from your pictures. And I can't begin to tell you how much I admire you and how much I've wanted to meet you."

Morris took a seat next to Purvis and spent the next hour asking questions. He was delighted to hear Purvis commend his movie for accuracy, and took it in stride when Purvis detected a false note in a scene when Morris went for a ride with his girlfriend instead of finding a phone to call headquarters. "Yes, that was a weak spot in the picture," Morris conceded. Like Morris, Harry Evans seemed smitten with the little man who had done big things. He wrote fondly of how Purvis loved good jokes, how he told good stories, how he liked standing around a piano singing along to songs in a voice that "is far better than that of the average bird who thinks he can warble a bit."

To Evans and Morris and anyone else who asked, it was clear even then that although Purvis was gracious in answering questions about his Bureau days, he was not particularly happy doing so. "He's not a great talker," Evans noted, "and says quite frankly that he's sick and tired of discussing his experiences as a G-man." Contrary to Hoover's portrayal of him as a crass publicity seeker, Purvis downplayed his part or referred to it not at all. Before long, he stopped talking about his Bureau days altogether.

Purvis next signed a deal to endorse Gillette safety razors, and appeared in ads headlined "Getting the Drop on Public Nuisance No. 1"—unsightly beard bristles. He also agreed to promote Dodge automobiles. "Famous G-Man Corners Dodge Economy," read the copy. But the deal that transformed him from a common celebrity to a cultural icon was his endorsement of a breakfast cereal. In 1932, Post Toasties tapped into the nation's growing interest in crime-fighting by debuting a clever marketing gimmick named Inspector Post. A fictional federal agent in a brown fedora, Inspector Post enlisted America's youth in his Junior Detective Corps, urging them to send two box tops to receive an official badge, instruction book, and decoder ring. Such clubs were enormously popular with children, who could choose among Quaker Puffed Rice's Dick Tracy Secret Service Patrol, Ovaltine's Captain Midnight Club, and the Lone Ranger Club sponsored by Cheerios—all of which sent them on far-flung adventures in their own neighborhoods. In 1934, however, these fictional adventures were overtaken by the real-life pursuit of gangsters like Dillinger and Floyd. Executives at Young and Rubicam, the giant New York City advertising agency that handled Post Toasties, saw a golden opportunity in 1935 when Melvin Purvis resigned from the Bureau. Purvis was comfortable in the role of spokesman to the nation's children—in 1936 he signed on to host a radio show called *Junior G-Men,* aimed at America's boys and girls. Purvis believed they should be made aware of the devastating effects of crime, both on society and on criminals, as a way to nudge them toward lawful and productive lives. When Young and Rubicam suggested replacing the fictional inspector with the real former G-man, Purvis jumped at the chance. In 1936 the Melvin Purvis Junior G-Man Club was formed.

By some accounts, Purvis received as much as $36,000 for endorsing Post Toasties, an enormous sum in that era and more than six times his last yearly salary with the Bureau. Even so, it was money well spent. The Melvin Purvis Junior G-Man Club became the most popular club of its kind, enrolling some 260,000 children in the United States. A cartoon likeness of Purvis—fedora tipped to one side, gentlemanly smile in place—appeared in hundreds of comic strips dramatizing his G-man exploits and depicting him chasing both real and fictional gangsters. "Stick 'em up, Joe Barkus!" orders Purvis in one strip, in a thinly veiled reference to the Barker-Karpis gang. "We've got you and your gang dead to rights this time!" The frightened crooks gulp, "It's Melvin Purvis!" and instantly surrender. By sending two cereal box tops kids could receive a special greeting from Melvin Purvis with the Junior G-Man pledge ("I pledge myself to obey the laws of my country . . . I further pledge to keep myself strong and fit for all duties of the Corps at all times"), a series of secret codes and signals, an official ring, a whistle, a fingerprint kit, and, most thrilling, a Junior G-Man badge. Parker Brothers even developed a Melvin Purvis G-Man Board Game, which sold for $1.50 and allowed youngsters to "run down the Public Enemy—Get Your Man!" Ironically, few people benefited from the Junior G-Man Corps as much as Hoover; the club increased the Bureau's popularity in a way that Hoover had been unable to accomplish. "The FBI's image as a grown-up version of the kids' breakfast cereal club," Richard Gid Powers wrote in *G-Men*, "was certainly one reason for Hoover's popularity with the younger set."

The next call came from Hollywood. Now free of the Bureau, Purvis was free to meet with movie executives. The papers reported that he was in line to serve as technical adviser to several pictures, and in 1937 it was announced the Samuel Goldwyn Company was close to signing him as a writer, adviser, and actor in a G-man movie called *Dead End*. "Purvis, we understand, is all but sold on this picture which deals with a group of boys in a New York slum, one of who[ck] grows up to be a G-Man, while his pal becomes a gangster," reported columnist Louella Parsons. "Even if the acting contract doesn't materialize there is a strong possibility that Purvis will . . . assist Lillian Hellman in preparing the screenplay." Meanwhile, when word got out that Purvis was in town, agents scrambled to have their clients photographed in his company. For a brief time, Purvis dated actress Jean Harlow but called it off because she was too cozy with the sort of marginal characters he spent his career putting away. Purvis also met and was befriended by actors Clark Gable and Fredric March. But a fetching print-model-turned-starlet from Texas became his most frequent West Coast companion.

Janice Jarrett, billed by papers as the country's most famous advertising model and best known as the Lucky Strike Girl, had just signed a contract to star in movies when she met Melvin Purvis. They were, according to one paper, "a model match." Reporters were on hand to see her warmly greet him when he arrived at the Los Angeles airport after a trip back East. "The two have been seen together frequently," one item announced. By March 1937 their romance was no longer secret. "Lucky Strike for Purvis," one headline declared. "Melvin Purvis Captured By Cupid," read another. Both denied reports they planned to marry, but not for long. In late March they announced they would wed on April 20, 1937. Plans were made to bake a multitiered cake, and more than 3,000 invitations were sent out, many to movie stars. A honeymoon in Acapulco was booked. It became the most highly anticipated celebrity wedding of the year.

By then Purvis had finally settled on a post-Bureau career. Despite the interest from Hollywood and his various endorsement deals,

Purvis had no real job, no office to go to. Other than his accidental education in criminology, he had only one expertise—the practice of law—and he decided to return to that career.

In April 1936 he flew to San Francisco, the city where he made one of his closest friends—Bartley Crum. Crum was a handsome and charming lawyer who would become known for defending blacklisted artists and serving as an adviser to Harry Truman. Crum had just started his own law practice when he befriended Purvis, and the two became frequent companions. Purvis spent many nights in Crum's San Francisco apartment, and in particular in the nursery, which had a large window with a spectacular view of San Francisco Bay. Crum's daughter Patricia recalled Purvis giving her and her brother Junior G-Man badges, which they pinned to their pajamas; she also remembered Purvis giving Bart Jr. piggyback rides around the apartment. One evening Purvis read to the children from his biography, *American Agent*. Some nights Purvis stayed over and slept on the living room couch.

His relationship with Crum helped convince Purvis that San Francisco was a good place to settle. He applied as an out-of-state attorney to be admitted to the California bar. In September 1936, a special session of the California Supreme Court determined that he was permitted to practice law in California. The former head of a 100-man crime-fighting squad opened a private law practice featuring only himself, settling into an office in the city's Crocker First National Bank Building. "I'm going to practice civil law," he told reporters. "No criminal cases and no divorce cases." Purvis rented an apartment on Lombard Street and was invited to join the city's exclusive Bohemian Club. Far from the tobacco fields of his youth and the hard streets of Chicago, Melvin Purvis had found himself a home.

———

It began with a crackle of static over the nation's radio waves, followed by the staccato intonation of an announcer. "Presenting the first of a new series of programs—*G-Men*," a deep voice declared at 8:30 in the evening of July 20, 1935. A scream in the night, a man yelling "Stop her!," the crack of gunfire, police sirens. "Tonight," the announcer said, "you will hear, for the first time, a dramatic interpretation of the life and death of John Dillinger."

J. Edgar Hoover's rewriting of history had begun.

Only eight days after Melvin Purvis resigned from the Bureau, the radio program *G-Men* aired on NBC radio. It was conceived while Purvis was still with the Bureau, and broadcast while his exploits were still fresh in the nation's memory. Yet the program launched a campaign that would not cease for the next three decades—the campaign to erase Purvis from the official story of the FBI.

The idea for the program came to Philip H. Lord, the producer of the popular radio show *Seth Parker*. Lord approached Hoover with a proposal for a series of shows about the Bureau's pursuit of gangsters, starting with the best-known gangster of all, John Dillinger. Both Hoover and Attorney General Cummings saw the benefit in dramatizing the work of the Bureau, as long as they could retain some measure of control over the show. With that in mind, Hoover agreed to help Lord but insisted that Rex Collier—a writer friendly to the Bureau—supervise its production. Collier developed a script that for the most part stuck to the facts of Dillinger's life and death, with two glaring exceptions—the script made not a single mention of Anna Sage, who provided the key tip that sealed Dillinger's fate. And it made no mention of Melvin Purvis.

This was a remarkably brazen act of revisionism, considering how well known Purvis was for his work on the case. Yet Hoover happily gave the script his blessing, and it remained in its original form until minutes before the live broadcast. Lord, a veteran storyteller, finally decided the omission of Purvis was simply too egregious—after all, the most memorable single detail of Dillinger's killing was Purvis lighting a cigar to signal his presence. Lord knew he did not have the authority to insert Purvis into the script, but he nevertheless hastily penciled in a change. A new character was created, and he would be the one to light the cigar. He could not be called Purvis—Hoover would not allow it. Instead, Lord named him Nellis.

Even so, Nellis was but a bit player in the drama. Its main character was inspector Sam Cowley. After a few minutes spent establishing Dillinger's criminal history, Cowley makes his entrance in the office of J. Edgar Hoover.

COWLEY: You sent for me Mr. Hoover?
HOOVER: Yes Cowley. That Dillinger gang has gotta be broken up.
 I want you to leave for Chicago immediately. Spare no expense.

Get all the men you need and get John Dillinger. He's clever, he's a killer. Get him alive if you can but get him.

COWLEY: Thank you sir. There's a plane that leaves within the hour.

In the show it is not Anna Sage who delivers Dillinger but rather a set of fingerprints that leads federal agents to one of Dillinger's molls.

Four days later Cowley deploys his men around the Biograph. In this scenario Cowley is not stationed across the street, as he was on July 22, 1934, but right next to the theater's front entrance, from which Dillinger will emerge. "He's a killer if ever there was one," an agent tells him. "Watch yourself Cowley." Cowley's reply: "You boys watch yourselves." Then the inspector happens to spot Nellis smoking a cigar. He has another brainstorm: "The only sure way to identify Dillinger is by the back of his head . . . as soon as [Nellis] sees him he'll lower his cigar. Watch for that cigar!"

Twenty minutes into the broadcast, Dillinger leaves the Biograph. Nellis lowers his cigar and disappears from the action. Cowley sees Dillinger start to run and yells, "Duck!" Bullets ring out; Dillinger drops to the ground. "Let's see him," says Cowley, first to the body. "Yes, Dillinger's dead. He had it coming to him. Pick up his gun Jerry. He'll never use it again." Ominous music closes the action before a final message from Philip Lord himself.

LORD: Crime doesn't pay. The G-Men never give up the hunt. With the passing of John Dillinger, Baby Face Nelson became Public Enemy No. 1 and Inspector Cowley directed the hunt for that member of the Dillinger gang.

So began the new Dillinger mythology, with Sam Cowley thrust into the role of action hero.

Of course, Hoover's scheme was possible only because Sam Cowley was dead. He was the perfect protagonist—someone who could neither dispute the retelling of the story nor benefit from it. The fact that Cowley had died in the line of duty made him an even more attractive figure, and Hoover took full advantage of his martyrdom, turning Cowley—who for most of his career had been bound to a desk—into an idealized version of a gun-toting, door-kicking agent. Another benefit to depicting Cowley as the hero was the credit and glory that funneled to Hoover himself. After all, Cowley was his handpicked man, and no future account of Cowley's heroics would fail to include the scene of Hoover shrewdly dispatching him to Chicago with orders to "get Dillinger."

Hoover had found a way to trump the media at its own game. He deftly manipulated the public's perception of events that had occurred, remarkably, only a few months earlier. The *G-Men* radio show spawned a series of FBI-endorsed *G-Men* comic strips, which once again retold the Dillinger story. This time Purvis did not even get a fake name and was referred to simply as "an agent" who lit his cigar "at Cowley's direction." In a 1938 FBI casebook issued with Hoover's approval and assembled by his top ghostwriter, Courtney Ryley Cooper, Purvis is not mentioned by name but rather referred to as "the regulation Field Officer of the Bureau." The casebook suggests this "Field Officer" was simply a decoy served up by the Bureau to divert the media's attention away from the man who was secretly honing in on Dillinger—Sam Cowley. "It was Sam Cowley . . . who deserved the credit," the casebook read. "His control was supreme in the Chicago region." All future FBI-sanctioned Bureau histories would similarly reduce or eliminate the role Melvin Purvis played. One book takes the speech Purvis gave to his men just before surrounding the Biograph and attributes it, word for word, to Cowley. Hoover's own book, *Persons in Hiding*, ghostwritten by Cooper in 1939, includes not a single reference to Purvis. This was, perhaps, Hoover's response to Purvis's earlier book, *American Agent*, which conspicuously failed to mentioned Hoover by name. In any case, Hoover used his book to blatantly rewrite one particular bit of Bureau history—he changed Purvis's resignation to a "termination with prejudice."

Hoover's Cowley mythology endured for decades. In 1956[ck]—nearly a quarter century after Dillinger was killed—Don Whitehead's Hoover-approved Bureau history, *The FBI Story*, did fleetingly mention Purvis in its account of the Dillinger case, but in an obvious slight failed to list him in its index. This policy of ignoring Purvis continued even after both Hoover and Purvis were dead. In 1975 former Assistant Director Louis B. Nichols, who had served as the Bureau's de facto publicist in the mid-1930s, told Hoover biographer Ovid Demaris that Purvis "was in water over his head. Sam

Cowley was the guy who actually handled the Dillinger case and Purvis was a figurehead." That same year, according to Hoover expert Richard Gid Powers, two Bureau officials preparing a Dillinger project discussed the importance of stressing Cowley's role while downplaying Purvis's contributions. "And then they just stopped and looked at each other and said, 'Why are we doing this?'" Powers noted. "They realized they were just on automatic pilot, that they were just doing what Hoover wanted them to do, even after Hoover was dead. And in this way Hoover's hostility to Purvis just continued forever. I doubt very much whether anybody in the Bureau even understood any reason for it. It just became Bureau gospel that Cowley was the hero and Purvis was the figurehead."

Hoover then turned his attack from Purvis's image to Purvis himself. He put Purvis under the sort of surveillance normally reserved for criminals. Although there is no record that Hoover ordered any such surveillance, it is clear from several hundred pages of FBI files that the practice became Bureau policy starting one day after Purvis resigned. The Bureau began gathering detailed intelligence on him and continued to do so for the next twenty-five years. FBI agents across the country dutifully sent Hoover reports on all of Purvis's personal and career moves. Any and every article about Purvis and his exploits was carefully catalogued in his personnel file. According to Hoover's niece Margaret Fennell, who was interviewed by Richard Hack for his biography of the director, *Puppetmaster,* Hoover became so obsessed with Purvis that "he repeatedly took home Purvis's file, updated weekly with reports from Tolson." This quarter century of scrutiny by a major federal law-enforcement agency, directed at someone who had neither committed a crime nor posed any threat of any kind, is extraordinary and possibly unprecedented in American history. It became a sort of reflex for agents to feed Hoover information about Purvis; more important, it became a sign of loyalty to the director, a way to curry favor. "There were a lot of little things like that where you could indicate you were part of the organization, and for a long time doing Purvis in was one of them," said Powers. "This meant Purvis was subject to a lot of deceit and cruelty, and from the FBI records you can tell it was a pretty brutal thing."

Those records reveal an animus toward Purvis that never subsided. The day after Purvis resigned, Hoover learned he was being considered for a job with New York's vice department. That such a

potential offer existed irritated Hoover, who scrawled on a memorandum, "Note the information re: Purvis' resignation was apparently known to [others] before it reached us." Three days later he
spoke with a movie producer who told him Darryl Zanuck, the
Twentieth Century Fox film mogul, wished to hire Purvis as a technical adviser on a gangster picture. Hoover had the producer tell
Zanuck that "I personally do not view with favor the use of a person
within or out of the Bureau in any way that becomes a matter of
commercial advertising." At the same time, Hoover volunteered a
Bureau agent to provide technical assistance for the movie, as long
as he approved of its subject matter. Hoover then ordered the spe-
cial-agents-in-charge in New York and Los Angeles to tell their Hollywood contacts that "representatives of this Bureau will be available
to give any technical advice" for any movie. Zanuck quickly learned
that hiring Purvis would be far more trouble than it was worth and
dropped the idea.

The reports about Purvis kept pouring in, and no detail was too
insignificant. An agent informed Hoover that Purvis stopped by the
Chicago office for five minutes a week after his resignation to pick
up his mail. He also told Hoover a call from a credit agency revealed
Purvis was planning to sell his Pierce-Arrow sedan, and that he listed
his occupation as "author." On July 19 a New York publisher tipped
off Hoover that Purvis was planning to write a book, and three days
later special agent Ladd, Purvis's replacement in Chicago and the
most consistent pipeline of information to Hoover, relayed that the
William Morris Theatrical Agency wanted Purvis to tour the country
giving speeches about his Bureau days. Hoover knew well in advance
that Purvis planned to publish a series of articles in *Redbook* and was
told the articles would be "a direct and vicious attack" on the Bureau. The news alarmed Hoover, who feared Purvis would divulge
his side of the Dillinger killing.

This meant any public appearance by Purvis was cause for concern. When he found out Purvis would be a guest on the *Rudy Valle
Variety Hour* on August 8, he had agents monitor the radio broadcast. Sure enough, Valle quickly brought up Dillinger. "How long
was it between [your first case] and the finish of Dillinger?" Valle
asked. Purvis answered, "I object. You weren't going to mention
Dillinger." "So I was," said Valle. "Objection sustained." And that was
it—Purvis was saving his version of the Dillinger case for his articles

and book. Nevertheless, Hoover found something in the broadcast
to slip into Purvis's file. A *Variety* item mentioned that Purvis "set
something of a precedent for radio: he let loose the first belch to go
over a national hook-up." Perhaps Purvis forgot to hit the cough
button on his microphone and belched on-air; perhaps the sound
was merely a cough or the rustling of a cable. In either case "it was
blown out of proportion by the Bureau," said Gid Powers. "The gossip columnists really played it up, and they probably got it in the first
place from Hoover."

Similarly, Hoover was concerned about a speech Purvis planned
to give at a luncheon hosted by *Redbook* at New York City's Waldorf-
Astoria Hotel. The word was it would be an "off-the-record" speech,
meaning Purvis might use the occasion finally to criticize Hoover
and the Bureau. Hoover hoped Walter Winchell would go to the
luncheon and report on the speech, but for Winchell the affair was
"too early in the morning" for him to attend and he sent a friend instead. Once again, Hoover's fears were unfounded. Purvis, addressing a ballroom packed with 300 executives of the McCall Company
publishers, "only spoke in the highest terms of the Department,"
Winchell's friend reported. "He pointed out that the Department
should receive the credit and no particular person . . . it was a happy
speech and nothing was said that would not help the Department."
Purvis even refused to take the bait when someone asked why he
quit the Bureau. "I resigned because I wanted to," was all he would
say.

Hoover was not assuaged by Purvis's discretion in his appearances. He seemed convinced it was only a matter of time before
Purvis took a shot at him. When Purvis was summoned to testify at
the Robinson kidnapping trial in Louisville in October 1935,
Hoover hatched a plan to discredit him should his testimony harm
the Bureau. He instructed Assistant Director Pop Nathan to have
the U.S. attorney prosecuting the case ask Purvis about a surveillance subject he had allowed to get away. "If it can be brought out
that the great No. 1 G-Man, Melvin Purvis, had flunked on this kind
of assignment, it would probably serve as a basis upon which the
jury could form their opinion as to what kind of G-Man he really
was," an October 9 memorandum stated. Hoover also told Nathan
to make sure that any agents in Louisville for the trial "were very cir-
cumspect in their dealings and contacts with Purvis." Despite this

order to stay away from their former colleague, several agents in the courtroom surrounded Purvis as soon as he entered, greeting him warmly and asking about his current plans. Once again, Purvis failed to live down to Hoover's poor estimation of him. His testimony, an October 10 memorandum noted, "was very conservative and did not hurt the case at all."

Hoover's hostility toward Purvis was such that merely being seen with him could put a person on the director's bad side. Hoover had agents snitch on other agents who were somehow linked to Purvis; such associations, once they were known to Hoover, could prove fatal to an agent's career. Hoover learned two agents in the Chicago office "are tied up and are very friendly with Melvin Purvis," a November 11 memo noted. "Therefore, [Hoover is] a little afraid of having them working on the . . . case with that connection." Hoover instructed that immediate steps be taken "to work them off the . . . case just as soon as possible, confidentially advising the Bureau when both of them have severed their connections with the case so that they might be transferred."

Conversely, speaking poorly of Purvis was a way to get in Hoover's good graces. Many agents found it an easy and convenient way to score points, never thinking that were Hoover's mood suddenly to change (as it often did), they could find themselves on Hoover's hit list just as quickly as Purvis had. Inspector W.H.D. Lester wrote several memos to Hoover that gleefully criticized Purvis. "I thought you might be interested to know that, on my recent speaking trip, many people made inquiry concerning Purvis's activities," he wrote in March 1936. "The general reaction of audiences to Mr. Purvis's activities seemed to be one of disgust . . . it has always been my belief that the old adage, 'Give a man enough rope and he will hang himself' will prove true in Purvis's case, and that the public will soon become tired of his 'trading upon his association with the Bureau.'" Later that month Lester wrote to Hoover again. "I recently received a letter from my mother in which she comments upon the recent actions of Melvin Purvis. . . . She writes, 'Did you see the numerous advertisements to which Purvis is selling his name? It seems very undignified, even piffling, to me.' I am inclined to agree with her that Purvis's actions are, at the best, rather piffling. For your confidential information, I suggest as a description for [Purvis]: 'The most expert blunderer the FBI has ever had.'"

Trashing Purvis could even advance an agent's fortunes. A November 4 memo noted that the special-agent-in-charge of the Omaha office asked Bureau headquarters for a raise to bring his salary in line with that of other agents-in-charge. He was told that since the Omaha office was relatively small, no raise was in order. But the memo continued that the Omaha agent "made rather disparaging remarks concerning Mr. Purvis and his resignation from the Bureau . . . he stated that he considered Mr. Purvis somewhat of a fool." The memo's author, S. J. Tracy, concluded, "I have been impressed by [the agent and] . . . with his loyalty to the Bureau and the Director . . . I feel that he has the interest of the Bureau at heart at all times, and it is recommended that further consideration be given to the possibility of increasing [his] compensation." The agent received his raise.

Hoover also wanted to prevent Purvis from flourishing in Hollywood. Purvis's resignation coincided with sweeping changes in the movie business. For years one of the staples of Hollywood was the gangster film, which glorified criminals in the same way the media made heroes of Dillinger and Floyd. Edward G. Robinson's turn as an Al Capone—like mobster in 1930's *Little Caesar* is a prime example. The definitive portrayal of a sympathetic criminal was in 1931's *Public Enemy*, one of more than fifty gangster pictures released that year alone. But in 1935 the Association of Motion Picture Producers issued a policy statement banning what it called "left-handed gangster pictures"—movies that glorified criminals. That same year James Cagney starred as a federal agent in *G-Men*, a celebration of Hoover's men. The movie was made without Hoover's cooperation; indeed, he distanced himself from it for fear he would be seen as exploiting the Bureau's successes. But *G-Men* drew large crowds and spawned a series of pictures about the Bureau, and movie producers went on the prowl for inside information about the workings of Hoover's crime-fighting force. The first person they turned to was not the director of that force but rather its recently retired star, Melvin Purvis.

Hoover had already quashed one Hollywood job for Purvis by scaring Darryl Zanuck away. Still, Hoover fretted that Purvis would land a deal before he had a chance to scuttle it. He ordered the special-agent-in-charge of the Los Angeles office to monitor the movie industry's interest in Purvis. There were rumors Purvis had signed a

$25,000 contract with a studio, for instance, and Hoover wanted confirmation. The Bureau's top man in Los Angeles, J.E.P. Dunn, was forced to devote time to tracking down leads about Purvis—and to keeping Hoover at bay. "I will continue to give very careful personal attention to this matter," he promised Hoover in September 9, 1935, "and I can assure you that through my various contacts and personal connections among studio executives . . . I will be able to gain, confidentially, first-hand knowledge concerning the activities of Mr. Purvis if and when he arrives in this community."

To help him keep tabs on Purvis, Dunn enlisted Joseph I. Breen of the Association of Motion Picture Producers, which was known as the Hays organization, after its director, Will Hays. Dunn had Breen talk producers out of hiring Purvis—Dunn began referring to him as "one of our former associates" so as not to name him in official letters—for their "special agent" pictures. The carrot Dunn dangled was full access to Hoover. "Mr. Breen informs me that he has on several occasions advised producers in the industry that there was no requirement that they hire a technical advisor for the reason that this organization and this office were available at all times for such service, and that you had repeatedly given assurance of your extreme willingness to cooperate in this regard," Dunn wrote Hoover on October 12, 1935. "I assured Mr. Breen of your continued interest to cooperate to the fullest possible extent." Purvis, through representatives, did in fact approach the Hays organization to line up a job as a technical adviser, but with Breen's help Hoover succeeded in having Purvis banned from getting any kind of job in Hollywood. Whenever producers inquired about hiring Purvis, one of Breen's men "exposed Purvis for the fakir that he was," an August 1936 Bureau memo to Clyde Tolson noted. "All of the prominent moving picture companies had made further inquiry [about hiring Purvis] and the policy of the industry, acting upon a suggestion from the office of Mr. Will Hays . . . was strictly 'hands off' so far as Purvis is concerned."

Reports about Purvis continued to land on the director's desk. A Chicago detective alerted Hoover that "Purvis is endeavoring to line up dissatisfied men in the service, those who have left of their own volition and those who have been discharged, and through their political affiliations oppose the Director," a Bureau memo noted,

though this proved an unfounded rumor. Surely Hoover enjoyed
learning that San Jose traffic policeman Tony Russo pulled Purvis
over for speeding in late 1936. When Purvis wrote to Hoover asking
him to compose a letter to California's bar examiners regarding his
legal work as a special agent, Hoover refused to put the letter over
his own signature, and had Assistant Director Nathan sign it instead.
When Purvis had his old friend Skipper McSwain telephone
Chicago special-agent-in-charge Ladd to find out the exact salary
Purvis made in his last year at the Bureau—information Purvis
needed to file his taxes—Hoover refused to help. "I suppose 'Advertising Mel' is too busy to figure it out himself," Hoover wrote at the
bottom of a memo file before lashing into Ladd for referring "such
a request to the Washington headquarters."

Nor did Hoover sit idly by when Purvis introduced his Post
Toasties G-man campaign. He had Tolson consult a judge about the
legality of the Junior G-Man badge, which "might fall within the pro-
visions of the recent Congressional statute prohibiting the repro-
duction of colorable imitations of any Federal badges," Ladd noted
in a March 1936 letter to Hoover. But a judge told Tolson "he did
not believe the Department is in a position at the present time to
object to the furnishing of these badges." Even so, Hoover had Post
Toasties remove any reference to the Bureau from its G-man campaign, and expressly insisted that Purvis be referred to as a *former*
agent of the Bureau.

Whatever Hoover could do to undermine Purvis, he did. When
he discovered Purvis was being courted as a speaker at functions
across the country, he offered his agents to speak at those functions
for free. Organizations that offered Purvis money to speak were denied access to Bureau agents, whether or not Purvis accepted the
engagement. In 1938 the Santa Anita racetrack wished to hire
Purvis as a supervisor of its police affairs. The racing industry, besieged by corruption and scandals, sought to bring in an authoritative figure to clean up the sport. Purvis seemed the perfect
choice—he had a solid law-enforcement background, a reputation
for integrity, and an abiding love of horses. Charles Strube, a racetrack official, telephoned the Bureau's Los Angeles office to ask if
Purvis would be a good man for the job. A special agent answered
the phone and parroted the Bureau's official line on Purvis—that

hiring him "would not be advantageous to the racing group," a
1938 Tolson memo noted. This, apparently, was not sufficiently
pejorative. Tolson immediately had the agent call Strube again to
elaborate on the subject. "I told [the agent] . . . to definitely advise
him that this Bureau could not recommend Purvis for this position,
and that it was felt it would be a mistake to appoint him," Tolson explained. The agent also was told to advise Strube that the Bureau
would not cooperate with the racetrack if Purvis was involved too,
"inasmuch as he is a persona non grata with this Bureau." Not much
later, Santa Anita officials dropped Purvis from consideration for
the job.

When Hoover sabotaged Purvis's employment by the racetrack in
January 1938, Purvis had been gone from the Bureau for two and a
half years. He would never be mistaken for an ordinary citizen, not
in 1938 or in any year to come, but by then Purvis was striving less to
capitalize on his fame than he was trying to put his past behind him
and move on. Nevertheless, Hoover's animosity toward him burned
bright as ever.

———

In April 1936, Hoover and his closest aide, Clyde Tolson, marched
confidently from the Department of Justice on Constitution Avenue, where they had brand-new offices on the fifth floor, to the
Capitol, to appear before an appropriations subcommittee to discuss the Bureau's budget. If he had his way, and he surely felt that
he would, Hoover would see his budget increased from the $2.58
million awarded for 1934 to an even $5 million. Seated at a table
facing the members of the subcommittee, dressed as he typically was
in an expensive suit, Hoover spoke of his many successes, of how his
men had cornered John Dillinger, had gunned down Pretty Boy
Floyd, had put an end to Baby Face Nelson, and to Doc Barker, Volney Davis, Machine Gun Kelly, and all the rest—nearly every major
gangster, save for Alvin Karpis. Posterboards with charts and
graphs—depicting precipitous drops in the crimes of kidnapping
and bank robbery—appeared on easels set before the senators. For
all practical purposes, Hoover testified, he and his agents had
turned the tide in the war on crime, though much meaningful work
remained and now was not the time to deny the Bureau the money

it needed. The near-doubling of his budget would be a sort of reward—and an affirmation of what Hoover valued most: his power.

But it was that factor—Hoover's growing power—that offended Democratic Senator Kenneth Douglas McKellar of Tennessee, a member of the Senate since 1917, who had long nursed a soreness for Hoover stemming from the director's refusal to appoint some of McKellar's constituents to the Bureau. Currying favor with politicians by making their constituents special agents was a common practice for Hoover in the 1920s when he was constructing his base of power and his reappointment to the directorship was not a foregone conclusion. But by the 1930s Hoover was unwilling to cede control over the Bureau's hiring practices. McKellar, for one, disapproved of Hoover's increasing insulation from political currents, and gladly assumed the role of his most outspoken critic. McKellar wanted to use the occasion of the subcommittee hearing to bring Hoover down a peg or two.

At first he questioned Hoover about his taste for publicity, suggesting the Bureau had unwisely exploited its own success to burnish its image. "Is any money directly or indirectly spent on advertising?" McKellar asked Hoover, who insisted he was not permitted to make such expenditures. Did the Bureau hire writers to help with favorable articles in the national press? None at all, Hoover replied—a narrowly true statement, in that Henry Suydam, the master publicist behind the Bureau's image enhancements of the early 1930s, drew his paychecks from the Justice Department. Well, McKellar continued, how many men, good and bad, had been killed under Hoover's watch? "I think there have been eight desperadoes killed by our agents and we have had four agents in our service killed by them," Hoover said.

"In other words," McKellar said, "the net effect of turning guns over to your department has been the killing of eight desperadoes and four G-men."

Again, the implication was that Hoover was mad for power and out of control. "I doubt very much whether you ought to have a law that permits you to go around the country armed as an army would," McKellar said, "and shoot down all the people that you suspect of being criminals." The courts and not Hoover, the senator declared, should deliver justice to gangsters.

"Even if he pulls a gun on you?" Hoover shot back. McKellar did not budge from his stance, prompting another senator to rally to Hoover's aid. "How would you catch them," Harry Truman asked McKellar, "if they commenced shooting at you?"

McKellar pushed on with his inquisition. What, he wondered, were Hoover's qualifications for the position of director? Unimpressed with the desk-bound jobs Hoover cited, McKellar put forth his question.

"Did you," he demanded in his booming voice, "ever make an arrest?" He would eventually ask this question four times, to drive his point across.

Initially Hoover did not let the question hang in the silence of hesitation. "No sir," he said quickly, "I have made investigations."

"How many arrests have you made," McKellar asked again, "and who were they?"

Hoover reached back to his early days with the Justice Department, when he helped round up immigrants suspected of Communist ties. "Did you make the arrests?" McKellar asked for a third time. "The arrests were made by the immigration officers under my supervision," Hoover replied.

"I am talking about the actual arrests," McKellar went on. "You never arrested them, actually?"

Not even Truman, the future president, could save Hoover from this one. The answer, he was forced to admit, was no. After the hearing ended, Hoover sent Clyde Tolson back to the office alone and called for a car to take him to his home on Seward Square. There, according to one biographer, he found consolation in the company of his mother and in a bottle of Johnny Walker Black Label scotch. This damned McKellar, this grandstanding senator, had challenged not only Hoover's efficiency but also his courage and character. Hoover's accomplishments were, at the time, close to astonishing—he had transformed a corrupt and ridiculed Bureau into his country's premier crime-fighting force. That he had done so from behind a desk seemed immaterial. But now it was a matter of public record: The top G-man of all had never made an arrest. Hoover, so keenly aware of his image, could hardly have been dealt a more hurtful blow.

All right, the director decided, if they wanted a Hoover who ran around with badge flashing and guns blazing, then that was the Hoover they were going to get. The next morning Hoover issued orders that he be notified immediately should Alvin Karpis be located.

No arrest was to be made until the director himself arrived at the scene. "Someone had to become the symbol of the crusade, and the Director decided that because of his position it was plainly up to him," Jack Alexander, a reporter for the *New Yorker*, dutifully reported in a 1937 three-part article on Hoover. "As he tells of it now, he was reluctant to accept the role because it meant sacrificing the personal privacy he had enjoyed before all the G-Man excitement began, but he felt that he was not justified in refusing it simply because it was distasteful. So he accepted."

Three weeks after the Senate hearing, Hoover got the phone call he had been waiting for. Alvin Karpis, Public Enemy Number One, had been found. Agents traced him to an apartment building just off the Jefferson Davis Parkway in New Orleans. Surveillance was set up around the apartment on Canal Street, with a raid planned for the following day, May 1. Hoover and Tolson chartered a TWA DC-3 to take them to New Orleans and rented rooms at the Roosevelt Hotel. The plan was for Hoover to stay out of sight until Karpis had been positively identified by agents, who would then summon the director to take part in the raid.

Alvin "Creepy" Karpis had proved a slippery prey. He was born Albin Karpowicz in Quebec, Canada, but grew up in Topeka, Kansas, on mean streets shared by pimps and petty gamblers. Sticking up a grocery store as a teen launched him into a fairly spectacular career of crime. "My profession was robbing banks, knocking off payrolls and kidnapping rich men," Karpis wrote in his 1971 autobiography. "I was good at it. Maybe the best in North America for five years, from 1931 to 1936 . . . I outthought, outwitted and just plain defeated enough cops and G-Men in my time to recognize that I was more knowledgeable about crime than any of them, including the number-one guy, J. Edgar Hoover."

Together with Freddie Barker, he formed the nucleus of the Barker-Karpis gang. Karpis, perhaps the most clever of all the gangsters, outlived them all—Dillinger, Floyd, Nelson, each of the Barkers. Yet he lacked the glamour and charisma of the other top criminals, so that when Hoover named him Public Enemy Number One, no one—not even Hoover's own agents—paid it much attention. Karpis roamed free for months, completely off the FBI's radar, before the efforts of another federal agency—the U.S. Post Office—helped Bureau agents track him to New Orleans.

A first-year special agent, Raymond Tollett, on a stakeout in an empty house across the street, spotted Karpis pull up to the Canal Street apartment in a red Essex Terraplane. That set the wheels in motion. Special agent Earl Connelley alerted Hoover and Tolson, who were on the scene by midafternoon May 1. When Karpis left the apartment with another man, Fred Hunter, and got into a Plymouth parked at the curb, Connelley made the first move, pulling his own car in front of the Plymouth. There are two versions of what happened next. According to Hoover, the director jumped from his car, reached into the Plymouth, and grabbed Karpis by the collar. "You're both under arrest," Hoover recalled saying. "Put up your hands." Karpis instantly complied. "Okay, okay," he said, "I'll surrender." Then Hoover ordered, "Put the cuffs on him boys," but not a single agent had handcuffs, and so Karpis's hands were fastened with a necktie. Finally, Hoover rode back to the FBI office with the captured gangsters. "Well, it took a lot of you to catch me," Karpis said. "After all, I was Public Enemy Number One." Hoover's reply: "You were nothing but Public Rat Number One."

That is Hoover's version, variations of which appeared in several articles and books over the next decades. The day after the arrest, Hoover was careful to provide reporters with details of his role in the raid. The press had no reason to disbelieve him. "Karpis Captured in New Orleans by Hoover Himself," the *New York Times* declared. It was a smashing victory for the Bureau and for its director, who only weeks before had been dressed down by a U.S. senator for never having made an arrest.

There is another version, however, told by the man on the other side of that arrest. Alvin Karpis spent thirty-three years in jail for kidnapping, most of them in Alcatraz. In that time he was asked the same question almost every day: "Did Hoover really arrest you personally?" Karpis's standard reply: "Why don't you ask Mr. Hoover?" Once he was paroled and deported to Canada in 1969, Karpis became more talkative. "The story of Hoover the Hero is false," he claimed in his book. "He didn't lead the attack on me. He hid until I was safely covered by many guns . . . then he came out to reap the glory." In a 1976 interview he elaborated: "Twenty-eight agents arrested me . . . I see a guy peeping around a corner . . . one of the agents shouted, 'We got him, Chief, we got him, we got him. Come on, everything's all right, we got him.' So here they come and it turned out to be Hoover and Clyde Tolson." According to Karpis, Hoover never grabbed him by the collar—in fact, never got anywhere near him. "I made Hoover's reputation as a fearless lawman," he wrote. "It's a reputation he doesn't deserve."

According to FBI files, Hoover was not hiding behind a corner but rather waiting in a car, as he claimed. Of course, these reports were based on testimony from Hoover and the agents on the scene, who were surely aware of Hoover's interest in personally arresting Karpis. Even so, not a single FBI report gave Hoover credit for arresting Karpis; Earl Connelley was first to the car. Thus it seems that Hoover's version was pure invention. When Hoover told his story to writer Quentin Reynolds for the Bureau-sanctioned 1954[ck] book *The FBI*, he made sure that not a single one of the two dozen agents on the scene the day of Karpis's arrest was named: not the rookie, Raymond Tollett, who first spotted Karpis; not Earl Connelley, who risked his life by pulling his car in front of the armed Karpis and then arresting him. Only Hoover and Clyde Tolson were named. The credit and the glory were finally right where Hoover wanted them.

His moment in the spotlight did not, however, diminish Hoover's resentment of Purvis. Purvis did not know it then, but the true measure of Hoover's animosity toward him had yet to be revealed. Somehow Hoover nursed that hatred over decades, so that when he summoned it, it was always there. "Hoover had terrible insecurities, and the root of his authoritarianism and acting like a martinet and all that came from his insecurities," said former agent William Turner. "I don't think he ever stopped being insecure. So that once Melvin Purvis got caught up in Hoover's ego, he could never get free."

14

"THE BIGGEST GIANT IN THE WORLD"

Spring 1937

In San Francisco, Melvin Purvis moved to an apartment on Telegraph Hill; from his window overlooking foggy San Francisco Bay, he could see Alcatraz Island, home, ironically, to some of the very criminals he helped put away. Like the infamous prison, Purvis's days as a G-man seemed distant and remote. He was a lawyer now, and he was building a new life for himself in California. At the center of that life was the beautiful woman he planned to marry, Janice Jarrett.

Two small-town people living big-city lives, they seemed to observers to be a perfect pair. "Jarrett's dark beauty has mowed down the popular expert on crime as effectively as his machine guns laid low our public enemies," wrote one reporter, who added that for two years running, New York's Annual Exhibition of Advertising Art had voted Jarrett "the country's most typical American girl." They reserved St. Mark's Episcopal Church in San Antonio, Texas, Jarrett's hometown, and planned their wedding for the evening of Thursday, April 29, 1937. Jarrett picked twelve bridesmaids, Purvis twelve groomsmen. Purvis used an assumed name to board a Braniff Airways flight from San Francisco to San Antonio on April 19; Jarrett was there at the airport to greet her future husband. Some socialites in the city, it was reported, were put off by the pageantry of the wedding—with the "present card" included in the invitation, and with the excessive number of invitations sent for a service in a church that barely held 500 people. Some accused the couple of "puttin' on the dog," which was frowned on in genteel Southern circles. Still, San Antonio was in a mood to celebrate as it held its week-long Fiesta de San Jacinto, and the Purvis-Jarrett wedding fit right in. The happy couple were seen all over the city attending social functions, and a prominent local doctor, James Nixon, announced he would throw them a dinner dance on July 26.

Several of Purvis's sisters flew down to San Antonio for the wedding; Purvis had written them insisting that they attend. "The truth is that his family was not 100% behind the wedding," said Dr. Robert Lathan, an Atlanta physician and the son of Melvin Purvis's sister Cal. "They saw it as a little bit of Melvin going Hollywood." Nevertheless, they came to be with him, and just three days before the wedding, Purvis sat down with his sisters in their hotel and made a startling admission. "Melvin told them that he was not sure he wanted to go through with the wedding," said Lathan. "Of course his sisters said that if he didn't want to, he didn't have to. It was not too late to call it off."

Late on April 26, Purvis met Jarrett in the hotel lobby. With some of her friends lingering nearby, Purvis pulled his fiancée aside. Curious bystanders in the lobby quickly realized the two were arguing. Jarrett stormed off. Purvis hurried to his room, packed his suitcase, and left the hotel through a private back entrance. He was on a train back to San Francisco at 3:20 A.M. Jarrett's mother told reporters the wedding was off.

The media had a grand time dissecting the disaster. "The argument was believed to have started when Miss Jarrett kept Purvis waiting and Purvis resented it," one paper speculated, while Walter Winchell gave readers "the lowdown why Janice Jarrett jilted Melvin Purvis: a famous San Antonio drug firm chief!" Jarrett fled San Antonio for the nearby ranch of a friend, and spent that summer with her sister and her husband. In July a rumor floated that Purvis and Jarrett would soon get together again, but it was only a rumor. In 1939 Jarrett married a San Antonio engineer named Thomas Deely. The small, quiet ceremony at St. Paul's Episcopal Church was limited to family and friends.

As for Purvis, he fled the relentless media by boarding the *Normandy* cruise ship and sailing to Europe on May 15. Two months later he returned stateside and made his way back West. He found something different about San Francisco; suddenly it did not feel much like home. Part of him yearned to return to his roots in South Carolina. The break with Jarrett, it would seem, marked the end of the great adventure that began when he was only twenty-three. Perhaps the time had come to go home.

On January 16, 1938, Purvis learned his father, Melvin Sr., had died. He had been battling pneumonia, but at sixty-eight he could battle no more, and his lungs, weakened from decades of smoking, finally gave way. Later that year, in spring 1938, Purvis traveled to Florence to see close friends, James and Floramay McLeod. When he walked into their house on Cherokee Road, he was startled to see another familiar face. "There was Rosanne, sitting in the living room," recalled Mamie Charles, a Florence native who was a close friend of Rosanne's and spent time with her during that trip to Florence. "She was still married to Archie Taylor, and she had her servant, Philip, drive her down from Baltimore to wait for her husband, who was coming in three days. And so she didn't have much to do and she went to Floramay's to have a bit of supper and the door opens and in walks Melvin Purvis." They hadn't seen each other in years, not since Purvis invited Rosanne to Washington when he worked in the Bureau's fingerprint department in the late 1920s. That spring evening Floramay sent Rosanne to buy stamps for her. "And Melvin went with her," said Mamie Charles. "That's when the romance started again."

Things happened quickly after that. Within days Rosanne told her husband their ten-year marriage was over. "He had a complete breakdown," Charles recalled. On May 17, 1938, Walter Winchell reported that Purvis "will wed a gal named Taylor from his home burg, Timmonsville." Rosanne and Archie officially divorced on August 13, 1938. One month later, at six o'clock on the evening of September 14, Melvin and Rosanne wed in the First Baptist Church in Charlotte, North Carolina; he was thirty-four, she was thirty. On the way out, the newlyweds mingled with a group of churchgoers who had heard the famous former G-man was getting married inside. By 8:15 that night they were on a Southern Railway train headed for New York City, from where they would board the cruise ship *Europa* for their European honeymoon.

My father did a curious thing on the morning of his wedding to my mother. Just hours before the twilight ceremony, he stopped by the local field office of the FBI. His purpose in doing so is not clear. "There was no apparent reason for his visit," Edward Scheidt, special-agent-in-charge of the Charlotte office, quickly wrote to Hoover. On what should have been the beginning of a promising future, my father felt some compulsion to reconnect with his past. Perhaps he missed the camaraderie he enjoyed during his time with the Bureau; perhaps he felt it would warmly receive him on this, his happiest of days. Whatever moved him to use his wedding day for such a visit, one thing seems apparent: Melvin Purvis could not cut the cord.

Still, he was in love, and these were largely carefree days. After the wedding and just before sailing off to Europe for their honeymoon, my parents spent a romantic evening in the restaurant at the Waldorf-Astoria in Manhattan. My father whispered to the piano player and sang "Now Is the Hour" to his beaming new wife. They returned to the fabled Purvis house in Timmonsville, with its memories both of the frolicsome childhoods of Melvin and his siblings and of the sorrow and suffering it saw after Melvin's mother died. My father was happy to be in Timmonsville: The call of home to the native son is a strong thing indeed, and my father was only too happy to dream backward—to imagine his own future as a reflection of how he was raised. He knew enough, however, to find his own house, and in August 1939 he leased a place on Cherokee Road in Florence, my mother's hometown. The plan was to secure a plot of land and on it build their dream home. The model was a famous mansion in Natchez, Mississippi, a spectacular, sprawling, columned structure, known to this day as Melrose. Soon a similar though smaller Melrose went up on Cherokee Road, on 200 acres of land once owned by the Willcox family. The name Melrose, of course, had a second, special meaning: Besides being a nod to its predecessor in Natchez, it combined the first names of my parents.

Now that he was clear of California—and any idea of making his living in the fickle business of movies—my father began to cast about for some new job to hold his interest. The practice of law alone did not fulfill him before he left for Washington, and it did not fulfill him when he resumed it in San Francisco. Comfortably back in his home state, my father must have believed he would have his pick of opportunities. Sure enough, in January 1939, just two months after moving home, word surfaced that he was being considered to organize a new state police system to be created by the South Carolina legislature. The governor, Burnet R. Maybank, envisioned a force based on the FBI. "Mr. Purvis's reputation with the Federal Bureau," he said during his inaugural address, "is a guarantee of what could be accomplished if our plan is carried out." Maybank was so enamored with Purvis that he marched him out in front of the legislators to give them a look at their new top cop. "His tone is almost ministerial." His appearance drew hearty applause, and the job seemed all but his.

He did not get it, and any disappointment he felt was neither the first nor the last of its kind. In this instance a subcommittee representing South Carolina's sheriffs opposed the nomination; they believed that having such a strong figure at the top of the force would usurp their power. The sheriffs "thought if Purvis was too big for the FBI, he certainly would be too big for them," the Charlotte special-agent-in-charge, Edward Scheidt, reported to Clyde Tolson. "They were not opposed so much to the idea of the State Police as they were to the fact that Purvis would probably head it." The governor's proposal died in committee. This sudden reversal of fortune bore the fingerprints of Hoover and his henchmen. Yet there is no record that Hoover fed derogatory information about Purvis to the sheriffs. There is only a reference in an FBI file that Hoover viewed the creation of such a state police force as an "agitation"—he was not in favor of contending with a mini-FBI in South Carolina, and certainly he was not keen on seeing his old nemesis as its chief. If Hoover did somehow influence the subcommittee vote on Maybank's proposal, he did so discreetly. Even so, my mother was convinced that Hoover had blocked my father from getting the job.

My father's next move was surprising. The man who had spent a career eluding reporters, and who ultimately had been undone by the media's fascination with him, suddenly decided to join the enemy. Buying some second-hand printing equipment in a building on Dargan Street, he launched the first evening newspaper in Florence—the *Evening Star*. Papers across the country were intrigued by the idea: "G-Editor," one headline announced; "Purvis Publisher!" said another. My father's goal, he told reporters, was to produce a paper that was "solid, appealing to the eye and dignified." He hired a veteran publisher, John A. Zeigler, who had previously worked for the only rival paper in the area, the *Florence Morning News*, and printed his inaugural issue on August 3, 1939. The irony of the endeavor was not lost on him. "As a G-man I sometimes had to dodge or hedge around reporters," he said, "and now I'm out to get all the news I can."

At first the *Evening Star* did well. "Purvis appears to be getting along fine . . . although meeting stiff competition in the morning field," an investigative report submitted to Hoover declared. "The paper appears to be gaining strength." Certainly my father was proud of his upstart *Evening Star*, and he wasted no time in giving his old boss a charter subscription. "It is a most interesting and fascinating job and I am very much pleased with it," he told Hoover. "I am taking the liberty of sending you the paper for a few weeks just to show you what it looks like and also in case you are not getting all the news up that way." Hoover's reply was gracious. "I shall certainly look forward with pleasure to reading the copies," he wrote in a letter signed "Edgar." "That is really what makes life worthwhile—when one can do the things that he likes best and which are interesting and not boring." Hoover probably did little but flip through a single issue before banning the *Evening Star* from the Bureau's offices. "Unless otherwise advised," he ordered in a January 1940 memo, "copies will not be brought to the Director's attention unless some article of interest to the Bureau appears therein." Why my father would have expected any other reaction is unfathomable, but if he wanted a single word of praise, it was never to come.

After an initial curiosity about it buoyed its early success, the *Evening Star*—like the press that printed it—sputtered. The second-hand printing and typesetting equipment my father bought broke down often, and he lacked the capital to make improvements or see the paper through a fallow season. Loyal fans of the *Morning News* were neither interested in switching papers nor reading two of them. Florence, it turned out, was a one-paper town. In summer

1941 my father sold his interest in the *Evening Star*; only six months later, it folded. My impression was that he lost quite a bit of money on the venture.

The position my father wanted most of all, however, had nothing to do with the media. In September 1940, South Carolina Congressman John L. McMillan endorsed my father for a federal judgeship. Once again, my father did not get the post. A 1944 Bureau investigative report stated that "[Purvis] sought an appointment as a Federal Judge, but Hoover blocked it," and that "Hoover had succeeded in preventing Purvis's appointment as Federal Judge." That same report, based on information from anonymous Bureau sources, included this comment: "The breach between Hoover and Purvis was said to be so deep and rancorous, at least on Hoover's part, that the informant did not believe it would ever heal." Although my father knew Hoover had intervened to ruin his chances, he was convinced the animosity between them was not as deep and permanent as others might believe.

In late summer 1940, my father paid his first visit to FBI headquarters since resigning from the Bureau. His goal was to see the director—after all, Hoover had earlier written, in his gracious letter about the *Evening Star*, that "should you be in this part of the country I hope that you will give me a ring." But in Washington my father was told Hoover was out of town. He made several such trips to the FBI, but never got past the door to Hoover's sprawling office. In 1951 he arrived in Washington and told Helen Gandy, Hoover's personal secretary, that "he would like very much to speak with Mr. Hoover if possible," Gandy noted. "I told Mr. Purvis Mr. Hoover is out and it is not known when he will be in his office." My father said he understood if Hoover did not want word of their meeting to get out, and that he was willing to meet him secretly. "He asked to be called if and when Mr. Hoover will speak with him," Gandy wrote. On the bottom of the memo Hoover scrawled, "I am not available."

My father held up well under the disappointments, and his decisions indicate he was not afraid to strike out in unlikely directions. In 1941 he surprised observers by buying part of WOLS, a radio station in Florence. Years later, he gave himself a spacious office on the second floor and spent much of his time entertaining visitors there. "Everyone came to see him in that office," remembered Ross Beard, who as a teenager ran errands for my father at the station. "Politi-

cians, bankers, law enforcement officials, everyone you can imagine.
People would fill the lobby waiting to be let up to his office. It was
quite a thing to meet Melvin Purvis."

The easy pace came to an end not long after the bombing of
Pearl Harbor. My father had a young son and another baby on the
way, and he could have declined to enlist without raising too many
eyebrows. Nevertheless, he entered the U.S. Army on January 31,
1942, and was to be commissioned as a captain. He worried,
though, that Hoover would try to block his commission. A Bureau
report revealed that my father "asked Hoover not to interfere with
his appointment as Captain in the Army." The commission went
through: Perhaps the press attention to my father's enlistment made
it impossible for Hoover to derail the appointment. Even so, when
the War Department advised Hoover it was considering Melvin
Purvis for a position in the Military Intelligence Division, and asked
"whether the Bureau's files contained any derogatory information
concerning Purvis," a Bureau memo noted, the director could
barely resist the opportunity. Hoover told an aide he didn't "want to
go on record as not recommending Purvis, but they should check
into him." It was not an explicit slur on my father's character, but
Hoover's intent was evident.

In the end my father joined the Provost Marshal's Office as a major; he began his officer training at the Arlington Cantonment in
Arlington, Virginia. He "is, as everyone knows, extremely quiet and
retiring," the *Washington Times-Herald* wrote in announcing the appointment, "but he possesses that certain ring of authority in his
voice which is never mistaken." At first my father was stationed in
several posts across the country and was able to travel with his wife
and their young son, Melvin. It was not always easy going. Their stay
in Washington, D.C., began miserably, "with Rosanne taking the flu
immediately upon arrival and the baby began with a cold," my father wrote to his friend James McLeod in March 1942. "Our house
would not warm up until about noon and that, with many other
things, made the house uninhabitable." A tour at Fort Custer in
Michigan did not go much better. "The weather has been terrible
and we have all had the flu," my father wrote. "Rosanne had it four
times . . . the little boy had it also and developed ear trouble." For a
while my father was director of the Officer Candidate School and
the Enlisted Men's Schools of the Provost Marshal General's Schools

at Fort Custer and Fort Oglethorpe in Georgia. Once again he found himself interviewing candidates for training—just as he had in his final weeks at the Bureau. Finally my father had had enough. He was named executive officer to the provost general, Joseph Dillen, and sent to Dillen's headquarters in North Africa. I later heard that my father did some maneuvering to get the assignment: He was accustomed to being in the thick of battle, and a series of stateside tours with his sickly family in tow probably was not what he had in mind when he enlisted. He departed in August 1943, a month before I was born.

In early 1944 my father—by then a lieutenant colonel in the U.S. Army and the deputy provost marshal general of the European Theater of Operations—received orders to interview General George Patton about the alleged misconduct of one of his colonels. Purvis, accompanied by his friend and former FBI agent Leon Turrou, then chief investigator and assistant director of the Army's Criminal Investigation Division, found Patton headquartered in Palermo at the lavish palace of Italy's former King Victor Emmanuel; the palace was seized during Patton's lightning-quick thirty-eight-day conquest of Sicily. Purvis and Turrou passed through the shimmering gold and ebony doors of the grand ballroom and glimpsed Patton across the cavernous room, seated behind a small desk. There was no furniture except for a few random chairs, and the ballroom's enormous crystal chandeliers were, incongruously, all lit. The sound of footsteps on the marble floor echoed loudly in the empty space. It was a long, odd walk to get to Patton, in his tight Eisenhower jacket and alone in his corner, particularly since the business at hand was so unpleasant.

"You've got a cozy little office here," Purvis said after shaking hands.

"It'll do," Patton answered. "I like a place to breathe in."

Then Patton quickly got down to business. "Look," he said, "I won't beat around the bush. I know what you two are really here for." Purvis had no idea what Patton meant. "For crissakes—don't play innocent!" the general yelled. "It's too important to me. I want to settle this one way or the other. I want to get back to the fight." In fact, Patton had been suspended from the fighting because he had been involved in an ugly incident with one of his soldiers. On a tour of the Palermo Army Hospital, Patton paused in front of a young man sitting on a windowsill and staring absently at the sky. He

thought the soldier seemed angry, and it galled him. Still he was
gentle, at least at first, asking the soldier how he was doing. However, when the man shrugged off Patton's question and refused to
look him in the eye, the general grew furious. He took out one of
his white gloves and slapped it twice across the young man's face.

The incident made the newspapers. Patton was sure this was why
he was ordered to stand down. "I admit that under the circumstances my hitting the boy was villainous," he told Purvis. "But it was
a reflex, an impulse. I was helpless to stop it." Then Patton, on his
feet and raging at what he perceived as an injustice, began to cry. "If
I hadn't seen Patton crying with my own eyes I wouldn't have believed it," Turrou wrote later. "But even the way he cried was a virile,
soldierly thing."

Purvis and Turrou never managed to convince Patton that the
sole purpose of their visit was to investigate a separate matter. Patton
could not be swayed from his belief that he was being persecuted.
Purvis met with Patton for seven straight days to update him on the
investigation of the colonel, but still Patton believed what he believed. Purvis could identify with Patton. The politics of power, the
importance of perception, the terrible frustration of being prevented from doing your duty—these were things Purvis well understood. His official report on the investigation cleared the colonel of
all charges, and also, as Turrou recalled, "said categorically that we
believed Patton's immobilization was an injustice to him as well as to
the war effort."

Patton had his personal pilot fly Purvis and Turrou back to Al-
giers. He would never know that they stood up for him so insistently
in their report. Not much later, Patton was back on the battlefield
and "on his way into history," Turrou said. "Purvis and I took pleasure in feeling that our recommendation may have had some slight
effect in swaying the decision of the High Command."

Unfortunately, this is one of the few stories from my father's time
in the Army that remains; his service records were destroyed years
later in a fire in St. Louis. Much information covering five years of
his life was lost forever. It is a significant gap, for aside from his time
with the Bureau, my father's military service represents the most
dramatic time of his life. We know he came to the rescue of his
friend Leon Turrou, who years earlier was fired from the Bureau by
Hoover for agreeing to cooperate on a series of newspaper articles.

Hoover blocked Turrou's commission as an Army officer, but when my father encountered him as a lowly enlistee at Fort Custer, he pushed to have him commissioned as a first lieutenant in the Military Police Corps. We know my father was briefly summoned back to Washington from overseas to help organize the War Crimes Office and serve as its deputy director. We know he spent a week with General Patton, and we know that after V-E day, he spent time in Heidelberg, Germany, searching for the worst war criminal of all—Adolf Hitler. His assignment was to discover whether Hitler had died in his bunker, as was believed, or had instead somehow escaped. We know my father instigated a surveillance of Martin Bormann, who he believed had access to a fortune stashed away by the führer. But the absence of records, maddeningly, prevents knowing precisely what came of these investigations.

We know my father was asked to help institute the protocols for the Nuremberg trials. It was in this capacity that he had one of his two unusual encounters with Hermann Göring. Their first meeting was in Berlin before the war, when my father traveled to Europe following his breakup with Janice Jarrett. At the time, Göring was a German aviation hero; later he would become head of the German Luftwaffe. Göring, fascinated with American gangsters, heard that Melvin Purvis was in Berlin and rang him at his hotel. "Hallo, beeg G-Man," he said. Göring invited my father to his estate just outside Berlin, and the two went on a wild boar hunt, galloping out on horseback holding lances. My father bagged his boar and returned stateside with its tusks and hair from its neck mounted as a memento. Göring also presented him with a sword. My father stayed at Göring's estate for several days and remembered him as a generous but pompous host.

Their second meeting was under far different circumstances. Soon after Göring's arraignment on charges of war crimes, my father, then attached to the Nuremberg trials, interrogated the unshaven and emaciated German in his cell. (Bizarrely, due to the housing shortage, my father was given Göring's private railroad car as his quarters during his stay in Nuremberg.) At first, Göring seemed not to recognize my father, but after striking his forehead several times he said, "Oh yes, beeg G-man." Perhaps believing their past hunting trip gave them a special kinship, Göring asked my father if there was any way he could avoid execution. My father said no, and after a brief interrogation walked away. Göring eventually swallowed a cyanide capsule.

My father was released from active service on February 7, 1946, having risen to the rank of colonel, and he received a commendation ribbon from the Judge Advocate General's office and another from the War Department. By any measure his service was distinguished. By any measure, that is, except the one entertained by J. Edgar Hoover. In June 1946, Hoover received a report from a Lieutenant Colonel Karl Nash, who spent time in the European Theater during the war. Nash supplied a vitriolic assessment of my father and Leon Turrou. "He stated that both men were incompetent and thoroughly despised and both had yellow streaks up their backs," Hoover's report of Nash's memo noted. "He stated that from personal observation of Purvis's cowardice . . . he definitely knew the reason why another man was substituted for Purvis to be in charge of the capture of Dillinger. [He] stated that both Turrou and Purvis were pathological liars." It did not matter to Hoover that these allegations were unsubstantiated, that no specific instances of cowardice or deceit were included, that both Purvis and Turrou received decorations after their service. He accepted Nash's assessments at face value because they corresponded with his own. "Well," he wrote at the bottom of the memo, "the truth will out." Hoover kept the memo tucked carefully in my father's personal file, and in later years used the allegations in attempts to prevent my father from getting jobs.

———

Melvin Purvis became my father without knowing it, at 10:30 A.M. on September 28, 1943. On the clear fall morning that my mother underwent a cesarean section at the McLeod infirmary in Florence, attended by Dr. McLeod, my father was an ocean away. The telegram announcing my birth found him somewhere in the north of Africa.

My mother's joy at seeing her new son was tempered by having to see him alone. Her recovery from the pregnancy was slow, and she had to receive blood transfusions to regain strength. She needed comfort from her husband, but this was impossible. Unaware that letters were often delayed, my mother felt more alone each day that passed without a response from him acknowledging my birth. She wrote hard, unhappy letters that she knew would worry my father, but they were a way to ease her anxiety. Many weeks passed before she could forgive him for not being there at my birth. "I am sorry if I wrote you letters to hurt you," she said on December 8, over two months after I was born. "You see that I did not hear from you until the little baby was nearly a month old. . . . It is always hard for a woman to have a baby and her husband not be there. It was worse for me because I love you so much and am so dependent on you. The strain made me very nervous and maybe subconsciously I resented you for not being here. I am well now and not nervous anymore and I won't write letters like that again."

My brother Melvin was almost four when I was born. Headstrong and hard to wrangle even when my father was home, he became a wild and woolly buck with only one parent around. "If you don't come home and never go back," Melvin wrote our father, "I am going to tie you with a long string." He was too young to understand why his father was missing, and so he gave vent to his frustration through outbursts of unruliness. At bath time he might thrash in the tub and shield his ears from my mother. "Did Daddy wash his ears?" he would ask, and only after hearing that he had would Melvin relent: "Okay, then wash mine."

My mother had never found the heart to spank him, and certainly did not find it after my father shipped overseas. Her son was ailing from the same melancholy she felt, and so she gave him room. Sometimes she complained that he was too rambunctious to handle. "He is such a swaggering little boy," she observed in one letter. "He is a man's little boy and too interested in guns and man's things. All he talks about is hunting." Secretly, though, it gave her pleasure to see Melvin—nicknamed Big Big—act as rowdily as he did. He did so in obvious homage to his father, which allowed my mother to see some part of the man she missed so much. The luckiest days were those when an air-mail letter arrived with my brother Melvin's name on it. He would make my mother read it over and over, then carry it in his pocket, envelope and all, for weeks. His idealization of our father intensified with each day they were apart. "He is aware you are a great man," my mother wrote to him. "He calls you 'the biggest giant in the world.'"

When my father finally returned from Europe, my brother Melvin was seven years old. I was nearly three when I saw my father for the first time. He made me nervous, and for many months after his arrival, I referred to my father as "Mr. Purvis."

Yet with him home, our family became whole, and our lives surely resembled those of a million other families. To someone not from the South, the biggest difference probably was the number of servants who lived with us. We were a blood family of only four, but our extended family was double or even triple that size. Most of the servants descended from families that were linked to those of my father and mother, stretching back as long as two centuries. Some of their ancestors had been slaves owned by my ancestors, and in many instances they had chosen to stay once slavery was ended rather than start over someplace else. This was the way it was then in the South: Everybody had servants. By the time I was born, our servants were considered as much a part of the family as any uncle or cousin, and no one treated them with more kindness and respect than did my father.

There was our wonderful Dolly, whose family became linked to ours in the mid-1800s. Dolly ran the house and particularly the kitchen, orchestrating elaborate meals with such authority that no one dared cross her—not my mother and certainly not my father, who though he loved fine food knew enough to defer to Dolly on all matters culinary. At a housewarming party of some friends, my father was invited to see their new kitchen. "Madam," my father said. "I have never seen my own."

There was Lawson James, whose relatives were linked to my mother's family, and there was Gertrude, who became known to us as CuCu because my younger brother Christopher could not pronounce her name and referred to her that way. I remember the story of Gertrude's husband, Willy Cyrus, who had been in touch with a witch doctor. One day, while working for mother's grandmother Martha Brunson, Willy attempted to scatter some special dust in her eyes while she was napping in the afternoon, convinced that this would cast a spell that would make her stay asleep and allow him to rob the house. My Aunt Mattie awoke suddenly, pushed Willy through a window, and shot him in the leg with a pistol as he was fleeing. She then took him to the local jail in the back of a buggy, and he soon received a lengthy prison sentence. After a year my aunt went to the prison and told his jailers, "He's had enough." She brought him back to the house where he spent the next fifty years in the family's employ.

There was Uncle Jimmy with his immense white beard, who one day simply ambled onto our property and moved into a vacant cabin. My father told him he could stay, and he stayed there until his death. There was Charlie Vivians, who worked as both a butler and chauffeur. To me he was nothing less than another brother. Charlie would go broke every two years or so, and my father would give him long lectures before bailing him out. Charlie was very sweet-natured except when he was around our yardman, Belton McClain, who lived in a house next to our barn with his wife Teresa. Belton was an ex-convict who had robbed a store in Tennessee. When he showed up at our house, my father liked him and helped get the charge against him dismissed. Belton was fond of us boys and built us a clubhouse made of two old schoolbuses; he even put a working stove inside. But Belton also liked his liquor and often fought with his wife. One night when I was inside the clubhouse I heard a tremendous racket coming from Belton's house. The next morning I saw him raking leaves in his yard. "Did you and Teresa have a fight?" I asked. "Tweren't no fight to it," he said. "Just gave her a good lickin'." Every now and then Belton and Charlie would mix it up, too. I remember them going at each other with pitchforks, and Teresa valiantly trying to break it up.

My father was as demanding of his servants as he was of his children, but he was also exceedingly kind and considerate to them. He would brook no disrespect directed at them because of their race. When my father was in the Army, he checked into a hotel in Michigan along with my mother and Dolly. The desk clerk refused to let Dolly stay. My father found the hotel manager and said, "Do you know who I am?" For someone who did not lightly brag of his Bureau days, this was an extraordinary tactic. "If you don't let her in," my father said, "I will make this a major case in every newspaper in this country. How dare you insult her?" Dolly soon had her own room. Another time a train steward stopped Dolly from getting into a Pullman car with my parents. My father told him he would have the train stopped immediately if she was not allowed in. My father always took care of his servants, even when money for his own family was tight. And as far as I could tell they loved him dearly for it.

They loved my mother, too, for she was affectionate and charming. My mother never got over losing her father at an early age, never shook off the terrible feeling of being abandoned. She harbored a fear of sudden catastrophe for the rest of her life. While this anxiety was a big part of her personality, manifest, perhaps, in a kind of skittishness, so, too, was an artistic streak that ran through her. She loved poetry and hosted poetry clubs, and she was a member of the Edna St. Vincent Millay Society. She kept a notebook filled with her writings—stories, poems, impressions. Sometimes it seemed my mother was not of this world. In contrast to my father—rigid, grounded, precise—my mother often seemed to float through her days.

Florence, once a mostly rural town of 18,000, was my mother's hometown, but it was my father who was most wonderfully in his element there. He could finally indulge what he gave up when he joined the Bureau—his love of horses. A superb rider, he kept several horses in a barn on the property. He had a magnificent gray Tennessee walker named Big John and another lovely palomino, and he took them out for morning canters over the grounds.

Horses were one way to spend time with my father; hunting was another. My brother Melvin was far more intrigued by it than I. One of my first hunts was for rabbits, and after stirring one up in the brush, Melvin's pack of howling beagles chased it in a long circular path covering over a mile. Eventually the rabbit returned to the spot where we started, and came into our sights. I shot a rabbit, my first kill, and approached it cautiously. The sight of it did not shock me, despite the blood, but when I reached down and touched the rabbit it was still warm, and after that I did not do much hunting. One time I found a dead, putrid squirrel and dragged it into the house as if I had slain it myself. For a while I believed that all good sons in the South were hunters, and I did not know what to make of my aversion. But then one day my father told me of a deer-hunting trip he had taken at the famous King Ranch in Texas. My father shot two deer and went to collect his prey. When he came up on them, he noticed one was still alive. He saw a tear dripping down its face. My father said that was the last deer he ever shot. I understood well what he meant, and more important, I felt he understood me.

Besides horses and hunting there was a third rite of passage we shared with our father—guns. My father enjoyed collecting many things—tin soldiers, rare coins, antique cars—but his primary passion was weaponry. He kept hundreds of guns in the house, gathered over the years and lovingly catalogued and displayed. There were Remington Elliot ring trigger derringers, half-nickel brass-framed pepperboys, Colt .38 lightning revolvers, wood-handled Waffenva-brik Mausers, German dueling pistols, Belgium Browning pistols, pristine gold-plated pistols, and rusty antique pistols. He had a Deutsche Werkerfurt caliber .765 mm automatic pistol that had been used in a murder in Chicago; a seven-shot revolver inscribed "Ejercito Mexicano" and given to him by a police officer in Texas; a .22-caliber automatic rifle left behind by the Dillinger gang at Little Bohemia; a Remington .22-caliber rim-fire pistol given to him by FBI inspector J. S. Egan; and a .45-caliber Colt automatic that was a gift from the Chicago chief of detectives and had once been carried by the gangster Gus Winkler. My father spent hours cleaning and ex-amining his guns, and many more hours shooting at targets at a nearby range or on the property. He set up a skeet-shooting range in the back, and when my brother and I were old enough, we joined him in target practice. My first gun was a BB gun; I think I was ten. Then I got my first shotgun, a .20-gauge Winchester, as a Christmas present from my father. I was twelve. I remember shooting skeet with my father, and I remember him sometimes using his pistol in-stead of a shotgun, with amazing accuracy.

In those pursuits, slowly I learned who my father was and what he had done. I cannot recall discovering it all at once; I absorbed it over time. Once I was old enough to understand his past, I became very curious about it. My father kept several thick scrapbooks about his Bureau days; they had been assembled for him by a secretary, and included many newspaper clippings and magazine articles about his G-man exploits. I pored over the books and saw my fa-ther's name in headlines—"Purvis Gets His Man," "Purvis Scourge of Gangsters." It was remarkable to a young child. Though I could not quite comprehend the importance of it, I did realize that there was something special about my father—that he had been known and admired by the world. I felt pride, as any son would, and some measure of awe, and delight, I am sure, and also a new respect. But I also felt a little resentful. I wanted my father for myself; I did not want to share him with all of these people who so admired him.

Even so, there was something very thrilling about discovering my father's past life. My brother and I often asked him about those days when we were young. He always had answers for us; he would tell us about stalking Dillinger at the Biograph, about reaching for his gun and popping the buttons on his jacket; he told us about chasing after Pretty Boy Floyd, and about how some apples he had stuffed in his pockets bumped against his legs as he ran. We felt proud to be his sons, particularly when other children in Florence asked us about him. At least in the beginning, being able to shrug when asked about your father's heroism was a fine thing indeed. As the years passed, though, my father's willingness to tell us about his FBI days diminished. He never sat us down and told us the whole story—what it was like to be shot at by a gangster, what the true experience had been—and instead had offered only stray details here and there. Ultimately we knew no more about what he had done than anyone else familiar with his past. It would take me many years to understand my father's reluctance to talk about his Bureau days with any real honesty or thoroughness—it was because he did not wish to glorify those days in the wide eyes of his young sons. He was deeply conflicted about them—on one hand proud of what he accomplished; on the other bitter about how it all ended. Eventually, without enough to engage us and make the experience of my father's heroism real to us, we simply stopped asking him about Dillinger and Floyd and the rest of the gangsters who remained to us no more than mere comic-strip villains.

One day I sat next to my father and told him I wanted to join the FBI when I got older. His face reddened and he said, "That's the stupidest thing you ever said." He told me that I should forget all about the FBI, that it was not a good career for me, and that anyway I had other talents I should pursue. He was not making a suggestion. He was issuing an order. Under no circumstances would his son ever follow in his footsteps. I had rarely seen him more serious. Instead he encouraged me to follow my own path; I think he was relieved I had another option besides following him to the FBI. He always asked me about my drawings and hung several of them on the walls of his office at the radio station.

The pleasure of his encouragement of my art stands out in my mind. In contrast to my mother, who was endlessly attentive and supportive, my father was often a distant parent. This is not to say he did not want his children to be happy and did not do his best to give them rich, rewarding lives, for this he certainly did. When I developed an interest in amateur radio, he bought me a complete ham-radio outfit, and had an engineer from the station advise me when I encountered especially difficult problems. I cannot think of an instance when he denied us something we wanted, at least not something that was truly important. My father was thoughtful and giving to a fault. I have many cousins who still speak of his generosity, of receiving a present from him in their first week away at college, of seeing him pull up in an antique car he then left behind as a gift. Still, his wife and sons expected more of him than mere generosity. The nourishment we needed was of another kind altogether. In this, my father had more trouble.

The result is that we never could get as close as we wanted to get. There always seemed to be a barrier. I have a vivid memory of a summer night when he returned from work and pulled up our driveway in a new gray Cadillac. He stepped from the car and we both stood there, admiring its shiny chrome. Suddenly my father put his hand on my shoulder, and we stayed that way for long seconds, bound by this casual gesture that to me was a milestone of my childhood. I remember that night so well because, as best as I can recall, this was one of the rare times my father touched me in such a warm, affectionate way.

As it turned out, my father was not incapable of sharing of himself; he just was reserved in doing it with his own sons. Many years later I learned that my father had indeed taken a young man under his wing, as a father might a son, and bestowed on him all the wonder and marvel of his Bureau days. The boy was named Ross Beard, and his father, a local policeman, was a close friend of my father's. Ross developed an interest in my father and approached him for a job. My father hired him to degrease his collection of guns. Ross, then ten years old, began cleaning his first gun and found a cartridge inside it when he broke it open. He went to my father, who told him, "You've got the job." It was a dummy cartridge, and its placement inside the gun a test. Ross spent the next few years stopping by our house nearly every week to clean the guns my father had mounted on the walls in the attic. He also spent hours at the radio station, where sometimes my father would sneak down the back stairs so he and Ross could go look at a gun Ross had found in some shop. It was Ross who studied the long wall of my father's office—awash with framed pictures of a dazzling array of people including politicians, movie stars, and even Anna Sage, the "Lady in Red"—and expressed amazement at the range of characters my father had known. "So few people comment on that wall," my father told Ross.

"But every morning I come in here and spend a few minutes staring at that wall. I have learned something from every person up there."

It was Ross, much more than my brothers and I, who witnessed my father's pride in his accomplishments with the Bureau. My father even discussed with him some of his frustration about Hoover, a subject he would never entertain with his sons. He told Ross how he never sought to be a hero, how all he wanted to do was his job. He spoke of the sense of betrayal he felt when he realized Hoover had turned on him. He spoke of his anger, of his deep and gnawing anger, and Ross could tell it had yet to subside. Ross saw not only the heroic side of my father, in all its glamour, but also the human side, in all its vulnerability. Ross got the chance to know my father in a more complete way—both to enjoy the thrill of his G-man days and to understand what they meant to him, the good and the bad. This candor was the crucial ingredient missing from his relationship with his sons. Perhaps my father felt he could not say anything to diminish our idealized impressions of him; perhaps he did not want us to see the depths of his frustration over what happened. In the end we received an incomplete version of events. He simply never found the right way to share these things with us. Perhaps he did not feel his legacy would weigh so heavily on Ross.

———

On February 2, 1950, my younger brother, Christopher Peronneau Purvis, was born. From the beginning it was clear that he was not nearly as tough-skinned as my brother Melvin or even me. He was younger than his brothers by many years, and he seemed to sense quite early that he was on his own. Like me, he also had to do without his father, at least in his early years.

In May 1951, my father answered the call to public service once again. Senator Olin D. Johnston, chairman of the Post Office and Civil Service Committee, asked my father to serve as counsel to a subcommittee investigating federal manpower policy. His job was to probe for graft and waste in the government's personnel system, and he assured a reporter he did not plan to conduct "a superficial screening." He left for Washington and booked a room at the Hotel Carlyle, where he often stayed while in the capital. Within days of his departure my mother assumed the duties of a long-suffering

wife, writing him a melancholy letter reminiscent of the painful
messages she sent him during the war.

Not surprisingly, Hoover did his best to block this assignment. Bureau records show the institutional dislike of Melvin Purvis continued unabated into the 1950s, no less fierce than it had been in
previous decades. In 1946, L. B. Nichols,[ck] Hoover's publicity genius, briefed a reporter on the myth of Melvin Purvis, clarifying for
him that it was "Sam Cowley who deserves the credit." Hoover's addition to the memo: "Whenever opportunity presents itself get over
[the] truth—Purvis did not kill Dillinger and had very little to do in
the case." In 1949 the commissioner of the Atomic Energy Commission called Hoover to ask about my father, whom he was considering
for a job. Purvis "had been in charge of our Chicago office and then
resigned and gave out a lot of magazine stories and advertised a
breakfast cereal in connection with G-Man work, etc., which was
very distasteful to all of us," Hoover told him. Purvis "might be a
problem from an administrative point of view or might be a problem subsequently if [he] left in regard to writing memoirs and so
forth."

When the Bureau learned my father was being considered to
study government efficiency, special agent T. D. Webb quickly called
Robert Ramspeck, chairman of the Civil Service Commission. Purvis
"is a publicity seeker and in my opinion didn't have a gut in his
body," Webb said. "In my opinion he would louse up any job he got
into. Mr. Ramspeck stated that he was glad to get this information,
inasmuch as he would be talking to Senator Johnston and the Senate Civil Service Committee in the very near future concerning this
matter." Webb scheduled a lunch with Ramspeck to "go into the
matter further with him." After that, Tolson ordered that all inquiries regarding my father be directed to his office for, as he put it
in a memo, "handling." The passage of time—my father had been
out of the Bureau for sixteen years when the appointment came
up—had done nothing to dull Hoover's animosity toward him.

But this time he got the job and was periodically away. We weathered his absences, as we always did, and we waited for him to come
home. It took him more than a year to conclude his investigation,
and more than two to produce a fourteen-volume report detailing
the gross inequities of reduction-in-force practices, the lack of incentive programs, personal favoritism, and other ills. Around the

time he was wrapping up his interviews, my father was again nominated for a federal judgeship, his dream job. Once again the Bureau was notified, and phone calls were made. Once again my father did not get the job.

Before my father returned to South Carolina, my mother, my brother Melvin, and I made a trip to see him in Washington. Along with a friend, Melvin and I took a tour of FBI headquarters. My father did not come with us, though it would have been a wonderful experience. An agent took us around to see the usual sights—we rolled our thumbs in ink in the fingerprinting division, and we fired Thompson submachine guns in the basement shooting range. The agent did not take us to the director's office. I remember Melvin enjoyed the tour more than I did. I sensed no connection between the Bureau's sterile halls and the adventures I attributed to my father.

15

FATHERS AND SONS

In 1959 the twenty-fifth anniversary of Dillinger's death rolled around. Naturally reporters sought out my father for comment. He obliged most of them, but there was more than a trace of bitterness in his remarks. He had kept the secret of who exactly killed Dillinger for a quarter century, and now he was being pestered finally to come clean. He would have none of it. "I have never told, and I assume none of the others have," he said to a *New York Daily News* reporter. "Most of us were young fellows. We had a feeling there was no great honor in taking part in killing a man." He added, "I wish I could just forget the whole horrible affair." Still, the reporters persisted: Did you shoot the fatal shot? "I have been credited with capturing him," he said. "I have been credited with killing him. All that I ever said is that I led the group that captured Dillinger. That's what I stand on. After all, does it really matter that much who killed him?"

There must have been a deep weariness in my father's voice as he reflected on that day at the Biograph Theater. The 1950s had been hard years. Both my parents began drinking far too much, and although I did not know it at the time, my father suffered from chronic depression, even undergoing shock therapy in an attempt to cure himself. He and my mother began to confront one another regularly. My father's relationship with us teenage sons disintegrated as well. One evening, during a particularly bitter dinner table argument between my parents, my brother Melvin stood up and threw a glass of milk in my father's face. My father calmly got to his feet, ordered Melvin into the den, and followed him in. From inside came no screaming or yelling, no crashing of furniture. My brother emerged without a mark on him. Later I asked him what had happened. "I'm disinherited," he said. My falling-out with my father occurred when he punished me excessively after I took my mother's car on a date instead of using my own car. After that I often tried to avoid him. All of this, along with his worsening physical health, reinforced my father's agony and frustration.

Late in 1959 my father summoned the strength for one final tour of duty in government. Senator Olin Johnston called again, to ask him to serve as legal counsel for a Senate subcommittee investigating the functioning of the federal courts. Another senator, James Eastland of Mississippi, requested that the FBI initiate an investigation into my father to determine if he was a worthy appointee. It was not mandatory that appointees be investigated, though occasionally the Bureau would oblige such requests. In my father's case it was entirely unnecessary; he had served in a similar role only eight years before, and his reputation in Washington—Hoover's efforts notwithstanding—was impeccable. Nevertheless, Hoover agreed to launch a full-scale investigation into my father and his activities dating back more than two decades. "Bureau specifies interviews should be conducted," an FBI memo noted, "so no charges of character assassination may be made." More than a dozen agents fanned out to pick apart the details of my father's past; reports came in concerning his shopping habits (he "purchased groceries at the store . . . and usually paid promptly, but on some occasions was slow in payment") and his long-ago citation for speeding ("He was fined $15 . . . for driving 45 miles per hour in a 25-mile zone"). Sketchy but negative assessments from people who knew my father only marginally were entertained. "Purvis was disliked by those who knew him, was arrogant and dictatorial," one informant declared. "He had heard numerous stories of a derogatory nature concerning Purvis . . . but he thought [they] were told by people who disliked Purvis and probably were untrue." In fact the vast majority of reports that came in were positive. Purvis "is a loyal American citizen and highly recommended . . . for a position of trust with the U.S. Government," one source said. Purvis "has an excellent and widespread reputation as being a man of utmost integrity," said another. In all, several hundred pages of files were used to compile the report.

A Bureau memo dated September 10, 1959, prepared for "transmittal to the Senate Committee on the Judiciary," made clear the director's conclusion. "His file . . . reflects Purvis capitalized extensively in respect to the Dillinger case," the memo stated. "He also claimed credit for handling certain cases which had actually been handled by former inspector Sam Cowley." Then the memo recycled the unsubstantiated claims of Colonel Frank Nash that my father and Leon Turrou were incompetent and cowardly. Despite these efforts, my father got the job, but even then Hoover did not stop trying to undermine the appointment. When my father interviewed Judge Warren E. Burger as part of his investigation, Hoover had Cartha DeLoach, his assistant director in charge of public relations, speak with Burger in advance. "I talked at some length with Judge Burger concerning Purvis," DeLoach wrote in a December 1959 memo. "The Judge appeared to be extremely appreciative of the information and indicated that my remarks would, of course, be kept in confidence. He intends to be most cautious in dealing with Purvis."

By the time my father undertook his investigation of the judiciary, he was a weak and debilitated man. He suffered chronic back pain and sometimes relied on morphine to dull the agony. He often felt lethargic and had trouble eating and sleeping. Before he left for Washington, his weakened state seemed to affect his way of thinking, and he became ruminant and philosophical, reflecting on the accidents of life. We in the family heard him wonder what might have happened had he been appointed to a federal judgeship. We heard him wonder how events might have been different had Anna Sage not contacted him. My father was in the throes of a terrible psychic struggle, and the breakdown of his body seemed to reflect his every wound.

Still, he gathered his strength and left again for Washington. In November 1959 he contracted a bad case of the Asian flu that he could not shake. He flew back to Florence for Christmas and to recuperate. On the way out of the airplane, he stumbled and nearly fell on the tarmac. There was a tiredness to him that I had never witnessed before.

On December 8, 1959, not long after my father returned to Florence, he got a call from New York City. He learned that his great friend Bartley Crum had committed suicide. Crum had been despondent and, like my father, obsessed with his own mortality. "Life is preposterous," Crum said to his family during a dinner party on his final night. "You go through the motions and then you wake up and realize something is missing—something big is missing." Crum, also like my father, had been persecuted by Hoover and once confided to my father that he had been under surveillance for many years. The strain of it all finally took its toll. My father received the news badly; he sank even deeper into his depression. As he paced through the house, I heard him for the first time make a derogatory remark about the director of the FBI. "Damn Hoover for this," he muttered. "Damn Hoover."

On the night of February 28, 1960, my father was in particularly bad shape. He had trouble getting from his room to the bathroom, and I remember having to get out of bed in the middle of the night to help him. As I held on to his frail arms, I breathed the odor of alcohol and morphine. I went back to bed angry and confused.

The next morning I rushed to dress for school. Despite our lack of physical contact, my father and I had one affectionate ritual: Every morning before school I would go into his bedroom and give him a quick kiss on the cheek. On this morning I hurried past his open bedroom door and down the stairs. I decided not to give him his customary kiss. I did not even say good morning or tell him goodbye. It was the first time I had ever left the house this way.

———

It is hard to describe the devastation my father's death wrought on our family. For my mother, the idea of it was incomprehensible. She had grown accustomed to losing him for long stretches, and the ache of her loneliness was tolerable then only because she knew it was bound to end. But now my father was gone forever, and a big part of my mother died that day too. There were times during their difficult years when my mother would say she'd have been happier had she stayed with her first husband, and not chosen my father instead. I do not believe she meant it. My mother and father were deeply in love, of this I am surer than of anything else I know. The hardships of their later lives, the terrible frustrations they both felt, do nothing to diminish this fact. It was not a perfect union, and we were not the perfect family. But there was an intensity to their bond that I think many people would have envied.

For my mother to find my father there, lying in his blood at the top of the stairs, was a trauma from which she never recovered. We children, too, saw things no child should see. Christopher was only ten when he saw his father's blood on the carpet hung to dry on a tree limb. All of us were drawn to see the spot where he died outside his bedroom, and there, too, we found the stains of his blood. I cannot recall all of my feelings on that day and in the weeks to come. My good friend Bill Ducker remembers that time better than I. Bill had been with me in the school cafeteria when the principal summoned me to his office. Bill sensed something was wrong and asked to know why I had been called. The teachers would not tell him. Bill parked himself outside the office of our principal, Carlyle Lever, and announced he would not leave until he was told what happened. An hour later Lever brought him inside and told him my father killed himself. Bill said, "I don't believe that." Lever assured him it was true, but Bill wouldn't have it. He walked to his house to tell his parents my father was dead, and then he walked to my house. He rarely left my side for the next few days.

Bill remembers our house being full of policemen, FBI agents too. We found refuge from the intrusion in the den, which had been my father's private room; we children had to knock on its door before entering. On a high shelf that ran the length of the darkly paneled room, my father had arrayed his collection of handsome tin soldiers. There must have been 100 of them, high on their little horses, tiny swords and rifles drawn. I told Bill that my father had given one of these soldiers to each and every child who had come into the den—to the sons of friends and relatives, to boys in the neighborhood, to anyone who showed the slightest interest in them. He had not, however, taken one down and given it to me. I had always wanted him to, and I still choose to hope that had I gone in and asked or even expressed an interest, he would have happily handed me an entire platoon. But I never pursued it, and so I never got one. Now that my father was gone, Bill and I took down the soldiers and played with them on the coffee table as policemen came and went around us.

A single day after my father's death, a taxi pulled into our driveway. I watched out the window as a woman got out. It was Dolly. She had seen news reports of my father's death in her home in Brooklyn, New York, and had put herself on the first plane for South Caro-

lina. She had left the family years before, when things were bad between my parents. No one asked her to come, and yet she knew that
she would be needed now, and so she came. She stayed with us for
the next two weeks, and put a cot next to Christie's bed so he could
sleep beside her. I can think of no gesture more touching, no display of love more moving, than Dolly's surprise arrival at our sad
and broken house that day.

A cold, miserable rain fell the morning of my father's funeral. I
dressed and went downstairs to wait for the procession to leave for
St. John's Episcopal Church. My brother Melvin was already downstairs, as blank-faced as I. But Christopher was nowhere to be seen.
Finally he came down, wearing a shaggy pair of blue jeans. Surely he
knew what was expected of him, even at age ten—he was to wear his
best suit and act like the man he was years away from becoming. But
Christopher would not abide that. He was the most sensitive of us
all, and so he surely felt the pain of my father's death more acutely,
even though he could least understand it. The blue jeans were a
cover to disguise his anguish, a show of disregard for conventions he
had no use for. Ross Beard walked straight to him and admonished
him, saying, "Christie, you go back upstairs and put on your suit and
come back down and show some respect for your father." Christopher did precisely that, and played along for the rest of the day. We
all played along that day. There is no solace in funerals, at least not
for children.

It seemed the whole city of Florence was at the funeral at Mount
Hope Cemetery, just a mile from our house. There were dozens of
police officers in uniform, and several who identified themselves as
FBI agents. Only later would I be made aware of how J. Edgar
Hoover scorned my father by not sending an official delegation to
the funeral. All of these agents, some active, some retired, had come
on their own to stand in the pouring rain. I remember feeling
proud of my father in a way I wish I had when he was alive. How I
missed him on that day.

Three days after the funeral, my mother sat her three sons down
at the kitchen table and composed a brief message to J. Edgar
Hoover. She sent it to him in a Western Union telegram on March 7,
1960. "We are honored that you ignored Melvin's death," it read.
"Your jealousy hurt him very much but until the end I think he
loved you."

The years to come would not be bright; they would get even darker. Without my father my mother was lost. We brothers, slowly drifting apart even while my father was alive, now felt the tethers of family loosen even more. I had already begun my escape, and now all that remained for me was to physically disappear, and this I did as soon as I reached college age. Less than two years after my father's death, I enrolled at Virginia Commonwealth University and went north to Richmond. I recall a great feeling of relief at embarking on a new life, tempered only by a slight stab of regret. I knew the family I was leaving behind was terribly fragile. But there was an element of self-preservation to what I was doing, and I saw no choice but to do it.

My brother Melvin had a harder time of it; he was bound to the family and to my father in ways that I perhaps was not. Having his father's name proved a fateful and complicated matter. He inherited from him a sense of grandeur and a tendency toward outsized ambition; the little boy who vowed to fight with lions became a man who felt he could conquer the world. It was as if he believed that his name alone entitled him to an uncommon and adventurous life. Enormously bright, articulate, humorous, and generous, when he didn't reach the pinnacles he sought, he always bounced back and set off toward another lofty goal. Melvin was a grand planner, a believer in big ideas and noble ideals—the inheritor of our father's larger-than-life persona.

Melvin strove mightily to find his niche. After my father died he briefly attended law school but soon decided this was not his calling. He then worked as a merchant seaman, but after working for a summer in the engine room of a tramp steamer on the South China Sea, he wisely discovered he was not suited for such a life. Afterward he worked as a speechwriter for the head of the Seafarers International Union, Paul Hall. Melvin was an exceptionally gifted writer, but eventually he fell out with Hall and moved on. He wrote a novel, but he became discouraged when an editor to whom he sent his manuscript sent it back with commentaries. Like many writers, Melvin could not tolerate being criticized. He worked in real estate, married, and had a wonderful daughter Marie, now a nurse and talented writer. This marriage ended in divorce, and he then became an evangelist minister. Though some people brushed him off, my brother believed deeply in his mission and served it with distinction. In 1984, Melvin ran for the Senate against no less a regional heavyweight than Strom Thurmond. Predictably, he lost. Still, he waged a fierce campaign, with no support from the Democratic Party machine in South Carolina but convinced that his famous name would carry more than its share of weight. After this foray into politics, he entered the oriental rug business.

Through the years Melvin struggled terribly with our father's legacy. The ambiguity of it was something he found untenable, and something he ultimately rejected. He needed desperately for our father to be an unqualified hero, and he held fast to an idealized image of the man. Melvin was the first of us to begin a book about our father—to attempt to clarify the legacy clouded by our father's refusal to share it with us. The first draft of his manuscript was to some extent fictitious in a touching effort to make my father larger than life. He wrote, for instance, that my father was a great friend of Winston Churchill. To my knowledge, the two men never met, but some of my relatives still believe it to be true.

In his book is the story my brother told of our trip to the FBI building as youngsters. In his version, he and I were accompanied by both my mother and my father as we toured the headquarters. At one point my father marched us straight to Hoover's office and was let in to see the director. When Hoover did not rise from his desk, my father, Melvin recalled, was outraged. "You son of a bitch," my father hissed, "when I bring my wife in here you stand up." Hoover, of course, did as he was told. My brother told this story so often that some of my relatives still repeat it, and it has become part of the family lore. Although I began to believe it myself, it always troubled me because, try as I might, I simply could not recall my father or mother being with us as we toured the FBI. As far as I knew, my father tried many times to see Hoover on his own, and was never permitted past Helen Gandy's desk. There was no storming in, no angry pronouncements: My father simply left and tried again in a year or two. Also, such an outburst would have been totally out of character for my father, at least as far as his relationship with Hoover was concerned. Finally I uncovered an FBI record of our long-ago visit. It stated that the two sons of Melvin Purvis accompanied by another boy were given a standard tour of the building, but it made no mention of our parents. The only conclusion I can reach is that they were not there, and that Melvin's reimagining of the incident was motivated by a need to make our father seem more heroic than he was, a touching attempt to complete the incomplete legacy our father left us.

Our younger brother Christopher grappled with the same themes, and he harbored some of the same delusions about our father. He had not known him as well as we had, and had lost him at an age when his opinion of him had not had a chance to form fully. This confusion manifested itself in quite a different way with Christie than it did with Melvin. Whereas Melvin believed himself to be invested with our father's greatness, Christie had a damaged sense of self-worth. He had a volatile temper and lashed out at the world. Christie saw little value in being the son of Melvin Purvis and seemed to reject society altogether in favor of a marginal existence. This exceedingly bright, intense, and kind-hearted boy—the handsomest of us all by far, and the most charismatic—became addicted to drugs by the time he was eighteen.

Our mother saw the worst expressions of this tragic addiction. While I was away—first at college in Virginia, then at the School of Visual Arts in New York, the University of Washington, and at Yale, and finally in the Netherlands—my mother and Christie lived in the house on Cherokee Road. Before long Christie, not himself, had begun taking things of value to pay for his cocaine habit. It became so bad that my friend Bill Ducker became his legal guardian. I would get late-night calls from my distraught mother, but there was little I could do. At some point I conveniently resigned myself to thinking that Christie was a lost cause, sadly beyond my help or anyone else's. It was for me, in retrospect, a selfish way out.

In 1978, my mother died of pancreatic cancer. Some months afterward Melvin called me to ask for my permission to sell some old bank checks signed by our father. After his death my father's things had been distributed among us; we all took what we most desired, and the rest remained with our mother. I took his scrapbooks and kept them with me wherever I traveled; they were, to me, the most graphic representation of his glory days. His checks, however, had not struck me as important memorabilia. Still, Melvin knew that my father's signature was marketable, and he wanted to sell the checks—both to make some money, he explained, and to get rid of them. I felt they were of no use to us and encouraged him to do as he saw fit. The whole matter seemed entirely inconsequential. I took the view at the time that the less I was involved with my family's affairs in South Carolina, the better.

I did not realize I had opened the floodgates. While I was away in the Netherlands and later in Boston, my brothers began the process of selling off many of my father's things. First Christie sold for $50,000 the prime items of the gun collection that he had chosen as part of his inheritance. Encouraged by Ross Beard, a group of friends and gun collectors purchased the remaining part of the collection and had it permanently placed in a special wing of the South Carolina Law Enforcement Division (SLED) at Columbia, South Carolina. Christie also sold myriad other items—photos from my father's Bureau days and from his life in Hollywood, letters, files, clippings, G-man collectibles—all for a fraction of what they were worth. "He was literally giving them away," said Wallace Bird, a Florence native who purchased many of the artifacts at higher prices. "He had this dealer he would bring things to and get $5 for them. Then the dealer would turn around and sell it for $500. I told Christie to at least take these things to a reputable dealer and get the $500 himself. But he didn't want to hear it. He just kept giving things away for pennies on the dollar."

Bill Ducker visited Christie one day and found him having a yard sale consisting solely of my father's things. Letters my father had sent to my mother during the war were scattered on the ground. Bill stopped the sale and gathered the things himself. But before he could haul them away, Melvin showed up to see Christie. Bill explained what had happened, and gave the possessions to Melvin. Less than a week later, Bill was surprised to see the artifacts in the window of a local antique dealer. "It was as if he couldn't wait to get rid of this stuff," Bill said later. "He didn't want any part of it. He didn't even want it in the house anymore. For some reason he was determined to be free of it."

How could these relics of our father have held so little significance for my brothers? Did not some part of them yearn to keep these things, to preserve them, to claim them as their own? Yet when I learned they were selling these items, I did nothing to prevent it. Though I wasn't the one dismantling the estate, I was its official executor, a role I had all but relinquished by leaving the country. And so I was a silent party with no remorse. I felt no outrage, no inclination to make things right. I simply shrugged and did not interfere. Who was I, after all, to judge them from half a world away? They were still there, in the thick of it, surrounded by sights and memories I had long ago conveniently escaped. Perhaps the only way for them to free themselves of the legacy was to obliterate it, or at least the physical manifestation of it. I believe that we did what we did out of an instinct for self-preservation. For my brothers, relief came from disposing of my father's things; for me, it came from turning a blind eye.

I wish I could say that purging themselves of my father's artifacts gave them some measure of lasting solace, but I do not believe it did. Christie continued on his tragic and increasingly helpless downward spiral, losing more and more of himself to drugs. He married and had an enchanting daughter, McKee, but he kept company with questionable characters, existing in the shadowy fringes of normal life. One day he and a friend wrapped a Corvette around a tree, and Christie was hurled through its windshield. How he survived that, I will never know. The crash, however, hastened his demise. Afterward he phoned me and asked to borrow money. I had lent him money in the past; it was a quick and easy way for me to alleviate my regret at not being there to help him through his troubles. When he decided to start a trucking business, both Melvin and I were happy to lend him some of the start-up funds. But this time I was convinced he needed the money for drugs. I told him I was short on cash at the moment, even though I had enough money to lend him. He hung up and we went on with our separate lives.

Two weeks later, on August 7, 1984, I received a late-night call at my apartment in Cambridge, Massachusetts. It was Melvin with news, terrible news. Christie was dead. He was thirty-four years old. Some people walking along a deserted road in a remote section of Florence came upon the parked second-hand Chevrolet sedan that Melvin had recently bought for him. Christie's body was behind the wheel, where it had sat in the sun for a week. What was left of him was unrecognizable, yet Melvin identified the body as Christie's nonetheless. An autopsy revealed that his wrists had been slit, and cause of death was determined as suicide.

This news was horrifying, but I cannot say I was surprised. I felt bad about not lending him money that last time. But his death was only the final stop on a journey, and perhaps the time for me to have done something had long passed. After a while all I could see in his hollowed, handsome face was an unbearable sadness. Perhaps I could have helped him overcome his despair and find a way to live his life. Perhaps not. We will never know, because I made the choice to pursue my own salvation as far from Florence as I could get.

After Christie's death—reminiscent as it was of my father's—Melvin and I became much closer than we had ever been before. As the survivors, we forged a new and profound kinship, finding much comfort in merely being there for each other to talk to. He seemed to me to be happier than he had ever been. He and his wife Judy were deeply in love and they had two children, Asher and Anna. Melvin was a happy family man now, creating for himself a life independent of our difficult past. By then I was teaching at Boston University, but I saw Melvin quite often, and he liked coming to Boston to see me. I was surprised but also pleased that he and I now got along as well as we did. We shared many experiences and even managed to laugh about some of the lighter events in our complicated family past.

Then, on October 18, 1986, the telephone rang in my apartment in Brookline. It was Judy. Melvin was dead. He was forty-eight years old. He was about to take a trip to Pakistan on business. The tickets had been purchased and an itinerary drawn up. Just one day prior to his departure, Melvin came home around noon and sat with his young son Asher, then only four, on his knee. Melvin fell to the floor. His heart simply stopped. Two years earlier Melvin had had surgery to repair a hole in his heart, a defect caused by a childhood bout with rheumatic fever. Surgeons drew the hole closed and sewed it with a fabric they said would last several lifetimes. It lasted only two years.

When I went to Florence for the funeral, I asked about my father's scrapbooks, which I had left in Melvin's care. Traveling with them had become cumbersome, and Melvin needed them for the book he had started on my father's life. But I was told that Melvin had sold them along with everything else. I learned of the urgency of these sales, of my brother's unshakable determination to remove these items from his life. Years later, Ross Beard found the scrapbooks in North Carolina. Although the owner refused to relinquish them, he did allow Ross to copy the pages. This he did on a hot summer day in a nearby country store.

I learned, also, that Christie had hastily rid himself of all of our father's things. Everything except for one possession—our grandfather clock. Christie knew that I had claimed it, and somehow he had
summoned the willpower not to sell it. This small but admirable gesture of loyalty touched me profoundly.

The devastation, then, was all but complete. Many of its memen-
tos were gone, and now its members were, too. Why had it all come
to this so quickly? My father was fifty-six when he died; Melvin was
forty-eight, Christie only thirty-four. Why was I all that was left?

These were difficult questions, and ones I was not ready to answer. After Melvin's death I returned to my life, but with a heavier
heart than I had ever felt before. Suddenly it was not so easy for me
to shrug off family matters, for now I was the only member of the
family left. Its absence actually made it harder for me to ignore it.
The losses we had endured as a family haunted me as I returned to
my life in Boston.

The birth of our son Alston in 1995 changed everything. For
many years I had dismissed my father's legacy, suppressing a faint
but nagging suspicion that it was relevant to my life. I now knew that
the events of my father's life were important because they would
matter to my son. How he perceived them was, I realized, my responsibility.

I had already begun gathering some of the loose strings of my father's life—a photograph here, a love letter there—but absently and
without purpose. The arrival of my son stirred me to action. "Dad,"
he seemed to say to me, "go and find your own father. He is out
there waiting for you. So go."

———

Over the years my father's death has become part of his legacy. He
has become known as the former darling of the Bureau who was
driven out—and driven to his death—by Hoover. His apparent suicide finalized his martyrdom—it confirmed the extent of Hoover's
treachery and even allowed him the opportunity for another atroc-
ity or two. It fit neatly with the arc of the narrative—my father rose
to the highest heights and plunged to the lowest depths. That he
shot himself with a gangster's gun only added to the symmetry of
the story.

But is this really what happened? Did my father take his own life because he was, among other things, bitter and despondent about what happened to him a quarter century before? Did Hoover's continuing persecution of my father—right through his attempts to derail my father's final public appointment only months before his death—so torment my father that he chose to end his life? And what does it say about my father if his death really was a suicide? Does it diminish the heroism he displayed in his earlier days? Does it affect how he should be perceived as a father? Does it hold the key to who he was, or is it incidental to it? None of these questions interested me in the least for more than three decades—as far as I was concerned, it was all behind me, and that was where it belonged.

But there is only so much room to run away from things. The true pain, we finally realize, is in leaving matters unresolved. Little Alston brought me full circle and face-to-face with these issues that I had successfully suppressed for so long. I needed to revisit the events of February 29, 1960, the day my mother found my father at the top of the stairs.

As I dredged up old records and spoke to people who had been close to my father around the time of his death, it became clear that I would never find an answer. The facts of my father's death are not in dispute. He was killed by a single bullet that entered through the bottom of his jaw and passed through his brain. The wound was self-inflicted. This was the conclusion reached by the jurors impaneled at the coroner's inquest, and none of the research I have done suggests otherwise. Yet the jurors reached no conclusion on whether or not the wound was *deliberately* inflicted. We have been left, all these years, with the possibility that the shooting was accidental. The question was no longer an evidentiary one—it could only be answered, if it could be answered at all, through deep introspection and reflection about my father's life. I have vacillated between feeling certain that his death was an accident and feeling just as convinced that it was suicide. It has become clear to me, however, that what matters most are not the circumstances surrounding my father's death but what he accomplished in life.

Nonetheless, nearly everyone I spoke to has a theory. Despite the evidence to the contrary, some are convinced that my father was murdered, and I have been urged to demand that an investigation into the death be opened. It is true that Roger Touhy—the gangster investigated by my father and possibly wrongly sent to prison for the kidnapping of John Factor in the early 1930s—was released from prison late in 1959. Twenty-three days later—and just a few weeks before my father's death—Touhy was murdered by assassins who were never caught. Could Touhy's murder and my father's death somehow be related? Certainly my father would not have dismissed the possibility that someone might have wanted to kill him. After Touhy's murder he brought a gun into his bedroom for the first time in years. The notion that he might have been murdered is not fanciful, but the facts of the case suggest it did not happen. There were no extraneous footprints, no sightings of strange men in the neighborhood, no evidence of a quick escape, no broken windows or open doors. My mother reached my father's body within seconds of hearing the shot, and she neither saw anyone nor heard retreating footsteps. The doctor who first examined him—my father's friend and physician, Walter R. Mead—found nothing to indicate that someone else had been involved. I trust completely that Mead would have sounded an alarm had he suspected my father was murdered.

After her initial shock at finding my father, my mother always maintained his death was an accident. She shared her story with Gordon A. Philips,[ck] editor of the *Grapevine,* the publication for former agents of the Bureau. "Melvin was a collector of old guns and the gun he had in his possession at the time of his death was from this collection," Philips[ck] recalled. "He arrived home from Washington on a Saturday and fell from the plane ramp while leaving the plane at Florence due to a bad case of the Asian flu. . . . All week he told his son that he had to give this old gun to a friend and intended to keep his promise the first part of the week. On Monday morning, Melvin was in fine spirits, enjoyed his breakfast and apparently decided to ready the gun for delivery to his friend." What happened next, my mother told Phillips, was accidental. "Mel was shot in the throat and apparently it was caused by his falling downstairs and the fact that he did not know this old gun was loaded."

There is one obvious error in this version: My father did not tumble down the stairs; he was found at the top of the stairway. But certainly he had been weakened by the flu. And it is true he told me he intended to lend Gus Winkler's pistol to a friend, Lyle McCain, to use in a display at a gun show. The idea that the shooting was accidental is entirely plausible.

First and foremost is the argument that he would never have chosen an automatic pistol to shoot himself. Ross Beard, who was called
before the coroner's jury as a weapons "expert," stressed that my father hated automatics that could feed bullets into the chamber immediately upon firing; he preferred revolvers that required bullets
be loaded into the gun one by one. When the Winkler automatic
was found beside my father's body, it contained a partially loaded
magazine with a bullet in the chamber ready to discharge. Anyone
who picked up the gun—including my mother, the first to the
scene—risked having it go off. Also, the shells remaining in the
chamber and magazine were tracer (incendiary) bullets that could
have been a fire hazard as well. It is hard for me to conceive of a situation in which my father—meticulous about gun safety—would
have disregarded the danger posed in using a loaded automatic pistol to shoot himself. Wouldn't he instead have loaded a single bullet
into his service revolver and used that, so that when it fell to the
floor it was empty and harmless?

Also, why would my father have chosen to place the pistol beneath
his jaw? "Anyone who has ever fired a gun at someone else, as your
father did, would never take the chance of shooting himself in the
neck area," said Beard, who believes strongly that my father's death
was accidental. "You could bleed to death or be paralyzed. Someone
who knows guns puts it against his temple or in his mouth." Furthermore, the very notion of my father choosing a gun to kill himself is
out of character. "He had a very great horror of pain," Dr. Edwin
Allen, a physician who lived near us and was good friends with my
parents, testified at the inquest. "Giving him a shot was a major procedure. He didn't like pain a bit and it seems to me like if he would
destroy himself it would be with an overdose of some medicine. It
just didn't seem to fit that he would shoot himself."

And why was there no suicide note? Why would my father not
spare us the torture of leaving no explanation? Hadn't he been in
good spirits, according to our maid and to others who spoke with
him the weekend before he died? And wasn't there some question
about the powder burns on his jaw—didn't they suggest the gun was
not pressed against it but rather was a few inches away?

Bill Ducker has another theory. One day a few weeks before my
father's death, Bill and I took three weapons from my father's collection—a German-manufactured automatic pistol, a .38-caliber

revolver, and the silver .45 automatic that had belonged to Gus Winkler. I knew I should not have taken these guns—my father didn't mind our shooting his pistols but forbade us to use anything more powerful than a .22—but I figured as long as we cleaned and replaced them, we would be fine. Bill and I finished our shooting around 5:00 P.M., and because we were in a rush, we decided we would clean the guns later. I never got around to it. The next week Bill asked me if I had cleaned them. I put it off again. Finally Bill came to my house and asked where the guns were. I told him I had put them in the gun cabinet in my father's den. This is where he kept show guns like the Winkler automatic. Bill and I could not clean them that day because my father was in the den with a friend. We put it off yet again.

Two days later my father was dead.

Bill speculates that on the evening before his death, my father finally saw the three uncleaned guns in the den cabinet. He believes my father retrieved the Winkler pistol and took it with him when he went upstairs that night. His intention, Bill believes, was to clean it the next day so that he could finally give it to his friend. All of the cleaning equipment was in the attic with the guns. Bill believes my father likely had the gun in his hand the next morning while he was pulling down the rope to lower the attic stairs. My father had suffered an injury the day before when one of our horses mashed his hoof down on his foot. "It takes some effort to get those stairs to come down," says Bill. "My feeling is that Mr. Purvis suddenly put his weight on his damaged foot and it just gave way. He stumbled and fell and the gun, which he did not know was loaded, pressed against his throat and went off." Bill pauses when he tells this story and stares down at the ground. "I hate this story," he says, "because we were participants in it."

Bill and I always had emptied and cleaned the guns we took from my father's collection. This was the first time we did not clean them, though I remember we made sure none of the guns had a bullet in its chamber. Still, it is possible that a few bullets somehow remained in the clip of the Winkler gun. If a weapon is not fully and properly cleaned, there is always a chance that bullets might get "stovepiped" inside it—that is, wedged inside the chamber in a way that is not visible to someone peering down the barrel. These bullets can then load into the chamber if the gun is jostled or dropped. If my father did indeed intend to clean the gun, he would have been holding it with his finger through the trigger ring and the barrel pointed toward his face, precisely so he could see if there was a bullet in the chamber. With the gun in that position—and a bullet lodged somewhere out of view—a stumble or a fall could very well have been fatal.

The thought that I indirectly caused my father's death is as terrible as the idea that he committed suicide. Yet for all of the indications that my father's death was accidental, there is equally strong evidence from the coroner's inquest for the opposite conclusion. "I had no other idea at the time that it was anything but suicide," Dr. Mead told the jury. "Mr. Purvis was very much depressed, had been so for several days, I might say even weeks before then." Mead had seen my father eight or nine times in those weeks, and on each occasion "he was very much depressed because of his inability to sleep, because of the constant pain that he was having in his back, his feeling that he was not gaining strength," Mead said. "He was also very much worried about the work that he was doing in Washington, that he didn't see how he could get well enough to carry on, and he expressed many times the feeling of futility, of trying to go ahead with so many circumstances against him." These discussions my father had with Mead clearly reflect the thoughts of a despondent man. Mead even recalled that sometime during the previous week my father "had been unusually hopeless in his outlook and he said, 'I just don't see any way out of this at all.'" Mead added that my father continued, "'But I am not thinking of the same thing you are.'"

But was he? The terrible futility he felt could surely have clouded his mind, to the point where he saw suicide as the only option. I could not begin to fathom the pain and torment my father must have felt in his final days. Perhaps the physical devastation was only part of it. Perhaps in those desperate hours he looked back over his life and deemed himself a failure. He had not been able to re-create the idyllic family of his youth; he had not been able to truly succeed in any endeavor after leaving the Bureau. He had not been able to find a way to reconcile with Hoover. He had not forged a true connection with his sons. Did all of this weigh on him in his self-imposed hour of reckoning? Did the suicide of his good friend Bartley Crum at once break his spirit and show him a way to alleviate his own pain?

Dr. Mead, the man to whom my father spoke most intimately about his anguish, believed that his death was a suicide. Mead's judgment carries much weight with me. He was extremely close with my father and always had his best interests in mind. But he was also a medical professional sworn to provide his truthful assessment of any situation. His certainty that it was suicide is hard to disregard. Others would argue that my father had been in high spirits, but they were not privy to the deepest, direst thoughts he shared with his doctor. I suspect that even my mother was not privy to these thoughts. But Dr. Mead was, and the six weeks between my father's death and the coroner's inquest provided him with no new evidence to diminish the importance he placed on my father's fragile state of mind.

During the coroner's inquest, Dr. Allen was asked repeatedly if he thought my father's death might have been an accident. Finally he threw up his hands. "I frankly don't know what it was," he said. "No one knows but Melvin." This strikes me as the truest thing anyone could have told the jury that day. Ultimately we cannot know what happened with any certainty—the evidence allows us to determine only so much.

I did decide, however, that if Melvin Purvis had been investigating his own death, he wouldn't have declared it a suicide unless the evidence supported it. And I know that he would have been more fascinated by the life that had been lived than by the ambiguous circumstances surrounding the death. If my son ever asks me how his grandfather died, I will tell him that I am not sure what happened. If he is interested enough, he will grow up and look into it on his own one day. In a way I hope that he does. But I also hope he spends as much time looking into how my father lived his life. This, I will assure him, is quite a story, quite a story indeed.

And when my son asks me, as I know he will, if my father was a hero, I will have an answer for him. I will tell him my father led men into battle, that he risked his life more than once. I will tell him my father believed in duty, honor, dignity. I will tell him he never boasted or bragged about the things he did. I will say, "Yes, my father was a hero."

Epilogue

In a pleasant residential complex along Atlanta's Northwest Parkway, in a lovely apartment near enough to a playground to hear the squeals of children, the last living witness to the Bureau's war on crime offers me a cup of tea. Doris Lockerman is a lively, beautiful woman in her nineties, as elegant and witty and headstrong today as she was in the early 1930s when she watched men as young as she risk their lives every day. "That is what people sometimes fail to realize," Doris told me. "We were all so very young. These men who were entrusted to catch the most dangerous criminals were sometimes barely out of college. They were all so youthful and fresh-scrubbed and suddenly they were asked to fight this menace no one had ever fought before. These were not hard men with years of crime-fighting experience. These were almost boys."

A few months earlier Doris's youngest son, C.B., had written to me after reading in *Boston* magazine that I was working on a book about my father. Did I know that his mother had been there in the early 1930s alongside my father as he searched for Floyd and Dillinger? I knew she had been his devoted secretary, but I did not know she was still alive. I certainly did not realize what an incredibly wise and eloquent testifier she would be to the events of seven decades past. This was thrilling news. I spoke with her on the telephone and was astonished at her recall—names, events, small details; they were all there, in her wonderful memory. As soon as I could I made my way to Atlanta to see her. It was one of several memorable meetings and many subsequent conversations. "Melvin's is a story that must be told," she said. "It is a more important story than the hunt for gangsters and all of that."

To my surprise Doris was often somewhat harsh in her judgments of my father. She did not spare me any of her thoughts about him, however difficult they were for me to hear. She had no interest in glorifying my father, and she warned me against striving to do so. "You must not depict your father as some sort of solitary hero," she insisted. "He was simply a man who did daring and devoted work, who always worked as part of a group, who never grandstanded. You must depict him as the leader of a corps but also as a part of that corps. You must never forget that there were many men who took the same risks as he, and that no one realized this more than your father. He loved his men and he worried every time he had to send them into harm's way. This was a brave and selfless squad of men. They were all heroes. And your father was one of them, and it was a hell of a thing to be."

My father came to life for me in Doris's apartment: I learned where he ate his lunches and what he liked to eat; I learned how he walked down a hallway, briskly and with his hat pulled low; I learned how he dashed into his waiting car in case gangsters were waiting to fire at him. I learned that he could be pompous one minute—he once summoned Doris by ringing a bell just to impress his sister Mary Beth—and human and vulnerable the next. When Doris reprimanded my father for allowing his agents to treat a female suspect harshly, he did not get angry with her or dismiss her opinion. He simply asked her, "What should I do?" She reaffirmed to me that my father was a gentleman, in every sense of the word. I learned that his agents called him "Purvis," in the casual way the employees of any office might refer to a coworker they admired.

Of course, I learned much more about my father, and much of it was painful to consider. Doris remained, seventy years later, indignant about what had happened, and her anger, rising in her voice as she recalled distant injustices, nurtured a long-suppressed anger of my own. "This ought to be an angry book; it *must* be an angry book," she told me. "There should be a boiling anger all the way through it. It is the story of a man whose littleness and meanness and smallness led him to destroy another man. It is a calumny of the worst order, and there is no way to recall it without raging against it. I watched your father work every day for three years; I was there every day when he made his decisions and went on raids with his men. And I saw that this was a man who was absolutely steadfast, brave, determined, focused and devoted to his work and to his men. And I am so *outraged* that this man had to die in disgrace. The real disgrace is that it happened at all, and that so many years have gone by without someone setting the record straight."

I had not cried for my father in more than thirty years, but on that first day with Doris I cried for him several times—for his sacrifices, for his bravery, and for the things he did not do to protect himself. The passion Doris felt about what happened to my father, the still-burning anger she felt toward Hoover, gave me all the motivation I needed to embark on my journey. The strength of her spirit filled me at every step along the way, and it is the reason I dedicated this book to her. Many times during our talk I could see that she was crying too. She told me the injustice she witnessed so long ago had haunted her and was haunting her still, and she told me she believed I was the one finally to get justice for my father. "This is not the isolated story of a single man," she said. "What happened, happened in a unique and specific time and place in our history." Doris paused to consider just how to send me on my way. "The rise and fall of Melvin Purvis *meant* something," she said. "It is up to you to discover what it was, and to tell that story to the world."

Notes

[TK]

Index

[TK]